Now!
Painting in Germany Today

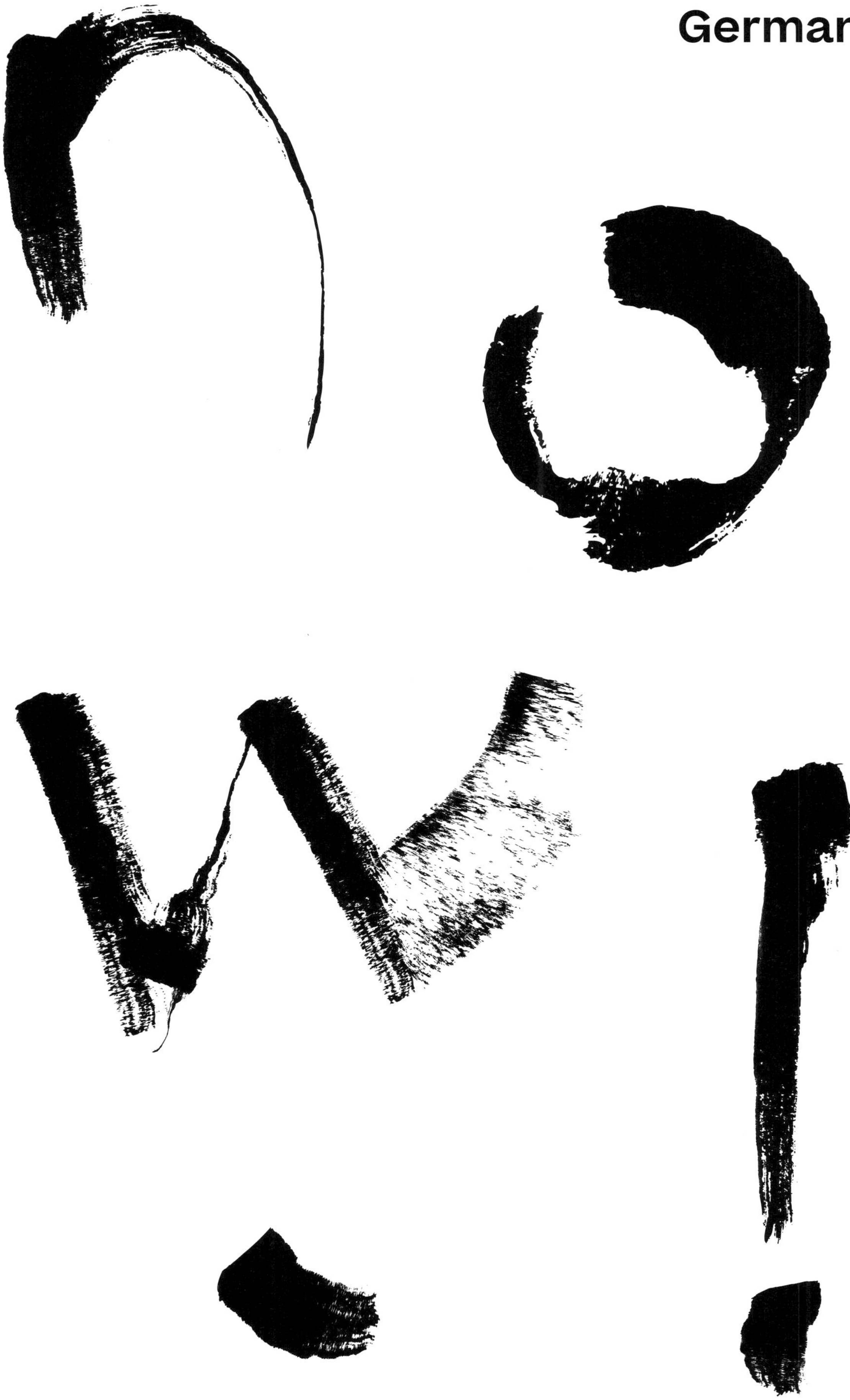

HIRMER

Contents

Now!
A Journey Through Recent Painting by Young Artists in Germany

No artistic medium has undergone as many negative or positive assessments as painting. The profusion of expectations and assumptions confronting the painted image ranges from jubilation of the undisputed "royal discipline" that always succeeds in transforming reality into just the right artistic style, to the distressing prognosis that it is a commercially corrupted commodity outmoded in aesthetics and in content. This negative finding is, on the one hand, the result of the medium's grandiose tradition. So much theorising has already taken place in this context, so much has been done that it seems, indeed, not easy to tease anything new out of this medium. On the other hand, painting has been chastised, especially in the twentieth century, for its easy marketability and this trait was suspected to be the medium's basic deficit.

The flatness and narrowness of the canvas or pictorial field not only serves as a cheap market accelerant, it also offers a reason why painting, despite all eulogies, is a highly energetic medium: the structural two-dimensionality of the pictorial field serves as a perfect dialectic foil of everything that happens within the pictorial field as a result of painterly means. Broadly speaking, one might claim that every painting lives off the productive paradox of creating its own space out of a sectional, non-dimensional image carrier. This basic dialectic process guarantees to a certain extent that painting may be regarded as the only and, until now, valid virtual medium. The effective force of the virtual reality needs to be rated even higher precisely because it does not operate in a total or immersive manner. Rather, it defines itself only as a section as long as it operates within the parameters of the canvas plane.

It is precisely this collision between the space created by painterly means and the context of a reality from which it differs starkly that constitutes the basis of the exhibition *Jetzt! – Junge Malerei in Deutschland (Now! Painting in Germany Today)*. It was organised in collaboration with the Kunstmuseum Bonn, Museum Wiesbaden and Kunstsammlungen Chemnitz – Museum Gunzenhauser and attempts to determine the present status of this medium. All three institutions – as well as the Deichtorhallen in Hamburg, which decided to show this joint exhibition after its first run – aim to present a valid cross section of paintings produced in Germany by young artists in recent years. All manifestations of the medium will be showcased without ideological or conceptual restraints.

This project is guided by three central premises. Firstly, with regard to what has been said above, the curation was restricted to positions that actually deal with the medium within the limited framework of the canvas panel. Consequently, this meant consciously leaving out all variations of the image in a broader sense such as painterly interventions of a spatial installation or multi-media explorations of paintings without paint. This focus struck us as crucial in order to arrive at reliable statements as to what potential the painted image still has today, especially against the backdrop of the overall spreading of digitisation. Furthermore, in view of the unprecedented expansion of artistic practice to all spheres of life, it begs the fundamental question as to whether an equally consistent expansion of painting may give the medium decisive impulses, or whether the conceptually viable position of painting today will not be found more likely at the juncture where painting must deal with its structural limitations on the flat picture carrier?

The second precondition concerns the age of the participants, who basically belong to the age group of around 1979, their ages ranging between thirty and forty. We are dealing with the first generation that has by and large grown up without the experience of a divided Germany. This, too, signifies a crucial focus of Jetzt! Very emphatically we did not want to unfold an historical panorama with this exhibition by specifying the various strands along which the medium developed in the two parts of Germany. In this respect, the title of the exhibition should be understood programmatically: the arena that becomes visible here is not legitimised by its embeddedness in an historically grown context, but stands its ground as an assessment of the contemporary condition which, in turn, raises its own questions and provides answers regarding the painted image.

The third precondition concerns the geographic framework of our area of exploration. Our focus on Germany should not to be understood as an indication of a common national visual language that we suspect is contained in the approaches we selected. Based on purely pragmatic grounds, this decision is the result of a needed delineation of the field to prevent the selection from becoming limitless and thus exchangeable. It was to our benefit that during the past twenty years –also on account of Berlin being so attractive – that the composition of artists living in Germany became increasingly international. Here they can fall back on one of the richest art landscapes in the world and also on vast resources of support.

Foreword

Within this framework we conducted our research as comprehensively as possible and did not rely simply rely our own competence, but had successful artists, colleagues, art critics, et al. supply us with valuable information. Consequently, from an overall field of 150 artistic approaches, a little more than 100 were chosen that we considered relevant enough to motivate us to supplement a first interest by a studio visit. Between the autumn of 2017 and the spring of 2019, changing teams travelled all over Germany to visit studios in Bremen, Berlin, Dresden, Hamburg, Munich, Stuttgart, Karlsruhe, Frankfurt, Leipzig, Cologne, Düsseldorf and other locations, but also destinations far removed from the metropolises. The journeys in and by themselves were their own rewarding projects: a tour d'horizon in which almost every visit was an adventure and a discovery. The size and location of the different studios alone could have provided sociological studies of their own. The spectrum ranged from 600-square-meter showrooms with the flair of grand bourgeois artisthood to tiny broom closets in crowded two-room apartments. The growing pressure on the housing and real estate markets as well as the explosive price increases in recent years pushed many artists to the outskirts of the cities – one more reason to expect communities to counter these developments by subsidising studio programmes. However, the experiences we had on the ground were rather sobering. It is true that every major German city offers communal affordable studios. But they are by no means sufficient, especially in Berlin, which loves to boast about its international artist community.

After long, enjoyable, occasionally controversial discussions, we selected fifty-three standpoints from the already condensed number of positions, each being represented with at least three works per exhibition venue of Jetzt! As we will open the exhibitions simultaneously in Bonn, Wiesbaden and Chemnitz, this comes to a total of 500 works on display that will be shown simultaneously for the duration of four months. Following these exhibitions, a selection of fifty-three approaches from the total collection of 500 works will be travelled to the Deichtorhallen in Hamburg. Thus, the claim of a genuine survey exhibition will be met and it will be shown in the west, the east and the northern parts of Germany. The decision to present the selected views via several works will provide a deeper insight into the different artistic approaches.

This current catalogue will provide additional elucidation and present introductory essays and short texts on each of the participating artists, as well as a selection of the works on display. A comprehensive accompanying programme will complement this project.

On behalf of the four participating institutions and the curator, we would like to thank most cordially all those who assisted, supported and subsidised this exhibition project. Our special thanks go to the artists, with whom we had many interesting studio conversations and to whom we owe a deep insight into the research laboratory that is contemporary painting.

Stephan Berg, Frédéric Bußmann, Alexander Klar, Dirk Luckow

Stephan Berg
Painting and the Productive Paradox of Marginal Phenomenon

The most interesting aspect of the current discussion of painting is possibly the fact that it actually exists – again. After theoretical discourse ignored the medium for a long time or – as in the case of Rosalind Krauss, for instance – categorically disputed the medium's ability to find a contemporary answer to today's artistic needs, the enthusiasm for a discursive debate with this obviously perpetually "undead medium", as the art critic Kolja Reichert calls it,[1] has grown again significantly in the meantime.

Looking at the most significant contemporary theoretical developments, it becomes apparent, however, that – as different as their trajectories may be in detail – most critics approach painting *ex negativo*, as it were. For instance, in his 1990 *Painting as Model*, Yve-Alain Bois looks at painting from the perspective of grieving over its constantly imminent, but frequently delayed, demise.[2] While Helmut Draxler, who draws an important distinction between the act of painting (which by the way he considers potentially obsolete) and painting (to which he definitely grants a future), sees the medium's merits mainly outside the fields of painting.[3] For David Joselit, painting is only still conceivable if it stands beside itself, quite literally and figuratively. In this context, the decisive factor is no longer what the image as a painted object contains but the transitive performance that it carries inside itself by design, in other words the connectedness with other fields outside of the image and its response to its constituent basic framework.[4] Finally, Isabelle Graw, who in the past ten years has worked systematically on painting as a medium, states in the introductory remarks to "Painting is Not the Issue", in *Texte zur Kunst*, published in 2010, that the issue is the "discussion of the practice of painting for which matter the crux is not the question of what constitutes painting at its core as a (guiding) medium within the arts, a specific genre and a symbolic institution."[5]

What all of these positions have in common is a quasi-paradox stance, whereby it is possible to detect currency and vitality in painting only by fading out the medium at the same time. One of the most significant reasons for the contradictory exorcising of the act of painting by shifting it to areas outside of the image and painting can still be seen in Clement Greenberg's both radical and problematic attempt to define painting. According to him, the essence of painting consists of its reduction to the elementary components of paint on the canvas and stretcher and, therefore, can be understood exclusively in terms of its media-specific "flatness", its structural flatness.[6]

Indeed, from today's perspective, Greenberg's much discussed thesis of painting, which dissolves in the thematisation of itself, must be considered fantastical. In addition, it was primarily a hegemonic assertion by American, more precisely New York, abstraction vis-à-vis the surreal-figurative tradition in Europe, predominantly that of Paris. Still, it is remarkable that the understandable opposition to such an essentialist reductive point of view also calls into question the legitimacy of a media-specific view of painting, as does Isabelle Graw, who considers the medial specifics of painting as "having migrated a long time ago into other genres such as the huge photographs of the Becher-Schule [Becher School]".[7] The unwillingness to discuss specific general conditions of painting, (at least) within the framework of the medium, has also been articulated in the exhibitions in recent years that were dedicated to painting. Starting with *deutsche malerei zweitausenddrei* (German painting 2003) in 2003, which was prompted by nothing more than the painterly production of a single year (just imagine if sculpture or photography had been treated in this way), to *Painting Forever!* (2013), a cooperative project in Berlin. In it, Kunstwerke Berlin showcased about eighty positions within painting close together in the ostentatious St Petersburg hanging style (in which works are clustered together), thus documenting the absolute insignificance of each individual painting and specific painterly expression in the context of the critical contextual "framing". Even *Painting 2.0* (2015) in the Brandhorst Museum Munich, most certainly the most ambitious and thoughtful exhibition on the current state of affairs of the medium, fell back in large sections on defining its subject matter as a structure of transitional networks. One can almost touch the mistrust toward all manner of immanent observation of painterly acts, not least Niklas Maak's reckoning with figurative painting, to whose adepts he attributes a "Galapagos syndrome" – that is, the state of living in a "biotope" untouched by the developments of an art-critical debate regarding the medium of painting in which criteria such as quality, authorship, incarnate and painterly virtuosity are asserted once again.[8]

Though attempts to isolate and extend privileges to the medium of painting need to be rejected, and aspirations to save painting by ahistorical means focusing exclusively on immanent factors are doomed to failure, it needs to be noted that entirely excluding the idiosyncratic properties of painting is not likely to achieve a particularly enlightening objective, either. Unless – see above – one were to accept the circular argument that no form of current painting still deals in any way with painting and that the act of painting no longer plays an integral part in constituting an image.

For instance, approaching Katharina Grosse's ambitious work, which explores and questions painterly properties, foundations and the challenges to the medium in a structural manner, it quickly becomes obvious that there are, indeed, ways to demonstrate the specificity of the medium without retreating into a romantic glorification of the act of painting. Looking at her work as a "convergence of a given surface with coloured material" (Ulrich Loock)[9] in which potentially the whole of reality may become the painting ground, her approach also honours a specific momentum of painting. It also rejects a purely self-reflective concealment in favour of always pointing to relationships and actions directed toward creating connexions. The paintings by Albert Oehlen, Christopher Wool or Charline van Heyl, to name just three of the highly praised positions in the discourse mentioned earlier, also veer in manifold ellipses and loops between questions that can, in truth, be resolved only in a painterly fashion and by claiming they might be connected with meta-painterly questions at the same time. Whoever claims the impulse of the paintings could solely be found in – as Isabelle Graw suggests – "the result of an external experimental arrangement",[10] reduces the complex and paradoxical-dialectical process of pictorial genesis to one factor among many.

Achim Hochdörfer and his newly coined term of "mark making" is already more helpful here, that is, the creation of pictorial signs that, as it were, name the elementary painterly practice without charging it either ideologically or teleologically.[11] A terminology such as this, which does not immediately engage in martial armament, would at least make it possible to speak of the properties of the brush and paint, in other words that which appears in the field of vision as a visible representation on the one hand, while, on the other, it remains an entirely abstract-autonomous layer of paint. This should happen in a way without again immediately interpreting this "iconic difference" (Gottfried Boehm) again as a signifier of the superiority of the alleged, and yet often toppled, royal discipline that is painting. The painterly marks would be applied here in the way of a non-judgemental difference strategy, as a marking of the medial difference that will need to be newly adjusted and interpreted regarding the meaning of the painting.

If one is prepared to concede that "no medium can be problematic in and by itself", as Isabelle Graw posited in a 2011 lecture,[12] this obviously needs to be true of painting as well, its immanent specifics once again deserving more attention. In this respect, Graw's thesis might be understood as the claim that the affective qualities of painting have something to do with the special materiality of its marks. The way she sees it, these in turn operate as a trigger for vitalist fantasies of painting: for instance, the idea that human properties could be directly transferred to the inanimate matter of the painting.[13] Whether this perspective is helpful in getting to the heart of the matter remains to be seen, especially as this form of animist thinking could also be transferred to certain aspects of sculpture.

Before this backdrop, it seems all the more urgent and fitting to once again bring the debate on painting back to the classic perspective, the "panel painting" – though not to the limited carrier canvas. In this sense, the concept of our exhibition cannot be understood as a revanchist or anachronistic attempt to tie the medium once again to historic boundaries that we thought were overcome a long time ago and confining them. On the contrary, this is about pointing to the origin of painterly imagery in a kind of narrowing of perspective, while fully acknowledging the need for context and delineation that the medium of painting has had to confront for a long time. Doing so will point to an accompanying vitality that is often lost within discussions on painting that, shying away from its own subject matter, cannot handle it head-on.

As we know, many attempts have been made to define the authentic property of the painted image: from starting with the dialectic relationship between plane and depth, and between representation and presentation, to the "impression of what can be seen in the painting" (Max Imdahl), in other words the asynchronicity of the visibility of the painting and the gradual deciphering of the visible by the viewer. One will have to realise that these, too, merely cover partial aspects of the medium. This is certainly true of the relationship between picture field and picture margin, to which, interestingly, far less attention has been paid attention than to the dialectic conceptual pairs mentioned above. Understanding the path of painting during the last five decades as a process that led from "combine painting to hybrid medium"[14] would make it clear that the greater part of the discussion on painting has always been carried out with a desire to remove it from its classical field of view, resulting in the painted image seeming to have only a limited claim to being considered open to the world and reality.

Furthermore, implying that the contemporary discourse on painting is as "critical of context as it is open to context",[15] raises the question of why the dialectics between self-centeredness and awareness of the world have not been discussed more forcefully at the juncture where materially they appear most dramatically and in a metaphorical sense at the crossroads – at the point where the image is separated from its location in the space surrounding it, and, on the other hand, also connected to it in a contradictory manner. Is it not, one might ask, this structural and unsolvable stress test that every image is subjected to on four sides by the margins that make the panel painting in its literal sense a marginal phenomenon and highly productive? In this manner, it thus becomes a virtual medium by asserting itself in a space that, as a rule, has no connexion at all to the reality of the painting; and, since a pictorial field defined in such a manner is always ready to declare its own totality, due to its paradoxical connexion between margin and content, it collides structurally with the demands of its surrounding spatial, and thus at the same time social, economic and political, realities. This collision would have been – the next assertion will claim – considered categorically different from a photographic or cinematic image, because the image margin of a photograph or a film runs between reality and is indexical with the connected image. The painterly reality, on the other hand, is inevitably designed as an invention that is categorically separated from reality, which would only apply in the case of photography or film if they were purely digital works.

Perhaps one should not assume that this "marginal phenomenon", if one may thus call it metaphorically, is not only or not entirely a problem of a historically obsolete definition of painting. On the contrary, this form of limited playing field needs to be understood as one of the central conditions of the indestructible productivity and topicality of the medium.

This hypothesis can be tested by this exhibition, which hopes for nothing more or less than a general acknowledgment that a medium does not have to be excluded from the current discourse simply because it refers (also) its own foundations and gains strength from them.

[1] Kolja Reichert, "Untot", in: *The Happy Fainting of Painting*, ed. by Hans-Jürgen Hafner and Gunter Reski, Cologne 2014.

[2] Yve-Alain Bois, *Painting as Model*, Cambridge 1990, pp. 229–244.

[3] Helmut Draxler, "Malerei als Dispositiv. Zwölf Thesen", in: *Texte zur Kunst*, issue 77, March 2010, pp. 39–45.

[4] David Joselit, "Painting Beside Itself", in: *October*, no. 130, 2009, pp. 125–134.

[5] Isabelle Graw and André Rottmann, Preface in: *Texte zur Kunst* 2010 (as note 3), p. 4.

[6] See Clement Greenberg, "Modernist Painting", in: *Forum Lectures*, "Voice of America", Washington, DC, 1960.

[7] "'Die Malerei gibt es nicht.' Ein Gespräch zwischen Isabelle Graw und Achim Hochdörfer", in: *Texte zur Kunst* 2010 (as note 3), p. 54.

[8] Niklas Maak, "Manufactum auf Leinwand", in: *Texte zur Kunst* 2010 (as note 3), p. 59.

[9] See Ulrich Loock, "Die Malerei von Katharina Grosse", in: *Katharina Grosse*, ed. by Ulrich Loock, Annika Reich and Katharina Grosse, Cologne 2013, p. 18.

[10] See Graw (as note 7), p. 54.

[11] Ibid.

[12] Isabelle Graw, "Malerei gegen Malerei? Vom Anti-Essenzialismus zum Subjektbild", in: *The Happy Fainting of Painting* 2014 (as note 1), p. 34.

[13] Isabelle Graw, *Die Liebe zur Malerei*, Zurich 2017, p. 22.

[14] Hans-Jürgen Hafner and Gunter Reski, "Synergieeffekte nach der Moderne?", in: *The Happy Fainting of Painting* 2014 (as note 1), p. 16.

[15] Kolja Reichert, "Untot", in: *The Happy Fainting of Painting* 2014 (as note 1), p. 31.

Lea Schäfer
The Material of Painting

The image as a communication tool for painting has been discussed in myriads ways and at countless venues. It seems that talk of its demise, of aspirations and suggestions while searching for a contemporary expression of the painterly image, has been the general theme of painting's self-perception from modernity until "Now".[1] It is not as if panel painting as an artistic medium steeped in art-historical traditions no longer enjoys great popularity even today, not only in the art market and among art connoisseurs, but also among art practitioners. The majority of painted images that we encounter today are rectangular, multicoloured and portable – much as in the days of Jan van Eyck.

Since its beginnings, panel painting was caught in a hierarchical configuration between its immaterial pictorial content and its materialisation through paint and support. In practical terms, a painting is first and foremost a crafted object. The painterly competence of the producer creates pictorial spaces on a flat, rigid or flexible image carrier. Until early modernity, a virtual ideal image preceded its material illustration as part of the artistic process in the physical world, which leads to a hierarchical mastery of the material. The latter becomes merely a carrier that translates the immaterial. It determines its translation but does not cause it.[2]

In the area of research, art historiography since the Renaissance has continued to define the "royal discipline" of painting as a history of dematerialisation that reached its peak in the idealistic art theory of the nineteenth century, where works of art were celebrated as transcending the material.[3] Although in its long history painting has been strongly associated with technical skills, the craft of painting and its materials, knowledge of materials was outsourced[4] to other technical scholarly fields – museum studies, conservation and technical art history. The emancipation of material as an autonomous carrier of meaning in post-war art added to the list of art-worthy materials and has been advancing the research on material iconography and the material aesthetics of modernity and contemporary art for several years.[5] The *Lexikon des künstlerischen Materials* (Lexicon of Art Materials) is the first handbook attempting to introduce material into the art-historical discourse. Monika Wagner explains the new research approach by observing that materials are involved in the effect and the meaning of a work, which enter consciousness only once "the canon of art-worthy materials has been broken".[6] In the meantime, the new attention on materials, the *material turn*, has also arrived in our discipline and introduced a new basic premise to the discourse: painting has no pre-material existence; it owes its significance and effect in large part to the materials and production processes from which it evolved.[7]

The works by the young painters in this exhibition demonstrate that, apart from all discussions on the wide-ranging varieties of the medium, the importance of colour material and image carrier is unbroken. The characteristics of panel painting continue to be used in the quest for the contemporary expression of painterly imagery. Consequently, the spectrum of painterly image production contains many facets, although it rests on the foundation of old conventions, as the great majority of young artists falls back on the original material used as image support, canvas. Up to the present, visual spaces are created on canvas, either by means of figuration or experimentation with materials. The textile image carrier seems to be in flux and is no longer the only one. Rather, it is an active function of medial self-reflexion and is employed in painting as material or metaphor.

In this regard, panel painting with its conventional painting materials – stretcher, canvas and paint – is driven to its existential limits by Franziska Reinbothe's (pp. 190–193) artistic work: the wooden skeleton of the canvas is broken and the fabric is folded as if designed for space-saving disposal. The classic image carrier is put into question by physical interventions or incursions during the process of painting that reflect the idea of paint on canvas. The act of destruction sets free a transformation into something new. Each of her works poses a question about painting and offers a potential response to it at the same time.

In the coloured works of Jens Einhorn (pp. 66–69), various fabrics are interwoven with the paintings' layers of paint. In an open production process, rough nets and distressed textile fragments are processed again and again, resulting in the viewer entering a graduated visual space through transparent lengths of fabric. The cutting and collaging are elementary ingredients of Einhorn's painterly practice. He knows how to utilise the diverse surface structures in a deliberate way, and how to highlight the appeal of the textiles as material and surface structure for his paintings.

Among the artistic views presented here, textiles serve not merely as a basic support or material, they are treated as pictorial content as well. Mona Ardeleanu demonstrates an interest in woven fabrics and clothing in her paintings. In his main work Der Stil (1860–1863), Gottfried Semper had already established theoretical positions on the origin of stylistic forms that he categorised according to material. In his first volume, Semper's starting point was the vital necessity for textile clothing.[8] He considered spinning and weaving *Urtechniken*, art techniques that created the discipline.[9] By interweaving threads or embroidery, textiles are frequently enhanced by decorative patterns – ornaments that carry meaning within a cultural context and transcend their basic practical use. Ardeleanu singles out these properties and composes – in the subtle style of Old Master paintings – figurations made of patterned, folded and gathered fabrics from different cultures (pp. 22–25). The peculiar seeming mixture of diverse textiles turns into a contemporary still life that makes the cultural significance of the fabrics visible.

Like dresses and fabrics, canvas paintings are surface planes that can serve as media of communication. The material-specific properties such as foldability, lightness, permeability and portability influence the substance of painting that may turn out to be both soft and flexible, yet robust. The reason why the classic canvas is still a preferred choice (for many young artists) may be found in the versatility and usability of the textile support. With Semper's concepts in mind, Hartmut Böhme refers to a "cultural 'fundamental connectedness of things'" underlying the "structure and order [...] that textile techniques generate".[10] Looking at the idiosyncratic structuring of the textiles, their own orthogonal surfaces that are generated by the interfacing thread system of warp and weft, he sees them as part of material culture and extrapolates them into overall structures of life. This is how our thinking about textiles became integrated into our speaking patterns: we spin or unpick ideas, take up a thread or lose it. Even in today's society dominated by new media, we are surrounded by terms from the domain of textile techniques, such as "tying together" or "networking".

The exhibition reaffirms the relevance of textiles for the contemporary status of painting: still today, the textile support is considered, apart from paint, an integral part of the fascination with painting. Although various artistic views demonstrate an intention to overcome panel painting and to transfer the paint from the window of the world to real life, the classic experimental set-up "paint onto canvas" has not lost its relevance today. On the contrary, material experiments and new techniques revive the old carrier and grant it a new function.

[1] See the contribution by Stephan Berg in this present volume, pp. 7–9.

[2] See Georges Didi-Huberman, "Die Ordnung des Materials – Plastizität, Unbehagen, Nachleben", in: *Vorträge aus dem Warburg Haus 3*, Berlin 1999, pp. 1–30.

[3] Ann-Sophie Lehmann, "Das Medium als Mediator", in: Zeitschrift für *Ästhetik und Allgemeine Kunstwissenschaft*, vol. 57, issue 1, 2012, ed. by Josef Früchtl and Maria Moog-Grünewald, pp. 69–88, here p. 71.

[4] For further information, see a study of oil painting by James Elkins, who states: "Few people besides artists know about oil colors. Even art historians and critics do not recognize them when they encounter them in pictures." James Elkins, *What Painting Is*, New York 1998, p. 68.

[5] E.g. Thomas Raff, *Die Sprache der Materialien – Anleitung zu einer Ikonologie der Werkstoffe*, Munich 1994 (Kunstwissenschaftliche Studien 61), and the research project on the research of material iconography and material aesthetics in Hamburg: Monika Wagner, *Das Material der Kunst – Eine andere Geschichte der Moderne*, Munich 2001; *Material in Kunst und Alltag*, ed. by Monika Wagner and Dietmar Rübel, Berlin 2002; *Materialästhetik – Quellentexte zu Kunst, Design und Architektur*, ed. by Dietmar Rübel, Monika Wagner and Vera Wolff, Berlin 2005; *Lexikon des künstlerischen Materials – Werkstoffe der modernen Kunst von Abfall bis Zinn*, ed. by Monika Wagner, Dietmar Rübel and Sebastian Hackenschmidt, 2nd edition, Munich 2010.

[6] *Lexikon des künstlerischen Materials* 2010 (as note 5), p. 7.

[7] See Lehmann 2012 (as note 3), p. 75.

[8] See Gottfried Semper, *Der Stil in den technischen und tektonischen Künsten oder praktische Ästhetik. Ein Handbuch für Techniker, Künstler und Kunstfreunde, vol. 1: Die textile Kunst für sich betrachtet und in Beziehung zur Baukunst*, Frankfurt a. M. 1860.

[9] See Gottfried Semper, *Der Stil. Einleitung* (1860–1863), in: *Materialästhetik* 2005 (as note 5), pp. 99–103, here p. 100.

[10] Hartmut Böhme, "Mythologie und Ästhetik des Textilen", in: *Kunst & Textil – Stoff als Material und Idee in der modernen Kunst von Klimt bis heute*, ed. by Markus Brüderlin, exh. cat. Kunstmuseen Wolfsburg, Ostfildern 2013, pp. 46–59, here p. 47.

Christoph Schreier
Consideration of a Constant – Painting in the Medium of the Picture

"In our 'pictorial imagery' we do have recourse to framed, rectangular pictures. To put it more precisely, in certain episodes of imaginative activity, the one which will draw the subject into pictures as they form and to which it becomes attached. The frame = as it were the superlative aspect of the picture, its completion. You could say that the imaginary perversion positively demands the frame, the rectangular passepartout, the outline. Compare enamoured ecstasy, love at first sight [...] = to be entranced by a picture [...] pictures like this are generally framed..."[1] Roland Barthes

Supported by the avant-garde impulse of non-compliance and border-crossing, and at the same time inspired by a longing to return to the bosom of society and hence of life which may seem rather oedipal at times, modernist painting has moved beyond the frame of the panel painting in order to explore new spaces of play beyond its boundaries. From El Lissitzky's PROUN Room designed in 1923 via Binky Palermo's wall paintings and drawings during the late 1960s and early 1970s, which have mostly survived only in documents, to Katherina Grosse's large-format spray works, which are draped across interior and exterior spaces like immaterial veils of colour, it is possible to construct an entire genealogy of expansive painting, the quality of which no one would seriously question. The only problematic element would seem to be the casual conclusion that the form of the picture was thus obsolete and would permit no further discoveries. After all, Wolfgang Riepl's law – that new media (including new, hybrid fusions of media) are by no means able to suppress traditional, in this case artistic, forms of communication entirely – also applies to the centuries-old panel painting.

This concept of progress is rather a naive one and already contradicts the empirical evidence, often neglected by the current aesthetic discourse, that even younger generations of artists unreservedly acknowledge the experimental field of the picture. It seems as if the panel picture, an externalised area protected against the liquefaction and volatilisation of all artistic activity, as it were, is nonetheless highly esteemed. The exhibition *Now! Painting in Germany Today* demonstrates in a convincing manner that the external limitation of the field of action is not associated with the curtailment of experimental freedoms.

[1] Roland Barthes, How to Live Together: Notes for a Lecture Course and Seminar at the Collège de France (1976–1977), New York 2013.

Thus the museums in Bonn, Chemnitz and Wiesbaden, and thereafter the Deichtorhallen in Hamburg, will present a varied exhibition in every respect, whose range with regard to both form and variety we can at best only begin to outline. In not always peaceful coexistence the semiotic reflections and visual structuring processes of a Tristan Wilczek and a Stefan Vogel encounter the gestures of ironic-feminist self-empowerment of a Kristina Schuldt; the pictorial-self-reflexive painting procedures of a Paul Czerlitzki meet the surreal hyper-realism of a Mona Ardeleanu; the apocalyptic worldview of a Hannes Michanek competes with the hardly less oppressive petit-bourgeois dystopias of a Simon Modersohn – to name just a few of the coordinates of the artistic positions represented in the exhibition.

Taken as a whole, all these approaches prove how diverse are the ways in which the instrument of visual art can be used, and which varied forms of expression can be gathered within its boundaries. This high degree of functionality – and not for example the flow of energy from outside, through the life-giving brushstroke of the artist who created it – is the guarantee for the survival of the panel painting as a genre, which in spite of its age still appears as both fresh and youthful-looking. It apparently offers the ideal platform for an artistic discourse which generations of painters have enriched and continue to enrich today. Because it seems as if new species are still able to grow in this biotope, as the exhibition demonstrates in impressive manner. It makes no attempt to pay homage to a fictitious, preferably hip "period style", but rather respects the breadth of an art production that proliferates in many directions and produces very different flowers. And so the principle behind the curatorial selection by the museums was thus not to prune the painterly biotope back to the measurements of an aesthetic monoculture, but to show the wealth, the diversity of species, and to direct our view towards that which is growing and blossoming side by side beyond all dogmas and ideologies.

Iconic diversity is a great strength of the contemporary painting scene, but it does not develop on its own, as any botanist knows. It needs the support of various institutions and individuals, as well as; sponsorship by galleries, art societies and the contributions of art lovers, who can also be purchasers. If we look at Germany, all these criteria are met, so that we have no reason to complain. The biotope of painting is tended by many hands and is thus flourishing brilliantly – in spite of the attempts to make it shrivel away by a few abstainers who are too heavy on theory!

Anja Richter
Now! All and Nothing

Painting is alive and kicking, its alleged demise simultaneously history and the beginning of new narratives. In its contemporary iteration, it speaks of gestural expressive energy, of conceptual themes that question painterly and material theories, of process-driven statements that deal with their genesis and narrative potential as well as their narrative visual content. Contemporary painting is characterised by fissures, border transgressions, queries, references and reformulations. It asks questions and initiates discourse.

The joy of experimentation and enthusiasm for diversity demonstrated by today's generation of young artists seems boundless and unfettered. Conceptual approaches have been moved to the fore and seem interchangeable at will with process-driven, content-defined painting motifs that transcend genre and style. In the process, inspiration is drawn from history and references are made over and over again to already created works, all the while attempting to drop the old and break with past traditions. The new generation of artists today is in a position to handle the potential of painting in a more casual way and to explore its possibilities, questions and scope. The artists operate "in-between", that is, between established invariables such as materiality and immateriality, accentuation of the surface and its dissolution, layering and disintegration, reality and fiction, concept and chance, openness and structure, image and ideal, visible and invisible, harmonies and dissonances, transparency and opaqueness, construction and deconstruction, geometric gridding and gestural free painting, narration and reflection, precision and lightness, layering and dissembling, system and chance, visibility and invisibility, abstraction and figuration, monochromaticity and polychromatism, momentum and stillness. It is a play with variables and the unquenchable thirst for mixing, modifying, innovating and reforming.

In this manner, paintings are emerging that we believe we know already, but they conceal unequivocal interpretation. Painting confirms reality or recreates it anew in an act of discord. It deals with being and non-being, it puts forward hypotheses and is capable of disproving them. Furthermore, painting can explore uncommon ways of seeing and open a new world view. Painting oscillates between a variety of its own achievements and reservoirs. Today, it moves back and forth between opposites and searches in its two-dimensional finiteness for liberties and free spaces. It oscillates between traditional categories and systems. Painting enables the transformation of the familiar and known into something special and alien. It lives off the casual handling of its resources and the infinite abundance of a free combination of themes, gestures and expressive ways. It is progressive because it amazes and shocks us, because it pretends to be readable unambiguously, while, in the final analysis, it manages to side-step a clear classification and categorisation.

Alexander Klar
What Matters in the End is that the Result is a Good Picture

The painting process

Painting is an act that requires not only skill but also imagination. At the start of a picture, the artist always has an idea of what he or she aims to achieve, but not necessarily what the result will look like. Paintings are created in a process which of necessity requires throughout its development the constant examination of what the artist is doing at any particular time. This means that it is essential that a picture distances itself from the original idea of what it might look like. This applies, mark you, to pictures of gestural abstraction as well as to figurative pictures. The former are created during a process of organic growth, while the latter develop as a rule from references which become less important as the painting process continues. In both cases the process of creation is subject to its own physical laws, whose precise procedures regularly escape from the artist's dominance over the form. This moment of controlled loss of control is at the same time the magical moment of a picture, and it is at this point that the dialogue between the painter and his or her picture can begin.

I remember the self-conception of a painter who was almost ashamed to admit to me that he was not a conceptual artist, but was simply a "poor sucker of a painter" who wanted to produce a good picture. During the course of our conversation, however, the conceptual aspect crept in willy-nilly, when he spoke about the start of his work while describing his working method. At the beginning of a picture, there is basically a goal, a sort of book of rules which all artists draw up for themselves. The internal composition of a painting is always based on an artistic decision, and it owes its creation accordingly to one (or more) guideline(s), which the artist gives himself/herself and which at the same time determine(s) the handwriting of the picture. The process of working on the picture is oriented towards these rules, and during this process something is created which is subjected to permanent investigation. It does not end until the result approaches the idea which he or she had at the beginning of the process.

The painting as handwriting

The particular value of a painting lies in its individuality, its singularity and its aura of the original. Paintings bear a signature which makes them unique and provides insight into the temperament and the sensitivity of their creators. This "human" aspect helps to give painting a personality which is surpassed in the world of objects only by sculpture. In contemporary art, however, since sculpture is only on rare occasions an object that has been formed by hand, the aspect of the handwriting is largely irrelevant. A painting represents the artist who created it, but serves at the same time as a projection surface for its viewers. There is nothing esoteric about entering into a dialogue with a painting. Paintings can arouse thoughts and feelings because they address both the intellect and the senses equally. "Address" should be taken literally here, because paintings are objects that can communicate and are thus linguistically gifted in a visual way. The exchange with the work itself and with its creator takes place in such a dialogue. The latter's personality is woven into the painting; it constitutes the personality of the artwork, which thereby rises considerably above the world of things. Pictures are personalities in their own right, with lives of their own. Their character is marked by their individual signature, their personality by the significance it acquires during the course of its lifetime. The life history of Picasso's Guernica teaches us that a picture is not only an object which can be written on as regards form; it is also a subject which has succeeded in writing world history by symbolising precisely that. The tour of the work through Europe and America in 1937–1939, the decades it spent in the Museum of Modern Art in New York, and its return to Spain in 1981 demonstrate the symbolic importance of this work over and above its artistic excellence. The picture radiates both painted content and an inherent significance which it received from the artist himself.

The picture as witness of an epoch

An artwork is an illustration of the present during the period when it was painted; it is an encoded time capsule, ambiguous during the moment when it was created, to be filled with meaning during the course of its career, as the example of Guernica has already illustrated. New paintings contain their presence within their subtext: they are incontestably pictures of their time, reflecting the present and telling us something about the status of a culture at the time they were created. The swarm intelligence of all artistic activities over a period gives rise to a certain style which will later leave its mark unchangeably on the image of the epoch. In the Dutch paintings of the sixteenth and seventeenth centuries, we not only look into rooms and situations of that period; we also look into these spaces through the spectacles of the artist who painted them.

The impression created constitutes our image of the time which is infinitely stronger than any which our powers of imagination might conjure up. At the same time it creates a reality of its own which differs from that of the historical situation. Although interiors from this period still exist today, with which we could compare the picture, and although man as the yardstick (albeit dressed differently) still exists unchanged, we remain with the painted picture as the witness of an epoch of which we know that it represents only a shadow of a past reality.

Our study of the picture itself – of the painting technique, the virtuosity and creativity of the painter instead of the subject of the picture – is considerably more instructive. In the Netherlandish painting of the Golden Age, the meticulous application of the paint and the painstaking recording of materials, fabrics and objects contrasts with the motionless figurines standing there as if spellbound, proclaiming an image of humanity whose ethos was characterised by restraint, the performance of duty, and humility. In a corresponding manner, paintings of the present day proclaim our world, freed from social constraints, from the contrast between analytical seriousness and playful pleasure in experimentation, and from the attitude towards the freedom thus gained in order to be able to make of a picture and of ourselves whatever we believe we are capable of being. Our Promethean age conjures up archetypes which in their self-given autonomy can become prototypes of our world image.

The new image

Curators are in the same position as everyone else when they view art. When studying a painting, they encounter an object which has developed during a long process of growth and whose result they have before them. In many cases, just a few moments of study determine acceptance or rejection, the application of subconscious parameters of taste rather than understanding or lack of it. The object was created within a certain period of time and is received within a period of time that is incomparably shorter, and it will not infrequently be misunderstood and rejected. The difference between the professional gaze and that of the less practised viewer of a picture lies in the fact that for the trained eye the picture can be compared against the background of a large internal catalogue and as a result of this comparison can receive a status within the existing picture cosmos. This will be useless, however, if we encounter something we have “never seen before”, pictures without references, paintings whose novelty must be dealt with.

One important insight that transpired during the course of our studio visits was the realisation that the division of painting into figuration and abstraction, which was established over a century ago, has become irrelevant. For the past twenty years, this separation into categories has no longer existed as a dogma. It replaces the realisation that today we are dealing with forms of painting which are effected in different ways but behind which there is no longer an ideological claim, so that neither abstraction nor figuration can be seen as more relevant to the times or more meaningful.

Mona Ardeleanu isolates potentially figural elements in her pictures to create forms which become patterns. Aneta Kajzer designs her pictures as canvases painted with areas of colour, from which she then “extracts” presumably figurative elements in painterly fashion, while David Lehmann fills his paintings with beings whose pictorial purpose is ornamental. Something similar occurs in the pictures of Monika Michalko: here they are vegetable forms whose natural character has been dissolved in favour of an existence as artificial nature. In the formal canon of Anna Nero we can find what appear to be objects that are, however, merely painted object-like manifestations. Moritz Schleime in turn paints his scenarios as an excess of colour and form in which the protagonist is not what he has painted, but the paint application itself. Albert Oehlen’s pseudo-category of “Post-non-representationalism” is echoed in the painterly attitude of many of the artists assembled in the exhibition.

During the selection process for Now! Painting in Germany Today we also came across positions which prompted discussions about the question of the expansion of the concept of painting within the circle of curators. One of them, for example, was the works of Dominik Halmer. A majority of curators regarded them as being in essence installations, so that they were not included in the selection. The argument that Halmer’s intention is always a painterly one failed to convince this circle of curators. His concern to continue the painting when necessary beyond the edge of the picture, on the wall and in the room, opens up a further dimension for the picture which is derived historically from the concept of the shaped canvas. However, opinions differed with regard to the question of the relationship between the painting and the form of the pictures within the room. Herein lies one of the most interesting dividing lines in the concept of our exhibition: the concentration on the panel painting aims to create a framework within which an incredibly broad spectrum of possibilities for innovation already exists. Abandoning this framework would have been at the expense of the concentration; in this respect, the limitation to the "picture on the wall" and its possibilities proved to be a wise decision.

Technique as a medium for pictorial invention

One of the most productive misunderstandings between the creator and the viewer is the following: painters want to solve painterly problems, while viewers want to see something in a picture with which they can establish a connection. As a general rule, pictures are the successful result of the artist's examination of his or her work, an examination which begins anew in the viewer on a different basis. Painting problems are usually of a technical kind; however, technical decisions can only be perceived as content within the picture when we are made aware of them. Here it should be noted that "technique" does not mean the question as whether it is "acrylic" or "oil on canvas", but the choice of certain resources, certain limitations, certain peculiarities which lead to a certain result. In the end it can be the decision to abandon the picture, as for example Paul Czerlitzki does, or on the other hand to reject the possibilities of paint and to paint with charcoal, as is the case with Peppi Bottrop. In the exhibition there are also two positions which arrive at an aesthetically similar result, from opposite directions: Franziska Reinbothe's deconstructed canvases with their broken stretcher frames and Daniel Schubert's painterly play with the stretcher frame as a picture subject take painting and/or the picture itself as their subject and offer visually exciting results. Cornelia Baltes's introduction of the sprayed surface is a technical decision, and so is Lukas Glinkowski's selection of tiles as a painting support. There was some discussion within the circle of curators about the work of Bastian Muhr, whose paintings are derived from an approach based on drawing. Composed from the painting style, his pictures retain an element of the ornamental and yet are two-dimensional, a contrast that transfers his pictures into a disquietingly quiet intermediate state. This quality is nurtured by the prudent transfer into his painting of certain technical parameters which Muhr has developed in the drawing.

The quality of the artwork

The characteristics of a painting are its composition, the choice of colour, its canon of forms and its size. Its quality derives from the arrangement of these characteristics as successfully as possible, as well as the persuasive power of its visual language. Paintings can be colourful or achromatic; they are elegant, unfathomable, austere, opulent, multicoloured or monochrome, large or small; they have a surface and a painted depth; their character can be jagged, edgy, garish and direct, or round, soft, harmonious and appealing. In their effect they are accordingly loud or quiet, aggressive or calming, monotonous or polyphonic, illustrative, figurative or abstract. The selection of these parameters may illustrate how far the framework for the assessment of the quality of a contemporary painting can be. The relationship of these parameters to each other, the use of painterly media and the credibility of a picture are the criteria by means of which its quality is determined. Here "quality" is a variable feature which can apparently also be reversed to its opposite, as for example in Bad Painting. Which criteria must "bad painting" fulfil in order to become "top-quality painting"? Which criteria apply to "bad" painting, when the successful painting is also the result of intentional "badness"? Are the blatantly classicistic figurines in Vivian Greven's paintings "good" or "bad" taste? And do Sebastian Gögel's colourful heads with their patches of colour belong in one of the two categories? It should be noted that Bad Painting was merely one possibility of producing the exact opposite of the claim to "great" painting. Its legacy is the option today of being able to paint supposedly badly as opposed to photorealistically or gesturally and expressively.

In the end, the question remains as to what, then, characterises a good picture – the quality of a painting. The reception of an artwork begins as a rule when it is viewed for the first time by someone who is not the artist. Partners, gallerists or curators are usually the first people who are allowed to pass judgement on a new picture. Their attitude and judgement are a first yardstick for the creator of the work. The different perspectives which the three "first viewers" I have to referred to bring to the table provide an indication of the difficulty of an absolute definition of quality which can be determined as the norm. Fortunately, however, the success of a work does not depend alone on the judgement of art historians or art critics. Paintings must stand out of the mass of today's wealth of images; they must stand up on Instagram as well as in museum spaces or on the walls of a gallery. They must find purchasers and imitators. Their "value", in addition to their inherent class, is also nourished from sources whose origins tend to lie in the arts supplements , such as mythical, original or scandalous details pertaining to the work or the artist in question. Paintings can develop a life of their own; they acquire quasi-human qualities and confront us with their own character. Correspondingly, their quality is a human one in the first instance: Do I like the picture? Is it intelligent? Attractive? Unique? Does it have something to say? Can it change something? If just one of these points applies, the painting is an important contribution to our culture; if they are all relevant, it is a masterpiece.

Mona Ardeleanu

"Bodies" is what Mona Ardeleanu calls the idiosyncratic and sometimes mysterious objects shown in her paintings. She composes their fanciful forms using various different combinations of patterned fabrics, lace, feathers, leather bands, laces or fur. The resulting mixture is non-hierarchical; in her intuitive yet sensitive arrangements, colourful juxtapositions are combined with various superimposed forms, colours and materials, so that the subjects are intertwined, interlaced, twirled or folded in a playful manner.
Ardeleanu works spontaneously, applying the paint directly to the canvas with a remarkable lightness of touch. Her impeccable technique permits her to pay careful attention to detail, so that the graphic precision of her skilfully composed paintings seems to echo the works of the Old Masters. Meticulously recorded folds and detailed, precisely executed patterns together with accurate silhouettes and lines hark back to the practice of earlier painting techniques.
With regard to her subjects, Ardeleanu finds all cultures that define themselves via fabric interesting. Traditional headdresses from the Black Forest, patterns from Delft and Japanese fabrics underline the importance of handicrafts in her works. The artist also uses geometric forms, especially motifs based on circles or rings, as examples of axial symmetry in undefined spaces. She sometimes supports them by making use of reflections, while on other occasions she interrupts or even destroys them by her painterly interventions.
For a number of years now, Ardeleanu has been expanding the tense relationship between body and space in her paintings. The form of the objects is dissolved as she unfolds them and spreads them out across the entire surface of the picture. This results in an all-over impression, whereby ornamental, even decorative, surfaces are shown to be riddles and therefore unreal. Ardeleanu consistently leaves all possibilities open, a process which she carries to extremes in her interplay of contrasts between figuration and abstraction, porosity and density. Every visual certainty is an illusion. Like visions, her pictures defy decryption. —— *Ulrike Groos*

Mona Ardeleanu was born in 1984 in Lörrach and currently lives and works in Stuttgart

Staatliche Akademie der Bildenden Künste Stuttgart, Diploma in Painting with Prof. Alexander Roob, 2010

2019 Mona Ardeleanu – fade, Galerie Thomas Fuchs Stuttgart (S)

2018 Ausbruch aus der Fläche – das Origami Prinzip in der zeitgenössischen Kunst, Museum MARTa Herford (G)

2017 Mona Ardeleanu – Kunsthalle Nürnberg (S)

Mona Ardeleanu – The Bow, Wetterling Gallery, Stockholm (S)

mona-ardeleanu.de

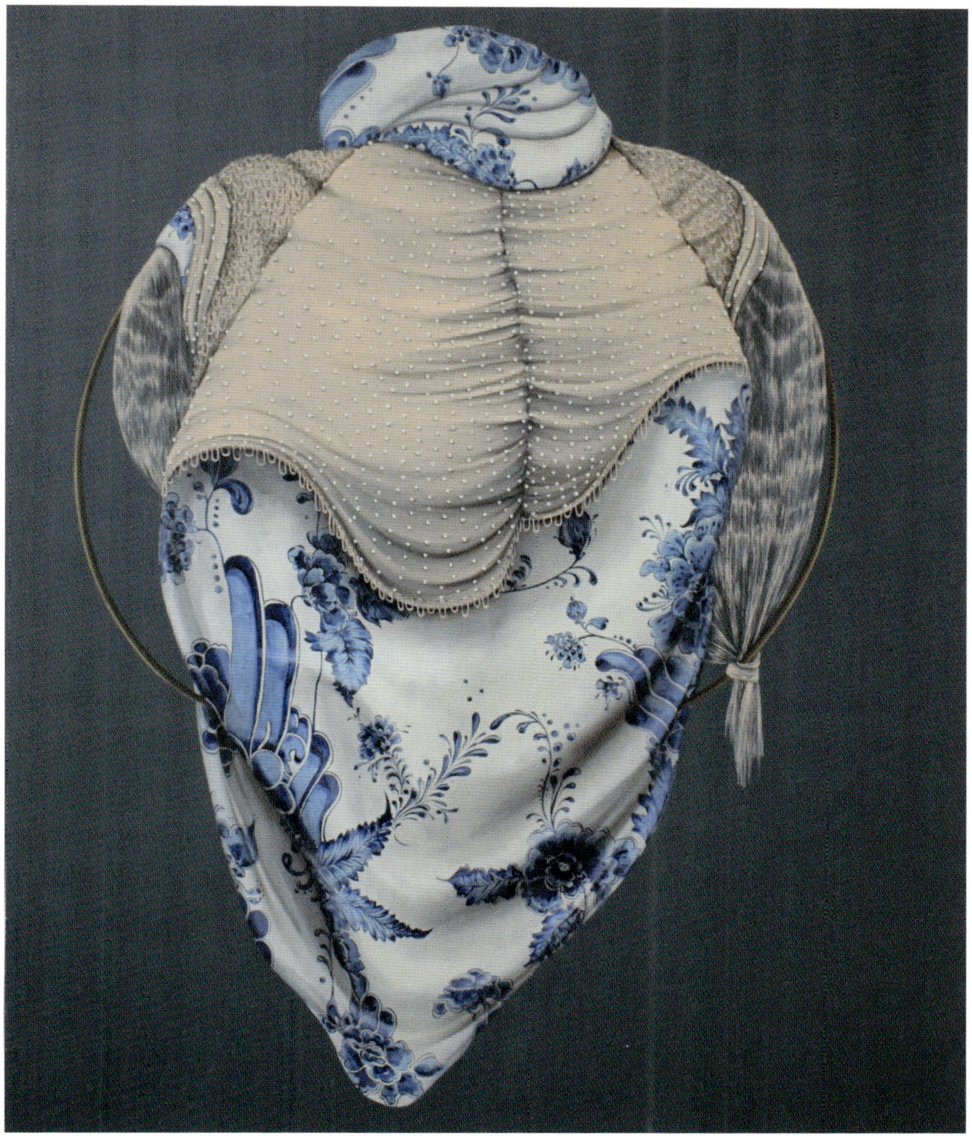

Kuro 2018/III 2018 Oil on canvas 140 × 120 cm Wiesbaden

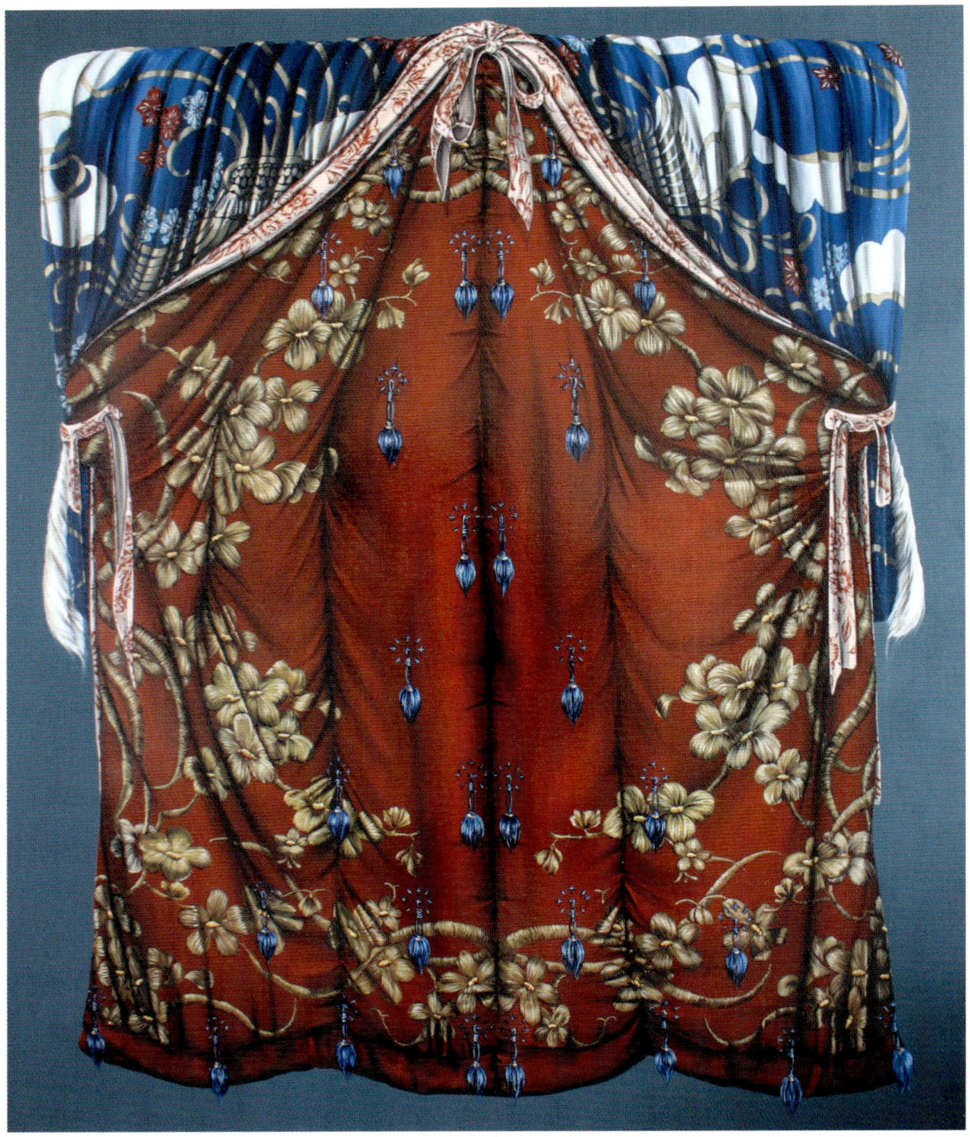

Kuro 2018/II 2018 Oil on canvas 140 × 120 cm Chemnitz

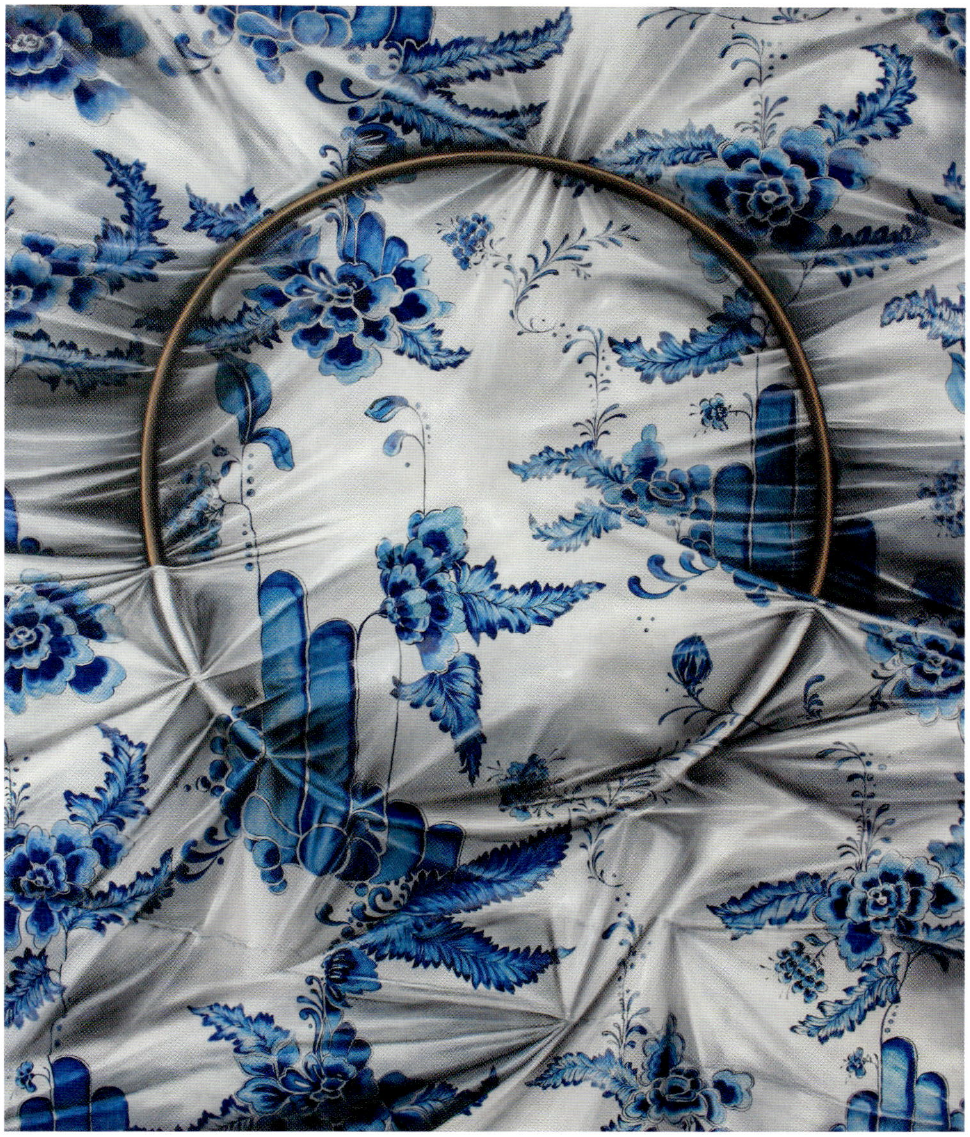

Kuro 2018/IV
2018
Oil on canvas
140 × 120 cm
Bonn

Israel Aten

Dust is the survivor of dramatic events. It's everywhere and it came from exploding stars. They blasted huge amounts of particles into space when they went ... błęmąśź! Motes of dust gently sticking together were the earliest building processes of our planet. Dust doesn't mean dirty. Dust means tiny and so much more than something to be cleaned up, washed off or wiped away. Soil, pollen or dead skin cells. They are dry and universal, they are anything made up of particles smaller than a grain of sand.

The liquid crystal display illuminates your face while you gently touch an icon on your smart device. Icons are symbols and they function as shortcuts to open applications and to navigate through an operating system. It is very much the same as how you navigate through the real-life system. Signs show you directions. Before GPS, before the compass, and before all those signs you encounter on a daily basis, your ancestors' main means of finding their way was to navigate by the stars. You move your eyes from your display. Sunbeams cut the swirling dust you set in motion. A full spectrum of light bounces off everything around you and finally hits your retina – a thin layer of tissue that lines the back of the eye on the inside. The light is converted into neural signals and, finally, your brain decides what the picture is.

You are surrounded by icons and they give you directions. You look up to them and they speak to you. Icons are Pictographs which were used as the earliest known form of writing. "Picto" means to make a picture or to paint, "grapho" to scratch or to draw a character. Dust mixed with egg yolk and applied as paint on a surface. Traces occur depending on the extent of force in the act of scratching dust from a surface – a constant application and erasure until touching the point of making an icon appear. Icons are shortcuts to your desires. —— *Tomasz Skibicki*

Israel Aten was born in 1986 in Detroit (USA) and currently lives and works in Düsseldorf

Kunstakademie Düsseldorf, Masterclass

2017 All Under Heaven, Natalia Hug, Cologne (S)

Peter Mertes Stipendium, Bonner Kunstverein, Bonn (C)

2016 RADAR: Blast Valiant, LWL-Museum für Kunst und Kultur und Westfälischer Kunstverein, Münster Selected (S)

Black Dahlia Quest, Garros Roland, Essen (G)

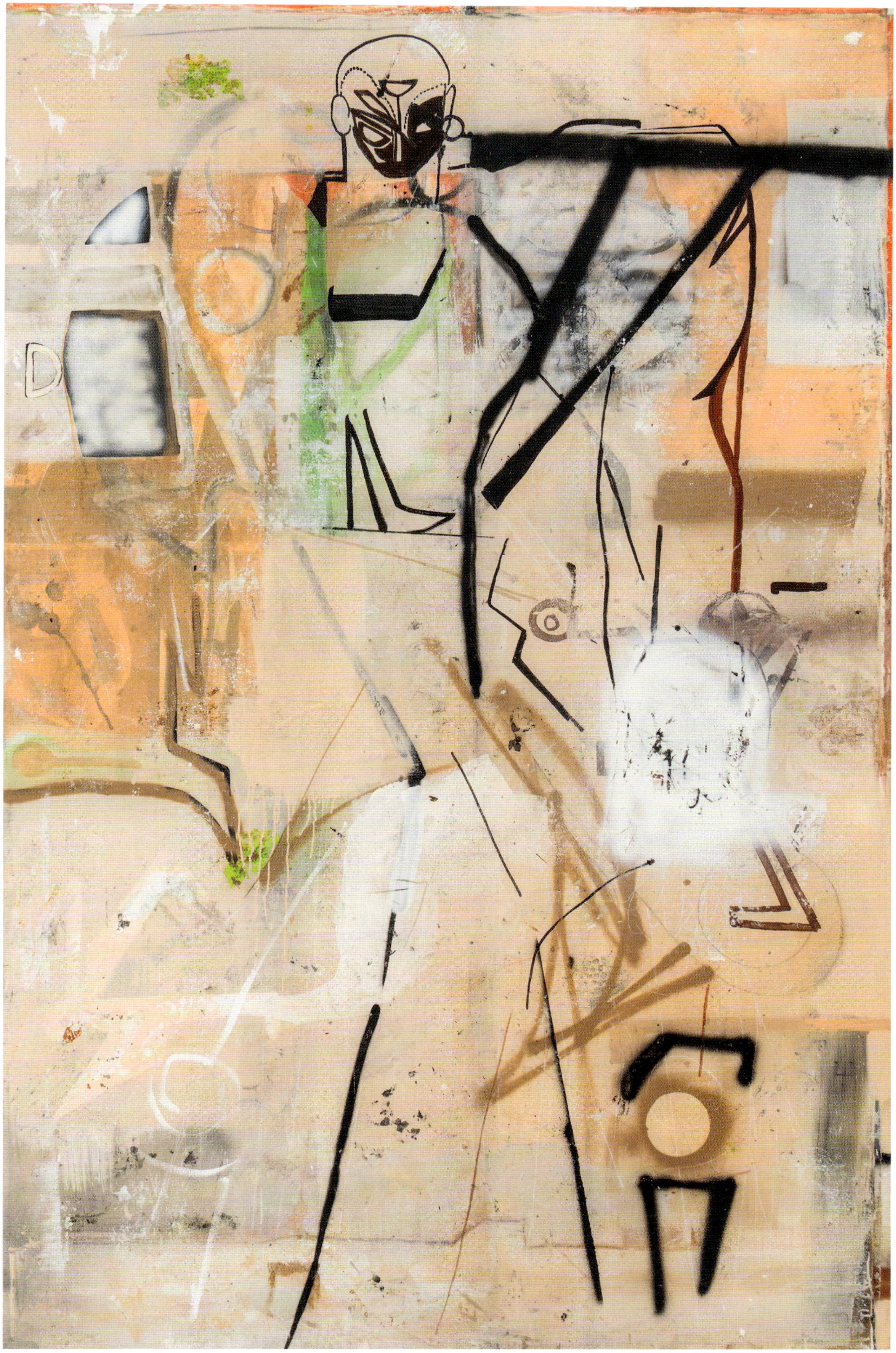

Evolution Rush 2019 Synthetic polymer, silver foil, graphite, pastel, spray paint on canvas 240 × 160 cm Chemnitz

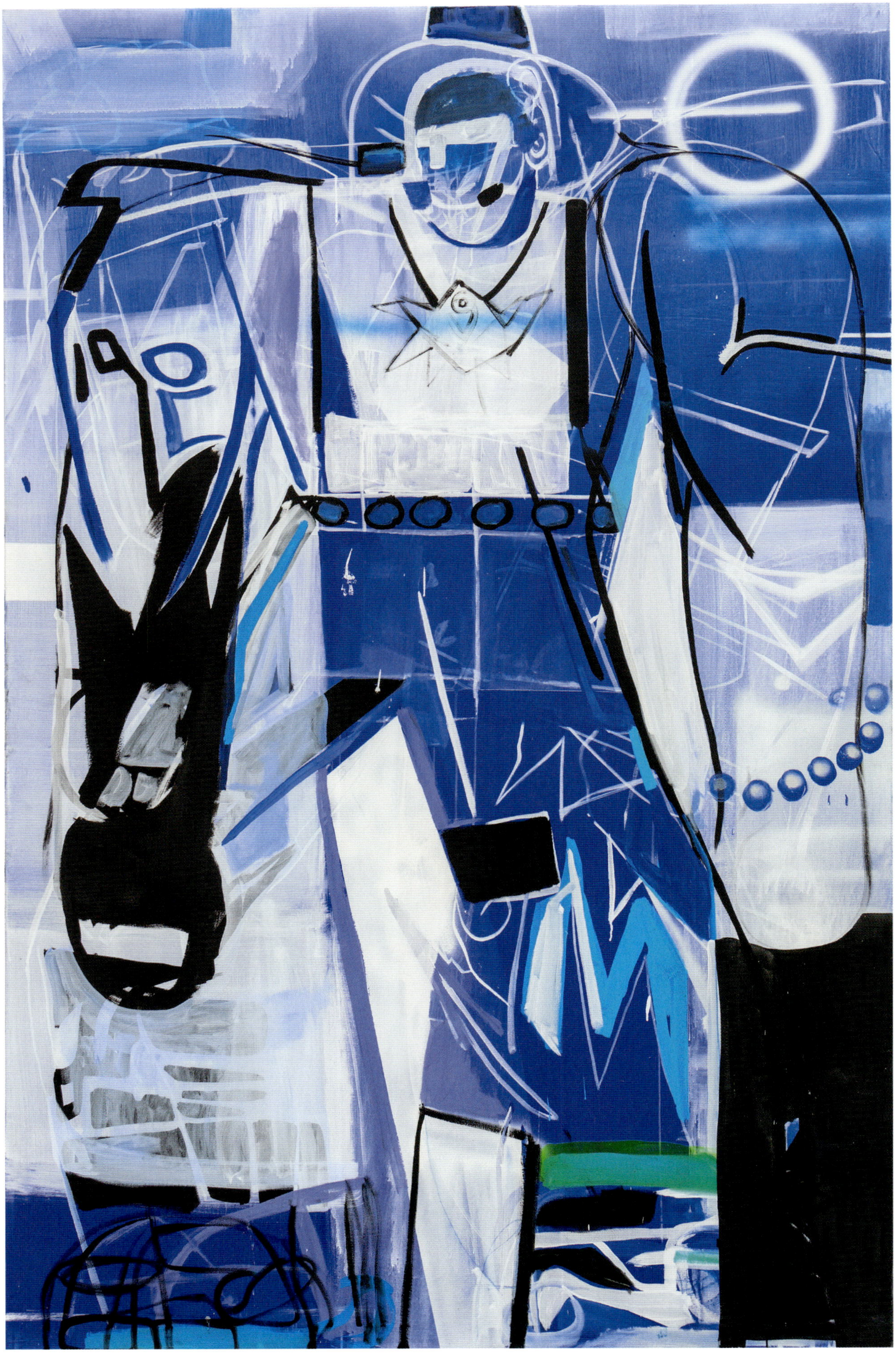

Untitled
2019
Synthetic polymer, spray paint on canvas
240 × 160 cm
Bonn

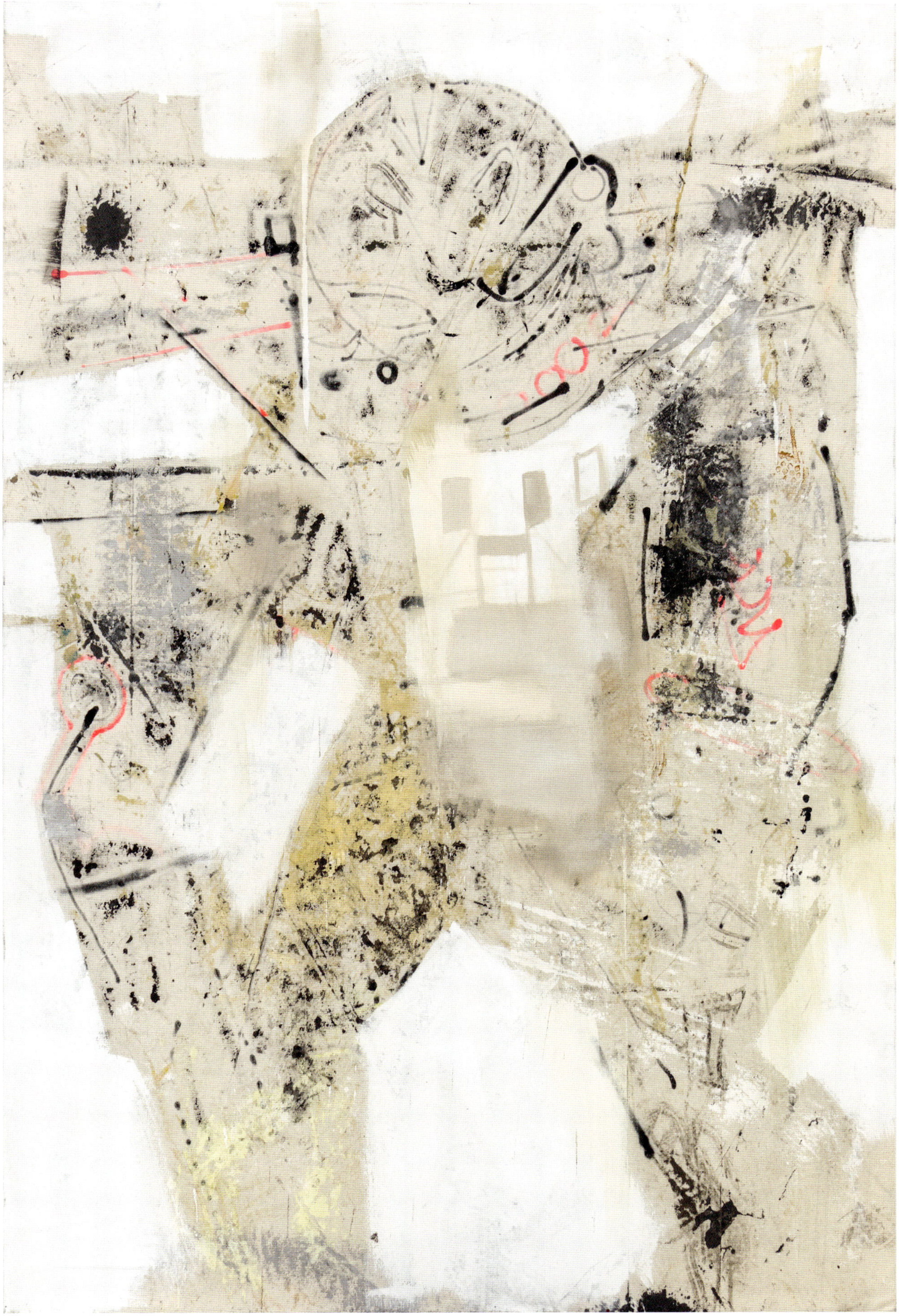

TG1r8 2019 Synthetic polymer, spray paint on canvas 240 × 165 cm Wiesbaden

Paula Baader

Paula Baader is a critical observer wherever she happens to be. While we often regard maps as objective representations of reality, the artist transfers her own, subjective view of her immediate surroundings onto the canvas. Holborn, Victoria Park, the Thames: Baader has lived in London and Hamburg since 2013 and translates concrete, location-specific associations, memories and recordings into delicate, abstract pictures which appear as structured as they are complex.
It is not clear what she is depicting. Nonetheless, her titles indicate a relationship with the places and their social, historical and political sub-texts which the artist explores in intensive forays. She traces these searches in mind maps, structuring snapshots, objects and notices without subjecting them to a specific order. They represent both documentation and working medium.
The artist regards this process as a necessary change of perspective in order to establish a certain distance between the work, the cartography of the location and memories. The method she employs in her artistic practice is also the continued use of the objects which she has selected, mostly symbolic little details which she subtly inserts into her pictures in order to make them aesthetically tangible. Pictorially speaking, her works resemble specific places with regard to their topographical details: the gestural brushstroke becomes intensified into streaks of colour evoking organic substances and providing at the same time associations with the structures of public spaces and private rooms – often seen from a bird's-eye view – with the aim of revealing the complex reality by means of equally complex graphic structures. In her works Paula Baader does not explore external, rigid appearances; her focus lies on the individual characteristics of the spaces concerned, the underlying rhythms – something which can really only be experienced through the temporal process of walking through them physically. —— *Jan Steinke*

Paula Baader was born in 1988 in Hamburg and currently lives and works in London and Hamburg
Royal College of Art, London, Master of Fine Arts, Painting, 2016

2018 Let Me Know Before You Arrive, Warbling, London (G)
Radical Residency, Unit 1 Gallery, London (G)
2017 salondergegenwart 2017, salondergegenwart, Hamburg (G)
ABSTRACT CONVERSATIONS, rosenfeld porcini, London (G)

paulabaader.de

Fabric Shop 2018 Mixed media on canvas 152.5 × 213.5 cm Bonn

Two Temple Place I+II
2019
Mixed Media on canvas
170 × 150 cm, each
Chemnitz

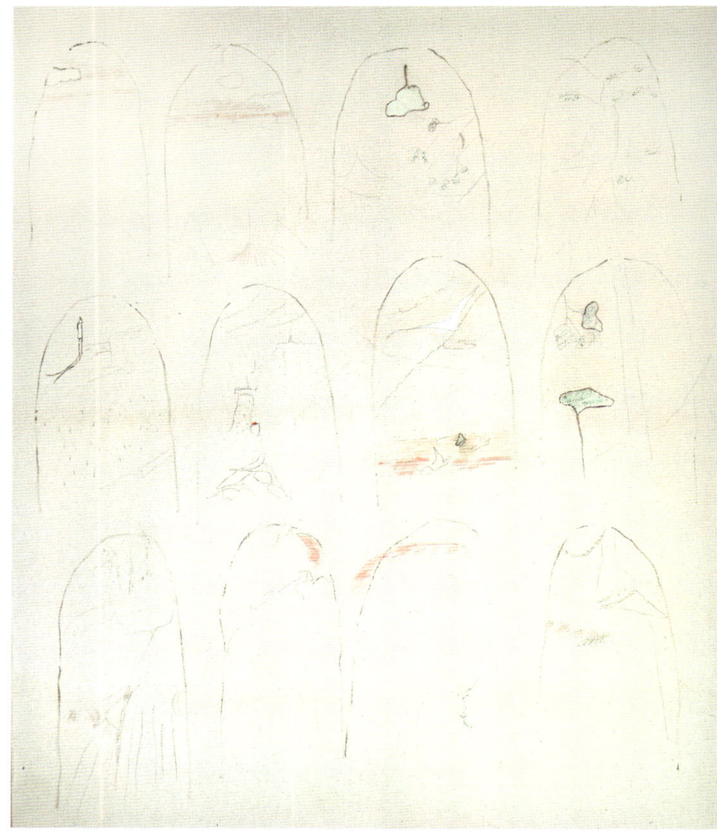

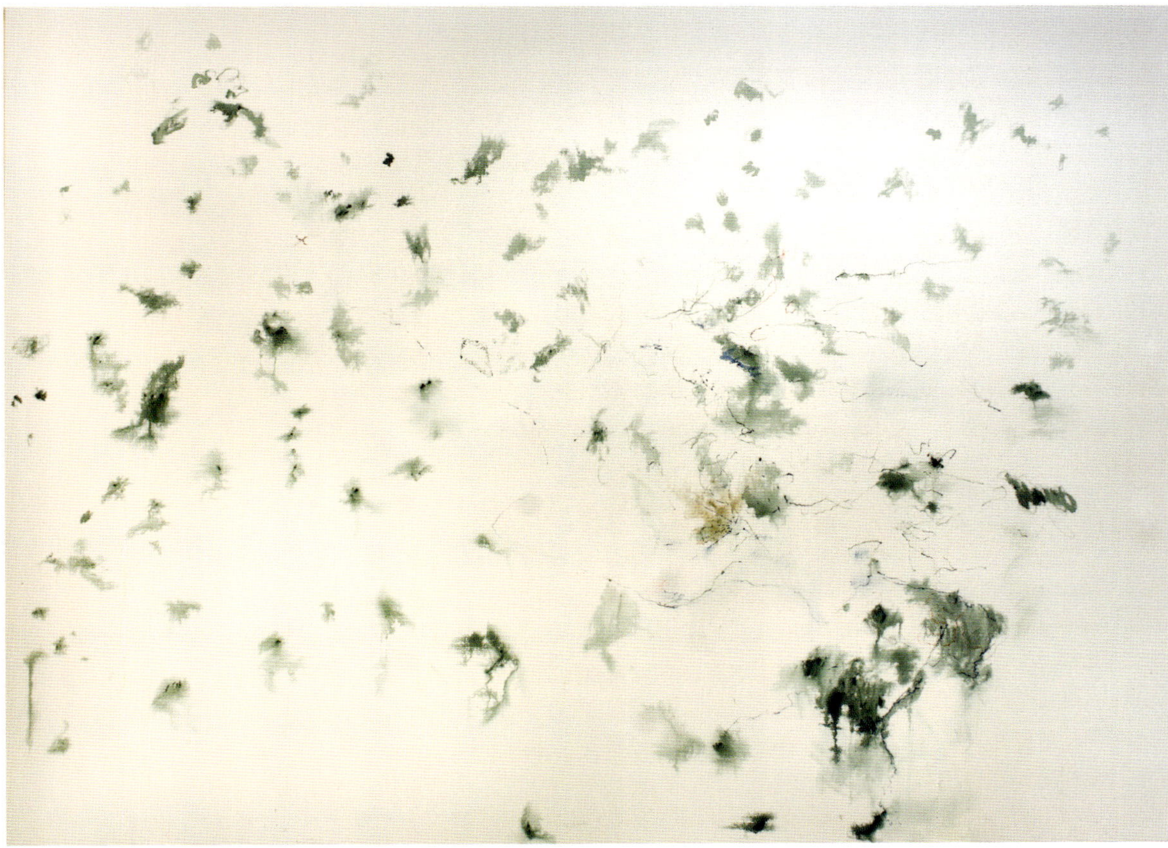

King Henry's Mound 2016 Acrylic on canvas 152.5 × 213.5 cm Wiesbaden

Lydia Balke

xxx (as I stood beside you in the studio, I thought [yet again]: "yes, that is how it has to be; that is how they need to stand and hang: ... beside the laundry.") (LK) xxx Of course they're scared of you. You're impolite. You paint like an old man and behave like a drunken teenager. (KG) xxx I would never have thought that it was you. It sounds very friendly. (ML) xxx You can also suppress everything and want to see more of the sun. Then you can't see the truth. I hope the truth doesn't eat you up. (SL) xxx Dear Lydia, I must confess, your e-mails mostly cause a bit of stress, and here I am not even referring to your flippant manner, but simply to the difficulty of finding out exactly what you mean. (PI) xxx Like Alice in Wonderland. In an anti-social manner. (MG) xxx And Lydia, it looks like you don't want to notice the communication, so the communication will end here. (SM) xxx And another request to you: We wish for clear, honest and fair dealings with our customers – and we are pleased to remain in dialogue with you. But please refrain from insulting us or other people. Thank you! (Customer Service Ing DiBa) xxx

---

Do you know who you are painting for? (LK)
Yes indeed! I am painting for nobody. To be precise, not "for nobody special" or "I don't care" or "anonymous mass nothing, who is really somebody" – but expressly, exclusively, grotesquely personified, for NOBODY. (LB)

"There is no true life within a false life." (Theodor W. Adorno)

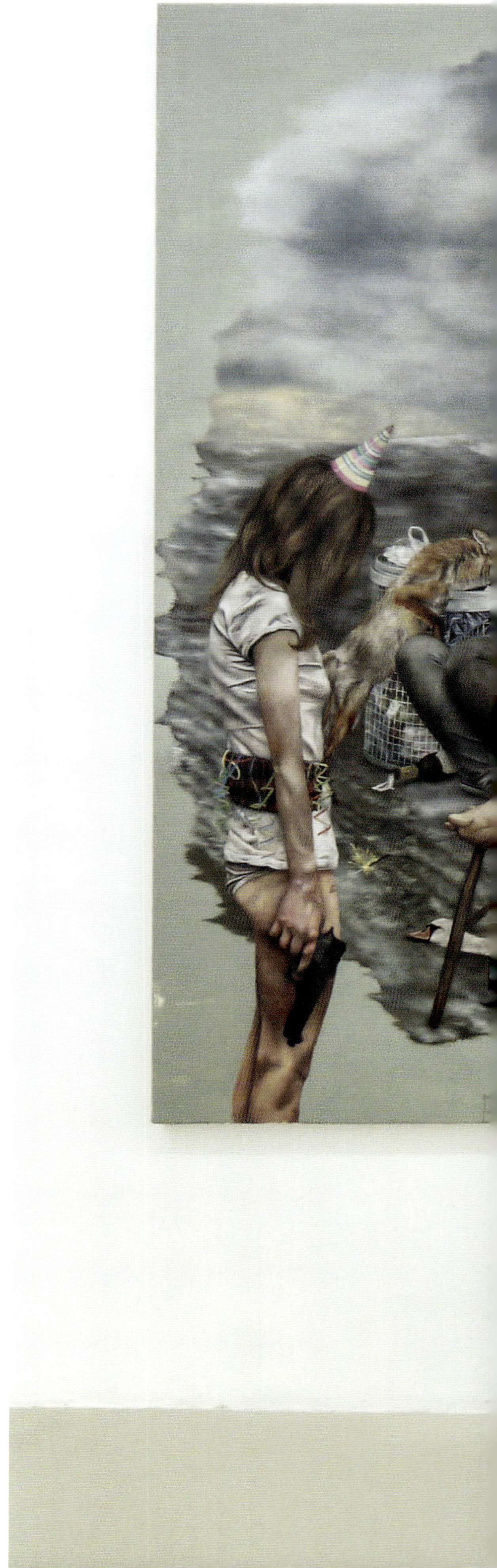

Lydia Balke was born in 1987 in Dresden and currently lives and works in Hamburg

Hochschule für Bildende Künste Hamburg, 2015

2017 Forgotten To Talk, W139, Amsterdam (G)
Angstfrei. Darmstädter Sezession, Kunstforum of the TU Darmstadt (G)

2016 NordArt, Kunstwerk Carlshütte, Rendsburg (G)

2015 MALEREI, BÖSE, Kunstverein Hamburg (G)

lydjuschka.de

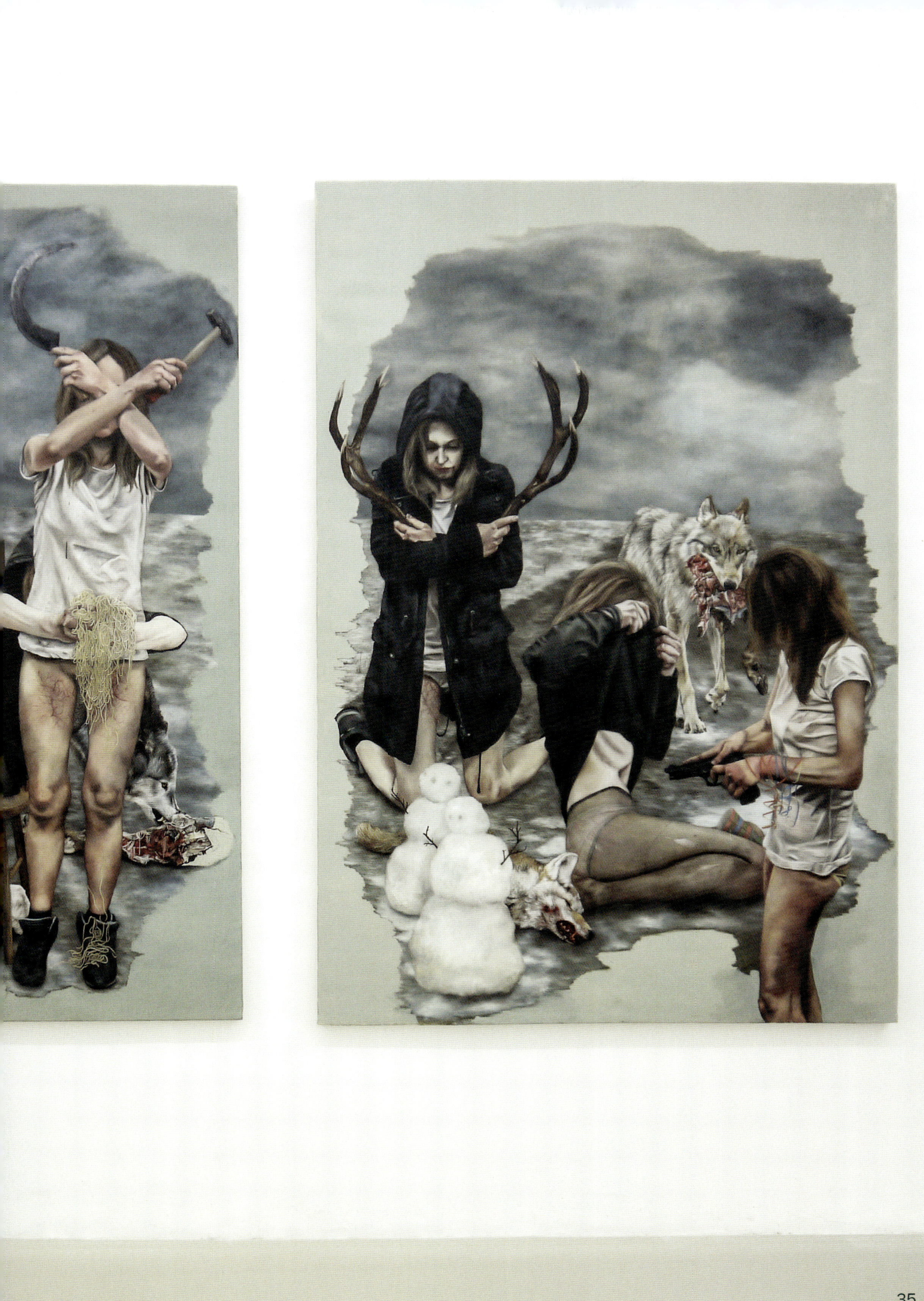

Her Fading. My Stumbling. Our Collapse.
(Hibernation Battlefield I)
A Stained Mattress. Two Frozen Bodies. One
Shattered Life. (Hibernation Battlefield II)

2017

Oil on muslin

230 × 160 cm, each

Bonn

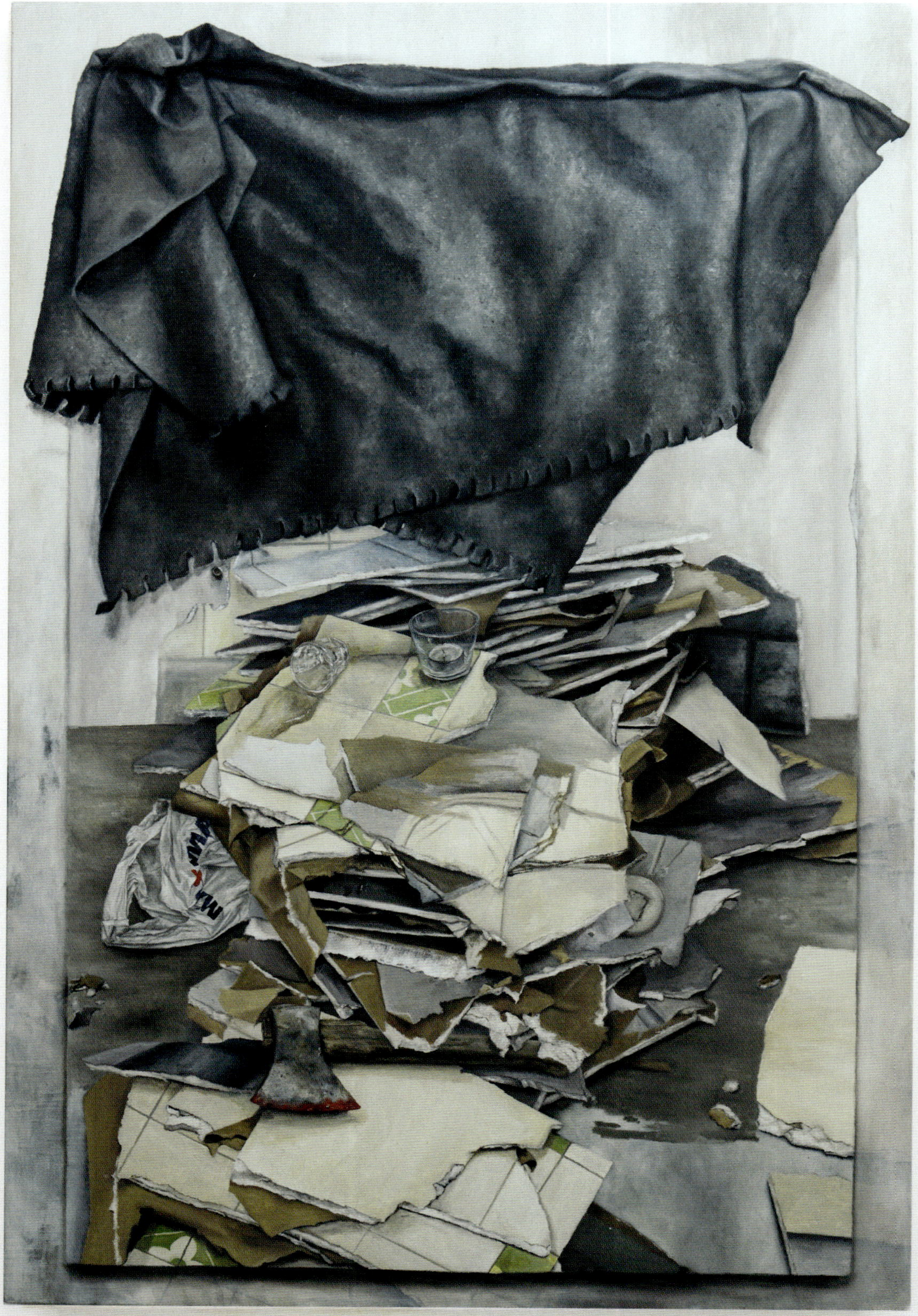

X 2018 Oil on muslin 160 × 110 cm Wiesbaden

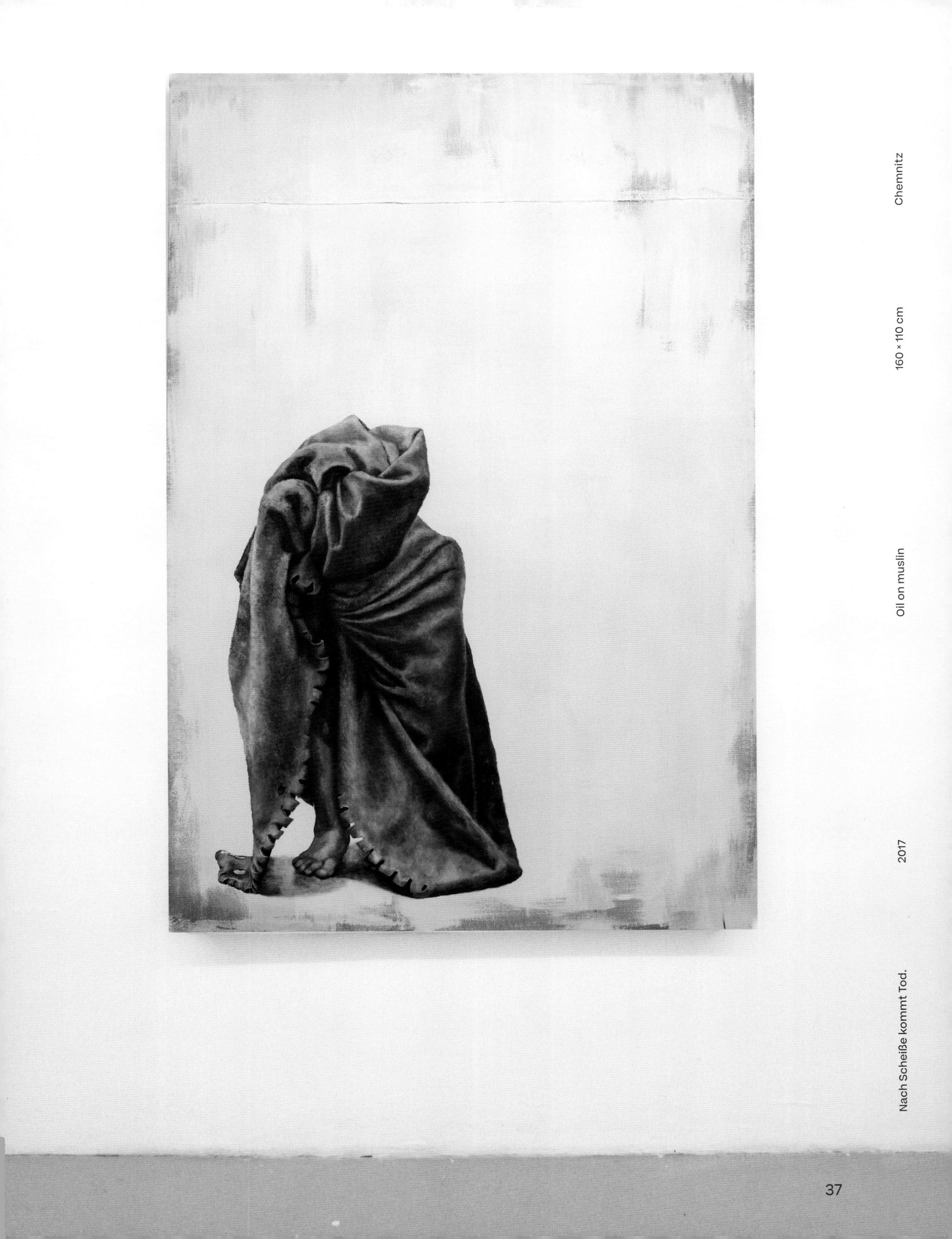

Nach Scheiße kommt Tod. 2017 Oil on muslin 160 × 110 cm Chemnitz

Cornelia Baltes

The artist Cornelia Baltes lives in Berlin. Like close-up photos, her pictures recall enlarged details of actual everyday subjects or recognisable patterns, but without settling on an unequivocal representationalism. The basis of her compositions lies in black sketches whose subjects hint at the silhouettes of objects and animals and the outline of human faces and body parts such as hands, hair or a knee in extremely simplified form. Using her cartoon-like aesthetic, Baltes's work questions the representative functions of painting and caricatures the seriousness of the medium.
These mostly intensely black forms, precisely painted with a paintbrush, stand out by virtue of their style against the coloured background, which Baltes applies to the canvases with spray paint. As monochrome areas or colour gradients in one or more colours, the colourful backgrounds – in bright green, yellow or orange – provide an optical contrast to the black motifs and create a new dialogue between colour and form in each individual painting.
In some pictures, details like colourful brushstrokes, ellipses, dots and chalk drawings create additional levels of content or form which either blend easily into the interplay between foreground and background, figuration and abstraction, or throw it off balance. Sculptural and haptic elements play a major role in Baltes's works. For location-specific projects she has them grow playfully from the canvas into the space and become objects. To achieve this, she placed her paintings on rollers, mounts them on a wall like a door, supports them at an angle on the floor or sets them on little feet. In this way her works, to which she gives names like *Immi, Takk* or *Ferl,* become abstract, three-dimensional portraits of fictional characters who appear as a group in the social space and yet never entirely reveal their identity. —— *Anna-Lena Werner*

Cornelia Baltes was born in 1978 in Mönchengladbach and currently lives and works in Berlin

Bergische Universität Wuppertal, 2000–2003

Folkwang Universität der Künste, Essen, 2003–2006

Slade School of Fine Art, London, Master of Fine Arts, 2009–2011

2018 Teamwork, Frutta, Glasgow (S)
Wallpaintings, Chapter Arts Centre, Cardiff (S)
Mingle Mime, Bolte Lang, Zürich (S)
2017 Capri, Galleri Nicolai Wallner, Copenhagen (S)

corneliabaltes.com

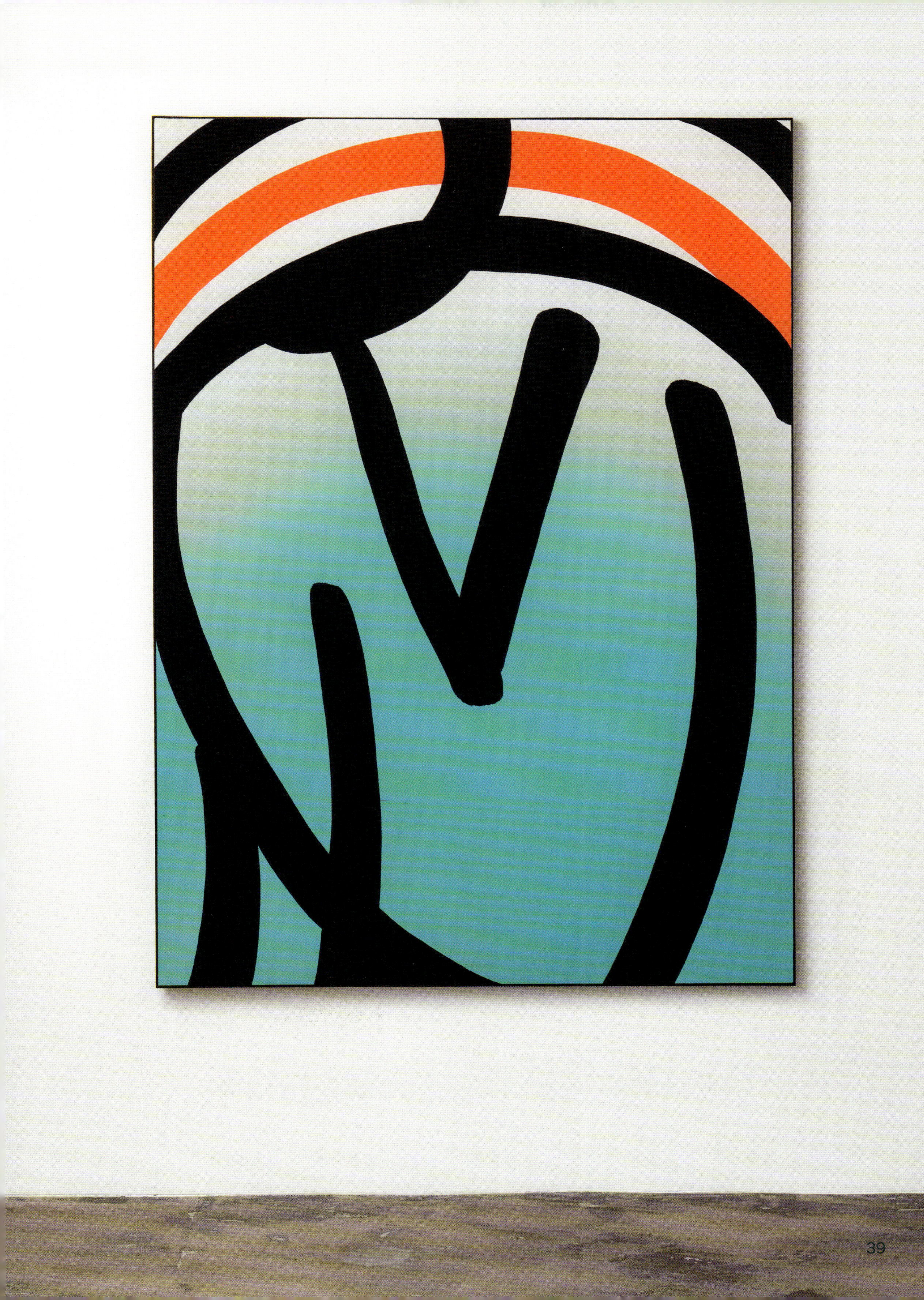

Loel 2019 Acrylic on canvas 190 × 140 cm Chemnitz

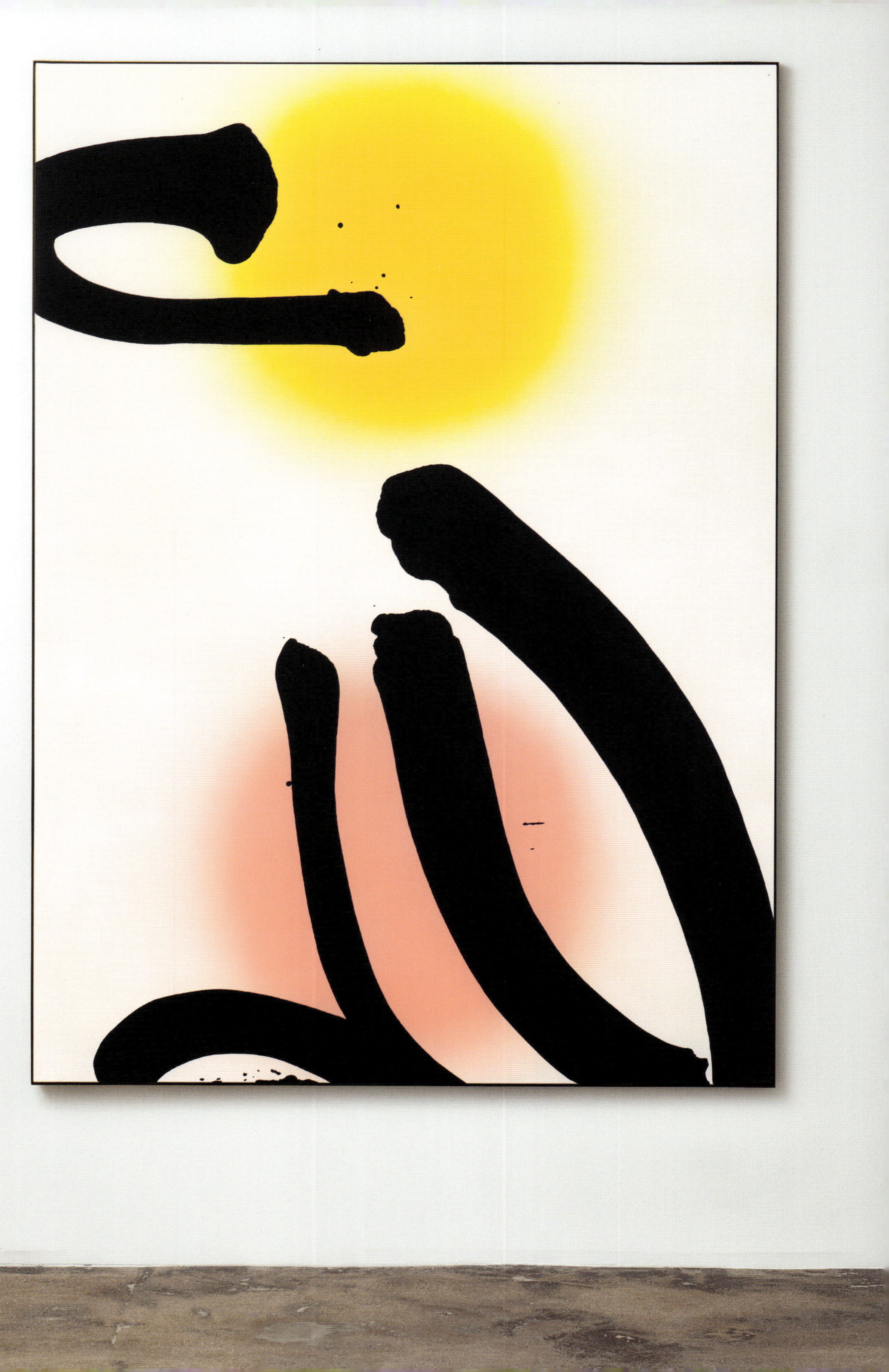

Olgh 2019 Acrylic on canvas 210 × 150 cm Bonn

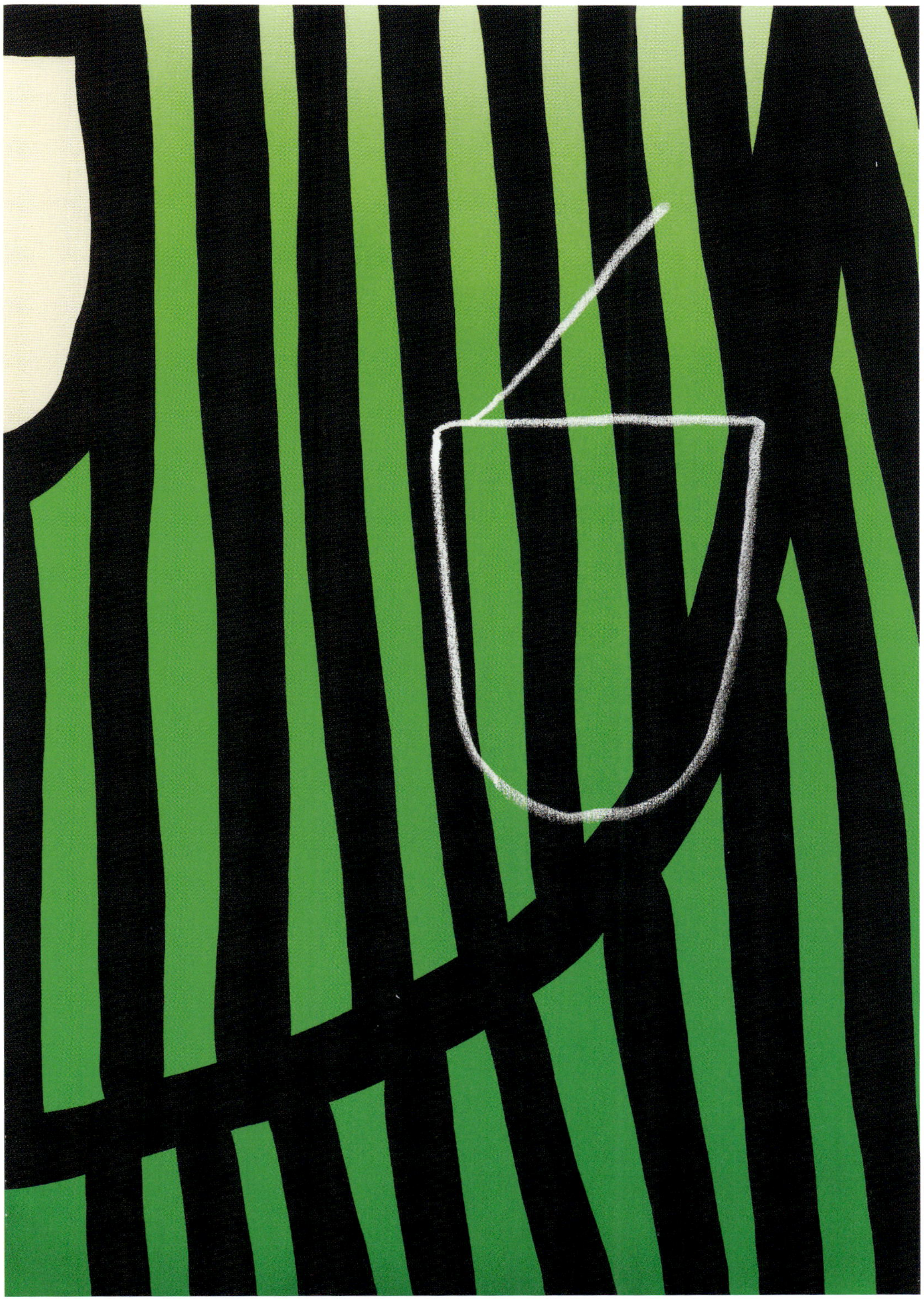

Takk 2019 Acrylic and oil stick on canvas 140 × 100 cm Wiesbaden

Jagoda Bednarsky

Jagoda Bednarsky was born in 1988 in Złotoryja (Poland) and currently lives and works in Berlin

Städelschule Frankfurt a.M., Meisterschülerin, 2014

2018 Introverterior/Extroverterior, Kunstverein Heppenheim (S)

Impression Management, Philipp Pflug Contemporary, Frankfurt a.M. (S)

2017 L.A. should die vor Glück, justmarried.one, Los Angeles (G)

Internship, Bundesbank Frankfurt a.M. (S)

The world consists of images and images never end. We think in images and all imaginable knowledge can be told in images. Jagoda Bednarsky's painting draws on this monstrous "archive" of past and possible, impossible, invented and actual images. She directs her questions towards history and brings it into the present, but is aiming at the future ... the connections she makes consist of a re-connection of all the images she has adopted and made her own.

She dissects what we take for granted and reassembles it quite openly. In a generous act of combination she skilfully and playfully creates her paintings from a multitude of visual set pieces and quotations of motifs. The result is idiosyncratic and variable, imaginative, touching, sensuous and absurd.

And yet what we see is evidently never what we at first take it to be. Enigmatically, apparently unambiguous references withdraw into the fabric of the overlapping textures of the picture. Only in the interplay of the subjects, colours and gestures can we gradually recognise Bednarsky's references. Between the pictures of what she found beforehand and her constructed pictures of "afterwards", which leave nothing to chance, she generates something new which updates history.

This new element is her present, what she feels, what she experiences – be it the "Shadowland" of motherhood, including "symphonic" milk pumps, despairing self-portraits and psycho-physical wellness mania, voyeurism, flirtatious masquerades and Art-Deco magazines, female role clichés and sealed book objects whose auspicious titles announce, for example, "J. Bednarsky" or which consist of second volumes without it being in the least clear what the first one was about.

Reflectively, poetically, Jagoda Bednarsky speculates in her pictures about a world of images which at times seems incomprehensible. From "disorder" she creates "order through [her painterly] repetition" (Jorge Luis Borges), an order which will perhaps enable us to see and understand a little more over time. —— *Christian Malycha*

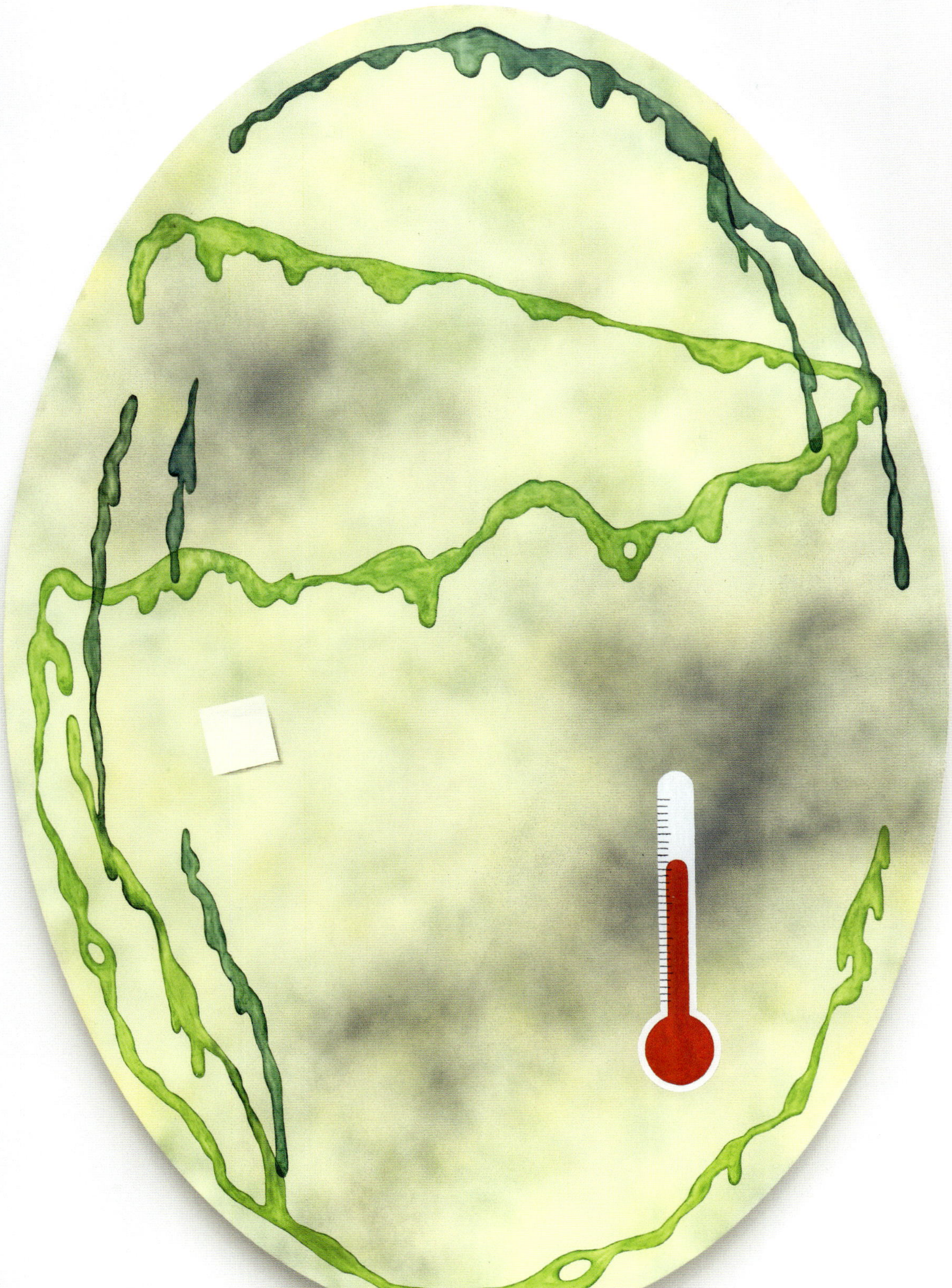

OPTIX (Temperature) 2018 Oil and spray paint on canvas 150 × 110 cm Chemnitz

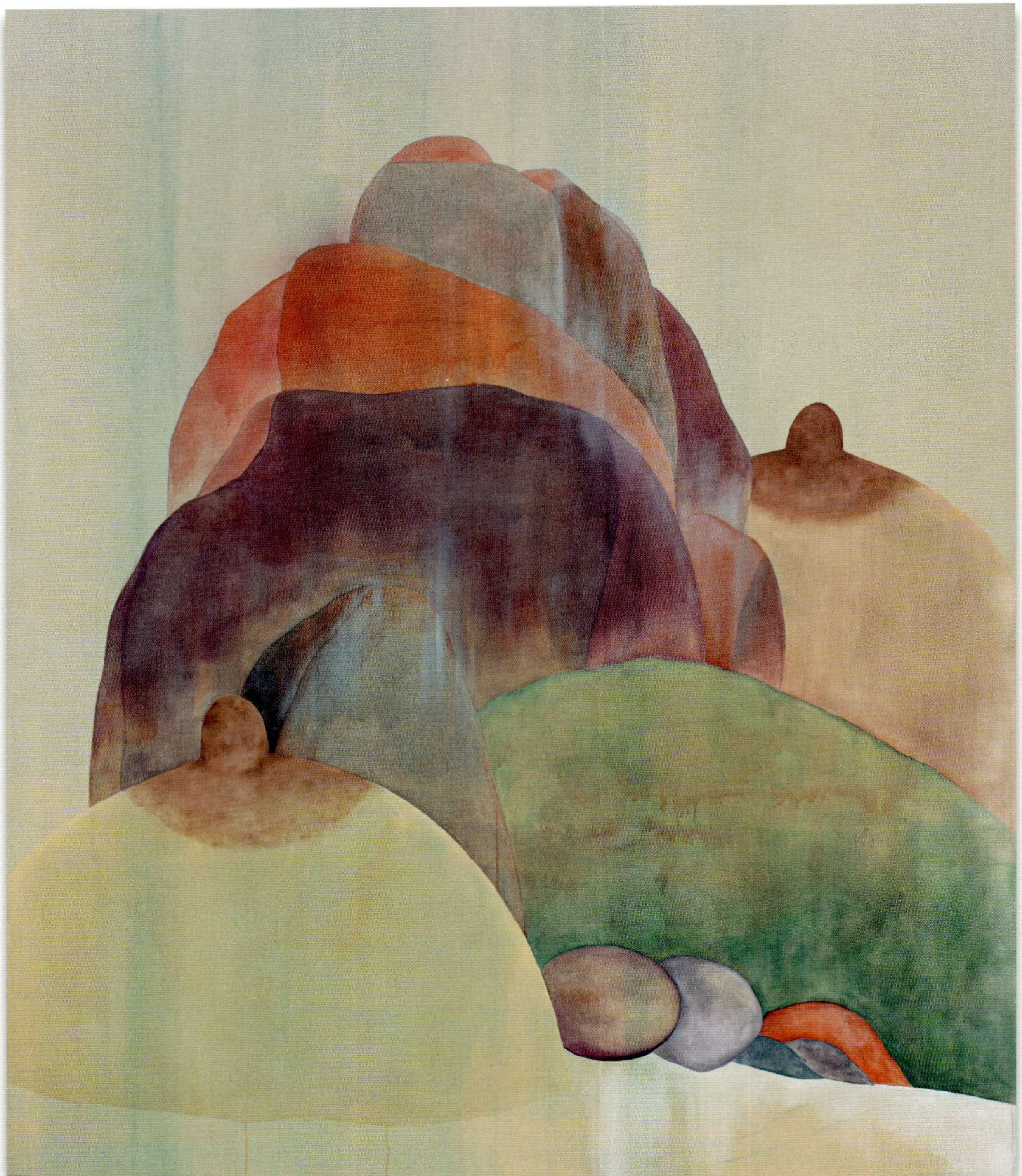

Shadowland

2019

Oil, gouache, acrylic and spray paint on canvas

220 × 190 cm

Bonn

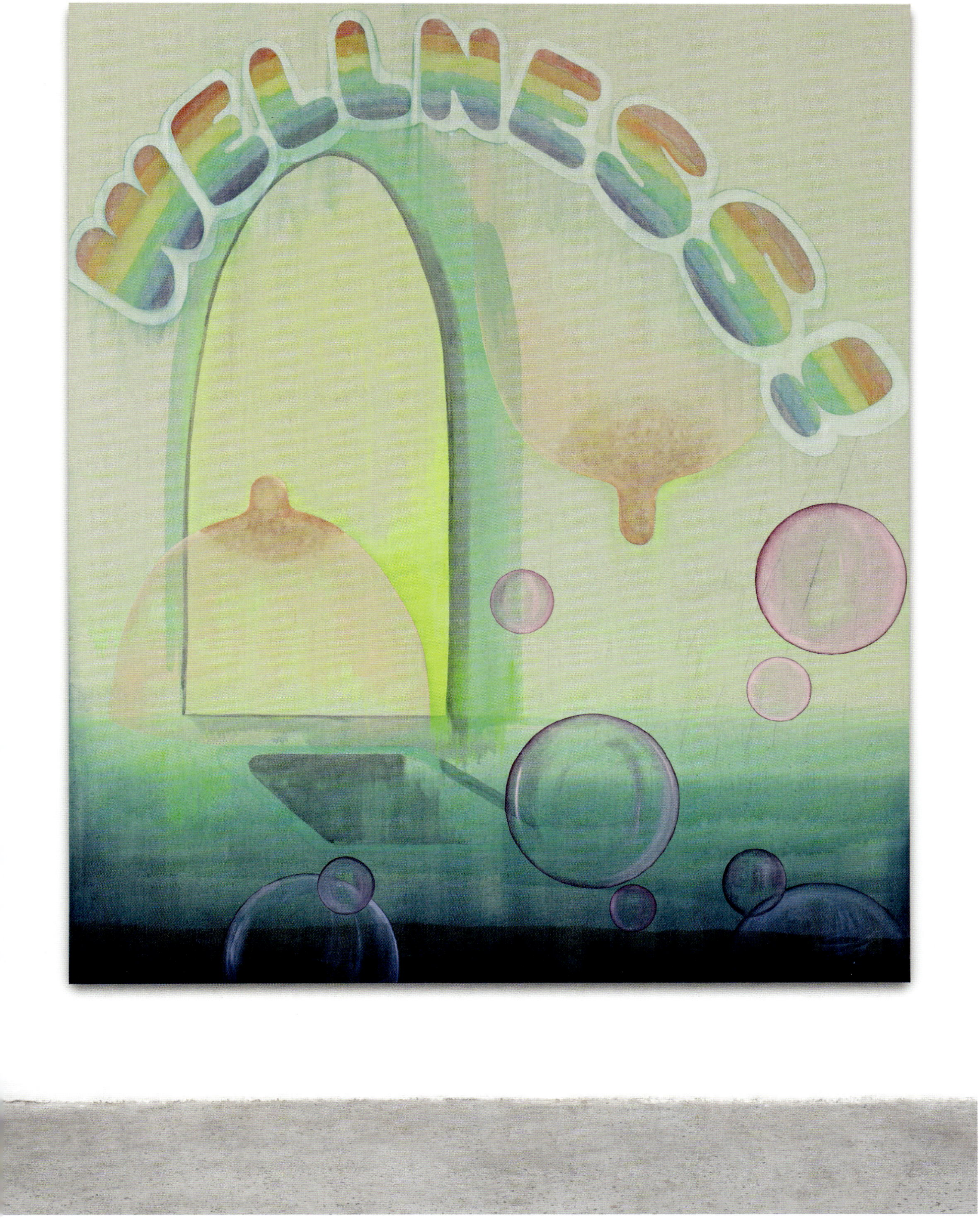

WELLNESS (Milk & Honey) 2019 Oil, acrylic, gouache and pastel on canvas 220 × 190 cm Wiesbaden

Viola Bittl

The sureness of awkwardness

It is difficult not to reflect on Viola Bittl's painting. At the same time, it seems impossible to conjure up the pictures accurately in one's mind's eye; they evaporate too quickly when they are no longer present, and it is too easy to fall into the trap of describing their form. And yet that is precisely what her painting starts out from: a form. And this form – whether circular or angular – acts on the painting. Surfaces are piled up on top of each other (or deposited?) to form a three-dimensional mass. Ovals that are scrunched up together or cut off stumble over each other or are combined to form a figure.
Viola Bittl's treatment of forms is diverse, precise and surprising – never random and in no way ostentatious. Her pictorial arrangements radiate an almost frightening awareness of what they aim to present. Here we see an artist at work who knows what she is doing, but who does not necessarily feel that she needs to demonstrate it. It is this pleasing restraint which makes us return to her pictures. No wailing and gnashing of teeth, but an intense conversation which begs to be continued. At any time and in any place. Bittl's pictures are confident, knowing, and lie beyond the realms of short-lived trends. They make their statements as mature paintings with the courage to be awkward. Edges break away, surfaces seem unable to find the form they are looking for, brushstrokes go a bit too far, edges of motifs which lie further down break through and irritate. These side stages of awkwardness bear witness to an attitude in painting which can also be found in the works of, for example, Suzan Frecon, Stanley Whitney and Gary Stephan. The painting of the picture remains alive, visible, comprehensible.
Viola Bittl's painting occurs before retouching and *cosmetic surgery*; it shows the world (painting) as it really is, with its scars, unevenness and deposits in the layers that have been covered up. Her gaze is always slightly displaced with a preference for the remote. ——
Tilo Schulz

Viola Bittl was born in 1980 in Eichstätt and currently lives and works in Frankfurt a. M.

Akademie der Bildenden Künste Munich with Prof. Sean Scully, 2004–2008
Kuvataideakatemia, Academy of Fine Arts, Helsinki, 2007

Städelschule Frankfurt a. M. with Prof. Christa Näher, 2008–2011, Meisterschülerin, 2011

2018 Hessische Kulturstiftung, Jahresstipendium New York

2017 basis.aperçu, Goethe-Institut Paris, Paris (G)
meaning gets unstable, Gallerie Doris Ghetta, Ortisei BZ (G)
gerissen/gefalzt/geschnitten/gezeichnet, Galerie Nanna Preußners, Hamburg (G)

violabittl.de

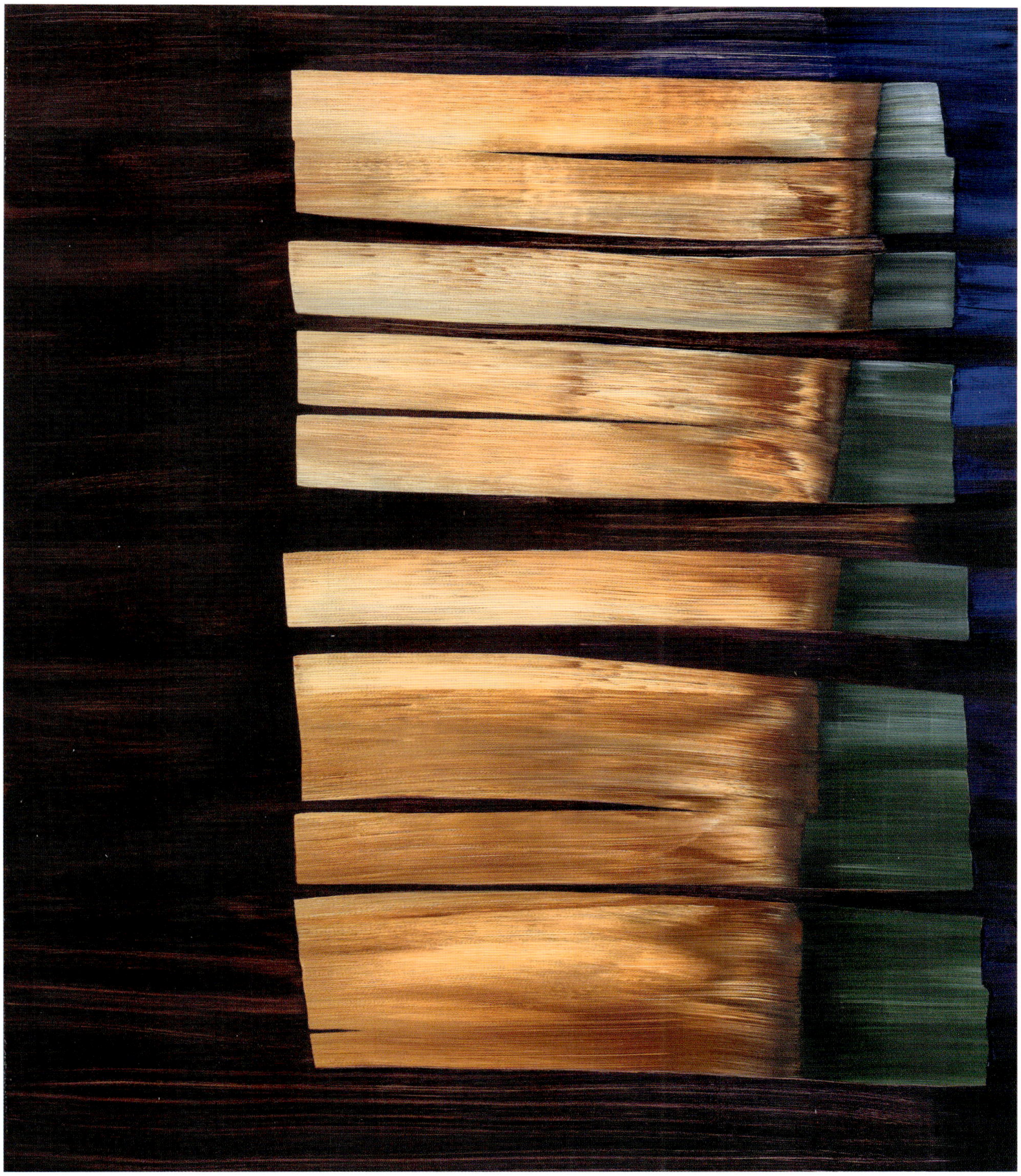

Untitled V   2017   Oil on canvas   180 × 160 cm   Chemnitz

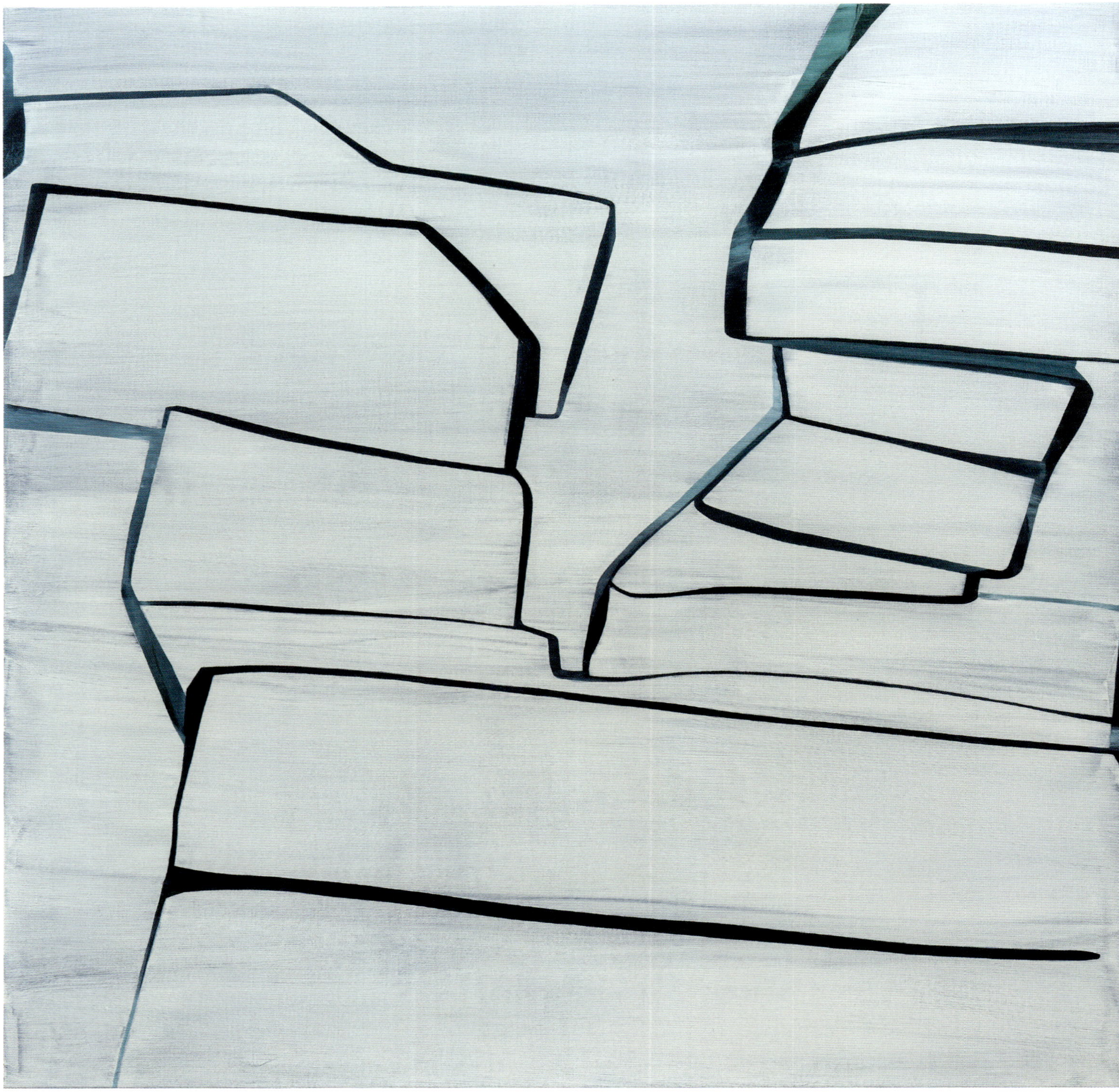

Untitled II 2019 Oil on canvas 190 × 200 cm Bonn

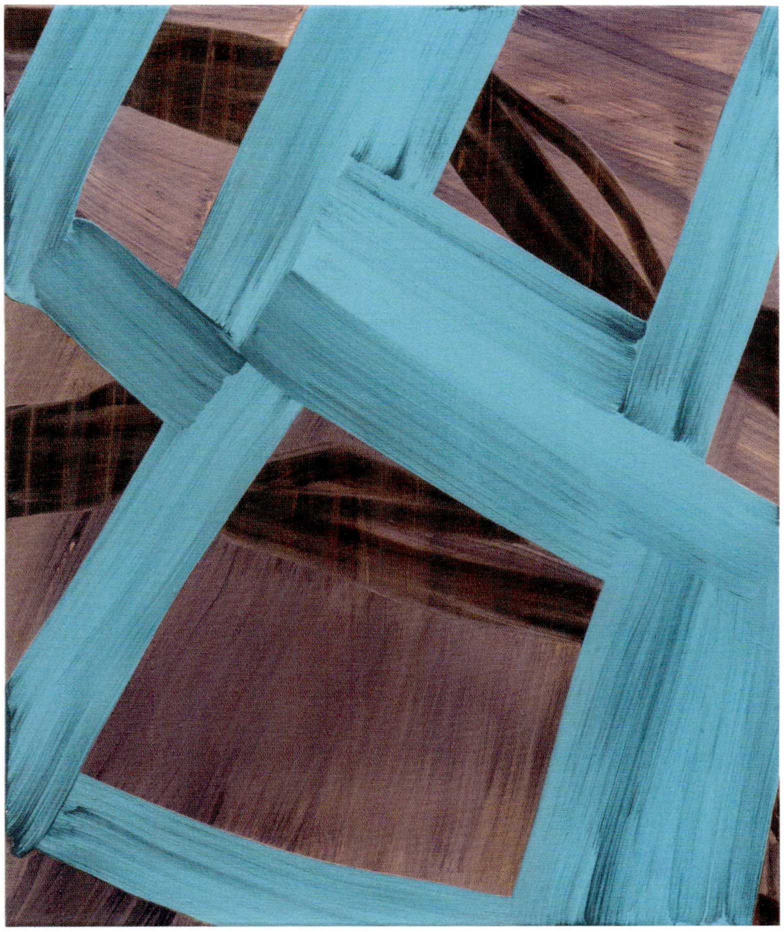

Untitled II 2018 Oil on canvas 70 × 60 cm Wiesbaden

Peppi Bottrop

If it is true that one criterion for the quality of a painter is his reliable recognisability, coupled at the same time with the largest possible development potential within the parameters he has set for himself, then Peppi Bottrop is among the best artists of his generation.

Even at his first solo exhibition at the gallery of Jan Kaps in Cologne in 2014, he demonstrated an unshakeable self-confidence. Someone had backed out of the gallerist's exhibition programme, leaving a gap. Instead of filling it with pictures from his studio, the artist he therefore invited at short notice decided that he would prefer to cover the walls of the gallery with canvases, to spend a night with, in front of and on them, and then call the result, succinctly and not without a suggestion of megalomania, *One Night In*.

And behold: it was already all there: the graphite pencil on the unprimed canvas, which seeks the pressure from both sides and which is always fixed during the act of painting (or drawing) directly to the wall without a stretcher frame. The basic geometric forms: squares, triangles, circles that recall children's building blocks in their brutal simplicity, were it not for the nervous line and the evident knowledge that it is in its very fragmentation that the whole world lies hidden.

What may seem to the viewer like Constructivism in a stage of advanced incompetence, could only be explained by others in biographical terms. Charcoal as a medium: what else should the boy from the mining town of Bottrop have chosen? Five years after his first exhibition, it is clear that Peppi Bottrop is a post-ironic painter through and through. If one of his works recalls a canvas by Giacometti in its graphic rigour and depth, that is in the first instance due to his process and his innate seriousness. In Bottrop's works, temporary aesthetic convergences are never of a conceptual nature, but arise from shared experiences during the act of painting and are in any case legible only for more sensitive souls; after all, a picture signed with Peppi Bottrop's name on the back can be recognised even at a distance as being by Peppi Bottrop.

Which brings us to another characteristic of his work: the undeniable striving for dominance. Whether he transforms tiny spaces into a work (2015 in the Kunstverein Heppenheim) or sees large spaces initially as an architectural challenge (as in his group exhibition with Albert Oehlen in 2018 in the Marciano Foundation Los Angeles) – as soon as it is a question of exhibiting, the painter becomes a "site-specific artist" par excellence.

Perhaps that – apart from the coal – is the most important legacy of his youth in the city whose name he bears so stoically: a "Don't-fuck-with-me" attitude, which was previously directed towards the boys from the wrong neighbourhood but today addresses all those who no longer want to believe in the eternal wonder of painting. —— *Cornelius Tittel*

Peppi Bottrop was born in 1986 in Bottrop and currently lives and works in Cologne

Kunstakademie Düsseldorf, Meisterschüler, 2014

2019 Concord, Gerhardsen Gerner Gallery, Oslo (S)

2018 linepackers, Marciano Art Foundation, Los Angeles (with Albert Oehlen) (S)

A ROUTINE TRIP TURNS INTO AN ENCHANTING ESCAPADE LUCKY #1, 7, 20, 34, 57, 44, Marc LeBlanc, Chicago (G)

2017 Der lange Löffel, Jan Kaps, Cologne (S)

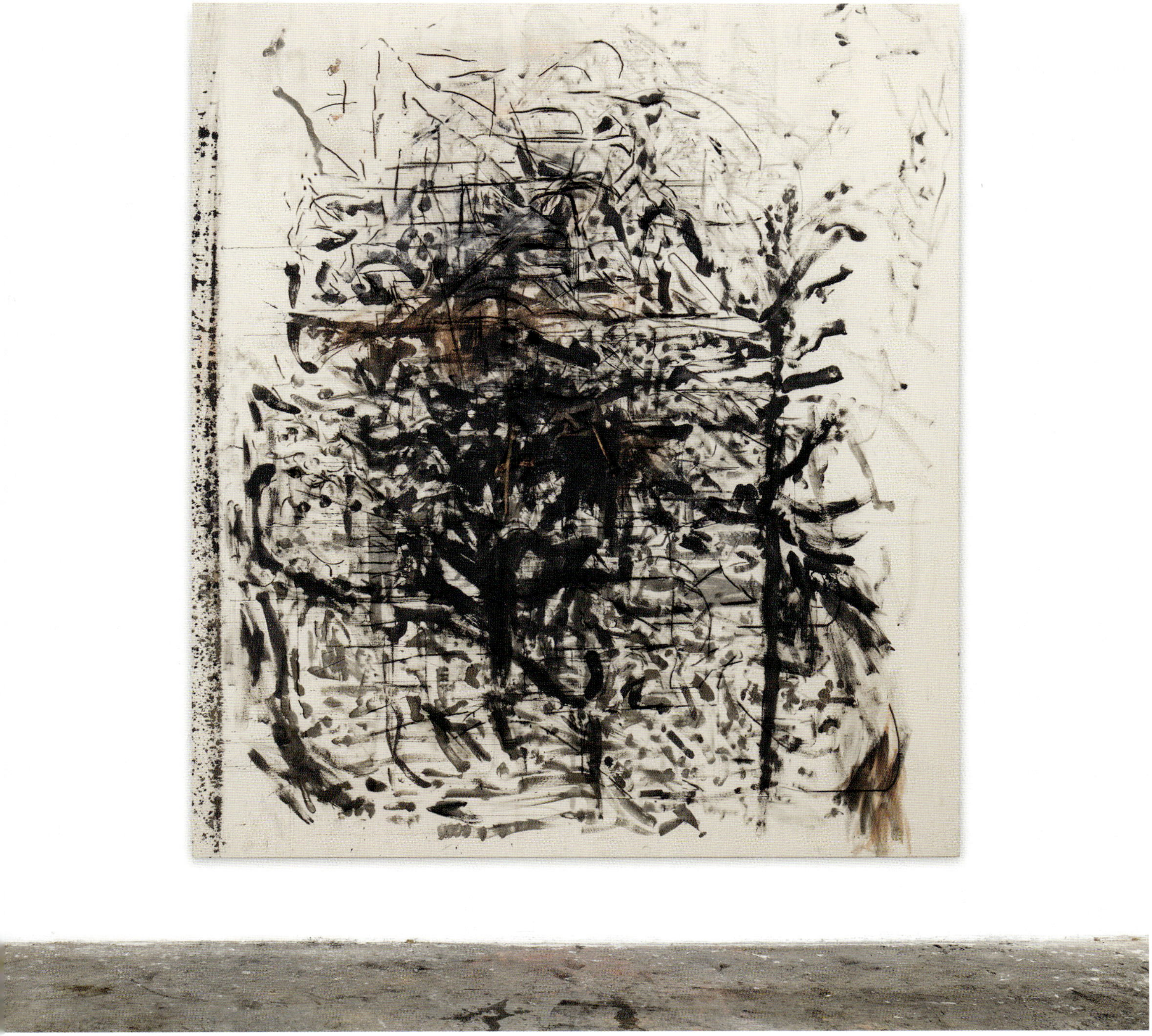

dis phen

2019

Graphite, copper pigment and
charcoal on canvas

310 × 280 cm

Chemnitz

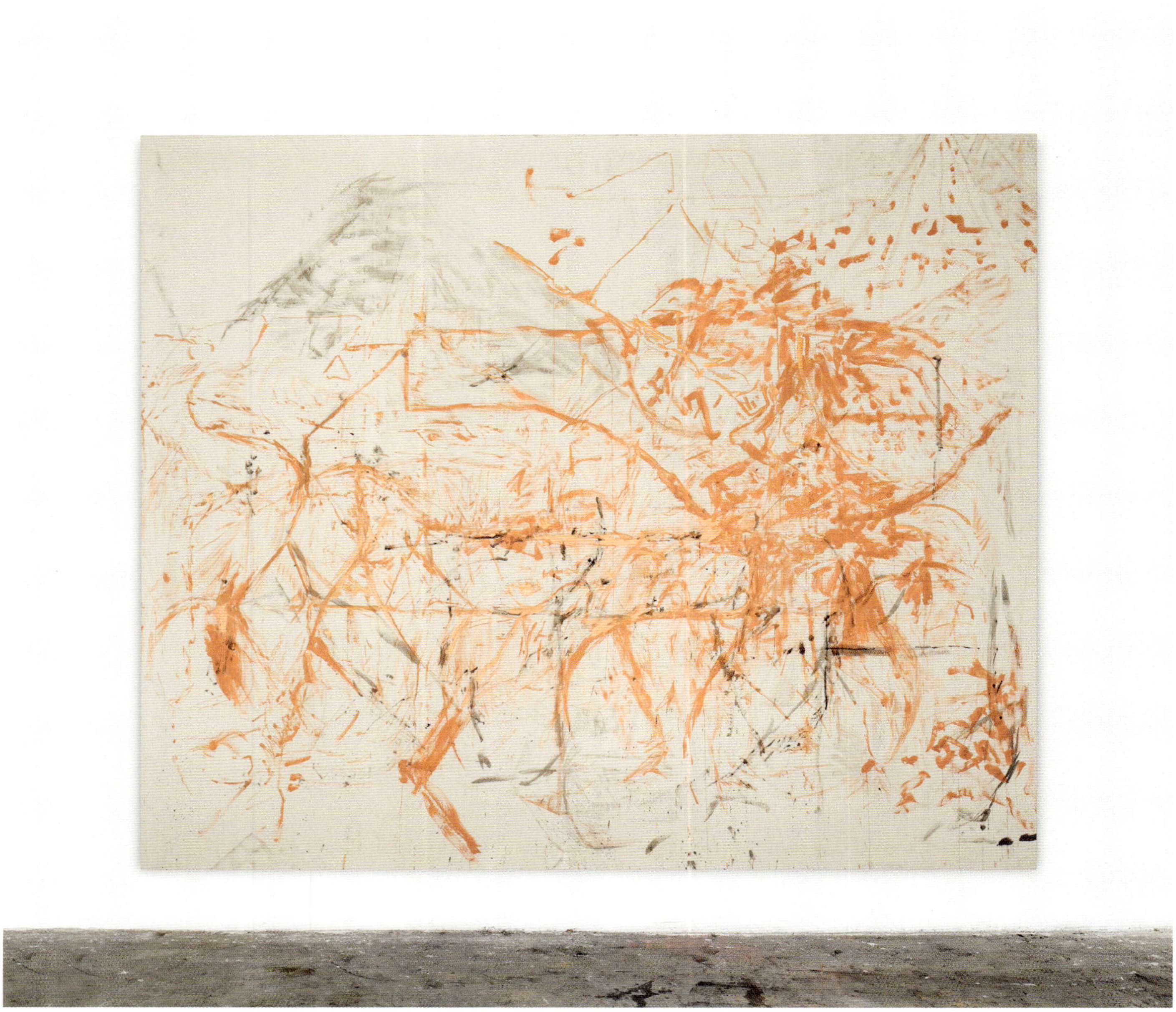

FFP

2019

Graphite, bronze pigment and charcoal on canvas

310 × 380 cm

Bonn

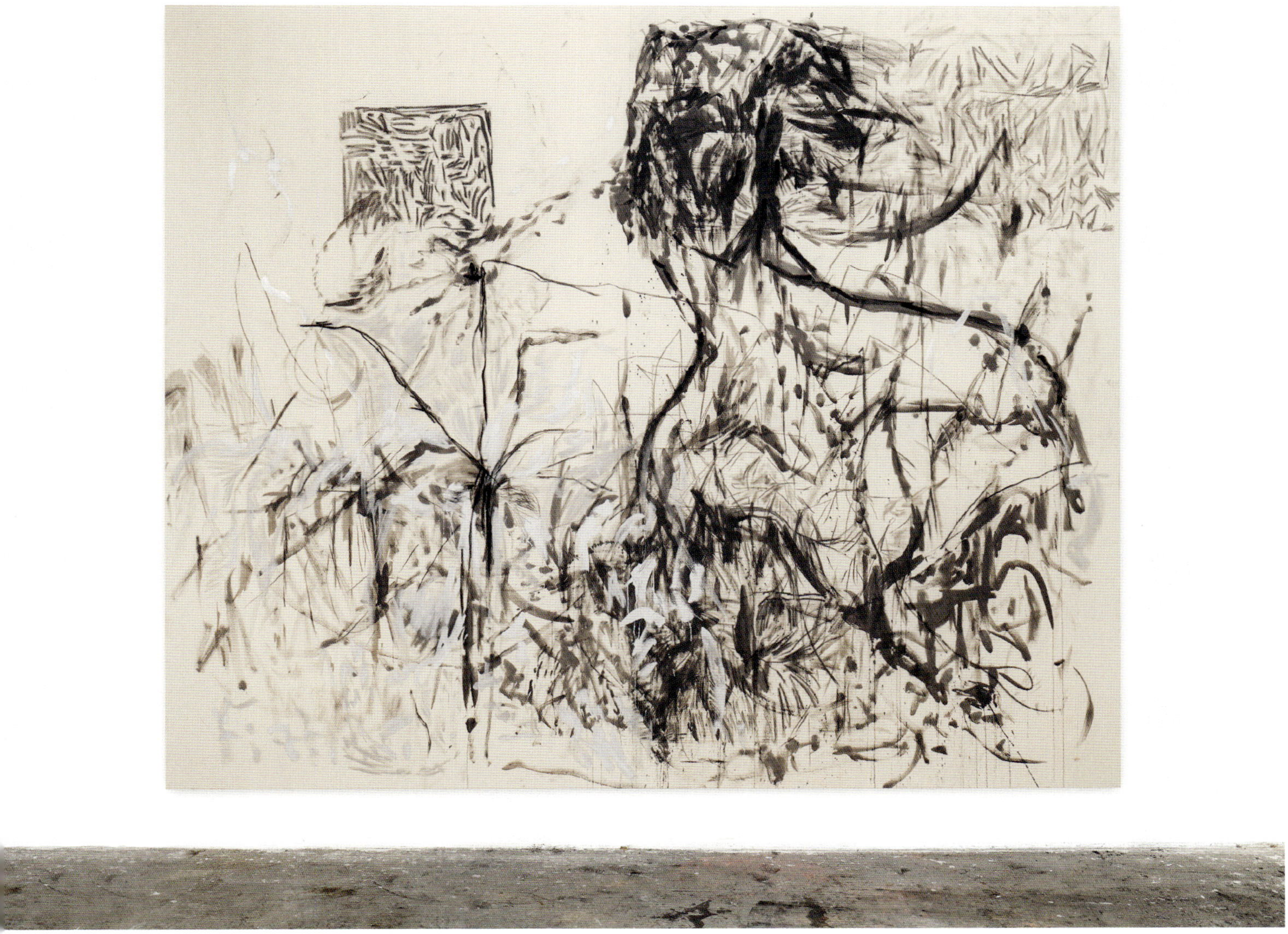

inef s.c.
2019
Graphite, aluminium pigment and charcoal on canvas
310 × 380 cm
Wiesbaden

Andreas Breunig

Everything that happens, happens only once. Everything fades away. Inexorably. And it takes time to realise what we have experienced.
Andreas Breunig's painting reveals this time. All representationalism dissolves against the unbroken white background as if against the light. Things recede on his "Hi>°<LoRes" pictures and where the material becomes porous, hazy or blurred, the colour itself appears.
But if reality is constantly escaping it becomes impossible simply to depict it. To express what was there it is necessary for fleeting impressions and emotions to have engraved themselves in our own experience – as a conscious echo of what is absent. Images permit our individual world of experience to recur, extract it from oblivion and bring it back into the present.
Breunig's pictures possess such a presence. They are wholly here and yet they are constantly being updated. Each picture begins with individual positions, but it is only the harmony that gives them their character. Every wave, every arch, every spot, every arc of colour responds to a strip, a block, a grid, an area of cross-hatching. The free ornamental pattern repeat is followed by a basic structure that gives the surface stability and orientation. Abundance and emptiness resonate in the same way as the contrasting colours. Rhythmically, Breunig contrasts different tempos and textures: roughness counterbalances velvet-smooth, fluid overlays dryness, and pastose elements contradict brittle ones. His paint demonstrates temperament; appearance is feeling, so to speak.
Andreas Breunig blends countless picture levels into each other as if they were films, curtains or draperies. They are positioned on the surface and strung up high. The pictures rise up and turn to meet us. It is a physical experience which he heightens by bringing them into space like an installation. The pictorial space reaches out beyond its boundaries to become a stereogram which makes use of all its experience to take a stand against the constant world loss.
—— *Christian Malycha*

Andreas Breunig was born in 1983 in Eberbach and currently lives and works in Düsseldorf

Kunstakademie Düsseldorf with Prof. Albert Oehlen

2019 The Windowing System – as a (hyperstatic) problem, Nino Mier Gallery, Los Angeles (S)

2018 Ein Tun ohne Bild, Kunstverein Reutlingen, Reutlingen (G)

VOTE (with Jana Schröder), Kunstverein Heppenheim, Heppenheim (S)

2017 Hi>°<LoRes (with Clemens Rathe), Warhus Rittershaus, Cologne (S)

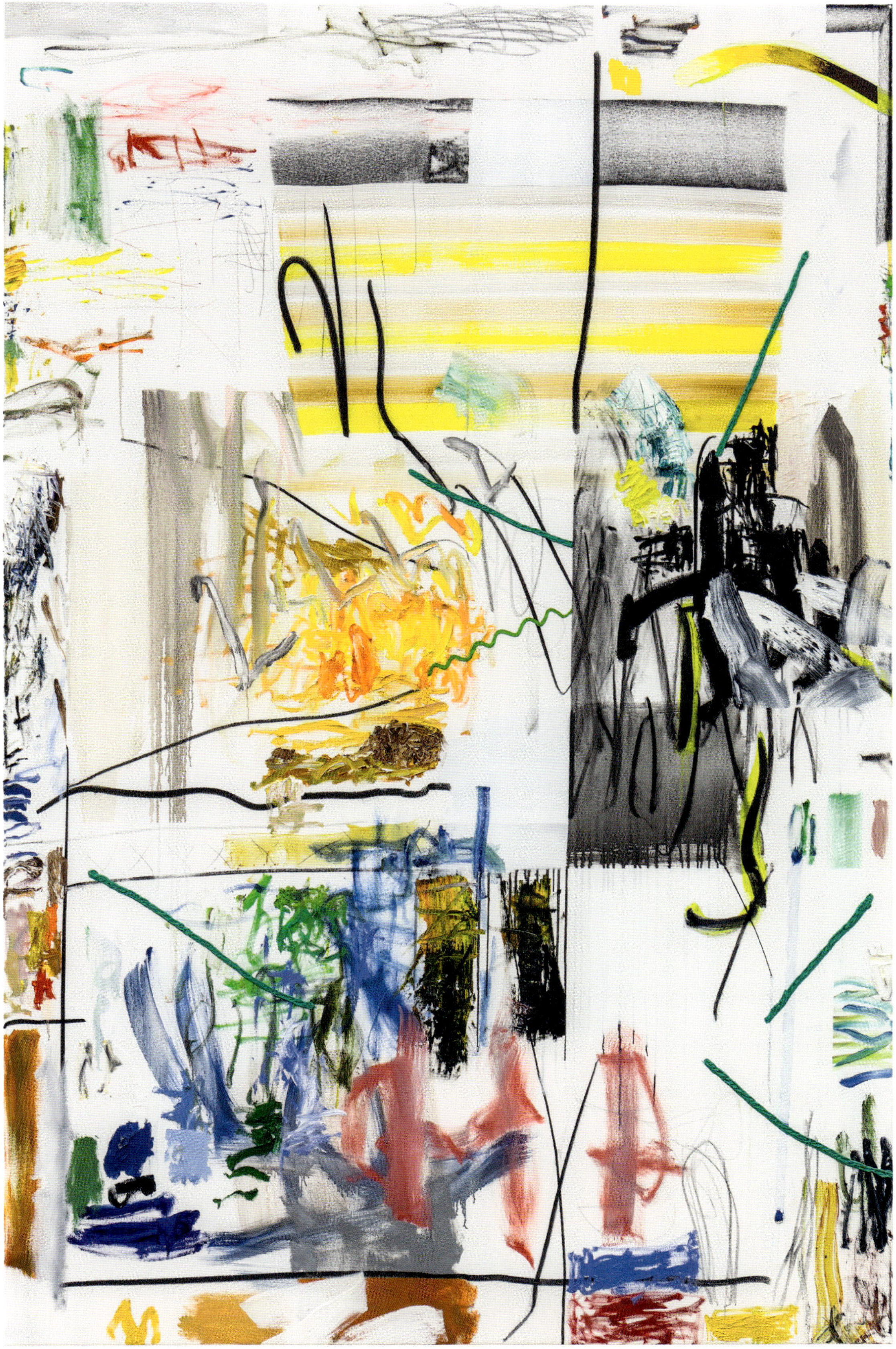

Hi >°< LoRes No. 66 2019 Oil, graphite and charcoal on canvas 210 × 140 cm Chemnitz

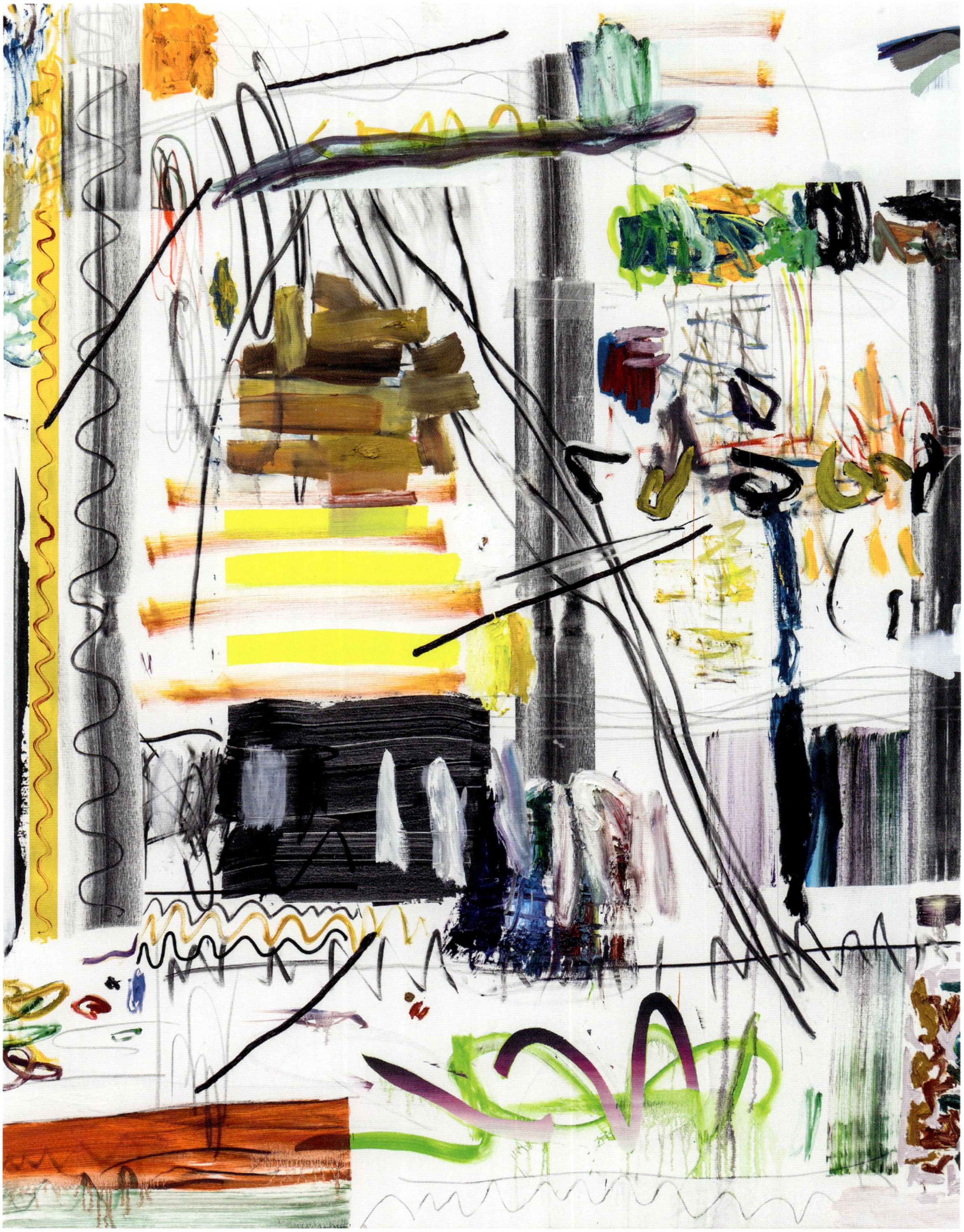

Hi & LoRes No. 56   2019   Oil, graphite and charcoal on canvas   210 × 170 cm   Bonn

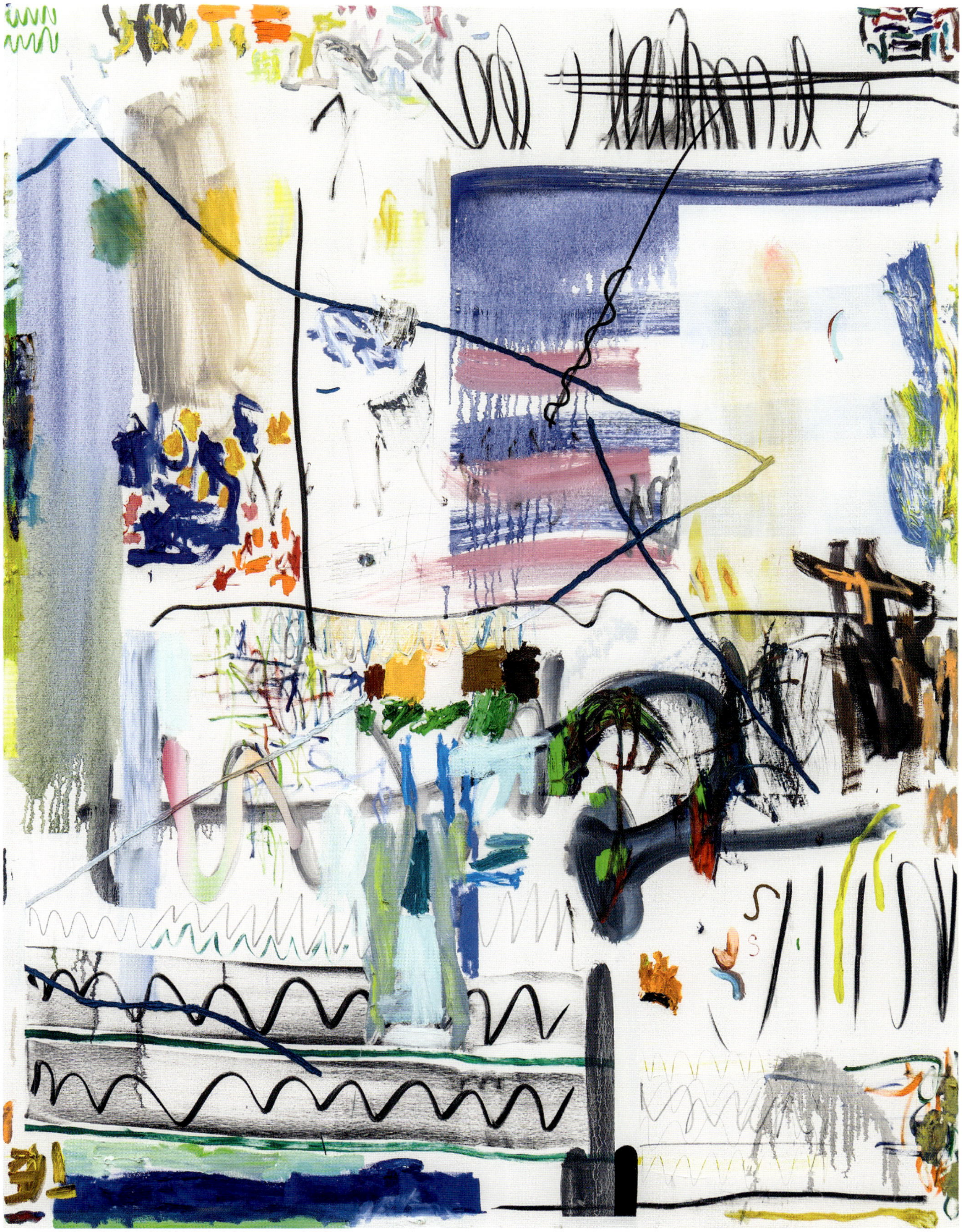

Hi >°< LoRes No. 62, 2019, Oil, graphite and charcoal on canvas, 210 × 170 cm, Wiesbaden

Paul Czerlitzki

Paul Czerlitzki belongs to the generation of post-medium artists who have been engaged in redefining painting's ontological status and its afterlife. His monochromatic canvases remind quasi-ancient statues, carved-in-stone anti-monuments, solid but vulnerable, fragmentary though autonomous, leaning against the wall like witnesses of heroic times long past. Their wrinkled surfaces simulate inevitable aging and ephemerality; in other cases, they dazzle with the polished greyness of what once acted as the sublime white of the nonrepresentational. Seemingly contradictory methods of reducing/erasing on the one hand, and accumulating/amassing on the other balance the artist's interest in excess and a void of the visual. *Nothing is more fragile than the surface,* chants Deleuze while architecturing the habitat of the logic of sense. *Plain Superficiality is the character of a speech,* he echoes after Lewis Carroll. Flatness governs the pictorial field of Czerlitzki's skin-like tableaux, performances of surface tensions. *The deepest is the skin,* as Deleuze articulates the paradox of pure becoming, composed of reversals that elude the present and question fixed identities. Czerlitzki's paintings are ruins in reverse, documents of silent temporalities and memories in suspense.

Manipulating with delay and postponement strategies, Czerlitzki appears as an archaeologist of painting: his processual installation mimics an excavation site and provides an insight to a breathing space of a painterly labour. Here it is: a painting stripped bare. An act of "delay" engineers a vivisection-like process of delayering: slicing through and across the matter, undressing layer by layer, dis-covering skin off the skin, a *mise-en-scène* of reality which, following Michel Serres, is imagined as veiled place. A displacement serves as a temporary method to postpone decision making and symbolic marking of a new life to come. Czerlitzki's painting is simultaneously an act of nonchalance and a slow-motion apology; a gesture of both a withdrawal and a devotion. —— *Adam Budak*

Paul Czerlitzki was born in 1986 in Gdansk (Poland) and currently lives and works in Düsseldorf

Kunstakademie Düsseldorf, Meisterschüler with Prof. Katharina Grosse, 2009–2014

2018 An, Galerie Konrad Fischer, Düsseldorf (S)
DELAY, annex14, Zürich (S)
06:16 SVIT, Prague (S)
Neuer Norden Zürich (G)

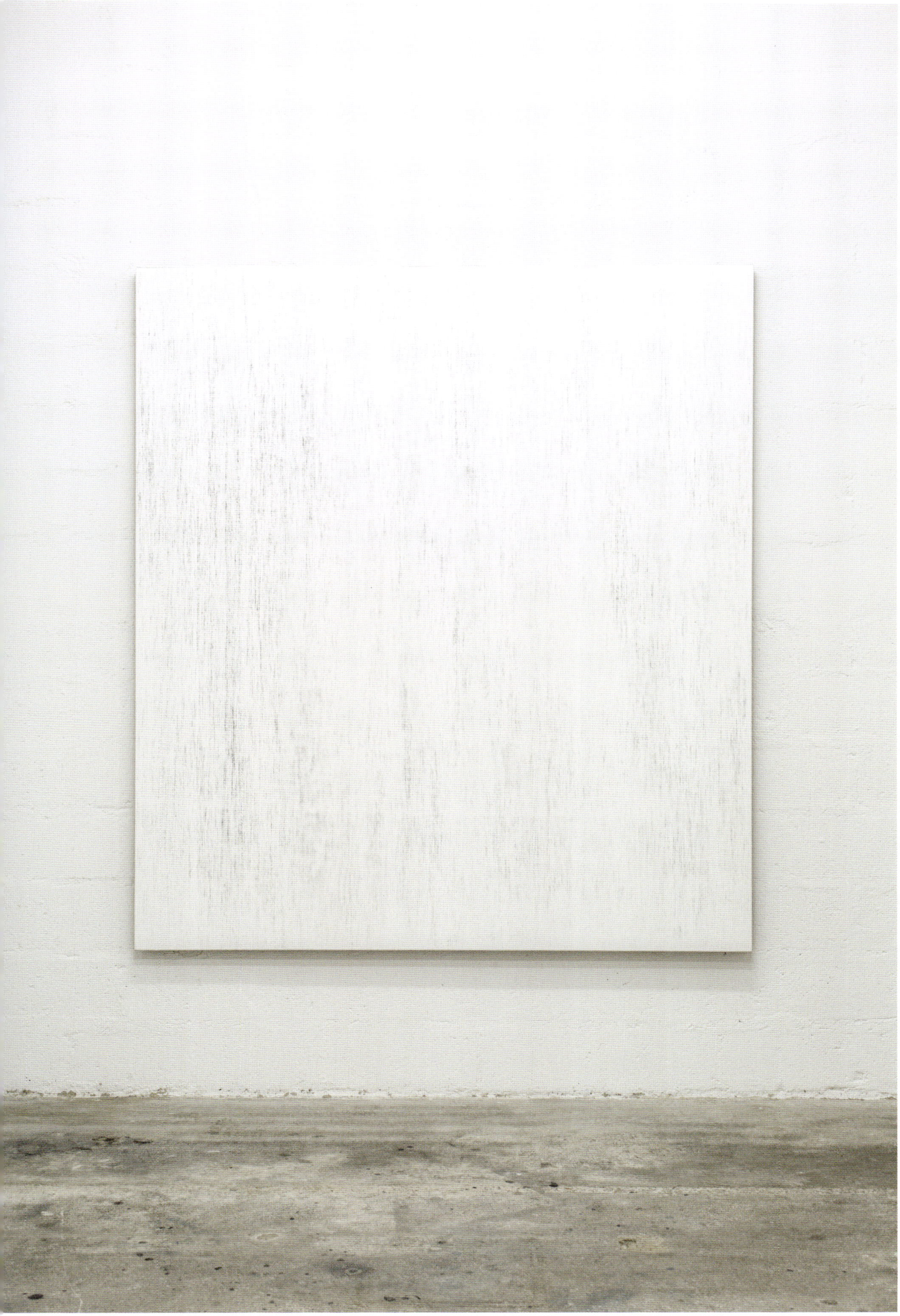

Untitled 2011–2019 Acrylic on canvas 210 × 190 cm Wiesbaden

Untitled 2011–2019 Acrylic on canvas 210 × 190 cm Chemnitz

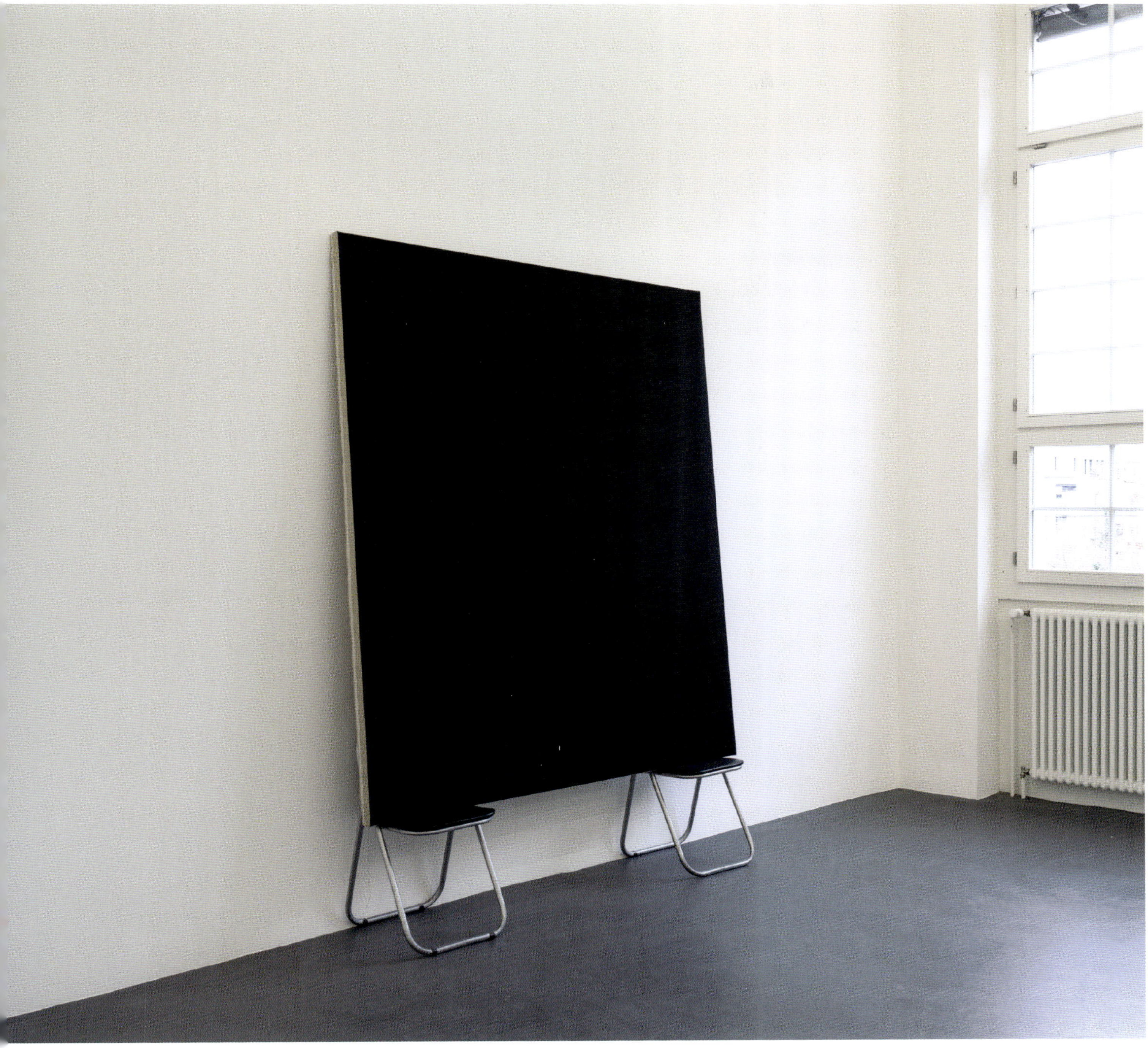

Delay 2019 Acrylic on canvas, folding chairs ca. 255 × 190 × 50 cm, total Bonn

Benjamin Dittrich

What are we actually looking at? The basic question whenever we find ourselves looking at art is posed yet again when we survey the works of Benjamin Dittrich. Distant memories of old television test cards are reawakened, reminiscences of classic science-fiction posters and computeresque retro-fantasies, intimations of worlds of technoid circuitry and physical cosmologies. It is not least the formal language of abstract modern art, mysterious and structured, which rears its head in these artistic parallel universes.
But Dittrich does not leave us in the dark; he needs no nebulous esotericism. His art is an exploration, a picture-making in the literal sense. What the natural sciences once created as a visualisation of world processes across the millennia – tables, spectra, waves – is divested of content and meaning, gutted and filled up again. The essence of the knowledge and information society lies in fragments, naked as it were before us, strangely familiar and at the same time alien. In this way, something that once claimed to represent a comprehensive portrait of the world is transformed into a coded graphical and geometric form, an artistic composition.
With the revelation of his sources – often encyclopaedias and scientific compendiums of former times whose content is now outdated – Dittrich succeeds in achieving a daring, logical turnaround: the dialectic relationship between art and the world, between human creation and supposedly objective science manifests itself starkly. The abstractions in the representations of nature and physics, caught up in the style and design of their time, become a contingent cultural technology which reveals the existence of the scientific object in the records of simplification, classification and combination.
By rearranging and showing the relationships between the existing fragments of those interpretations of the world in a playful manner like a puzzle, but without the claims of strict conceptual art, Dittrich permits us to examine their fragile innermost being – thereby granting us access to a new world. —— *Maximilian Haase*

Benjamin Dittrich was born in 1987 in Düsseldorf and currently lives and works in Leipzig

Hochschule für Grafik und Buchkunst Leipzig, Meisterschüler with Prof. Annette Schröter, 2015

2019 Erholung, aber wo, Thaler Originalgrafik, Leipzig (S)

2018 Zarter Fels, Museum der bildenden Künste Leipzig (S)

Dünner Pelz, Galerie b2_, Leipzig (S)

2017 Black Sugar, Städtisches Kunstmuseum Spendhaus Reutlingen (G)

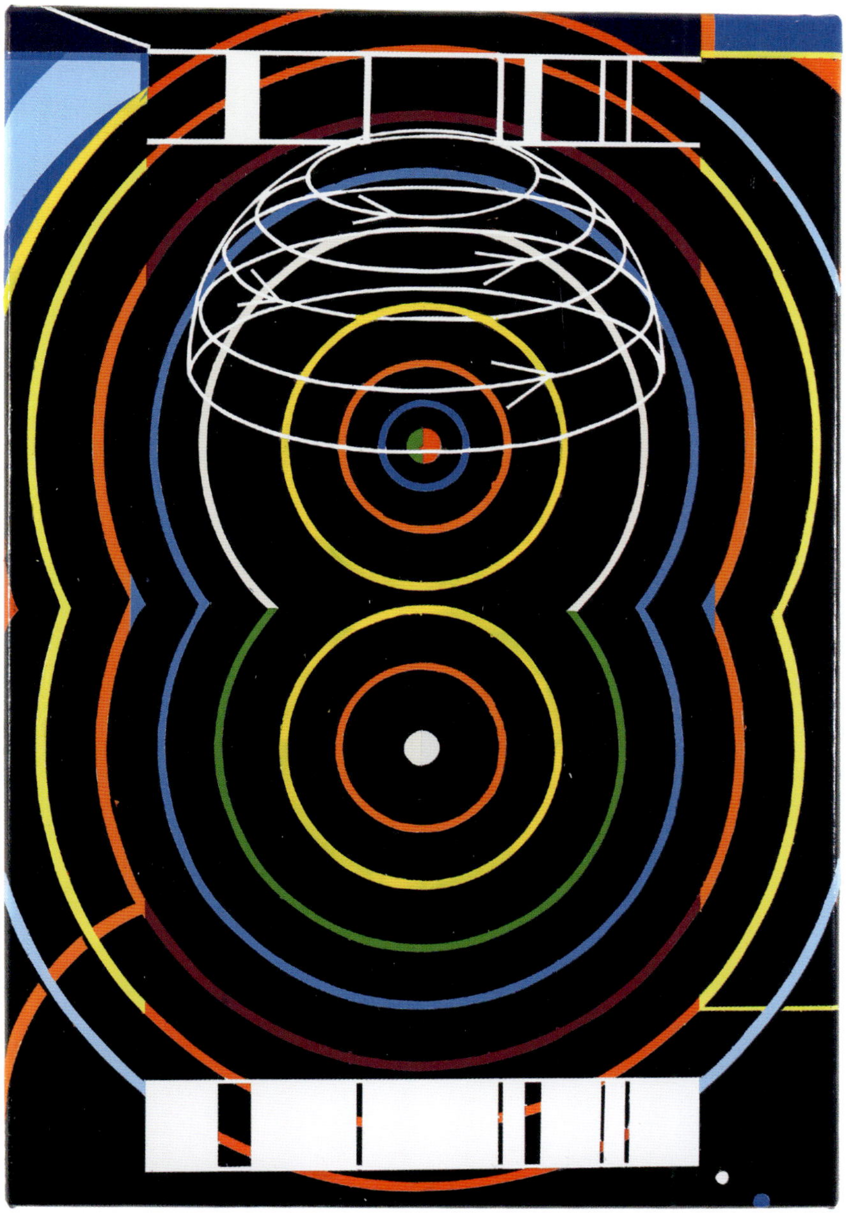

DHE3 2017 Lacquer on canvas 50 × 35 cm Chemnitz

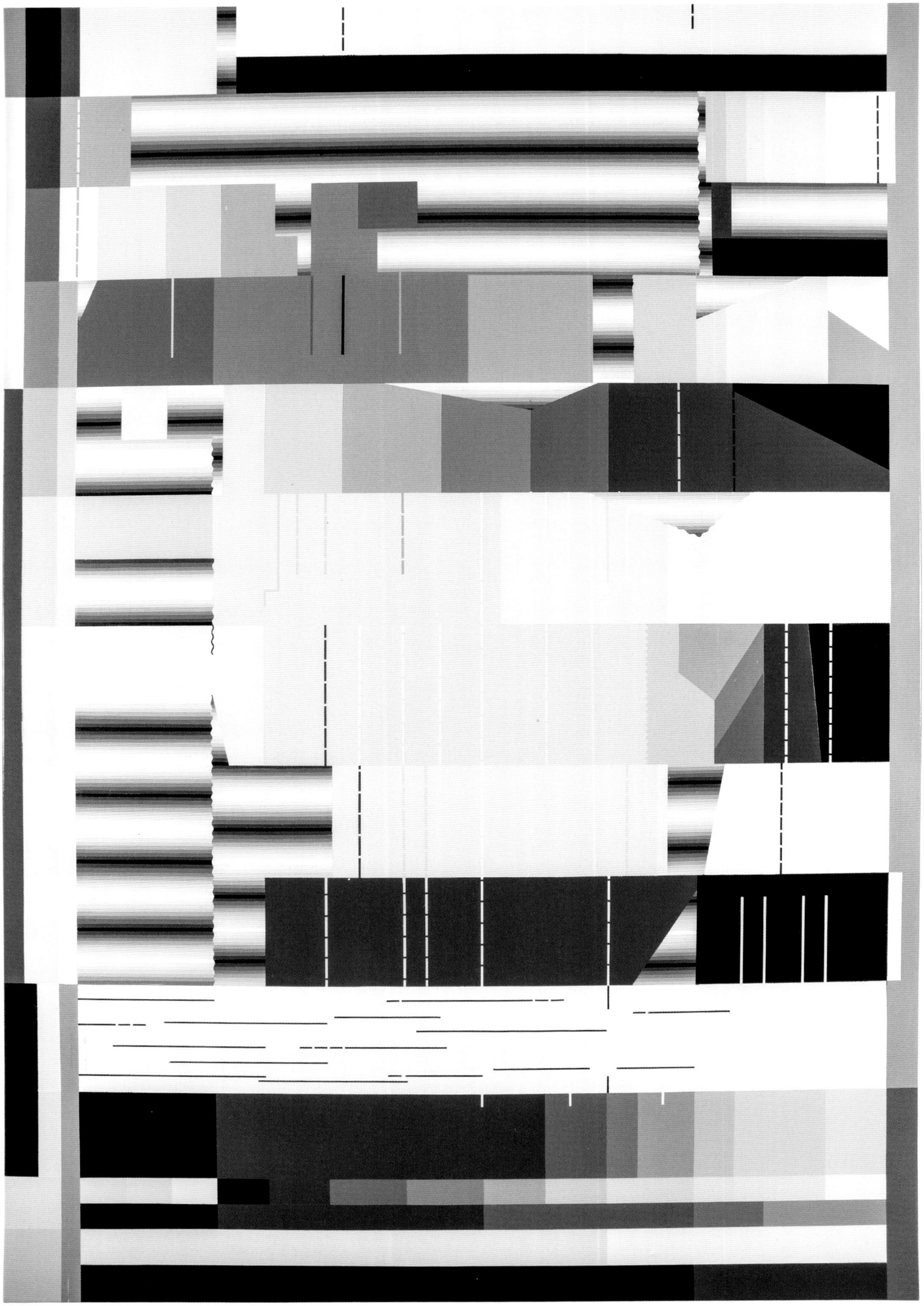

Karb.
2018
Lacquer on canvas
200 × 140 cm
Bonn

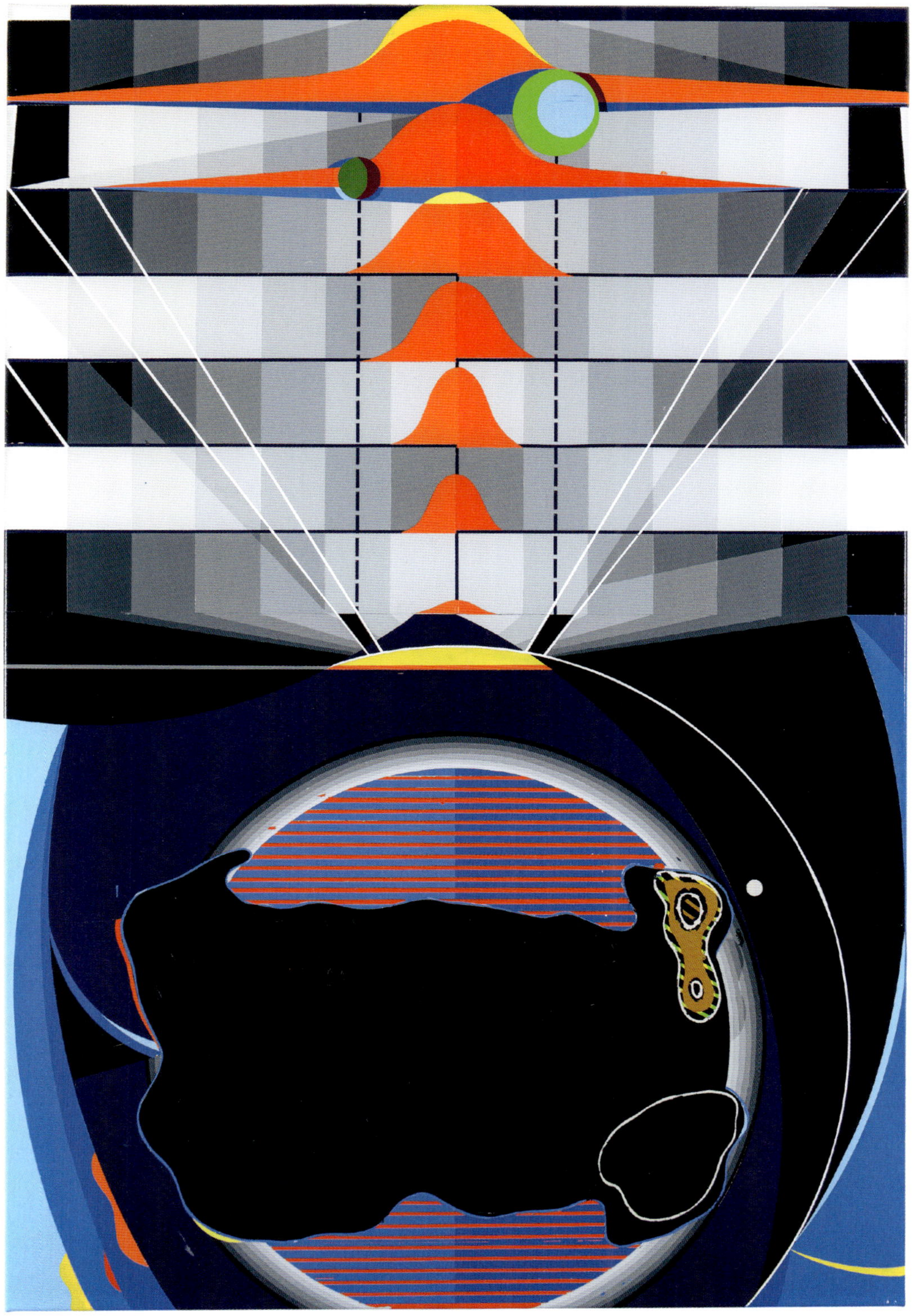

SUE3 2017 Lacquer on canvas 115 × 80 cm Wiesbaden

Jens Einhorn

Teen spirit

Jens Einhorn's process-oriented artistic practice seems like a breath of fresh air. A place in which doubt and contradictions are welcome. The pictures radiate a mixture of pure enthusiasm and disagreement.
Ripped nets and fabrics lie on top of a colourful background and are repeatedly overpainted and pasted over, cut out and inserted into other pictures. Einhorn's working process resembles a performance. Everything seems to be moving, somewhat chaotically and wildly, in order to come together in a state of harmony at the end.
His pictures resemble a handful of teenagers lounging around at a bus stop. Slightly hung over, they dream of next summer and scribble a few grimaces on the wall. On the floor, last year's chewing gum is slowly petrifying and there is a smell of sweet wine and apple schnapps.
There are echoes of a certain "teen spirit" in Einhorn's works and his picture titles. The figures in his paintings roar in a stolen car with *Benzin Und Kartoffelchips* (Petrol and Potato Crisps) on the *Straße Der Jugend* (Street of Youth) through a *Kaugummiwelt* (Chewing-Gum World). Conversations about meaning take place *Auf Der Treppe Vor Dem Haus* (On the Front Doorstep).
Einen Schritt Weiter (One Step Further) they have sex in the ruins, dream and *Starren Löcher In Die Wand* (Stare Holes in the Wall).
Everything is of equal value. What is here is true.
Shoeprints, blotches of colour and frayed fragments from previous pictures are not prettified but are invited to tell their stories. Like a wanderer, the artist instinctively follows the path of digression into a playfully constructed world of painting that constantly re-invents and re-interprets itself. He has taken into account the fact that in the end it can all lead to Nichts (Nothingness). After the concert we shall see what has the makings of an earworm; the rest will be swept up and will celebrate its merry revival in the next picture. —— *Julia Colavita*

Jens Einhorn was born in 1980 in Döbeln and currently lives and works in Berlin

Kunstakademie Düsseldorf, Meisterschüler with Prof. Tal R, 2014

2018 Raw Vision II, Olsen Gallery, Sydney (S)
Porzellan Und Vulkan, Gerhard Hofland, Amsterdam (S)
Raw Vision, Olsen Gruin Gallery, New York (S)

2017 Tracing Remains, Duve Berlin (S)

jenseinhorn.de

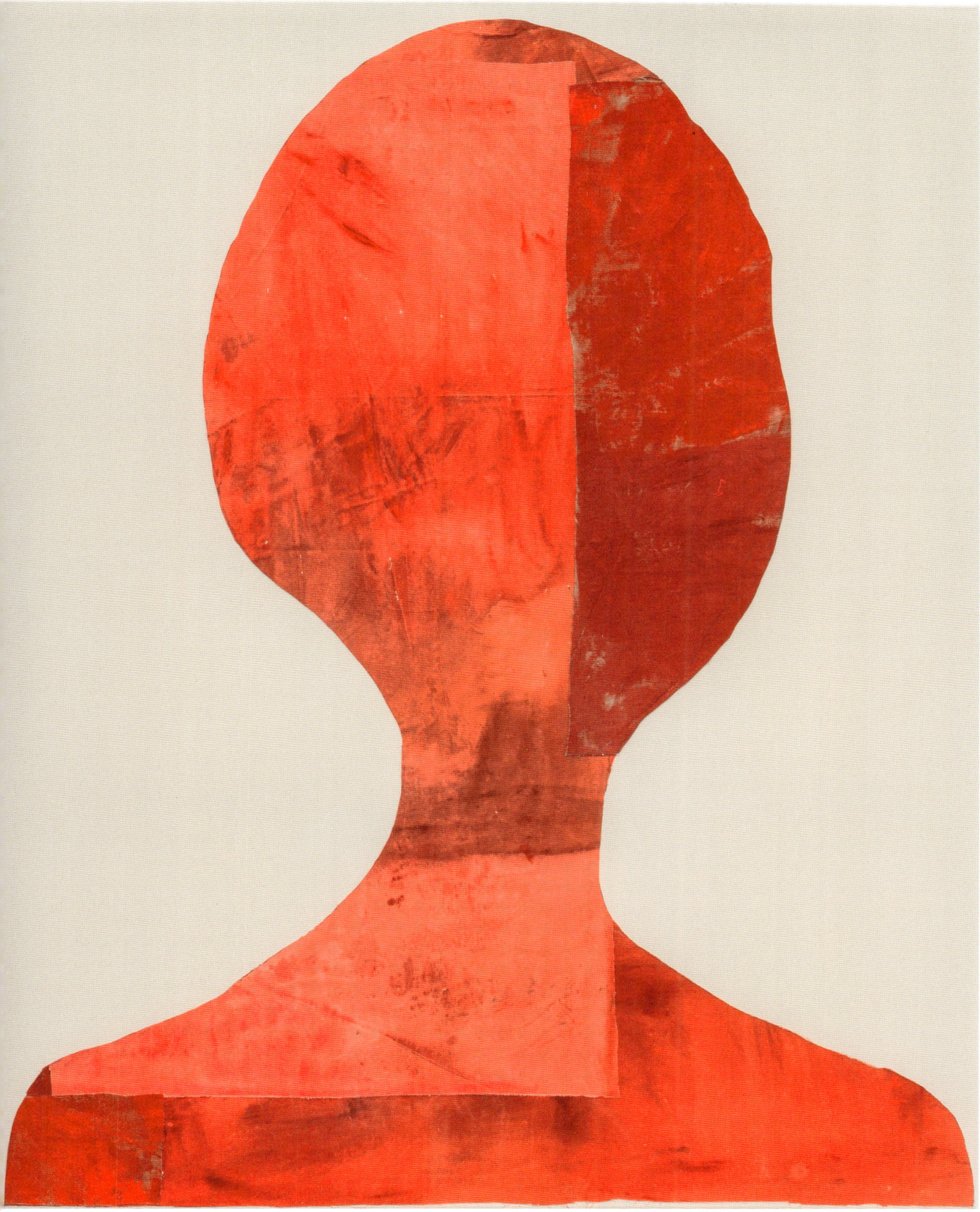

Tag Ohne Schatten 2019 Acrylic, linen, muslin, canvas, cotton, collage on canvas 220 × 180 cm Bonn

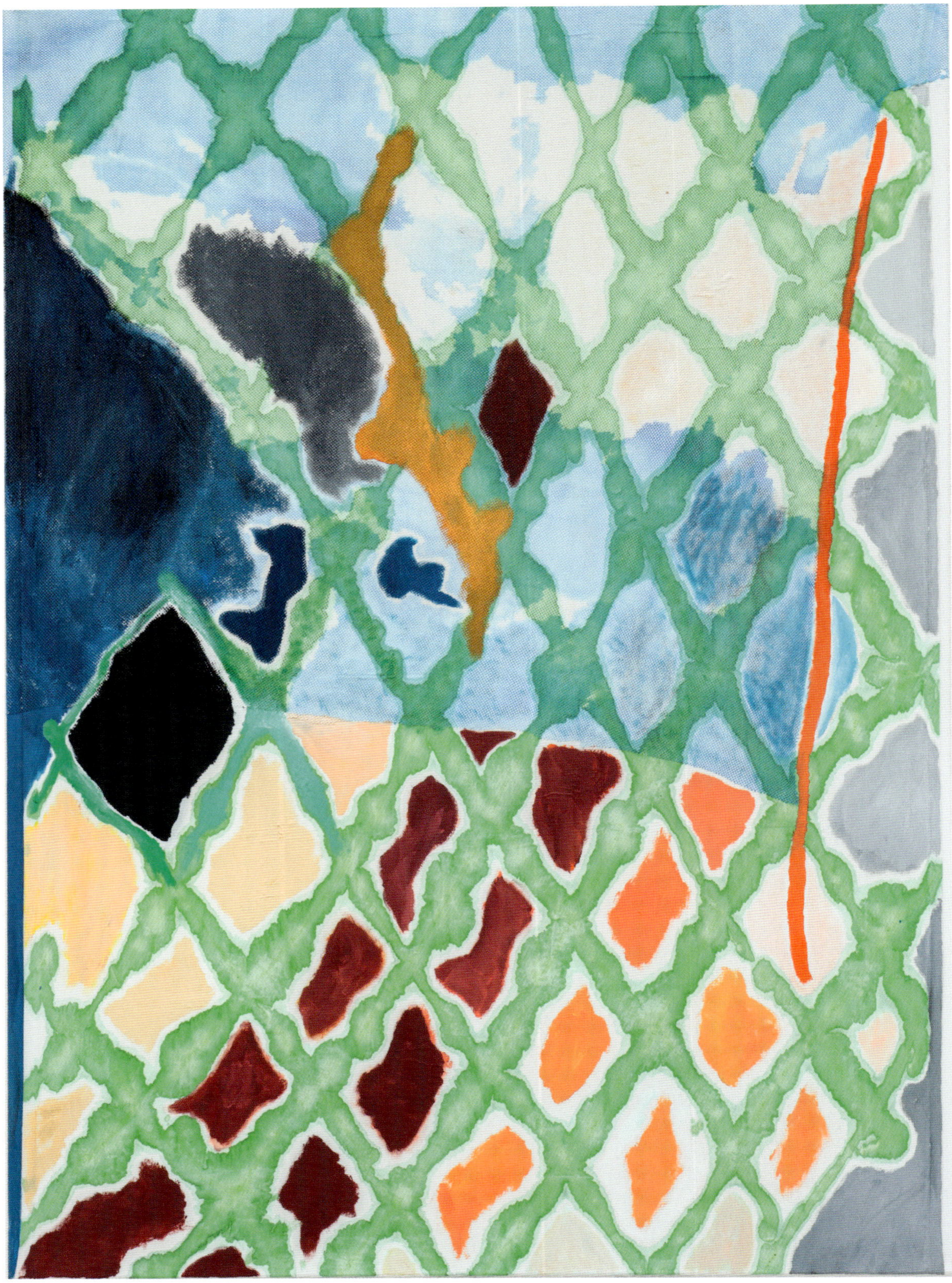

Einen Schritt Weiter

2019

Mesh material, polyester fabric, oil, acrylics, gesso, glue, collage on canvas

200 × 150 cm

Chemnitz

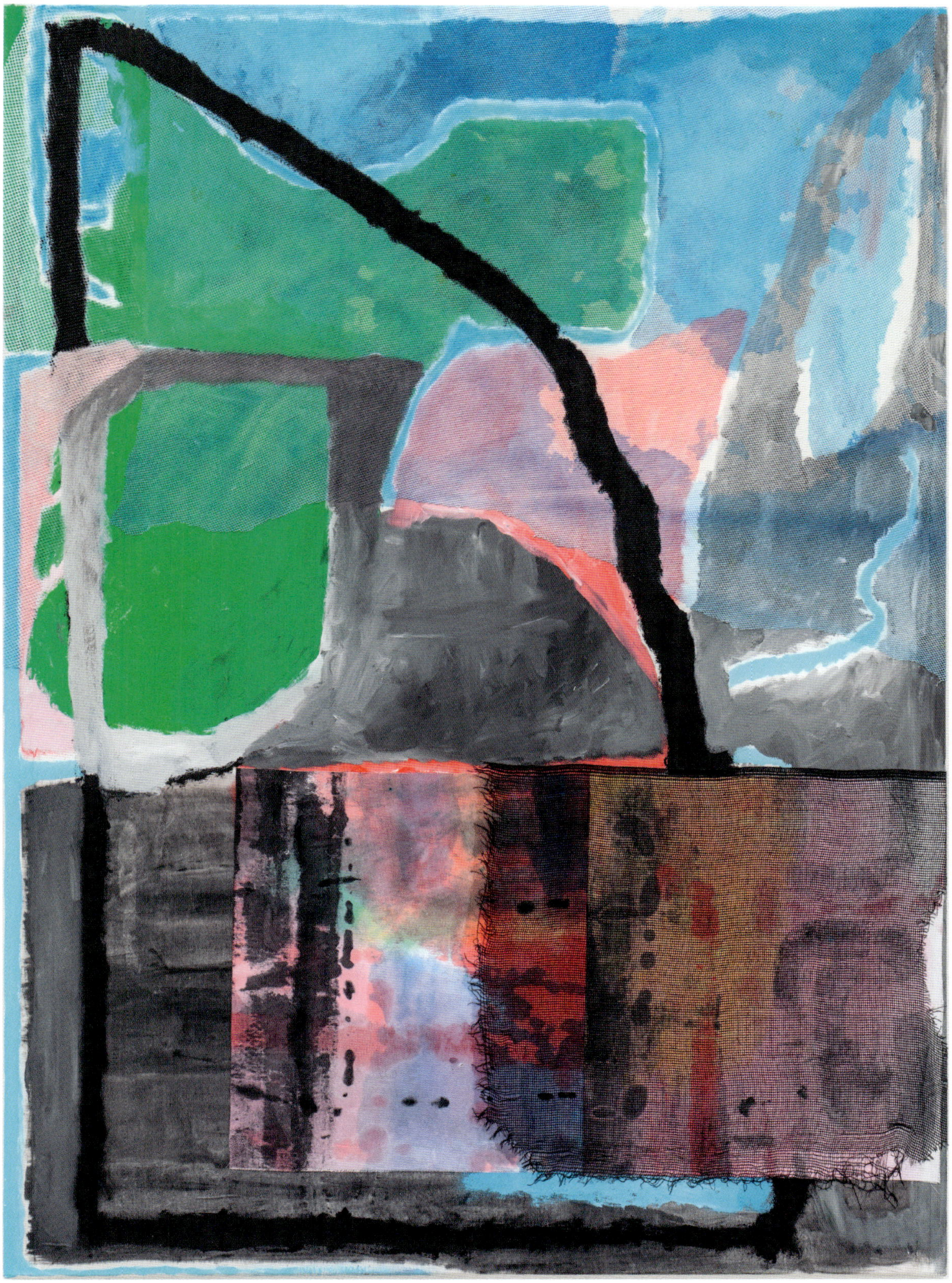

Auf Der Treppe Vor Dem Haus

2019

Acrylic, oil, ink, gesso, cotton, linen, polyester fabric, mesh material, glue, collage on canvas

200 × 150 cm

Wiesbaden

Jenny Forster

Galaxies, cosmic mist, dying suns, fragmented and interlocking spaces can be seen on the large-format paintings of Jenny Forster. Painted in brilliant colours, her images open up entire universes, permit our eyes to slide into the depths of the cosmos or to lose themselves in the possibilities of space – always driven by the artist's curious gaze behind the appearances of the world. What lies beyond the surface that we see and regard as reality? How can we approximate an understanding of "what holds the world together in its innermost core", when we assume that ultimately everything is matter?
Jenny Forster's painting is reflection crystallised in colour that vacillates formally between representationalism and abstraction. Her compositions are fixed pictorially for now, but at any moment they could start moving again, because "all we can see could also be otherwise" (Ludwig Wittgenstein). For the moment, however, controlled chance has given the pictures this precise form: like a multi-layered web of gossamer, powdered pigment, glazes, transparencies, splatters of paint and stress marks create a pictorial space which seems to stretch into infinity. They bear witness to a productive destruction, a game of adding and then removing once more. Colours, forms and structures complement each other to form a whole which reveals a fascination for materiality.
The autonomy of colour links up with the investigative interest of the artist to create a form of sensuous thinking. The series in particular show how she repeatedly manipulates an idea. As if looking through a kaleidoscope, she reassembles the forms and colours on each occasion to create a similar and yet different picture which always remains open. Instead of prescribed points of view, the pictures offer viewers subjective experience spaces which they are invited to discover. —— *Anne Simone Krüger*

Jenny Forster was born in 1979 in Landshut and currently lives and works in Munich

Akademie der Bildenden Künste Munich, Diploma and Meisterschülerin with Prof. Karin Kneffel, 2012

2019 Gestaltenwechsel. fluid figures., Neue Galerie Landshut (with Bärbel Praun) (S)

2018 spaces, Galerie Lesmeister Regensburg (with Jeremy Holmes) (S)

super flat layers, 3331 Arts Chiyoda, Tokyo (G)

2017 kokoro, kuratiert von Petra Hetzler und Dina Renniger, Verein für Originalradierung Munich (with Daniel Man) (S)

jennyforster.de

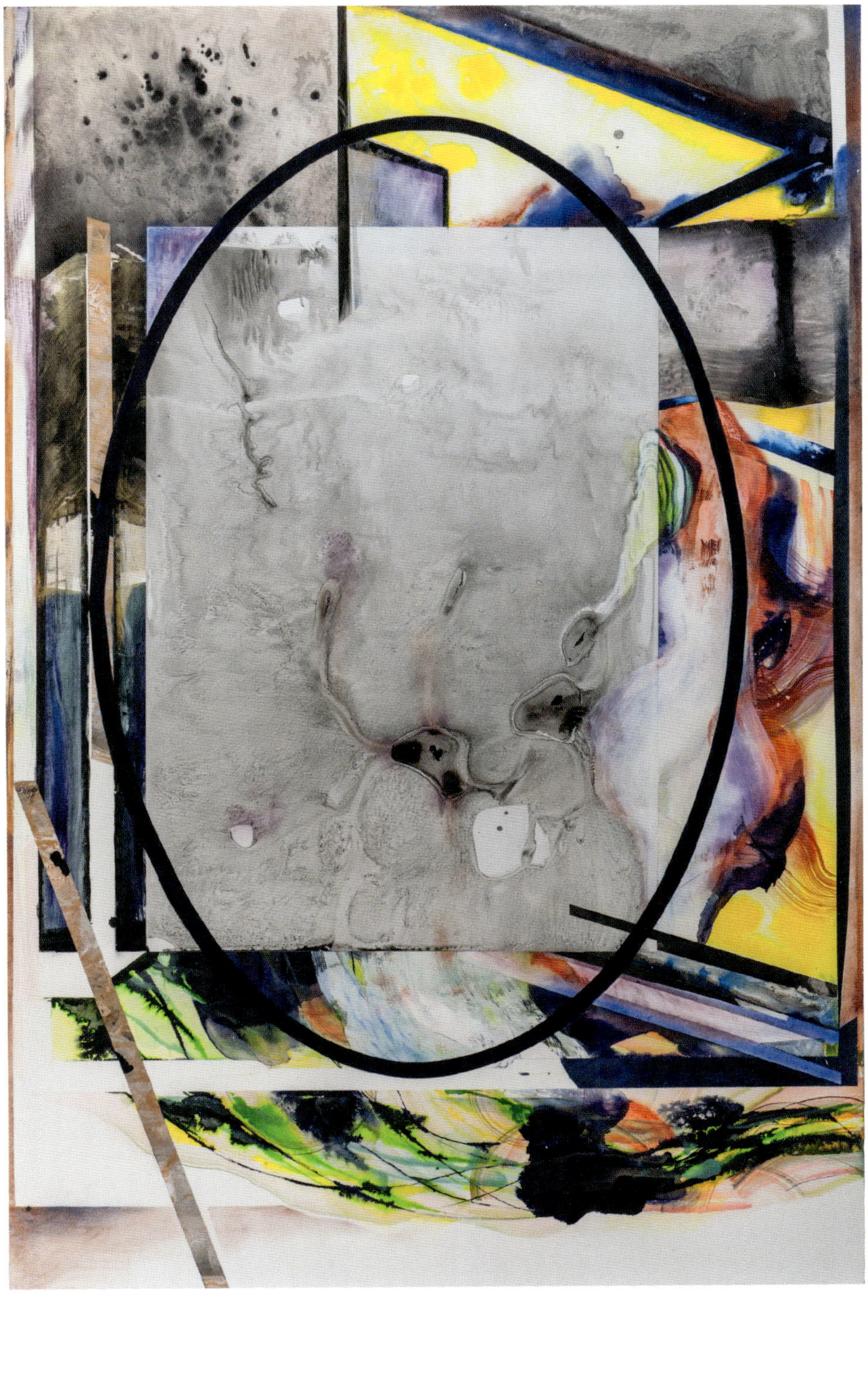

Port 2017/18 Mixed media on paper laid on wood 180 × 120 cm Wiesbaden

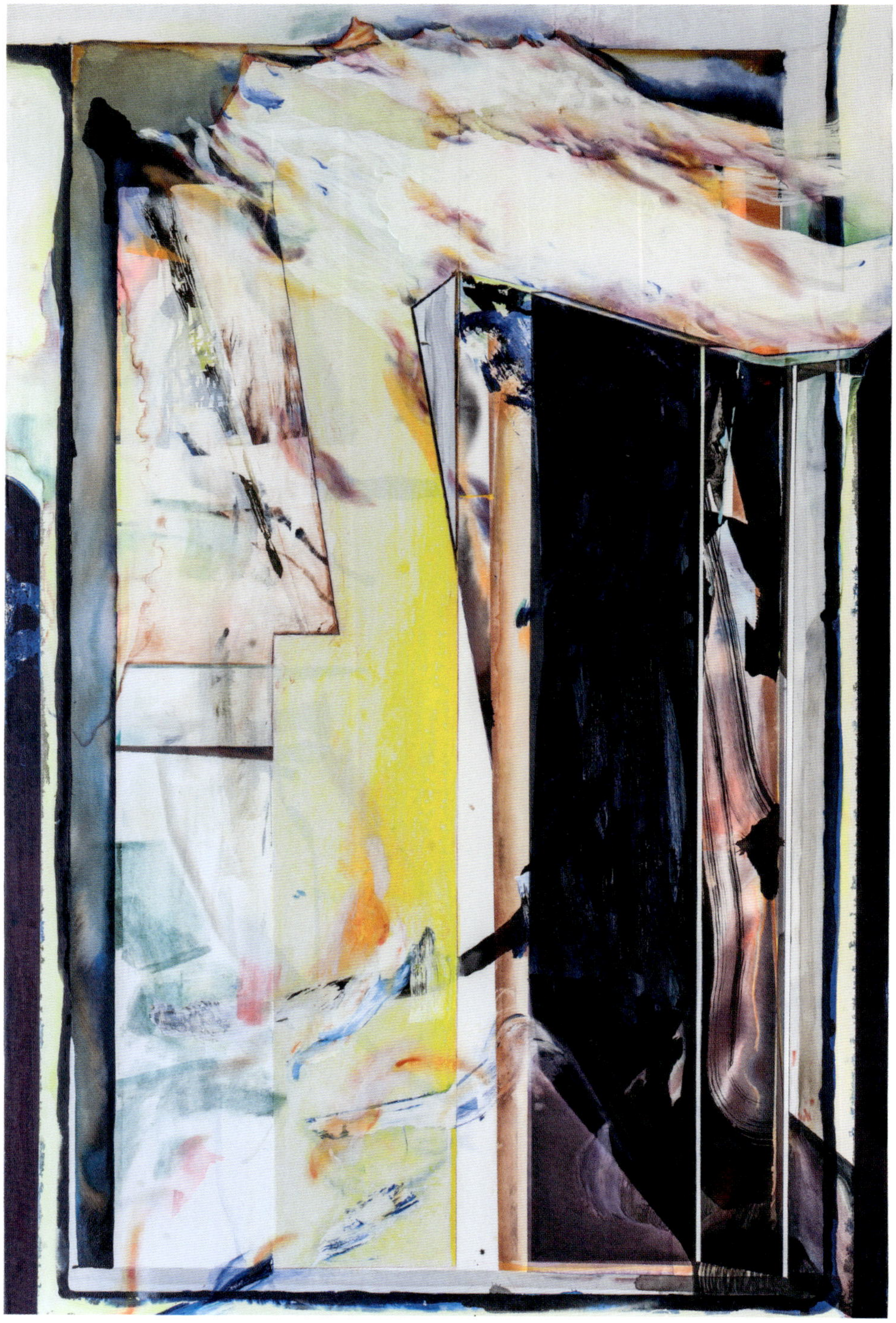

Paravent_II 2016 Mixed media on paper laid on wood 180 × 120 cm Chemnitz

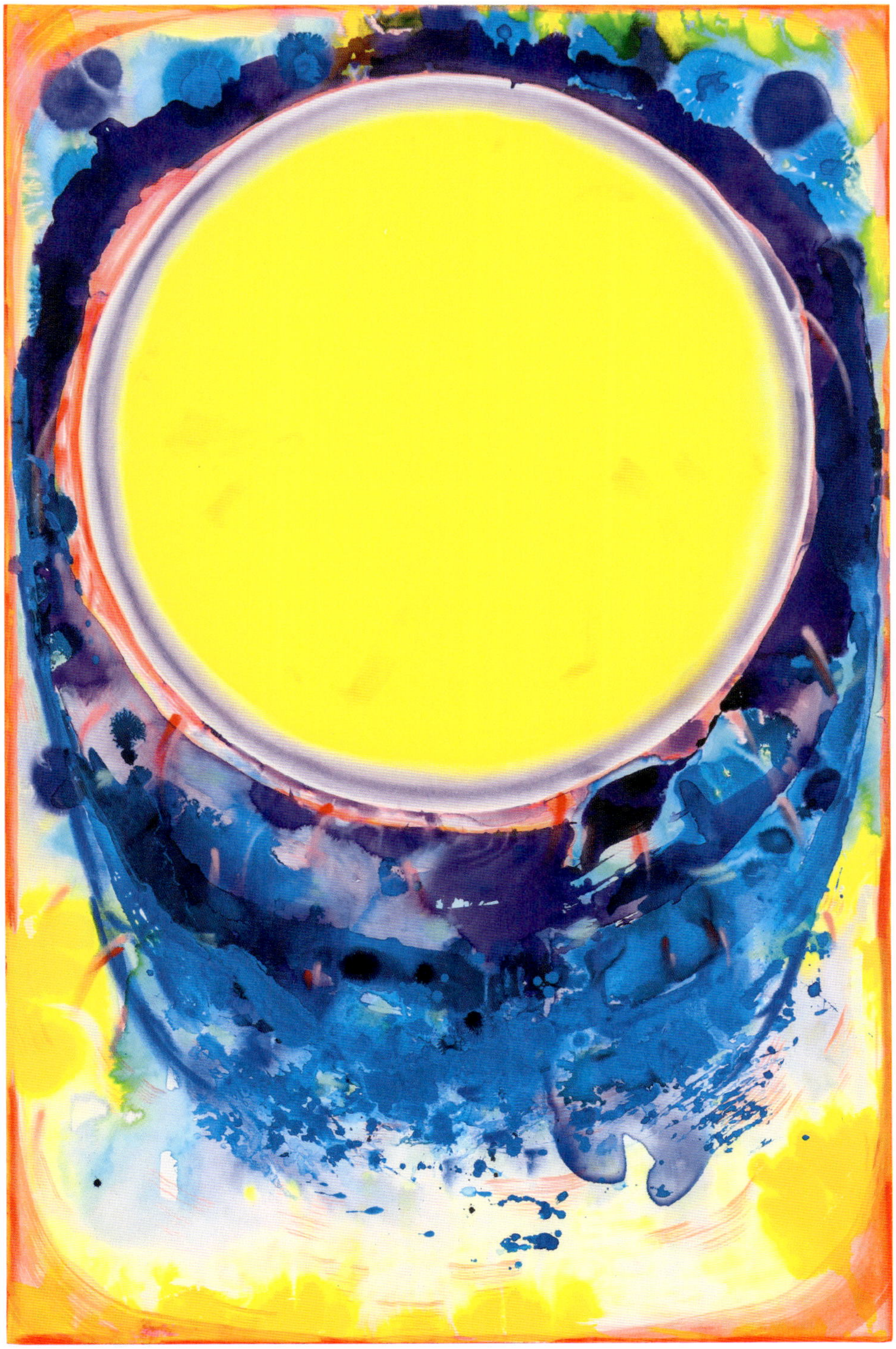

Gestirn_V   2018   Mixed media on paper laid on wood   180 × 120 cm   Bonn

Pius Fox

Pius Fox was born in 1983 and currently lives and works in Berlin

Universität der Künste Berlin, Meisterschüler with Prof. Pia Fries, 2010

2019	Der Trommler, 104GALERIE, Tokyo (S)
	Coral Reef, Pablo's Birthday Gallery, New York (S)
2017	Alvar, Patrick Heide Contemporary Art, London (S)
	Le Divan des Murmures, FRAC Auvergne, Clermont-Ferrand (G)

piusfox.com

The painter Pius Fox mostly works in an abstract manner, but in his pictures we repeatedly find references to the human need to organise the world. In his reduced paintings, which are often inspired by photographic studies, fragmented elements of architecture seem to develop a life of their own. Windows, doors, blinds and grids make an appearance and then withdraw again. They are transition spaces. They permit glimpses inside as well as vistas; they draw the viewer into the depths of the picture. At the same time our gaze comes up against walls of colour.

Titles like *Berge über Berge* (Mountains over Mountains) and *Pyramid Song* refer to the amazed gaze at monumental horizons, while *Fensterfall* (Window Fall) and *Türschwelle* (Threshold) provide views of less grandiose interior landscapes. In his pictures on paper the noble and the everyday are equally relevant. Patterns are not playful ornaments, but are instead an arrangement of forms which assert themselves in a confident manner.

The artist, who studied at the Berlin University of the Arts (UdK), demonstrates a feeling for situations in which the space around us is dismantled into geometry and yet cannot be entirely described by its forms.

Fox's painting is also interested in the history of its medium. His colours are not the clear shades of a digital present with their demands for attention, but are rather reminiscent of the subtle colour palette and patina of the paintings of the Old Masters. One of the surprises in his work is that it seems to have less in common with the tradition of Minimalism than with that of the fresco. The paint is applied directly to the wet plaster on the wall – thereby creating an indissoluble link between painting and architecture.

The small-format pictures look at times like a zoom into the unspecific regions of other paintings, a sharp glimpse of the periphery of art history, into backstage rooms of colour. Even the grainy surface which time leaves on a picture puts in an appearance in abstract form.

Pius Fox's paintings seem like details of other works and they appear never to end at the edges of the paper, but to point beyond their material boundaries. In spite of their modest measurements, they contain an intimation of infinity.

—— *Saskia Trebing*

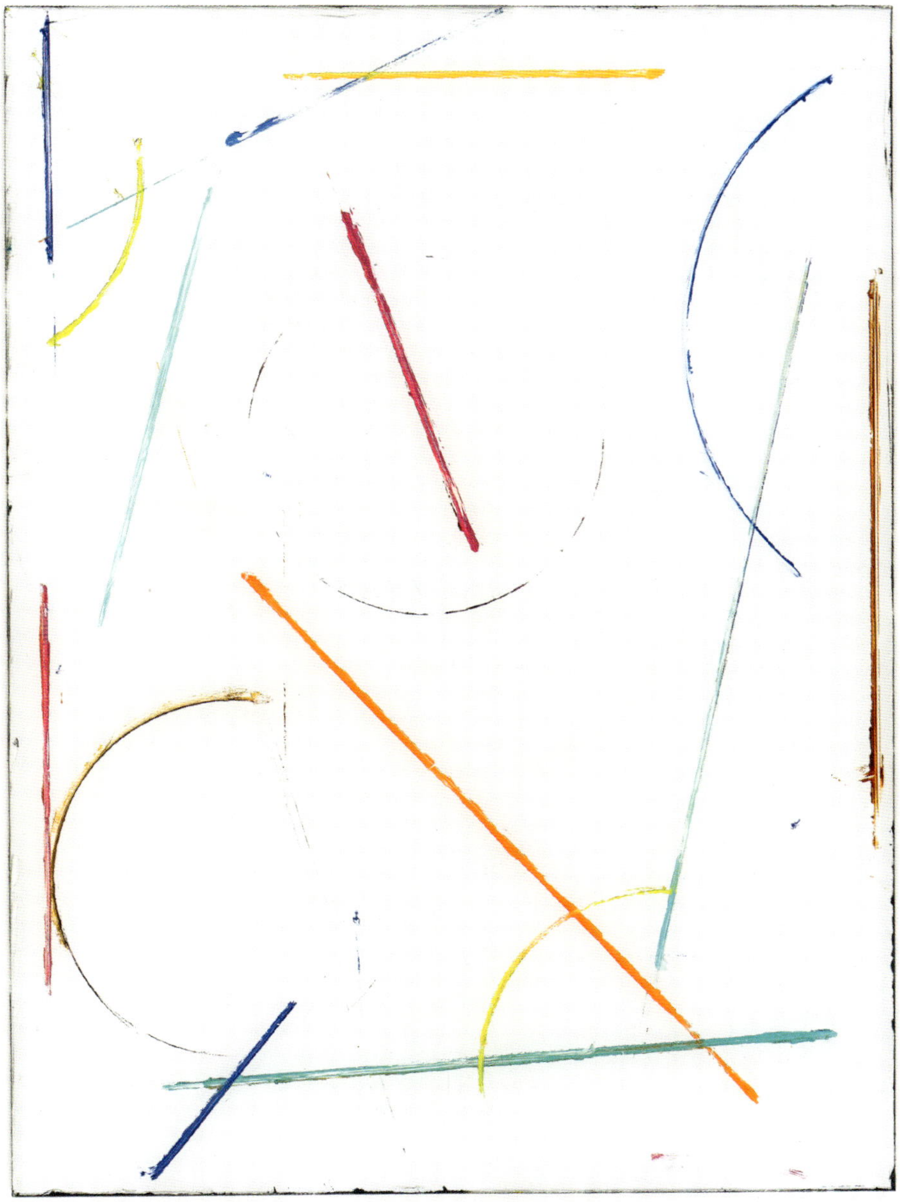

Aufgewirbelt 2015 Oil on glass 40 × 30 cm Bonn

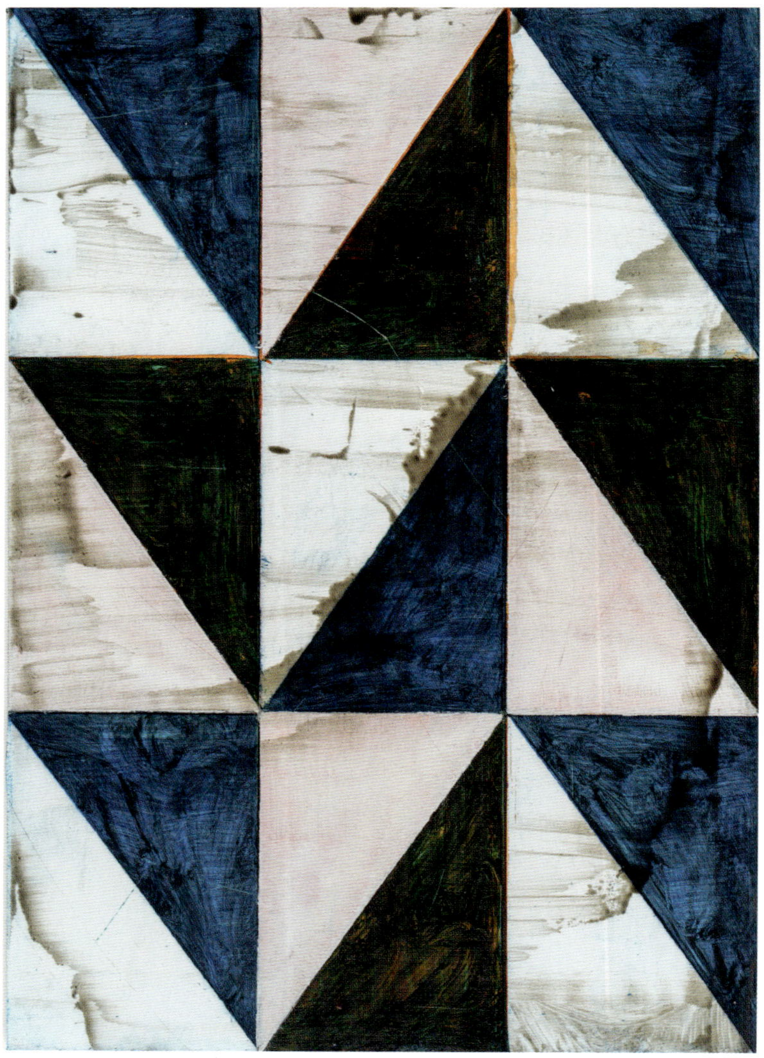

Berge über Berge 2019 Egg tempera and oil on paper 28 × 20 cm Chemnitz

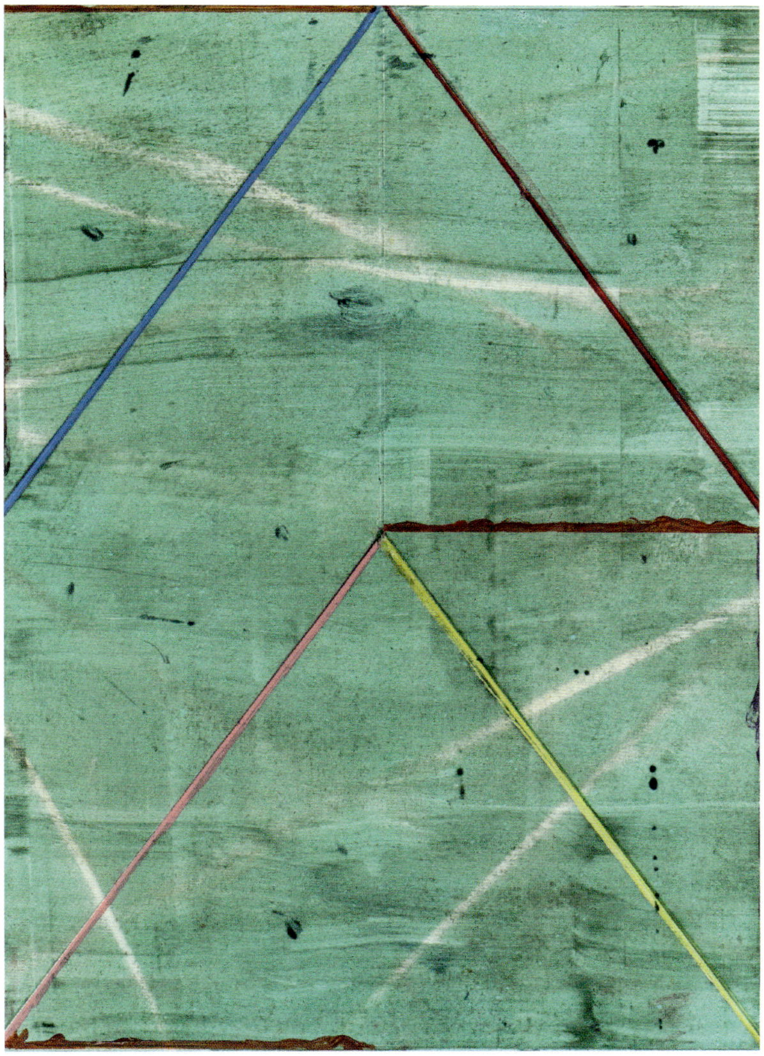

Maya 2019 Egg tempera and oil on paper 24 × 18 cm Wiesbaden

Max Frintrop

Drawing at the base

On the canvases of Max Frintrop, things lend their colours, which they never possessed, to the half-century whose impassive witnesses they were. The colours explode; they are brilliant and endlessly nuanced, colours with their own space and their own attitude. Frintrop documents their will with an artistic style that is in opposition to an abstract painting that got lost in the unpricked bubbles of the abstraction of its artistic ego carapace.
This attitude is implemented skilfully through the material. The flexible acrylic paint and the dark China ink are mixed with solvents and applied to the canvas lying on the ground. The home-made paintbrushes are no longer an extension of the artistic *idea*. They are sparring partners with a will of their own, large and unwieldy, more resistant than the badger-hair brushes sold in the shops.
If the free gesture of Abstract Expressionism is to stand for the free American individual, what sort of individual does Frintrop intend? He is in any case not quite as free as a *Drip* by Jackson Pollock, but rather drifts in firm structures.
Frintrop wants to draw our attention to the potency of colour, to the fact that it can do everything: be light and space, digital disruption and semiotic approach. And yet the alphabet, which brings so much knowledge into the world, remains typographically unstable. We are constantly hovering between what we see and what it suggests. Some colours actually collapse on the canvas, while others dance across it. In Max Frintrop's work an S can also be a Z. Or neither of the two. It is only meaningful as an image.
That which normally takes a space, holds it together, is its consistent quantifiable quality: space can be measured. This space expands. Not into the infinite, but into the undeclined. And man inside it? Perhaps an existence as a single portion, who can only suspect that the great globalised abstractions are highly concrete.
—— *Anja Schürmann*

Max Frintrop was born in 1982 in Oberhausen and currently lives and works in Düsseldorf

Kunstakademie Düsseldorf, Diploma, Meisterschüler with Prof. Albert Oehlen, 2009

2018 Lardo, Berthold Pott Galerie, Cologne (S)
Chansons dans le vide, Galerie Albert Baronian, Brussels (S)

2017 Mi par d´udir ancora, AplusB Galerie, Brescia (S)
Keine Welt, Kunstverein Heppenheim (S)

max-frintrop.de

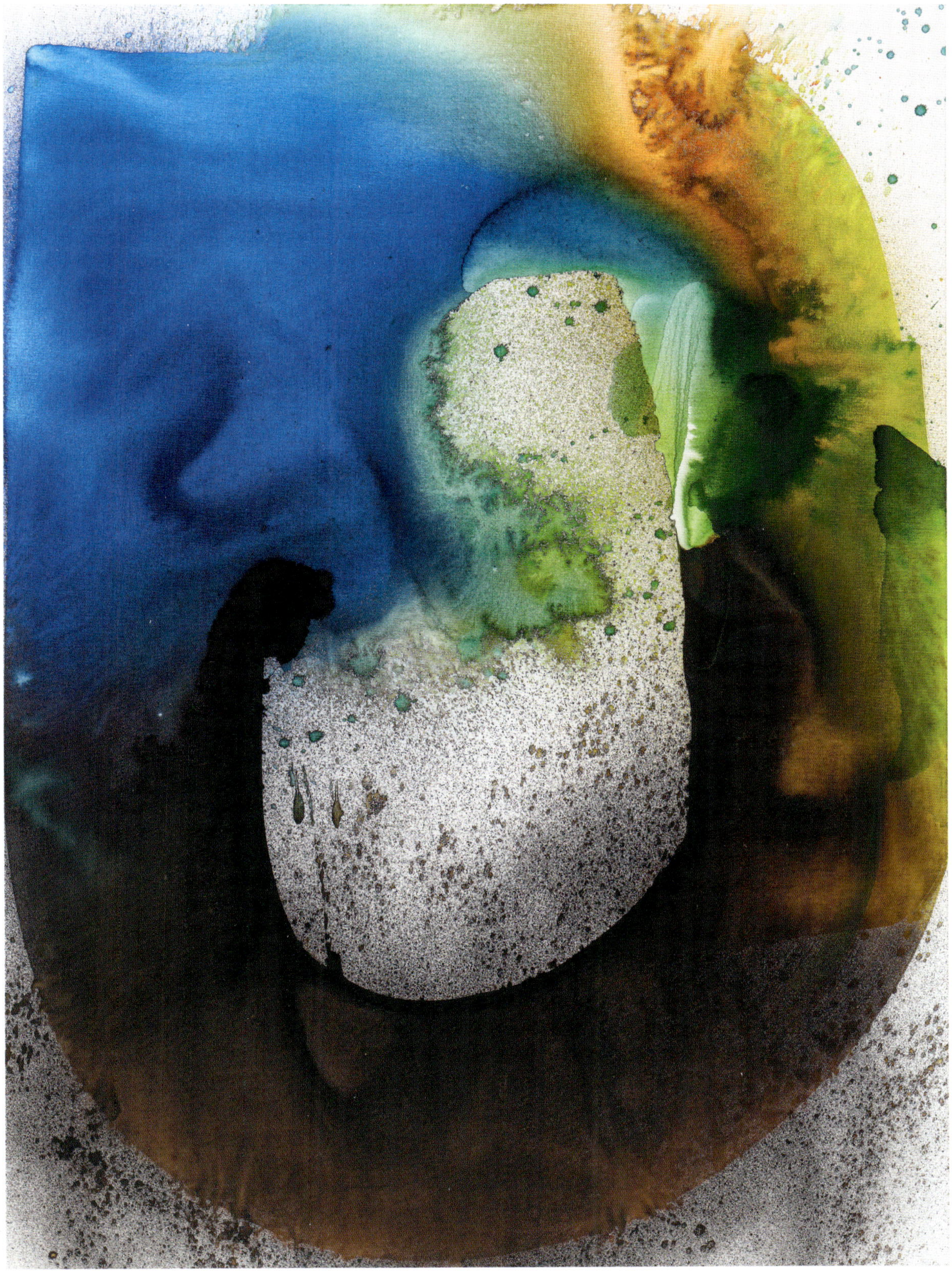

Untitled (Dizzy) 2019 Ink, acrylic, pigments on canvas 200 × 150 cm Wiesbaden

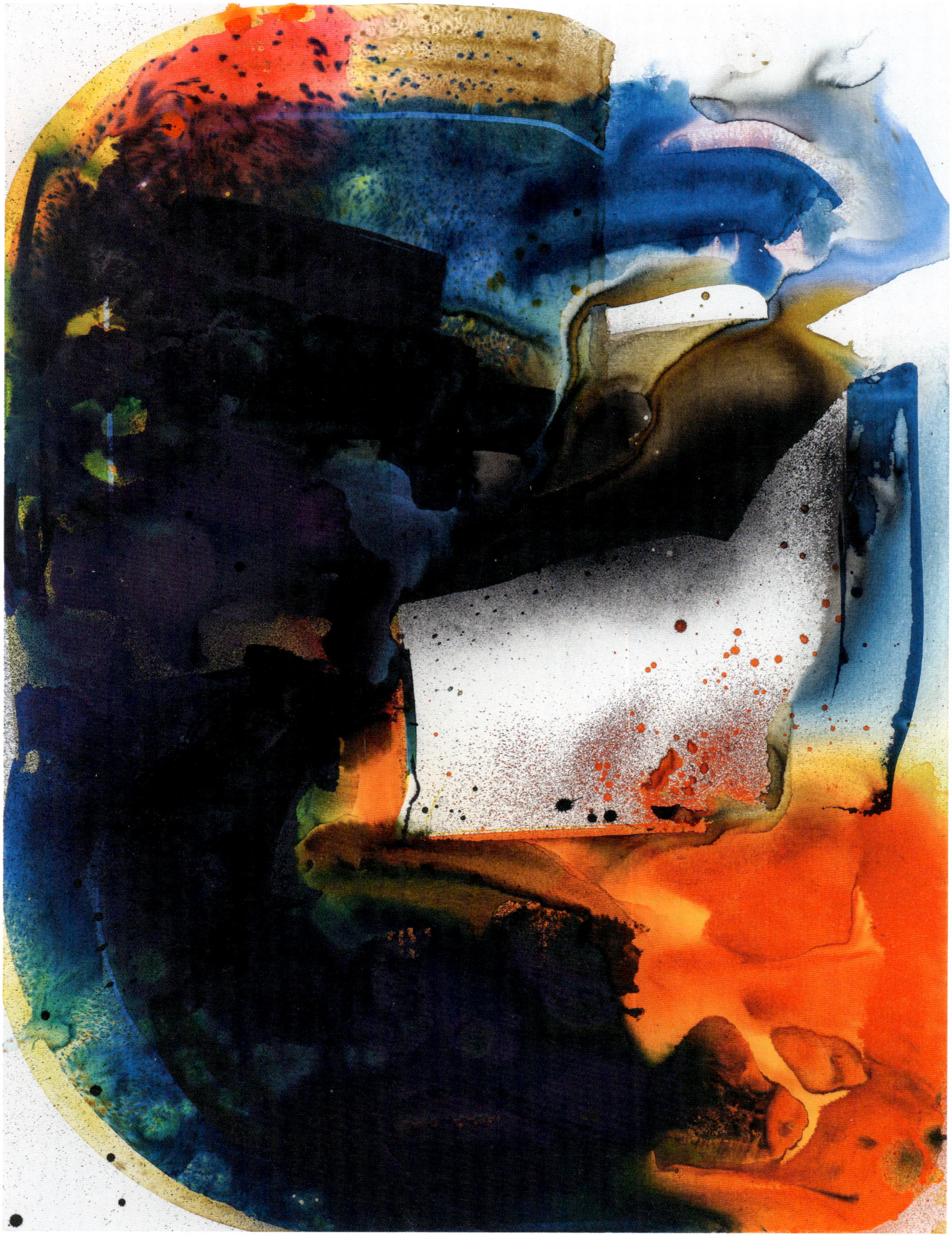

Untitled (Aphex Twin) 2019 Ink, acrylic, pigments on canvas 220 × 170 cm Bonn

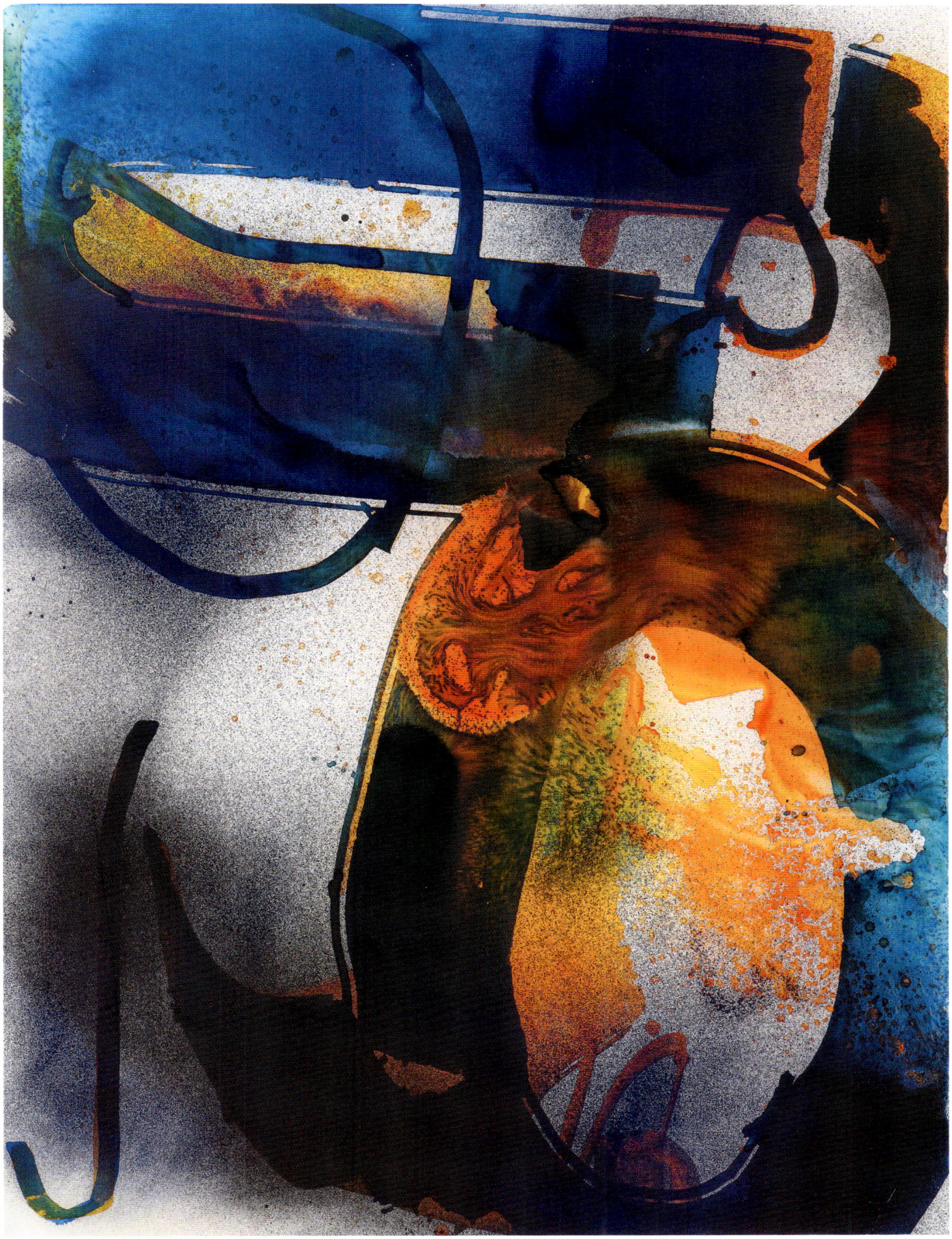

Untitled (Spandau) 2019 Ink, acrylic, pigments on canvas 220 × 170 cm Chemnitz

Sabrina Fritsch

Sabrina Fritsch's painting challenges the viewer. In the first moment it is obvious and clear, a combination of monochrome or geometrically subdivided surfaces as the variation of a shade of colour or the opposite of two structures. But if we allow our gaze to roam from one picture to another, a process is set in motion which begins with the feeling of the surface and the haptic perception of its texture by the eye and culminates in an analytical combination.
We begin to recognise pairings, correspondences or reversals, which however are never symmetrical reflections but are always a continuation, a reaction. Sabrina Fritsch frequently confronts her pictures with opposite numbers, responds to crowded, dense conditions in one with a picture of emptiness and reduction in the next, or contrasts sharp contours with decomposed, blurred images. The procedure recalls mathematical equations in which different variables stand on each side of the equals sign. She also follows this principle with the allocation of colour: achromatic colours, dull washed-out shades in all their nuances, black and white dominate the field on one side, with pure, sharply contrasting colours on the other.
Sabrina Fritsch uses colour both as colouration and as a material in the sculptural sense. Sometimes she places it neat and completely smooth on the canvas, and sometimes she leaves it standing like a three-dimensional excrescence in a strip on the surface. The relief-like structure is further enhanced by woven material, sand or the textile fibres of the picture carrier which penetrate the layers of paint. The concept of duality pervades her work, linking not only the individual pictures in the room; it also defines her work *within* the picture – the relationship between edge and line, detail and totality – and *with* a picture, the dialogue, the debate between classification and intuition, into which she enters with each work and then hands over to the viewer. —— *Leonie Pfennig*

Sabrina Fritsch was born in 1979 in Neunkirchen and currently lives and works in Cologne

Kunsthochschule Mainz with Prof. Anne Berning and Prof. Winfried Virnich, 2005

Kunstakademie Düsseldorf, Meisterschülerin with Prof. Peter Doig, 2008

2018 Skin, VAN HORN, Düsseldorf (S)
Fragen an das Medium, Kunsthaus NRW, Kornelimünster (G)

2017 Chrom, Städtische Galerie, Viersen (S, C)
Every Cult its Castle, Die Sammlung Philara in der Spinnerei Leipzig (G)

sabrinafritsch.com

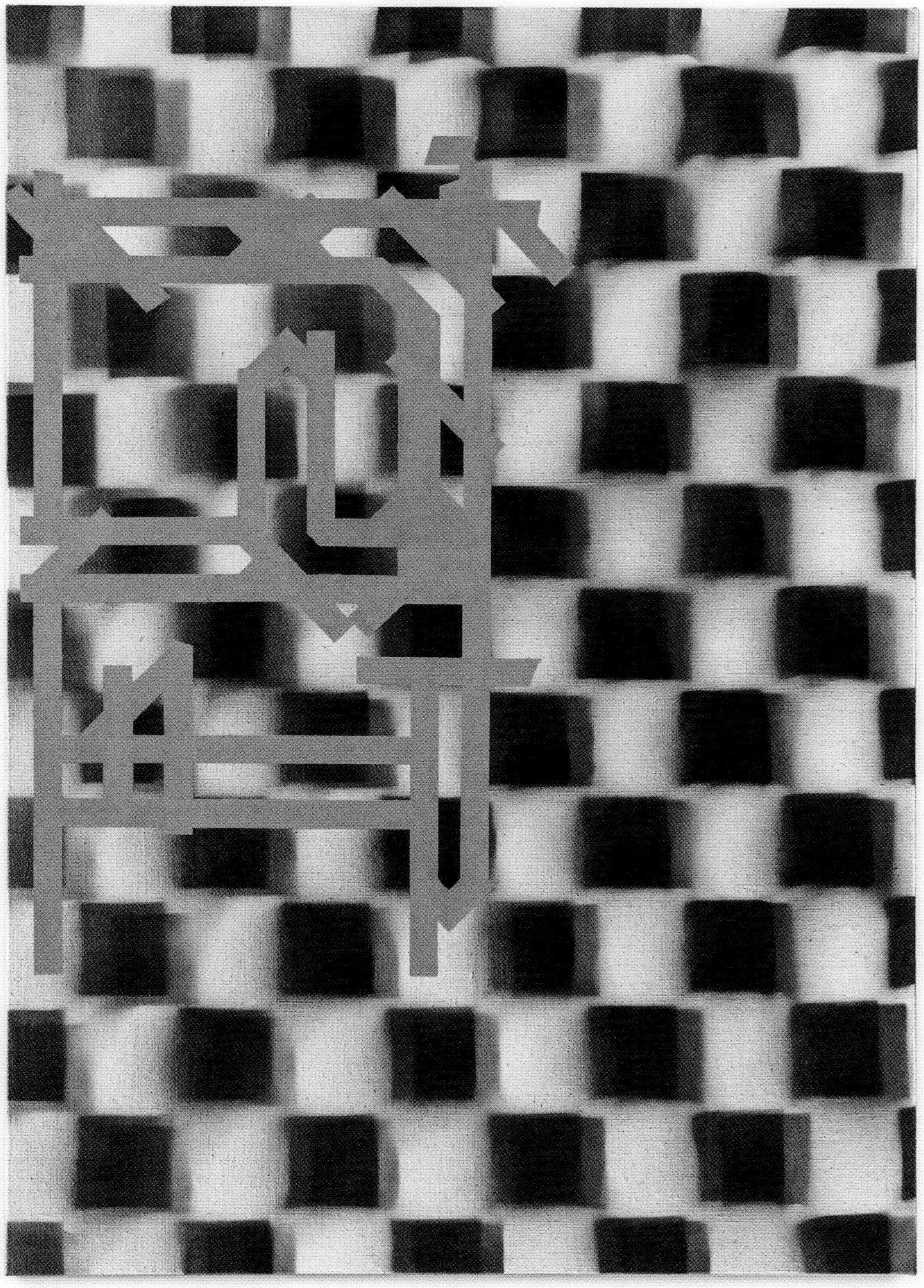

play II 2018 Acrylic on canvas 180 × 130 cm Chemnitz

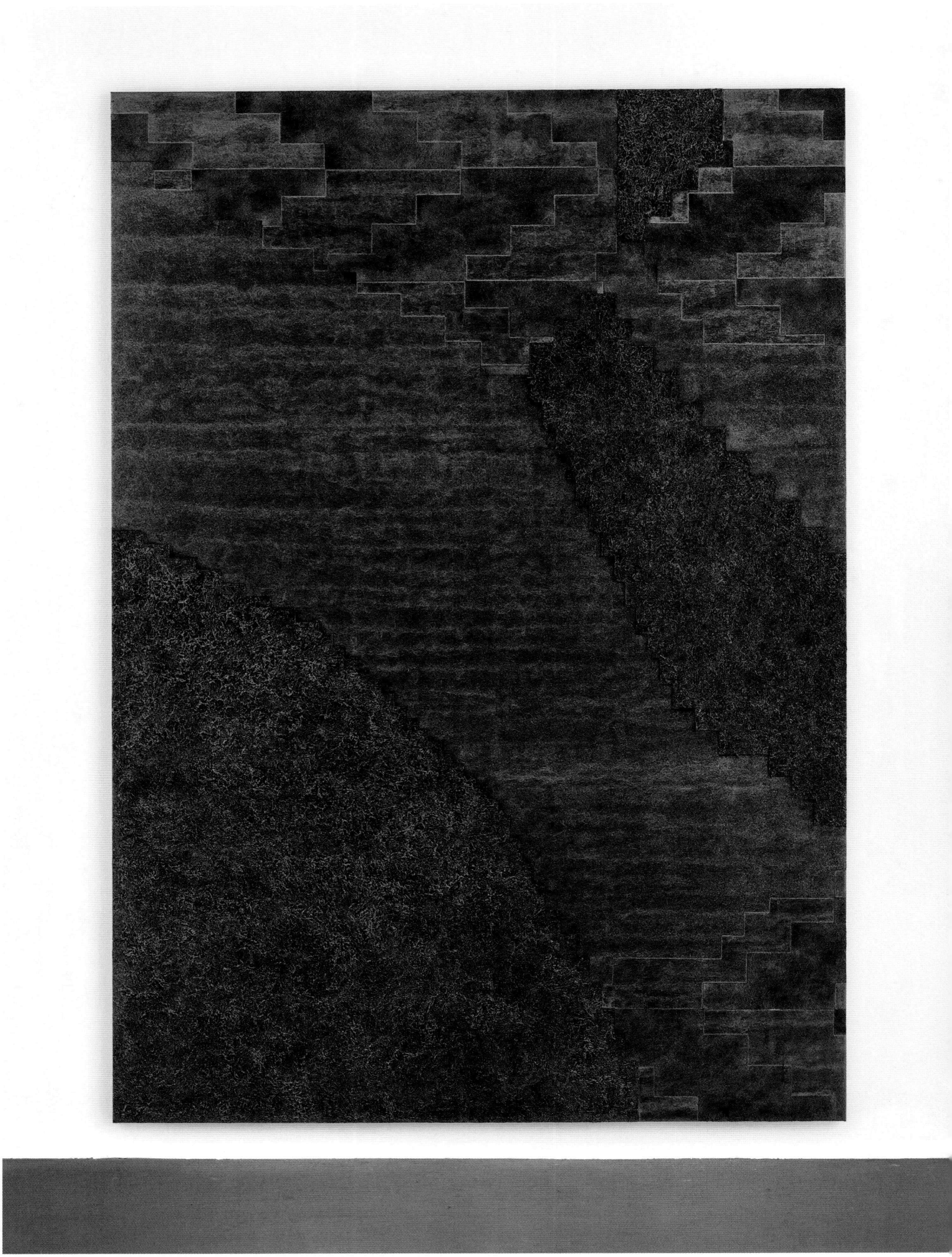

sltlalhl 2019 Acrylic on canvas 280 × 200 cm Wiesbaden

Nyx 2018 Oil, acrylic on jute 280 × 200 cm Bonn

Ina Gerken

The precision of chance

In a slender volume which Roland Barthes wrote about the works of Cy Twombly, the author differentiates between signs, message and gestures. In contrast to the other codes listed, a gesture produces without having ever pursued this goal (see Roland Barthes, *Cy Twombly*, Paris 1983). It is specifically the casualness of the production which similarly characterises the brushwork of Ina Gerken. Here we do not mean that her style loses itself in arbitrariness, but that the placing of the brushstrokes is sustained by a *determining* lightness. Every line sits.

Sometimes they appear as individual protagonists on the picture surface and create the impression that the paintbrush merely streaked across the canvas by chance. In other cases the canvas is covered by various markings, so that the eye gets lost amongst them. Although no representationalism is conveyed here, the composition results in the formation of loose formations within the arrangements. While some brushstrokes seem to continue the structure of the picture carrier, others form a coalition with other markings or recall letters of the alphabet. In any case the movements of Ina Gerken are evident, for they leave their mark on her pictures in the same way as a signature. The dynamics form the guiding thread running through her work, moulding every surface which she appropriates.

If we study the paintings at close quarters, we recognise that no surface is untouched. With surgical precision, fine layers of Japan paper have been inserted into the canvas. They never have an external character and do not look like a collage, but like another, even finer layer of the picture carrier. With this method, Ina Gerken seems to want to make visible something that is past, which however reveals itself to be an addition. That is also reflected in the different applications of paint which the artist wipes or scratches free or even sets in the middle of her works like a blind spot. She reaches ever deeper into the originality of her pictures, makes her own traces visible or lays false trails. She unmasks the surface and reveals that true precision lies hidden in the apparent randomness of expressive painting. —— *Carina Bukuts*

Ina Gerken was born in 1987 in Speyer and currently lives and works in Düsseldorf

Kunsthochschule Mainz, 1. Staatsexamen with Prof. Winfried Virnich, 2014

Kunstakademie Düsseldorf, Meisterschülerin with Prof. Katharina Grosse, 2016

2018 What a Feeling, Makasiini Contemporary, Turku (S)
Carolin Eidner, Ina Gerken, Sophie Reinhold, Galerie Tobias Naehring, Leipzig (G)
Blank Spots, Achenbach Hagemeier, Düsseldorf (S)

2017 Quintessenz, Galerie Guido Baudach, Berlin (G)

ina-gerken.com

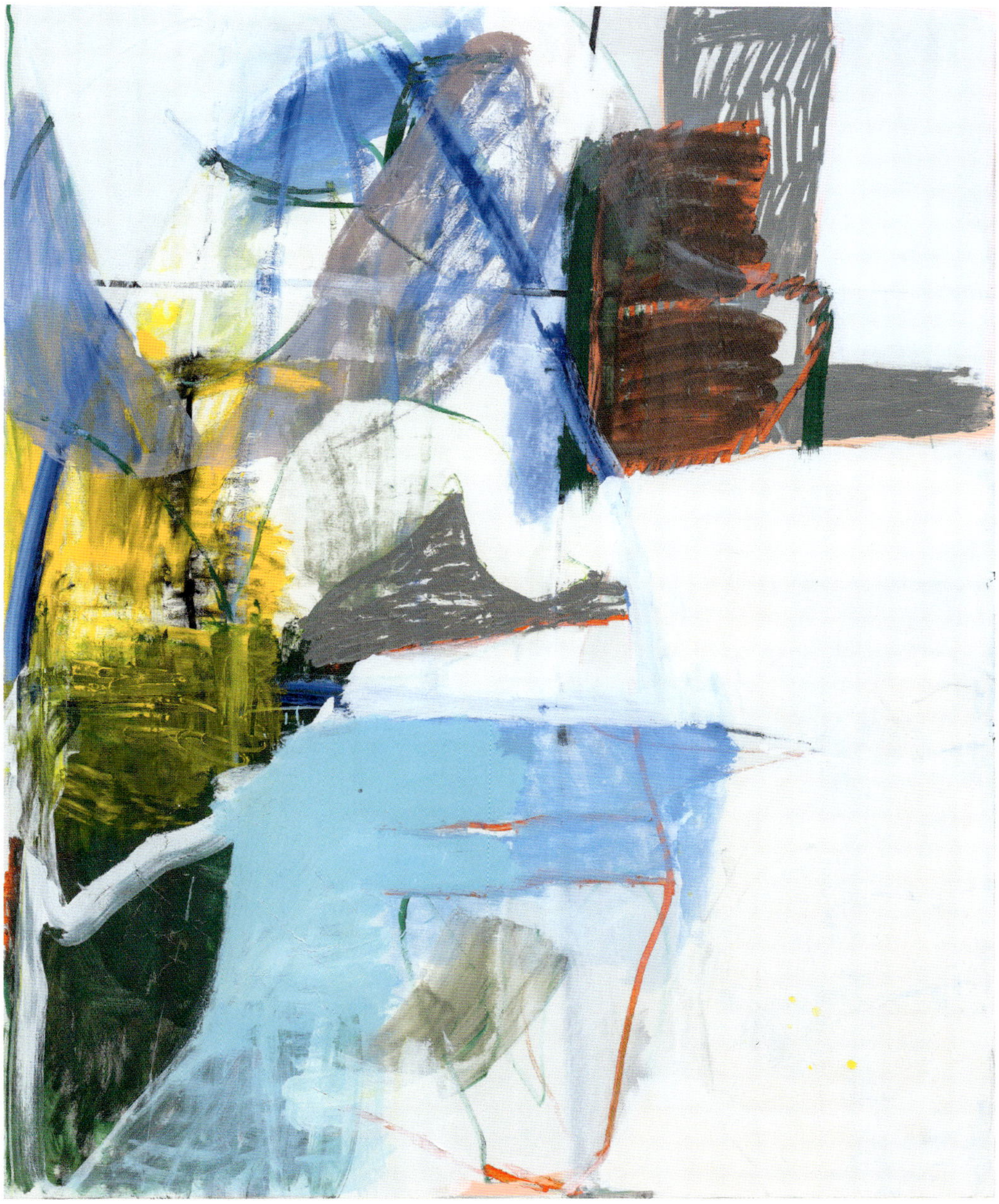

Untitled (Imitationen) 2019 Acrylic and Japan paper on polyester canvas 180 × 150 cm Wiesbaden

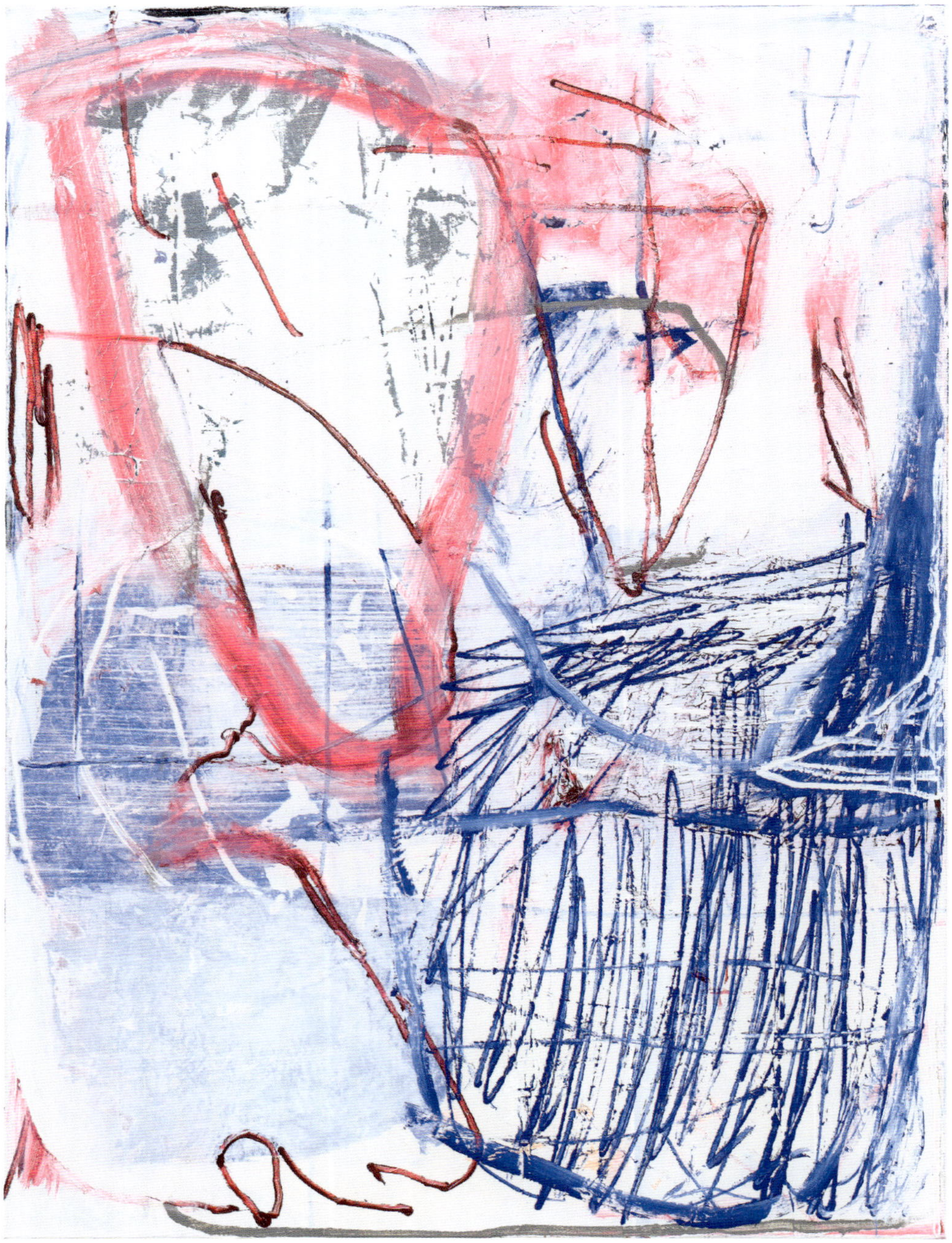

Untitled (Efflorescent)

2019

Acrylic and Japan paper on polyester canvas

130 × 100 cm

Bonn

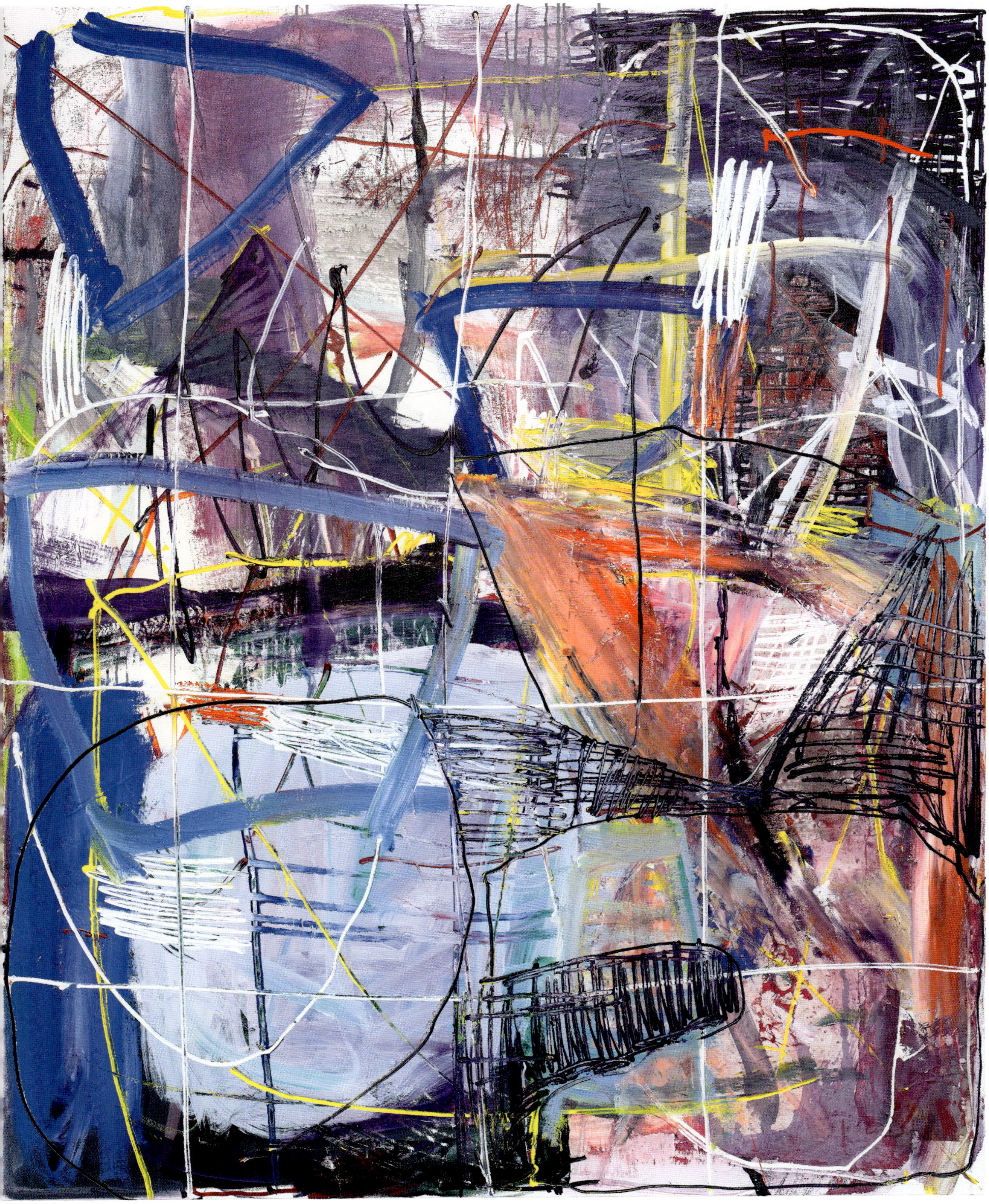

Untitled (After Laughter) 2019 Acrylic and Japan paper on polyester canvas 180 × 150 cm Chemnitz

Fabian Ginsberg

Raw patches of colour, capital letters the size of a hand, glued to paper on canvas; writing on the inside of the sheet of Perspex, always projecting, always with a view of the wall; ordinary wooden battens screwed together to make a frame – that is how Fabian Ginsberg shows his picture objects. Although it gives the picture its title, the carrier of the letters, applied in scattered fashion, collides with the traces of paint pressed on and unrolled by his own body.
Before the sheet closes off the picture module in the frame, and thus initiates its function as a device, it is painted on the reverse and given meaning with an extended signature the width of a brushstroke. In other groups of pictures, an exaggerated connection with the printed images is constructed when product advertising is used as a subject. Reflection and superimposition with simultaneous separation of the layers is programmatic (text, body, text, object, actual space) and serves as a valid model of a new imagery raised to become a concept.
The work of art aims to be epistemic, constant operationalisation, continuous continuation. A representation of the production of a representation, as Ginsberg says. His concern, once again, is the category of the oeuvre; he presents the individual work in permanent interconnection with the conditions of art, actor and self. Each pictorial object is designed to fit human proportions; the hanging height forms part of the picture and is an indicator and embodiment of his installation instructions.
He opens up another field with the completed remains of the exhibition and concept, in which he copies his sketches of floor plans and distributes them shrewdly and unquestioningly as a legend under coloured film, closing them and re-opening them again. Fabian Ginsberg shows aspiration and method as part of the problem. His work is proof of the refusal and part of the solution. —— *Klaus Merkel*

Fabian Ginsberg was born in 1983 in Freiburg and currently lives and works in Berlin

2019 Time as Activity 3, GELD, London (S)

2018 Strategien der Aufstandsbekämpfung, Antiimperialistische Kunst in Baden-Württemberg, Städtische Galerie Villingen-Schwenningen (S)

Augen, Kunstverein Zlin (with Stefan Hayn) (S)

2017 Disruption, NOUSMOULES, Vienna (S)

fabianginsberg.de

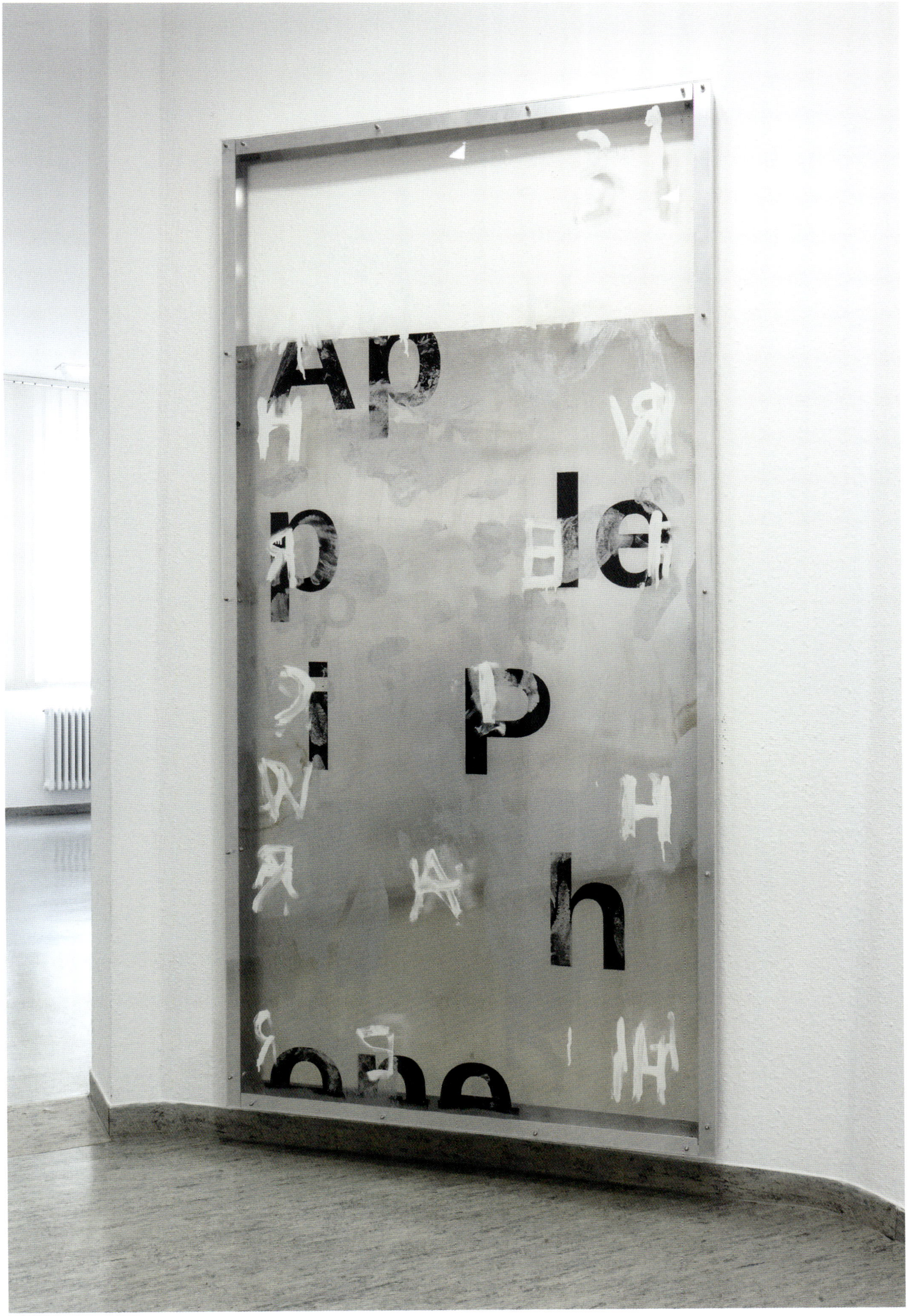

Untitled (Apple, Serie IN)
2018
Acrylic and lacquer on aluminium, Plexiglass, wood
190 × 96 × 6.5 cm
Bonn

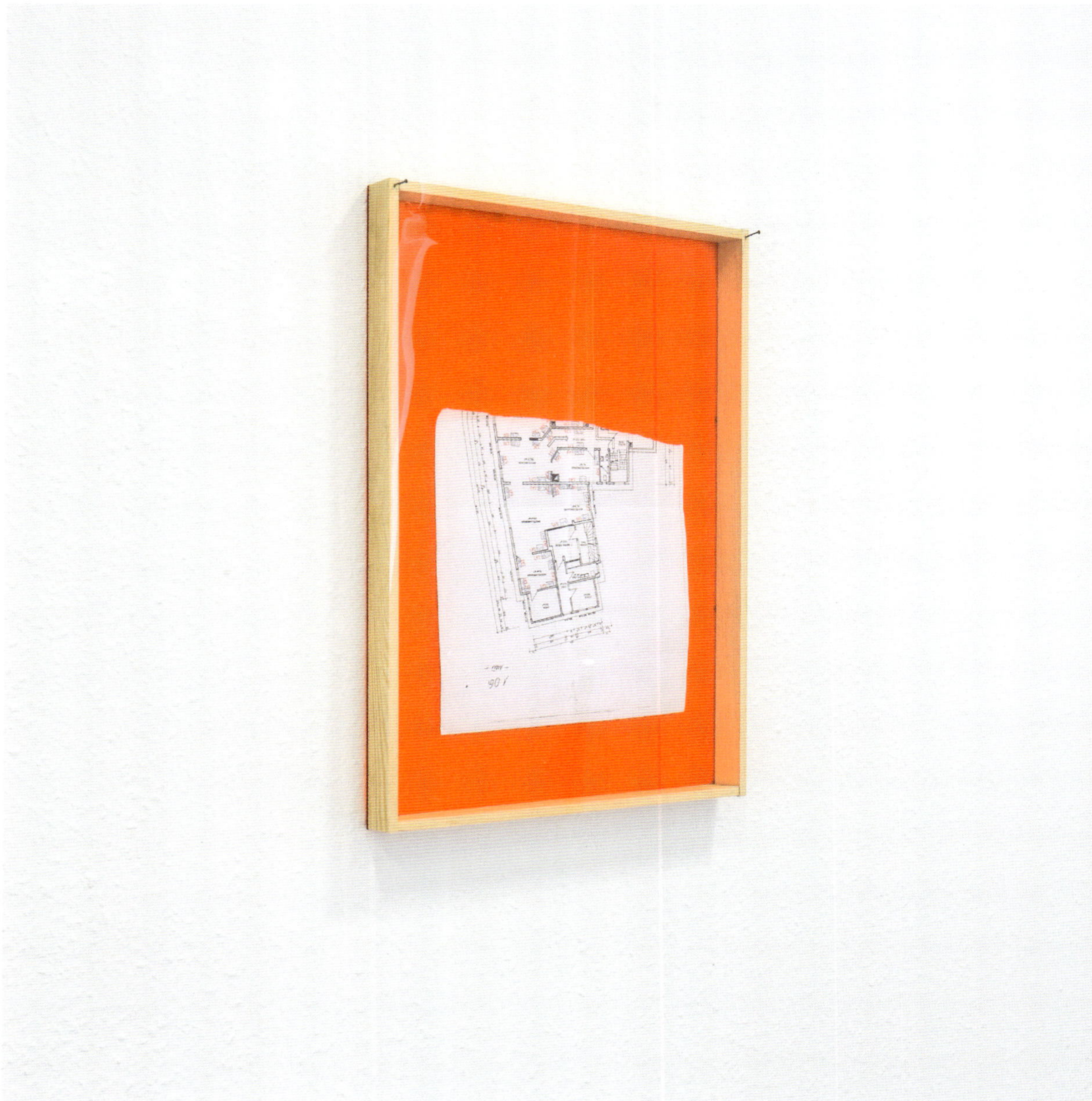

Untitled (Grundriss Städtische Galerie Villingen-Schwenningen, Serie R)

2018

Digital print on paper, Plexiglass, oil, wood

58.1 × 42.2 × 4.1 cm

Chemnitz

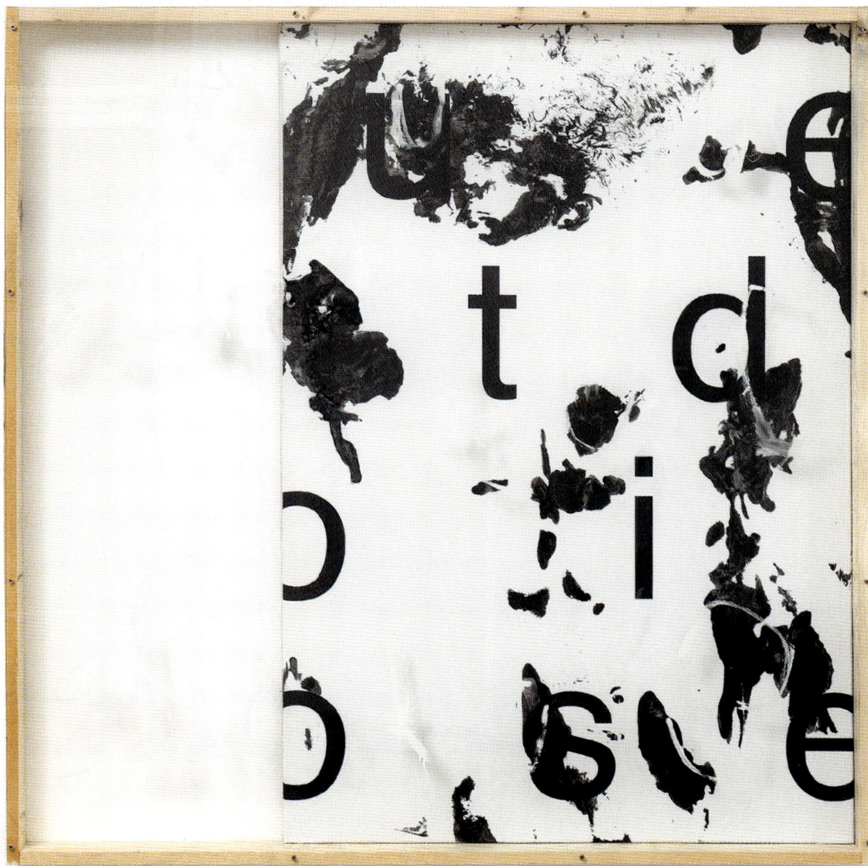

Untitled (outside, Serie IS)
2017/2019
Digital print on paper laid on jute,
lacquer, acrylic, wood, Plexiglass
134 × 136 × 8 cm
Wiesbaden

Gregor Gleiwitz

It stands to reason that the pictures of Gregor Gleiwitz can be described as non-representational, abstract images. Possibly we would be thinking in the tradition of figuration if we were to say that his pictures are "abstract": they seem like abstract pictures ... and yet if we observe them from an abstract point of view, they seem like figurative paintings. It is evidently not a matter of abstraction in the sense of an artistic reduction of reality as we perceive it, but rather an attempt to form it into a living opposite through painting. With this aim, each picture is created in a concentrated "painting session".
As soon as the picture confronts the artist, its first viewer and critic, he stops painting. When the work becomes a picture – is declared to be finished, that is – he gives it its date of production as a title. One picture was created on 2 May 2016. There was another successful attempt on 5 December 2017. And again on 19 September 2018. Before, between and thereafter a picture was successful on some occasions, but not on others. Gleiwitz's painting practice explains the diversity of his pictures; each picture is a unit, unique and hence different. *02.05.2016* is dark brownish with light patches which shine through and form an oval, centrifugal structure which looks like a face on a neck, almost Cubist. On the right there is even a green "eye", with a brownish-red "lid". A portrait? *05.12.2017* is more a window than a mirror. Colourful rainbows appear through a light surface, bending vertically and horizontally and growing up from bottom left to top right. A cheerful mood has been created in the picture, but scattered dark elements have been scratched and swallow up, negate, contradict the refraction of the light in the landscape. *19.09.2018* is jazzy; various flickering coloured bands (verses?) recall the late Mondrian. But the colourful graphic elements encounter soft forms of sky-blue and pink scribblings; behind, we can make out light green structured shadows. Each picture is the result of the flow of the "now", is hence a "today". But each day is individual. Unique. Different. Each day is today, was tomorrow, and has become yesterday. Gregor Gleiwitzs' pictures reflect the experience of time. In each picture he records a piece of reality.
—— *Michal B. Ron*

Gregor Gleiwitz was born in 1977 and currently lives and works in Berlin

Kunstakademie Mainz, 2000
Kunstakademie Münster, Meisterschüler with Prof. Mechtild Frisch, 2007

2019 Monstera – I'm sitting on the edge of my eye, SETAREH, Düsseldorf (S,C)

2018 Glass Tambourine. Guggenheim Gallery at Chapman University, Orange, California, (G)

2016 Faun's Fount, ACME, Los Angeles (S)

2014 Predator, HUS Gallery, London (S)

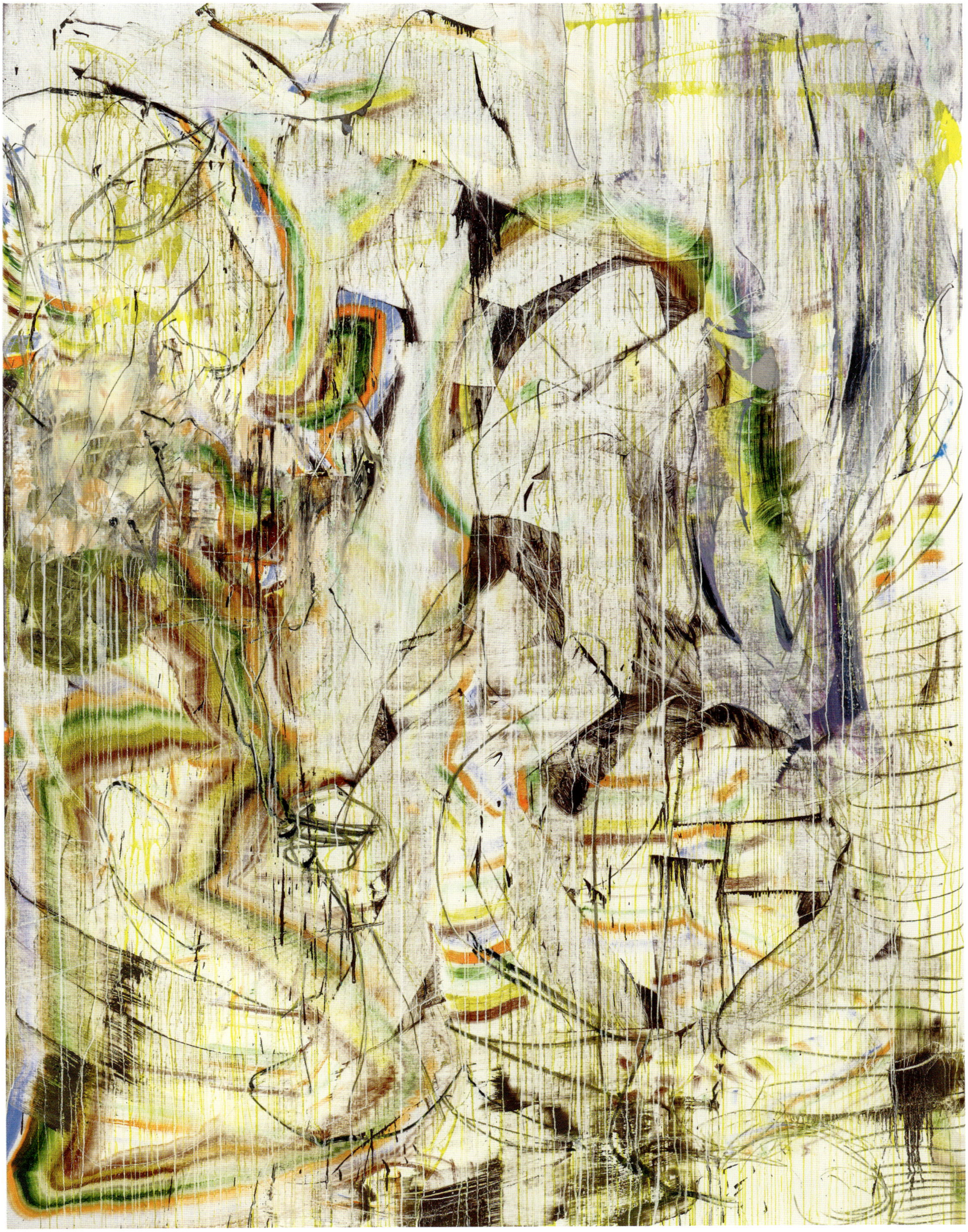

05.12.2017 2017 Oil on canvas 240 × 190 cm Chemnitz

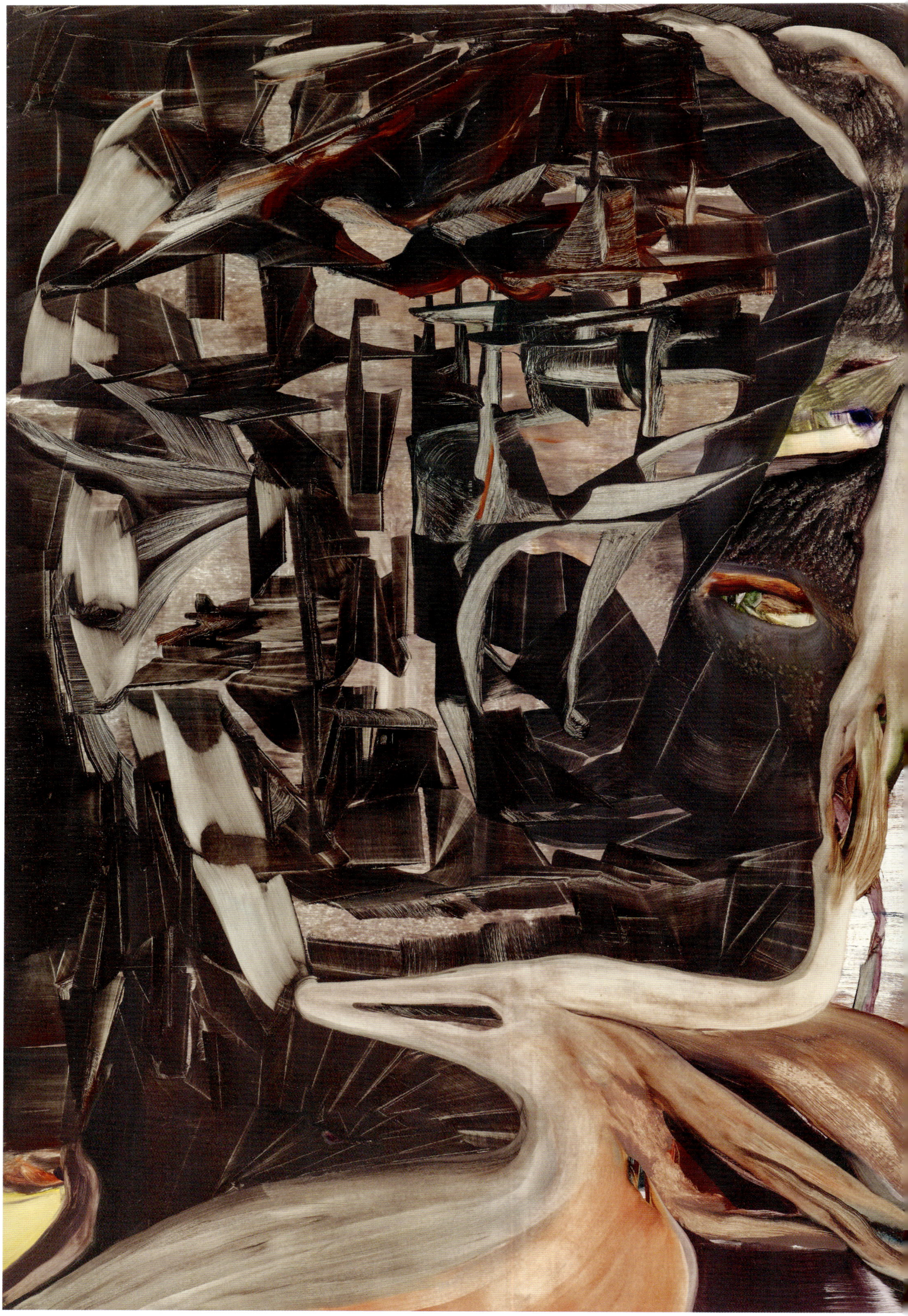

02.05.2016 2016 Oil on canvas 269.1 × 191.3 cm Bonn

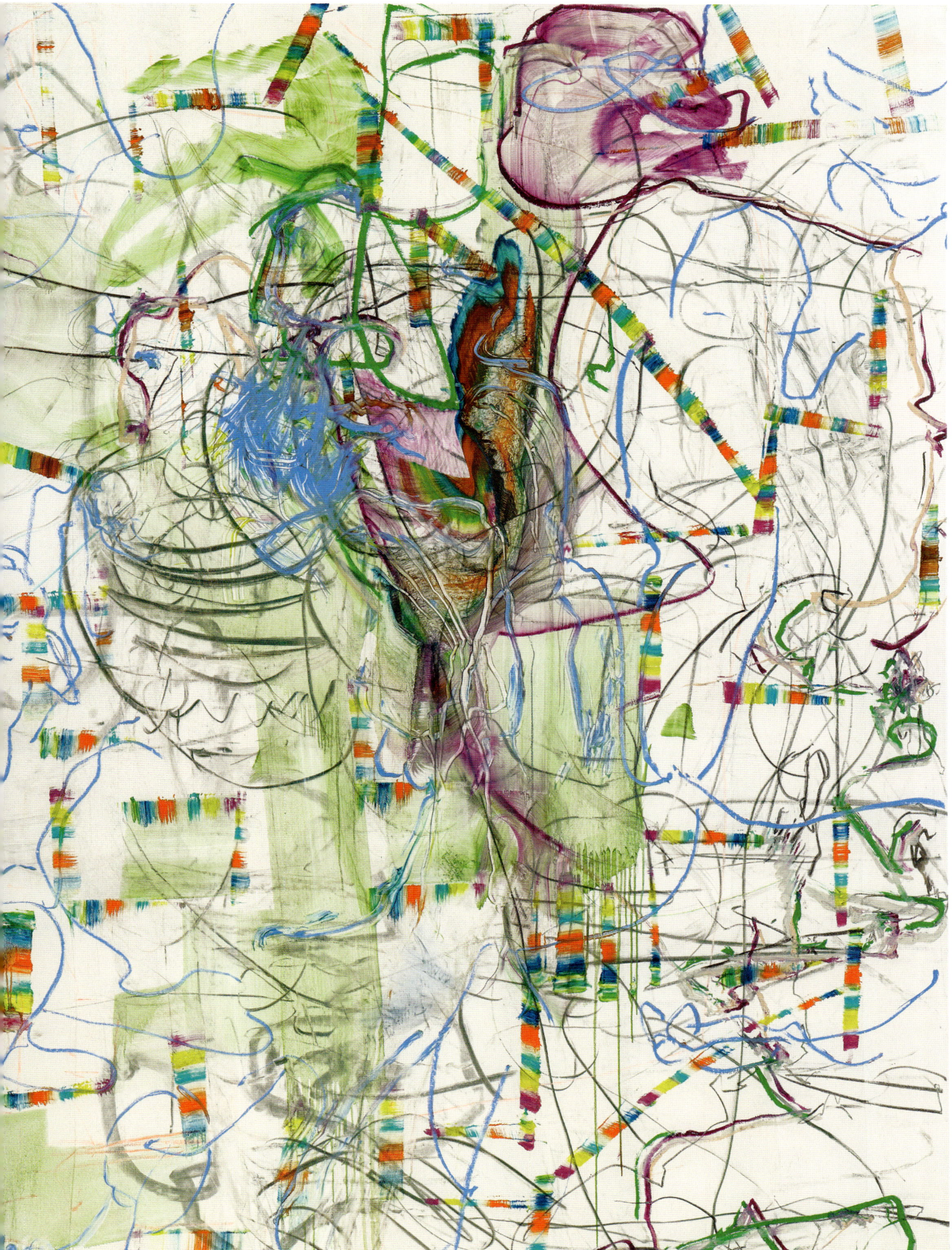

19.09.2018 2018 Oil on canvas 264.5 × 200 cm Wiesbaden

Lukas Glinkowski

Pump up the colour

There are countless unanswered questions in painting. The painter Lukas Glinkowski, who lives in Berlin but was born in Poland and trained in Düsseldorf, does not even try to answer them. Instead, he constantly asks himself, and us, new ones.
Analogous to sampling in music, he presents a visual mash-up in his works. Fragments and props are transformed into a new whole whose meaning the viewers configure themselves: art-historical quotations and contemporary references are aesthetic or conceptual pointers without a pointing finger. In Glinkowski's painting it is not a matter of proposing a harmonious, coherent meaning, but of individual access, in which the viewpoint of the artist and that of the viewer need not necessarily coincide. This decidedly postmodern approach creates space for him to play with our seeing and thinking habits, a game which simultaneously permits chance, chaos and plurality or even brings the incommensurable together. Lukas Glinkowski transports us into a pictorial world which derives from his everyday observations and experiences, sometimes perhaps also dreams or idealisation: urban spaces, films, track lists, cartoons, video games, pop and club culture. In recent years he has increasingly abandoned the canvas; tiles, photographic and woodchip wallpaper, mirror tiles and films, wood and glass have become the carriers for his painting. And because he is particularly interested in subculture, the places he conjures up are often as morbid as they are trashy, and his constructions consist of ordinary industrial products. The texture of the objects he constructs himself thus determine a "spatial occupation" by his painting, which in any case is not restricted to the hanging on the wall – sometimes the visitors to the exhibition are even invited to (participate in the) paint(ing). Possibly in order to show us that his world is actually one which we can discover anew with our own eyes by seeing it his way. He does not want to explain it to us, but as so often in life, well-posed questions are more illuminating than precise answers. —— *Peter Ungeheuer*

Lukas Glinkowski was born in 1984 in Chełmno (Poland) and currently lives and works in Berlin

Kunstakademie Düsseldorf, Akademiebrief and Meisterschüler with Prof. Katharina Grosse, 2014

2019 Not so a white cube, Lage Egal, Berlin (G)
2018 Kleiner Raum für aktuelles Nichts, Berlin (S)
Single Party, KanyaKage, Berlin (S)
2017 I like disco & disco likes me, Bruch & Dallas, Cologne (S)

lukasglinkowski.de

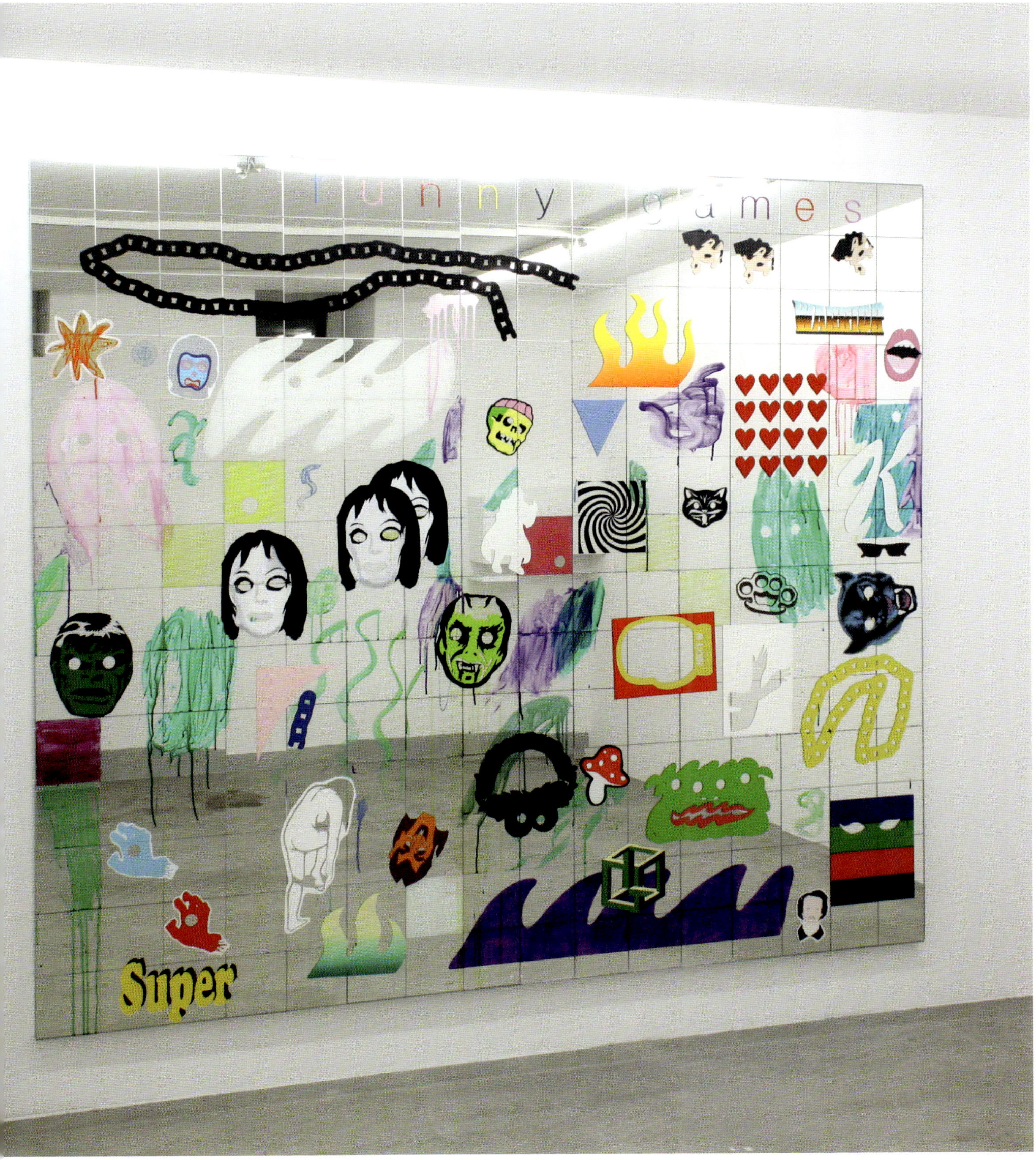

Funny Games

2018

Oil and glass paint, mirror tiles
on four-part wood construction

210 × 240 × 4 cm

Bonn

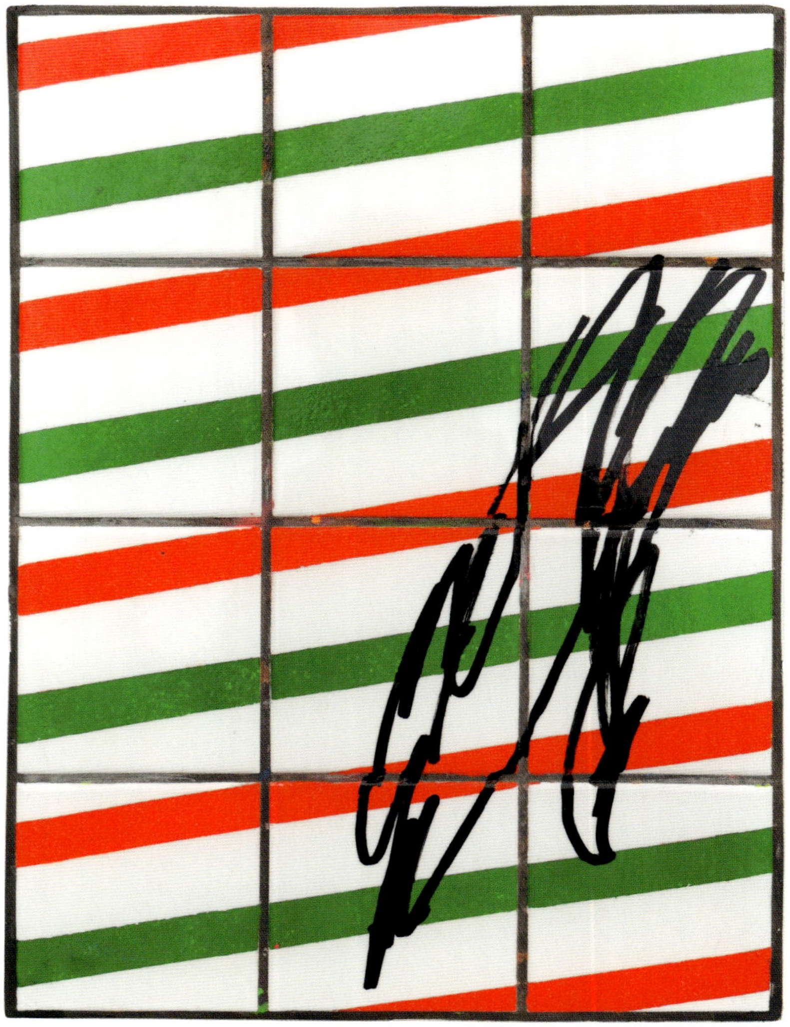

Margherita

2019

Lacquer, markers, tiles
on wood construction

40 × 30 × 3 cm

Wiesbaden

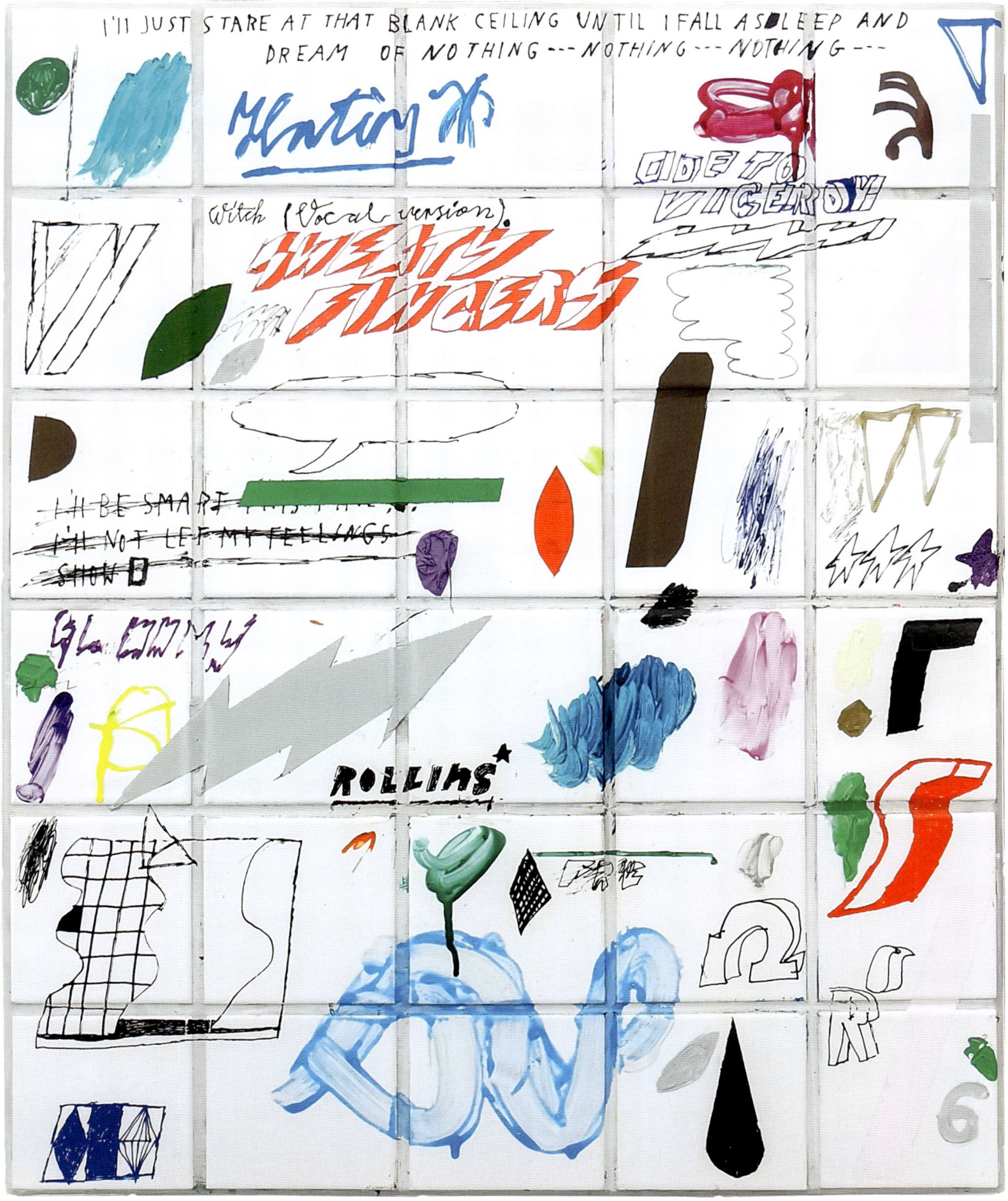

Eau de toilette VI 2018 Oil and glass paint, markers, tiles on wood construction 60 × 50 × 3 cm Chemnitz

Sebastian Gögel

Pictures from the family of the homunculus

The debate regarding artificial intelligence and the use of robots has long since found its way into the major discussion forums and is met with anxiety – an emotionality which does not testify to a regressive attitude. This justifiable anxiety stimulates images regarded as anachronistic which conjure up Frankenstein's monster as a prominent representative in the ancestral gallery of the homunculus. The anxiety also calls to mind images of the early culture of prostheses, with which medical technology attempted to restore functionality to maimed bodies. Drastic representations by Dix and Grosz show that it was another form of "progress", that of war technology, which turned people into cripples. This leads to the conclusion that ultimately there is an asynchronous correspondence between man and technology.
Gögel shows damaged specimens that resemble crash-test dummies, between ensoulment and unmasking. In *Hyperchron* (Hyperchronous), such a figure seems to be coming alive, because honey-coloured shading is spreading across its chest like streams of warmth, contrasting with the cold blue of the overall. In *Spalt* (Cleavage), a clone warrior figure is sitting on an office chair. It has removed its warlike helmet and instead of the eye-slit we are made aware of a thoughtful gaze. In the background, a precise cut has divided the spherical veil of colour. The line looks like a dissecting operation which seems to have cut off the controls. The cleavage looks like a break because its appearance uncompromisingly opposes the painterly style of the picture. Not only here does melancholy wear black and cast a shadow over every other colour. *Leumund* (Reputation) shows two seemingly armoured figures, whereby the dark-coloured one is tipsily embracing the other one. The apparently friendly gesture degenerates into a fracas, because the fleshy fingers are feeling for the larynx of the figure he is embracing. The mouths demonstrate that both steely figures could bite. Their body armour is not only protection against the outside world; it is also a corset that imprisons the emotions. Both have revealed their true colours in their interaction, which exposes all the depravity in the communication between eating and being eaten. Here the toast must be enriched by a large dose of cynicism. —— *Hans-Werner Schmidt*

Sebastian Gögel was born in 1978 in Sonneberg and currently lives and works in Leipzig

Hochschule für Grafik und Buchkunst Leipzig, Diploma and Meisterschüler with Prof. Sighard Gille, 1997–2005

2019 Grote Straat, Hoorn&Reniers, The Hague (S)
Circlus, Thaler Originalgrafik, Leipzig (G)

2018 Leipziger Blätter, Thaler Original Grafik, Leipzig (G)
Krakauer Blätter, Gallery Potencja, Krakow (G)

sebgoegel.com

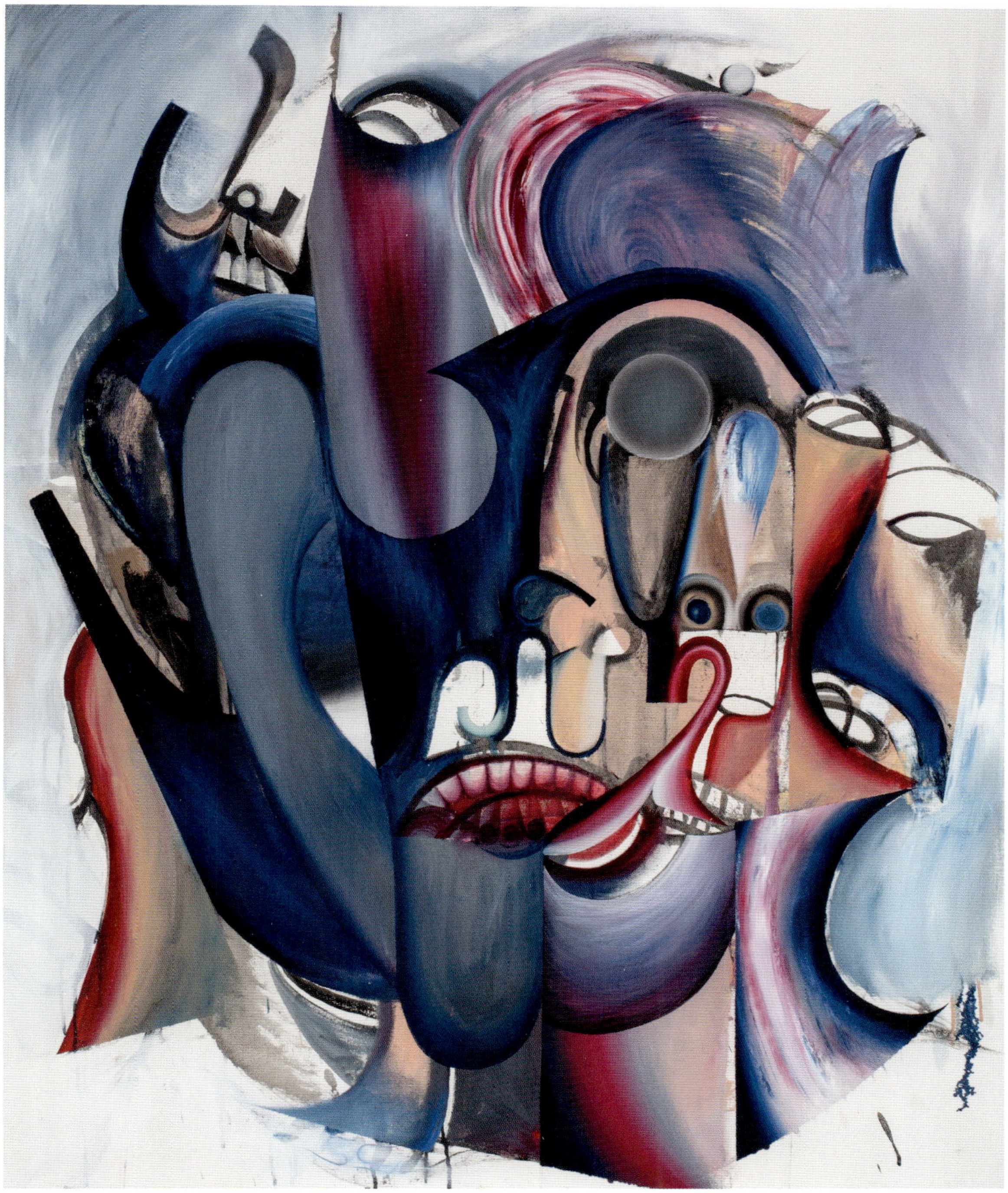

Elements 2017 Oil on canvas 130 × 110 cm Chemnitz

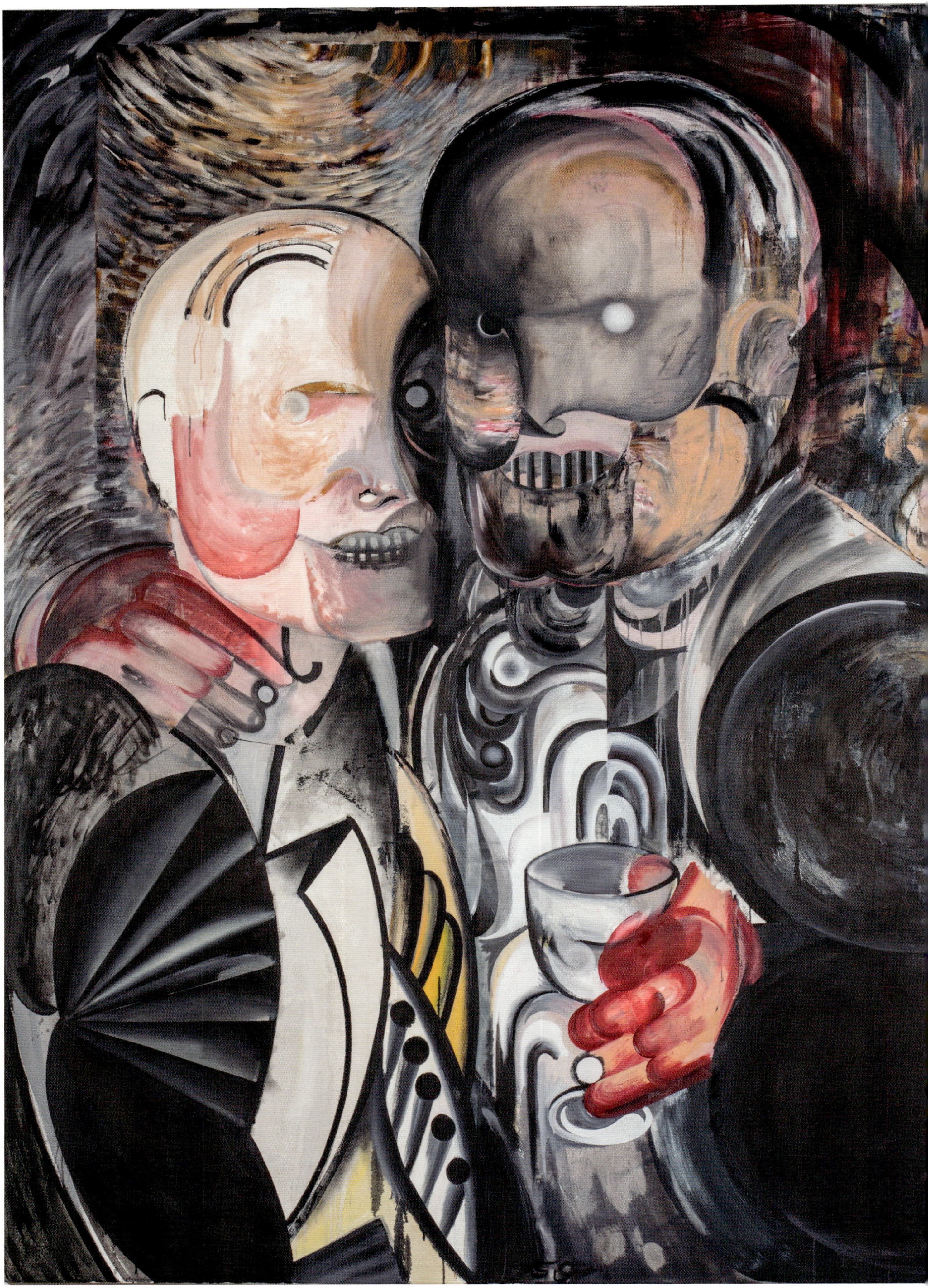

Leumund 2017 Oil on canvas 270 × 190 cm Bonn

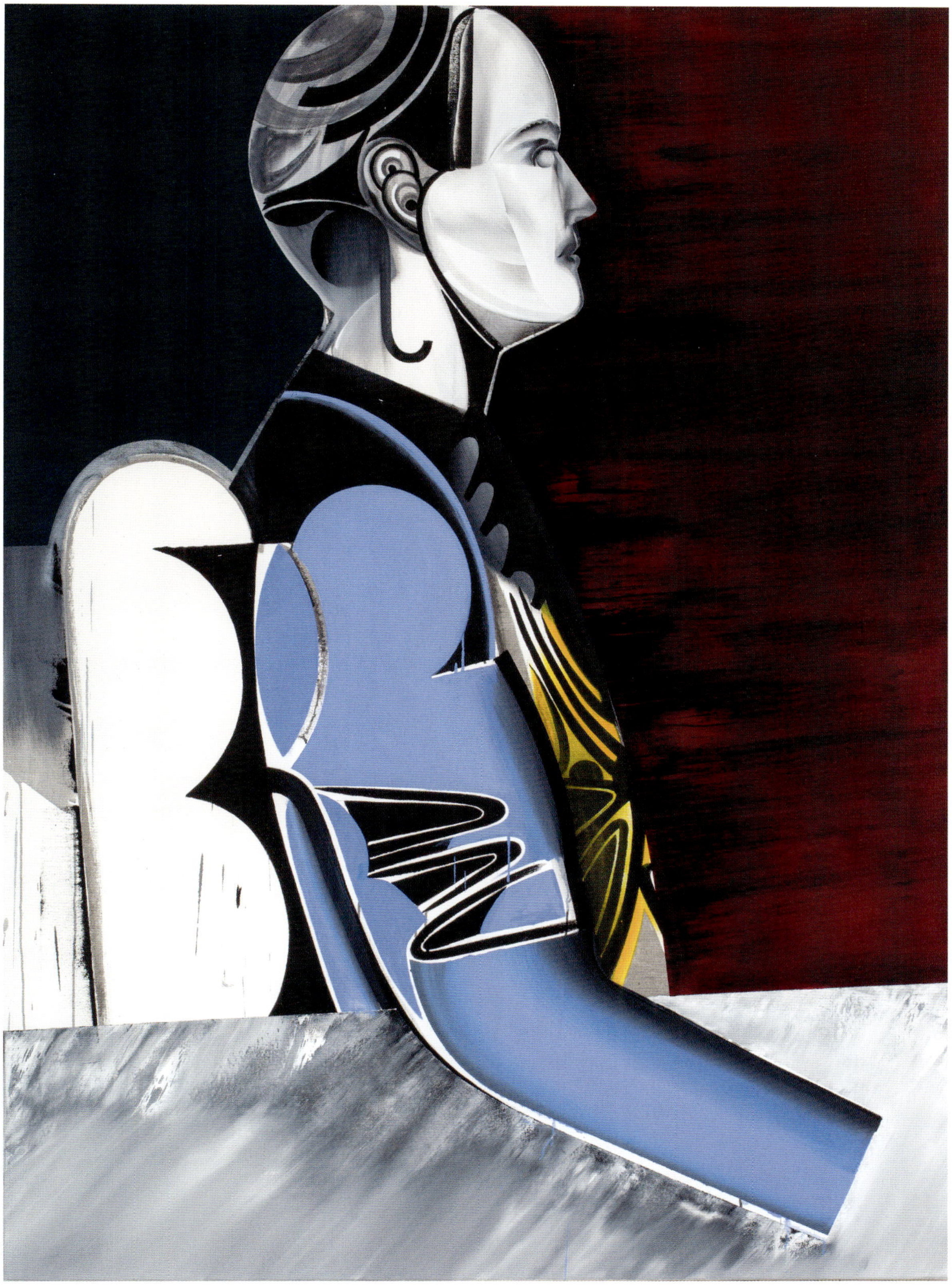

Hyperchon 2019 Oil on canvas 200 × 150 cm Wiesbaden

Henriette Grahnert

In works like *The painters table* or *Stillaleiftäbel*, Henriette Grahnert refers to the painting genre of the still life. Forms, decor and objects are assembled on small cocktail tables reminiscent of the 1950s to create anarchic little world theatres with an unknown stage plot. Comparable with a stage in which the dramatic action is layered into the depths, Grahnert develops a visual space with an explicit "in front of" and "behind".
Numerous references and allusions can be discovered in these assemblages. In some cases, as in *My son my sun*, Henriette Grahnert quotes her own works as a picture-within-a-picture. In others, Matisse, Picasso and other heroes of art history join forces. However, the reference is not limited to a skilled treatment of quotations. The artist also juggles cleverly with a wide range of painting traditions: her pictures quote Pop Art and Bad Painting, American Color Field Painting and classical abstraction, minimalist traditions and Concrete Painting. With cryptic humour she links these opposing forces to form an individual pictorial cosmos. And yet, none of the styles mentioned truly stands for what it claims to be. Instead, it is a nuanced discourse on the subject of painting itself, discussing the elementary questions about form and structure, spatiality and the distribution of surfaces, colour and composition.
The delight in quotations and ambiguities also takes place on a linguistic level. Henriette Grahnert's picture titles convey a specific humour which offers further levels of reception. One instance, for example, is the painting *The tricky thing with the right balance*. The square in this abstract composition becomes the protagonist by means of the narrative title. The viewer willingly imagines human traits and a diffuse feeling of empathy and solidarity arises. Similarly, the ghostly being in the painting *The cute ghost* immediately wins over the sympathy of the viewer. We are inclined to beg of the ghost, in the words of Rio Reiser: My friend, be my friend, be my friend, be my friend, my friend. —— *Harriet Zilch*

Henriette Grahnert was born in 1977 in Dresden and currently lives and works in Leipzig

Hochschule für Grafik und Buchkunst Leipzig, Diploma with Prof. Arno Rink, 2004

2018 Sammlung Reydan Weiss. Ohne Etikett fühle ich mich freier, Herzog Anton Ulrich Museum, Braunschweig (G)

MdbK meets G2. Malerei aus Leipzig ab 2000, Museum der bildenden Künste, Leipzig (G)

2017 Viva la natura morta / Es lebe das Stillleben, Galerie Kleindienst Leipzig (S)

My abstract world, Me Collectors Room, Berlin (G)

henriettegrahnert.de
galeriekleindienst.de

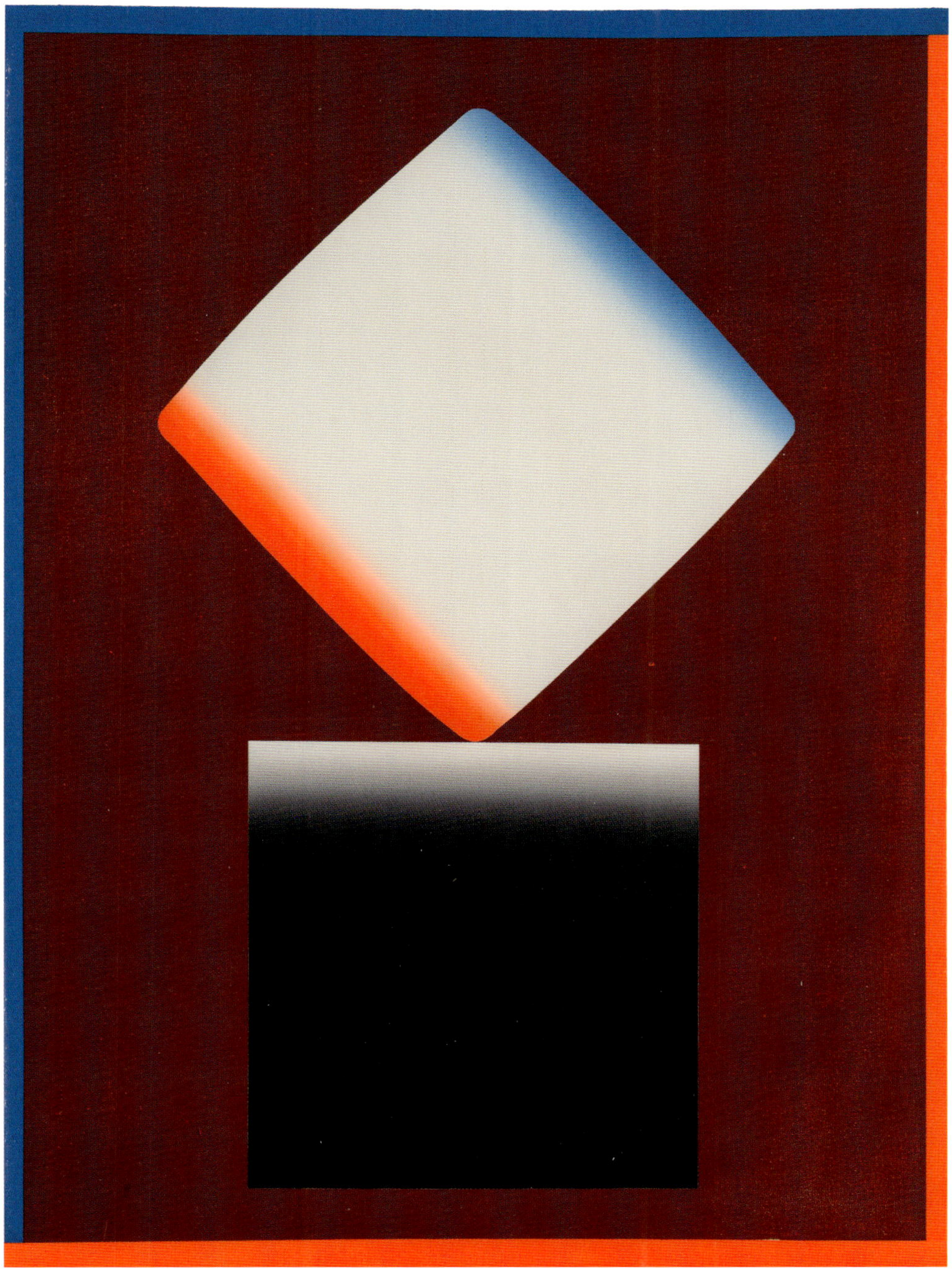

The tricky thing with the right balance 2017 Acrylic on canvas 120 × 90 cm Wiesbaden

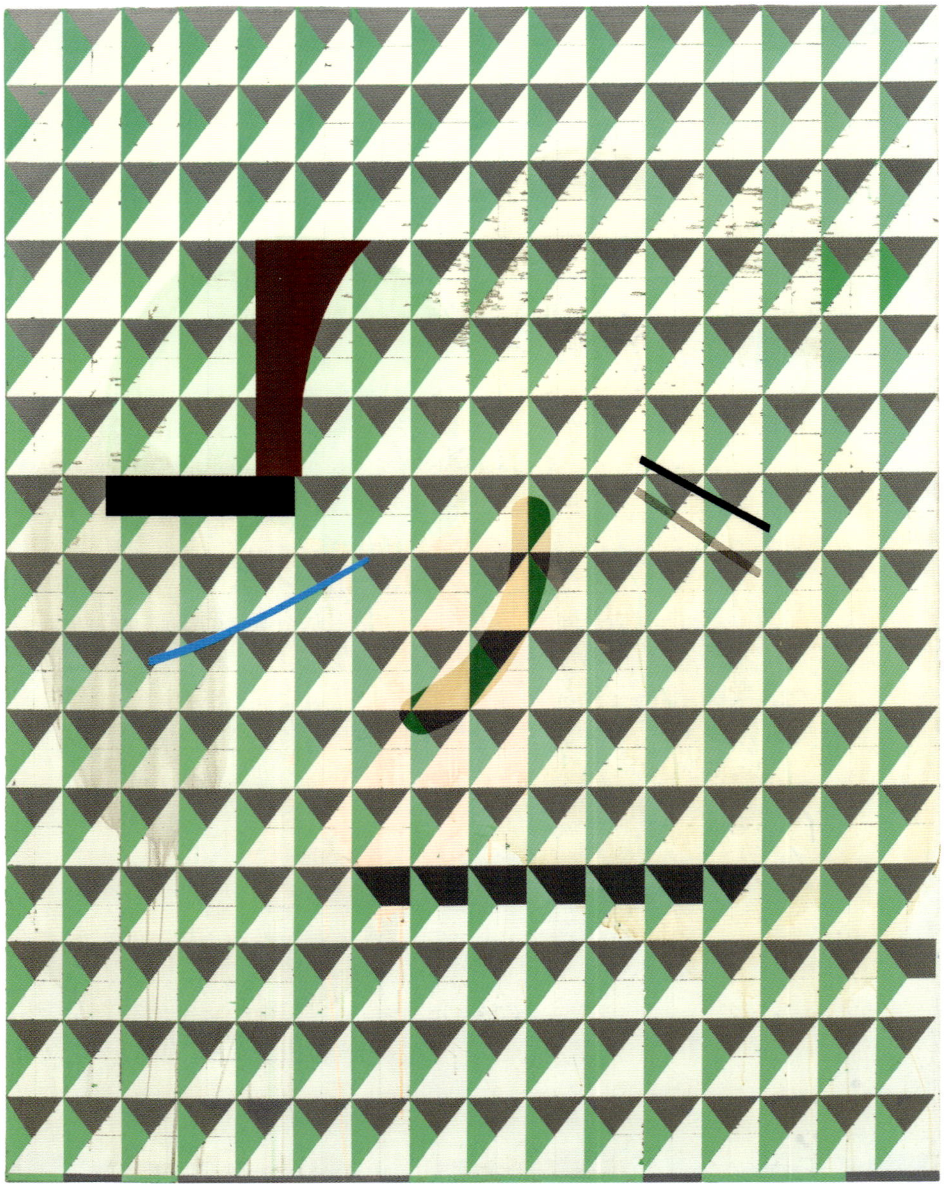

The cute ghost 2017 Acrylic on canvas 150 × 120 cm Chemnitz

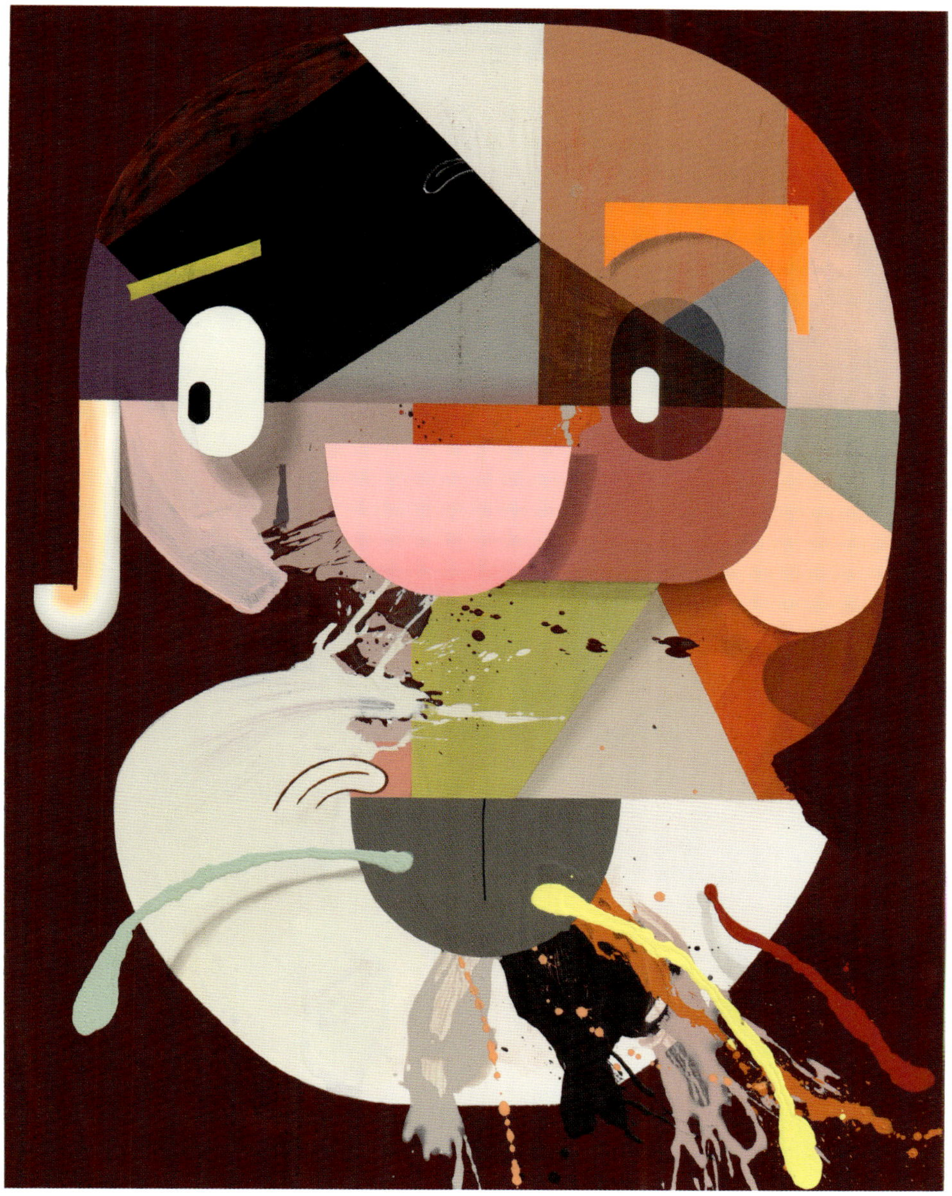

Doubleface 2019 Acrylic on canvas 150 × 120 cm Bonn

Dana Greiner

The watchfulness with which Dana Greiner investigates the character of form, material and colour is a decisive characteristic of her artistic work. Multi-layered realities appear through the use of different painting techniques and painting materials that she often produces herself, including wax, acrylic media, oil, graphite, lacquer, resins and unbound pigment, thereby permitting a variety of pictorial inventions. Picture carriers like wood, canvas or Perspex, and their characteristics as carriers, are worked in different ways and often come to the fore themselves.
In her search for what the material holds and what type of interaction it can produce, she develops compositions directly on the medium. The structure of the material, form, colour and space is formed in a dialectic-reflexive process that is searching for concentration and unification. The brilliant and nuanced colours, the symmetry which is in some places interrupted, the blurring of contrasts – all these open up an entire cosmos for the viewer, in that he or she can understand the artist's reflexions layer by layer. The viewer is also challenged to his or her own act of productive seeing. The necessary freedom of the visual experience is made possible through the absence of an iconographical form or interpretation.
Greiner's works are influenced by literature, film, music and theatre. This can also be seen in the choice of her titles. *o. T. (tria balette)*, for example, recalls Oskar Schlemmer's *Triadisches Ballett* (Triadic Ballet), whereby the work captures not only the visual but also the tonal aspects in an almost synaesthetic manner. The artistic worlds of Dana Greiner are presented as mysterious. Installations contain pictorial elements; in her casts the boundaries between object and painting are blurred and in some exhibitions her pictures themselves become actors in a performative situation.
—— *Andrei Yagoubov and Sophie-Charlotte Bombeck*

Dana Greiner was born in 1988 in Munich and currently lives and works in Munich
Akademie der bildenden Künste Munich, Diploma, 2017, Meisterschülerin with Prof. Pia Fries

2018 yrwšlm, Parallel light installation in mosques, churches and synagogues (USA, ES, IT; S)
Between Sheraton and Hilton, IGCA North Gallery, Anchorage (S)
2017 Die Vertreterin, Galerie Karin Wimmer/ Young art space, Munich (S)
Sanctuary, Einraumhaus, Mannheim (S)

danagreiner.com
yrwslm.com

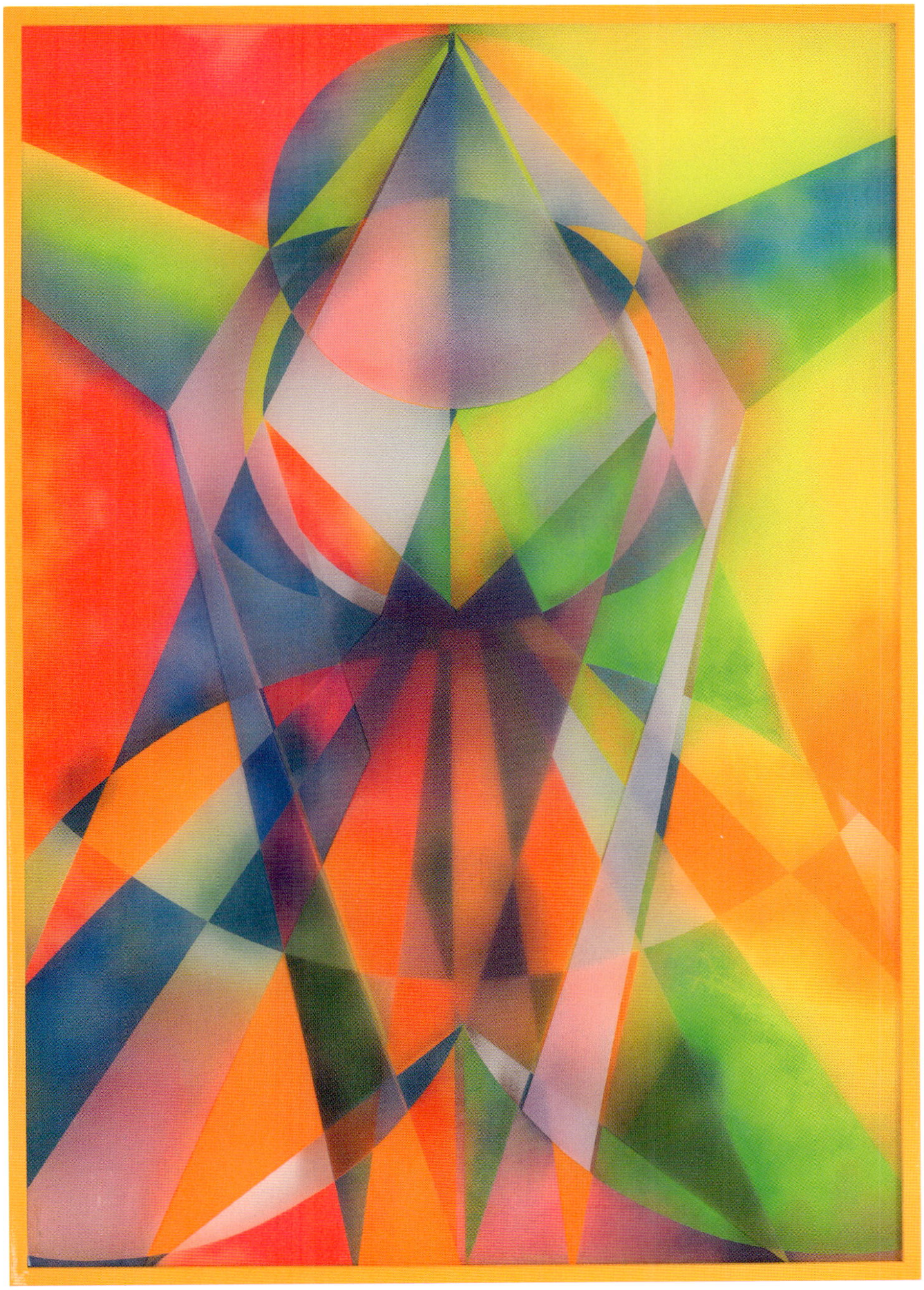

preplex xiii

2019

Spray paint on acrylic glass

125 × 85 cm

Chemnitz

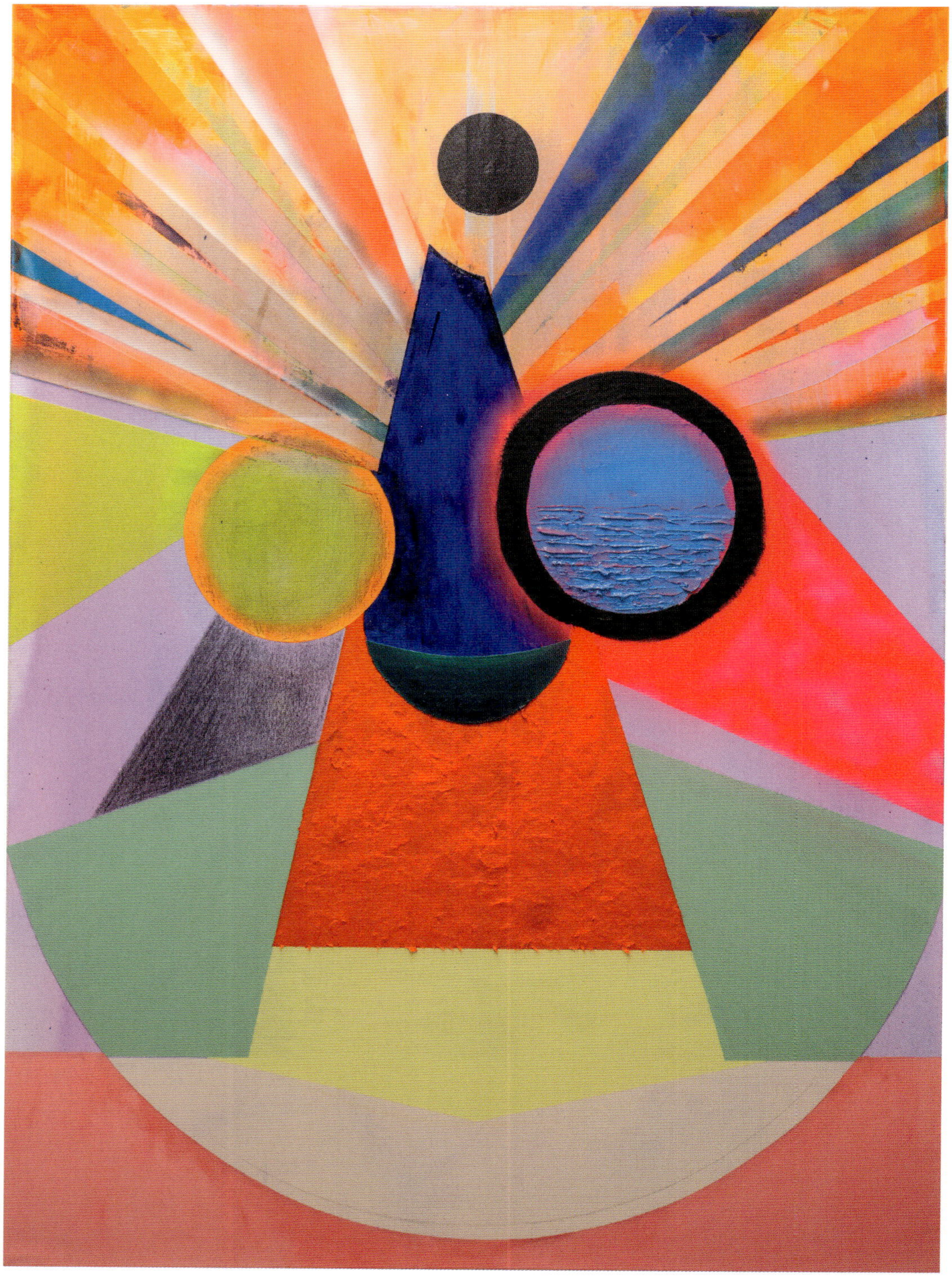

Untitled (querelle)

2019

Acrylic media, oil, spray paint, lacquer, vinyl, graphite, rope on wood laid on canvas

180 × 135 cm

Wiesbaden

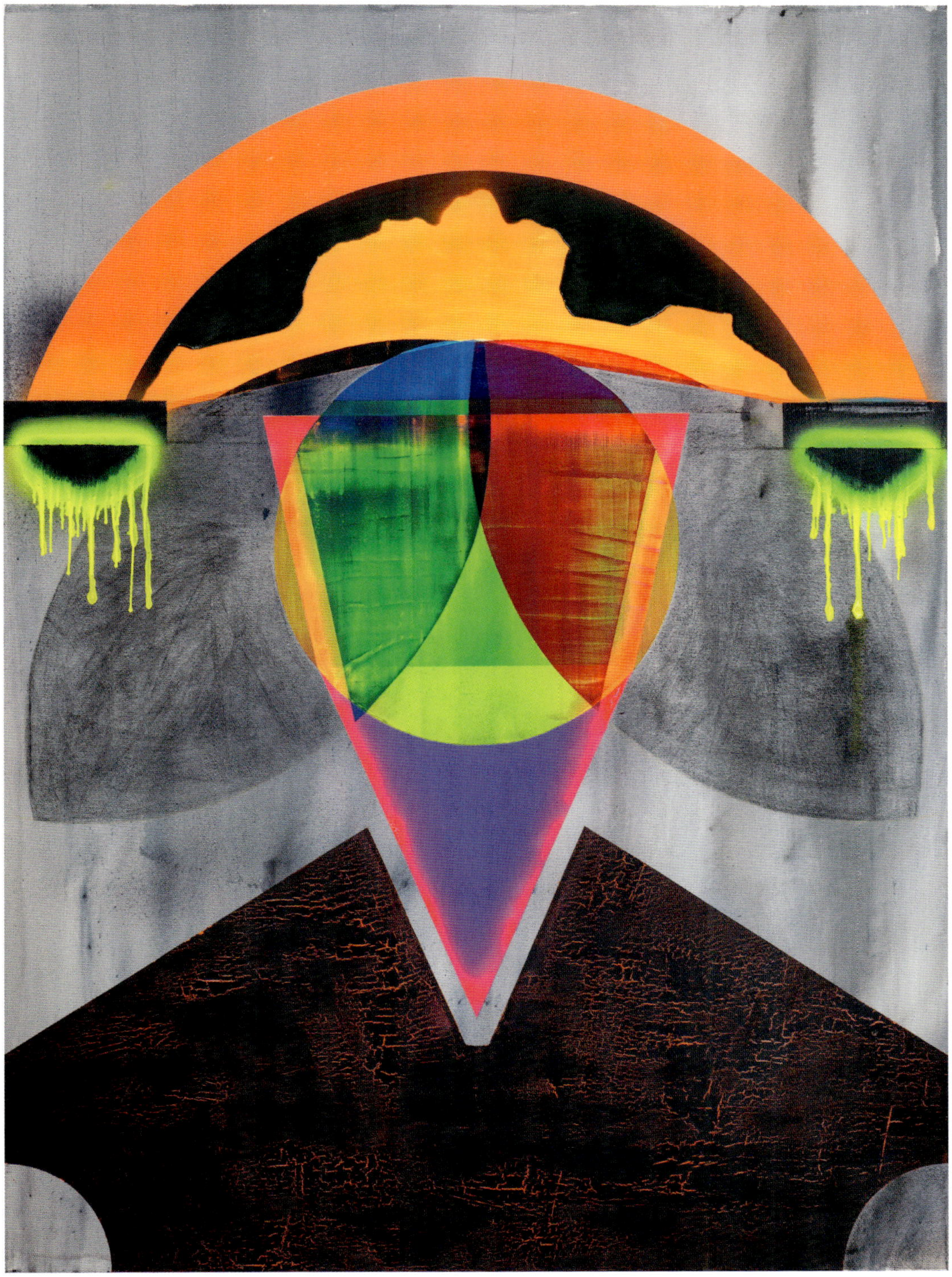

Untitled (tria balette) 2019 Acrylic media, epoxy resin, spray paint, graphite on canvas 180 × 135 cm Bonn

Vivian Greven

Corporeality, countenance and transjective matrixiality

When considering the current art-historical classification of Vivian Greven, we can establish a matrix consisting of six elements. Firstly, there is the excellent manual skill (*Handwerklichkeit*/Hw) of a painting characterised by conceptual and three-dimensional qualities, in which delicately executed flesh tones encounter monochrome colours and volumes meet disembodied surfaces. Secondly, we can emphasise the atemporality (*Atemporalität*/At) and thirdly the hybridity (*Hybridität*/Hy) of her works: the recombining of different stylistic concepts linked with the dissolution of hierarchies between original, reproduction and simulation. Fourthly, we may refer to the painterly emphasis of an interstitial spatiality (*Zwischenräumlichkeit*/Zw) similar to that of cut-outs (as the absence of the other in the sense of a trace); and fifthly, the role which our corporeality (*Leiblichkeit*/Lb) plays with regard to thinking, perception, awareness and our existence in the world as a whole, always linked with (sixthly) the question regarding the countenance (*Antlitz*/Al) of the other. Emmanuel Levinas wrote on this subject: "The caress is the unit of approach and of closeness. In it, closeness is always simultaneously absence. What else does the tenderness of the caressed skin consist of, but the disparity between expectation and present?" (Emmanuel Levinas, "Sprache und Nähe", in: *Die Spur des Anderen,* Freiburg 1999, p. 283). A border-linking transjectivity is created in the hiatus whose echo is reflected in the matrixial interstitiality of the works of Vivian Greven, which by creating a universe thereby connect in a highly topical manner the aesthetic and ethical questions of our time. —— *Georg Herzberg*

$$\begin{bmatrix} \text{Hw} & \text{At} & \text{Hy} \\ \text{Zw} & \text{Lb} & \text{Al} \end{bmatrix}$$

Vivian Greven was born in 1985 in Bonn and currently lives and works in Düsseldorf

Kunstakademie Düsseldorf, Akademiebrief with Prof. Thomas Grünfeld, 2015
Meisterschülerin with Prof. Siegfried Anzinger, 2012

2019	0 V / Kadel Willborn, Düsseldorf (S)
2018	Insane in the Membrane, Sammlung Philara, Düsseldorf (G)
	a m o r e, Aurel Scheibler, Berlin (S)
	Ekstase, Kunstmuseum Stuttgart (G)

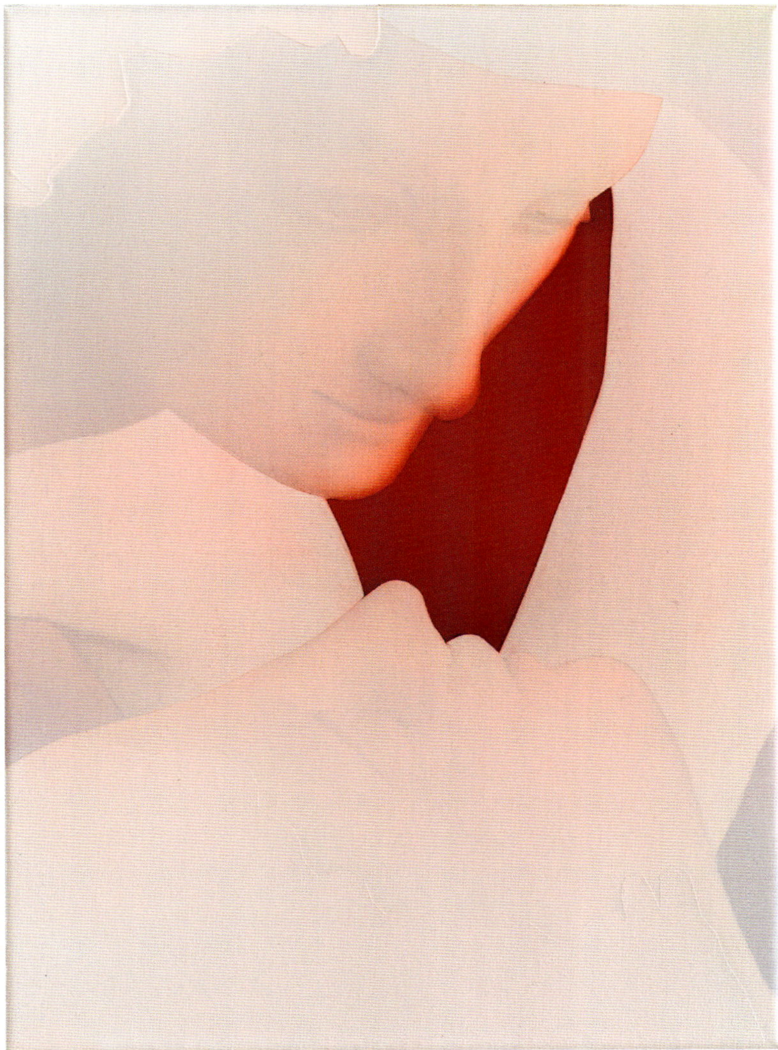

Lamia 2017 Oil on canvas 43 × 32 cm Chemnitz

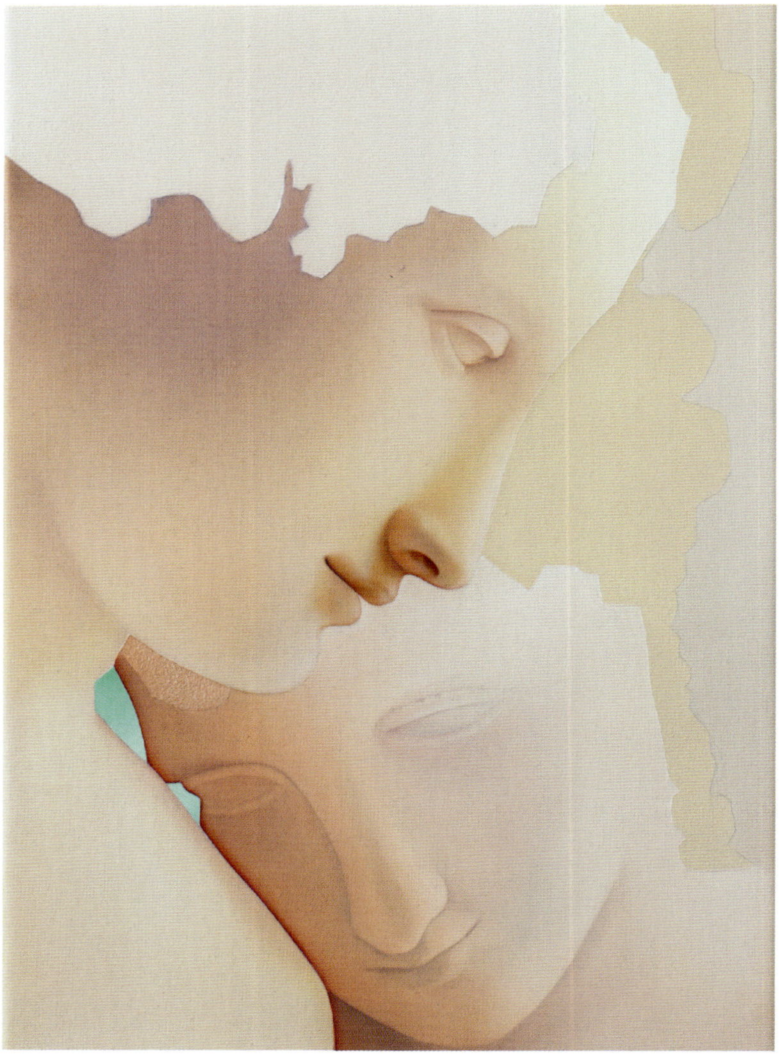

Tru I 2018 Oil and acrylic on canvas 49 × 35 cm Wiesbaden

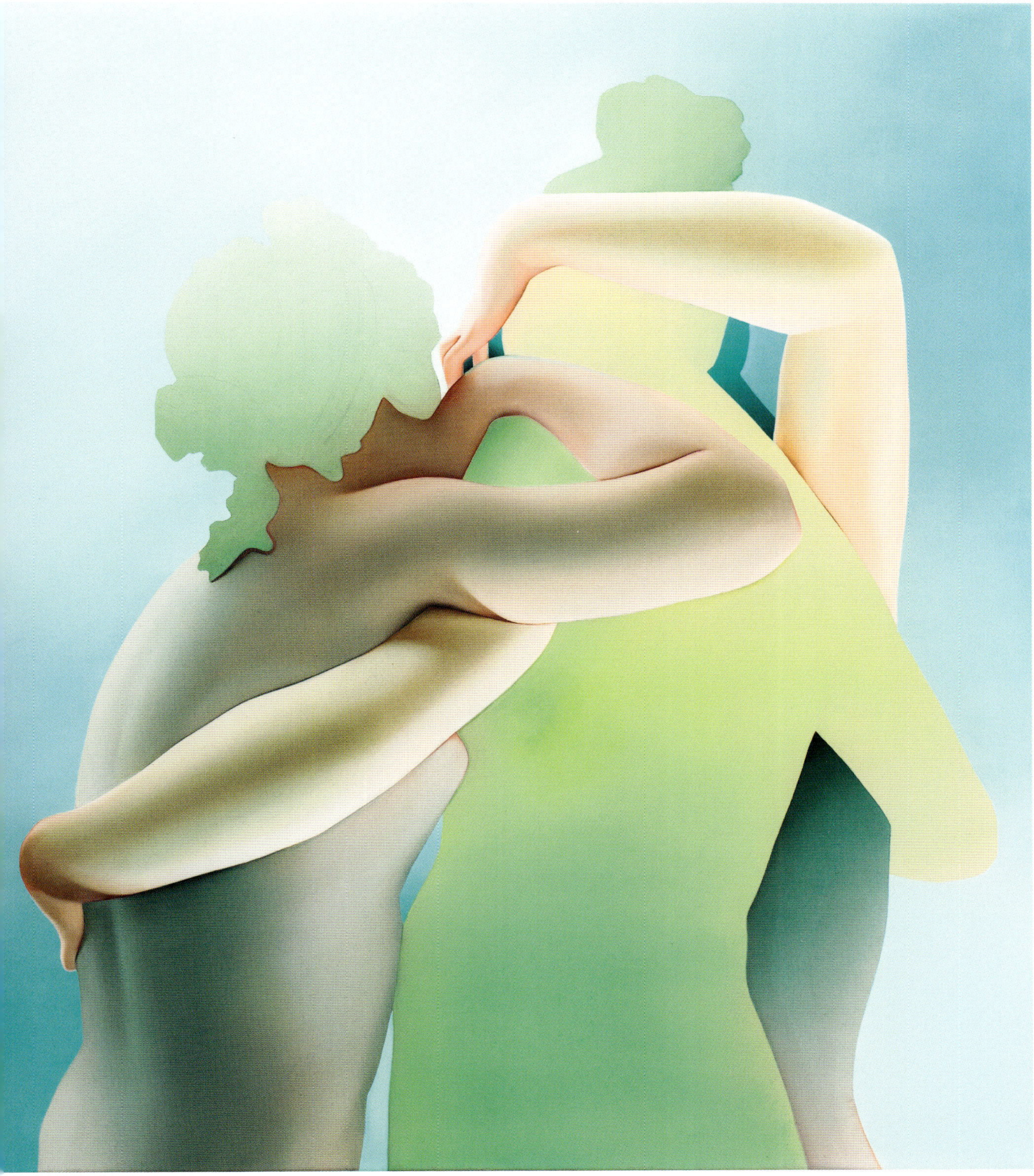

Leea 2017 Oil on canvas 120 × 110 cm Bonn

Toulu Hassani

In Toulu Hassani's practice to date, we can distinguish two technical approaches to painting. Firstly, classic oil painting, and secondly the casting process with epoxy resin mixed with pigment. The latter process is characterised by a more sculptural style, but in both painterly methods, Hassani declines the paradigmatic vocabulary of Modernism using the subject's abstraction, monochrome and grid. Drawings and semiotic systems in a figurative sense are frequently inscribed in her oil paintings. In the way in which the artist approaches the processing of the surface with fine brushstrokes, we are almost tempted to suspect a *horror vacui*. In concentrated, detailed steps she fills the canvas with meandering ornaments which I understand as variations of the grid in the diversity of their styles of execution. These grids extend so densely across the canvas that, in spite of a broad spectrum of colours, the picture appears like a black, red or green monochrome surface when seen as a whole. The staccato-like rhythms of the colour gradients make the surface of the picture oscillate like the shiny chitin carapace of a beetle. The oil paintings stand in contrast to the pictures cast in epoxy resin, which acquire the character of objects as a result of their spatial layers of paint. The relief provides the dominant connecting element between the two groups of works. In the painterly illusion of high points and depths, shadows and incident light the creation of relief in the oil paintings appears like the quotation of a classical trompe-l'œil effect. In the objects, by contrast, the relief is the component which provides the structure with its spatial formation. Ultimately, the positive and negative forms create the casting technique for the objects. In their essence, they ultimately refuse to be clearly assigned to the categories "painting" and "object" and complement each other together with the oil paintings to create Hassani's artistic signature. —— *Elmas Senol*

Toulu Hassani was born in 1984 in Ahva
(Iran) and currently lives and works in Hannover

Facultad de Bellas Artes, Universidad Valencia, Spain, 2008–2009

Braunschweig University of Art, 2005–2011
Meisterschülerin with Prof. Walter Dahr
2012

2018 "Deutschland ist keine Insel", Sammlung zeitgenössischer Kunst der Bundesrepublik Deutschland, Ankäufe von 2012 b
2016, Bundeskunsthalle, Bonn (G

2017 Iteration, Rudolf-Scharpf-Galerie
Wilhelm-Hack-Museum, Ludwigshafen (S)

VG Stipendium 2017, Kestner Gesellschaft, Hannover (G)

2016/17
Minus Something, Sprengel-Preis für Bildende Kunst 2016, Sprenge
Museum Hannover (S)

Untitled 2018 Mechanical pencil and oil on canvas 50 × 39 cm Chemnitz

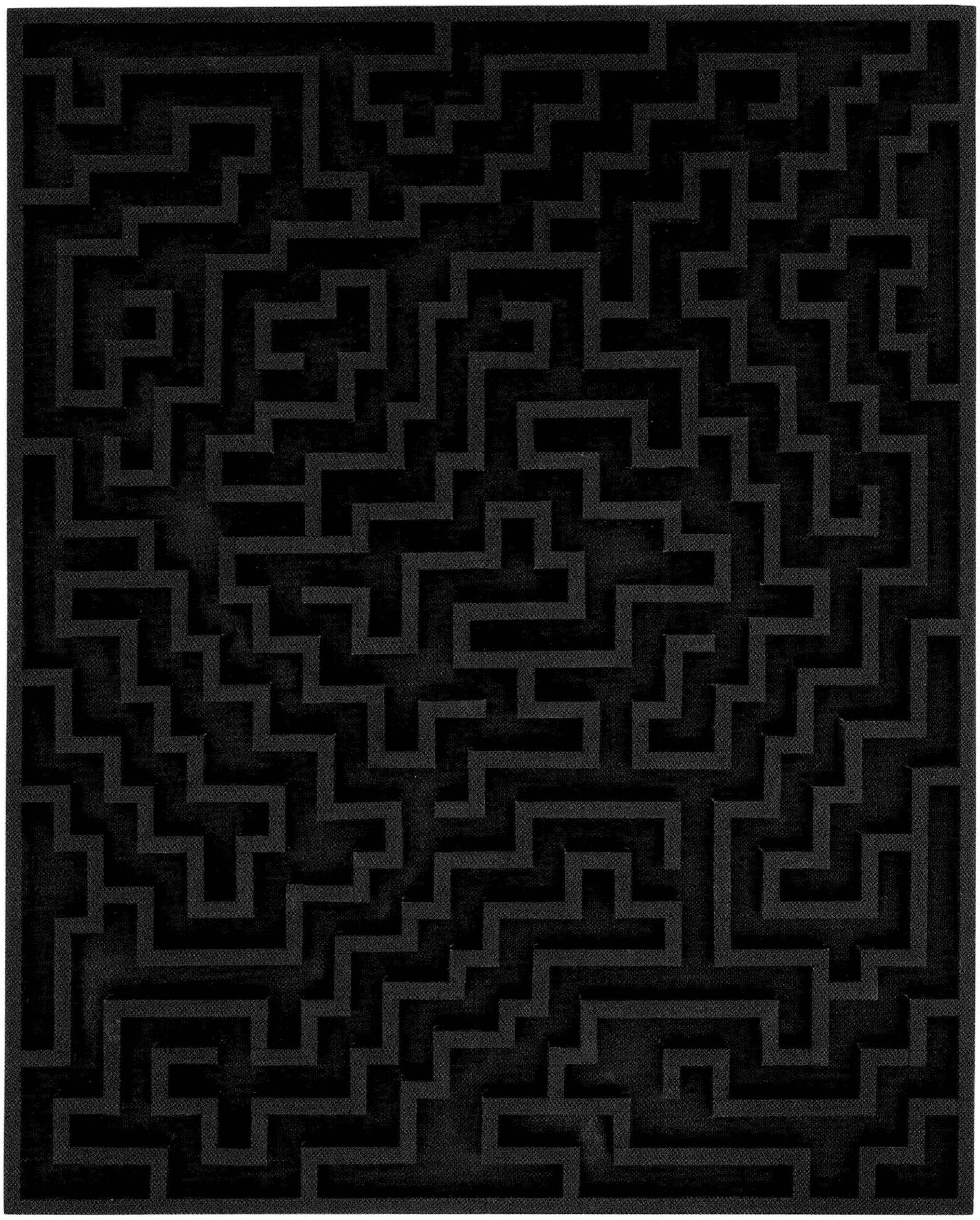

Untitled 2017 Epoxy resin and pigment 65.7 × 53 cm Wiesbaden

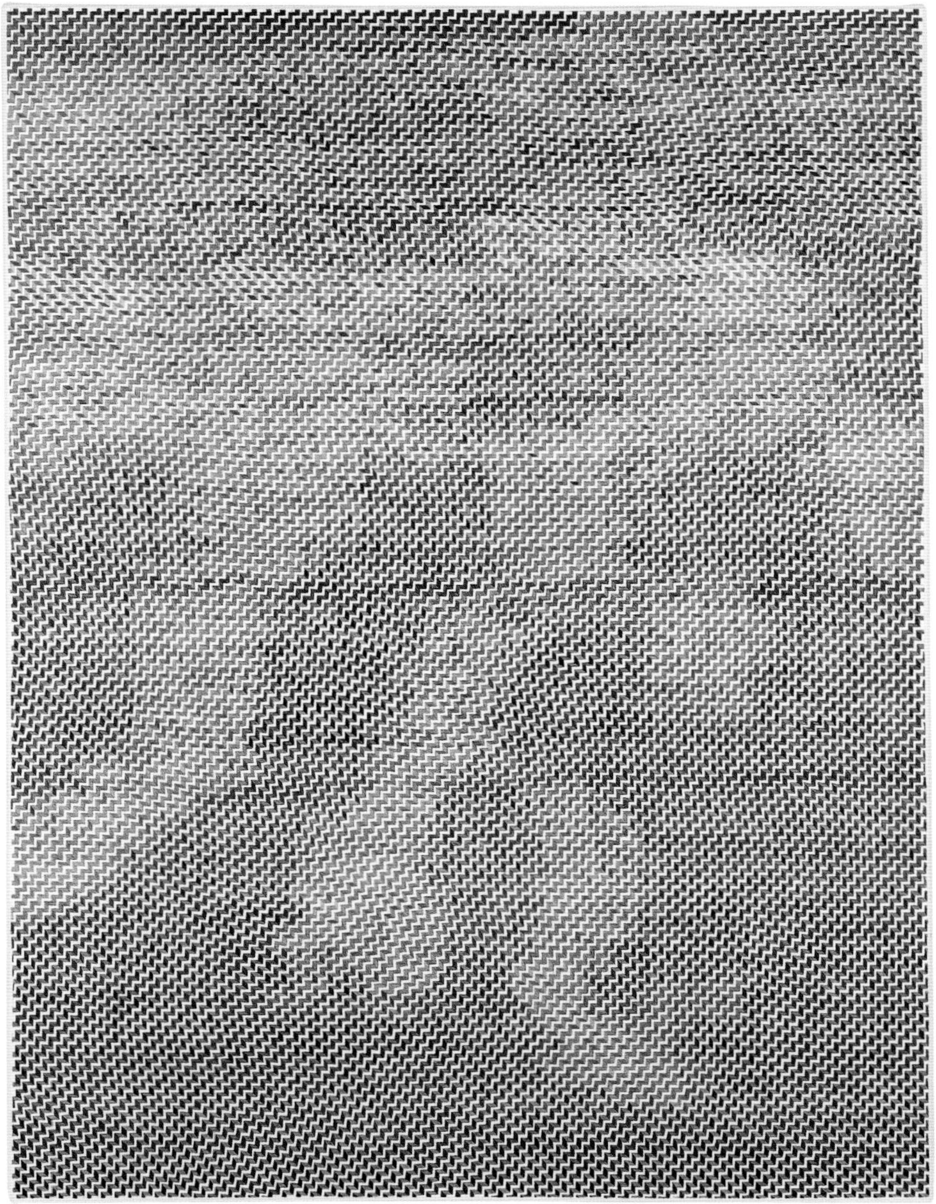

Untitled 2017 Nitro-frottage, oil on canvas 50 × 39 cm Bonn

Sabrina Haunsperg

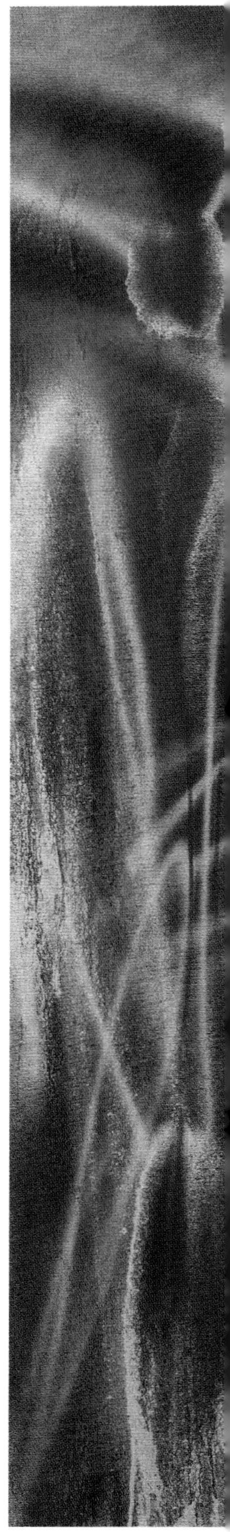

The painting of Sabrina Haunsperg represents one of the main positions in the non-representational painting of the present day. From a repertoire of the numerous different techniques for the application of paint, the artist has established for herself a single one in which streaks, surfaces, runs, pourings, spraying and traces of gestural positioning cohere into constellations which appear both tectonic and airy, determined not only by a long temporality but also by the instantaneousness of an arrangement which may take on another form in the next moment. This configuration, discovered spontaneously anew in every picture, explains the inner tension and freshness of her painting. Its universal quality is her original and precise approach to colour, which brings together the use of old colour recipes which have been rediscovered with the new materials of our century. —— *Robert Fleck*

Sabrina Haunsperg was born in 1980 in Hallein (Austria), and currently lives and works in Düsseldorf

Kunstakademie Düsseldorf, Meisterschülerin with Prof. Herbert Brandl, 2008

2018 Sabrina Haunsperg – Werke 2008–2018, SCHAUWERK Sindelfingen (S)

One day paintings, Kopfermann-Fuhrmann Stiftung, Düsseldorf (S)

2017 Malerei, Sammlung Mondstudio Collection, Bad Homburg (G) (with Richard Artschwager, Herbert Brandl, Katharina Grosse, David Reed, Joseph Marioni)

sabrinahaunsperg.com

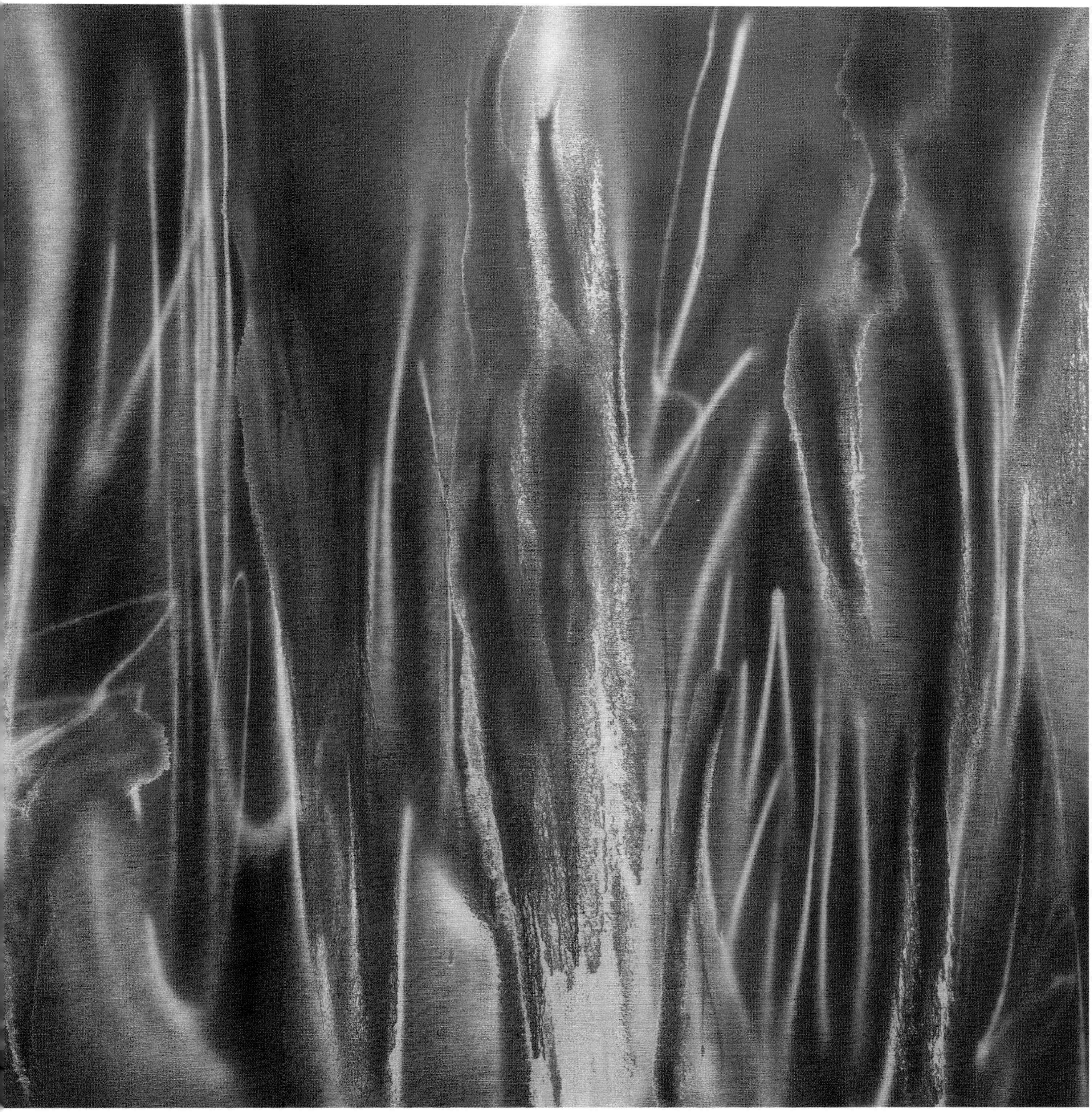

Untitled (040319) 2019 Oil on canvas 240 × 300 cm Bonn

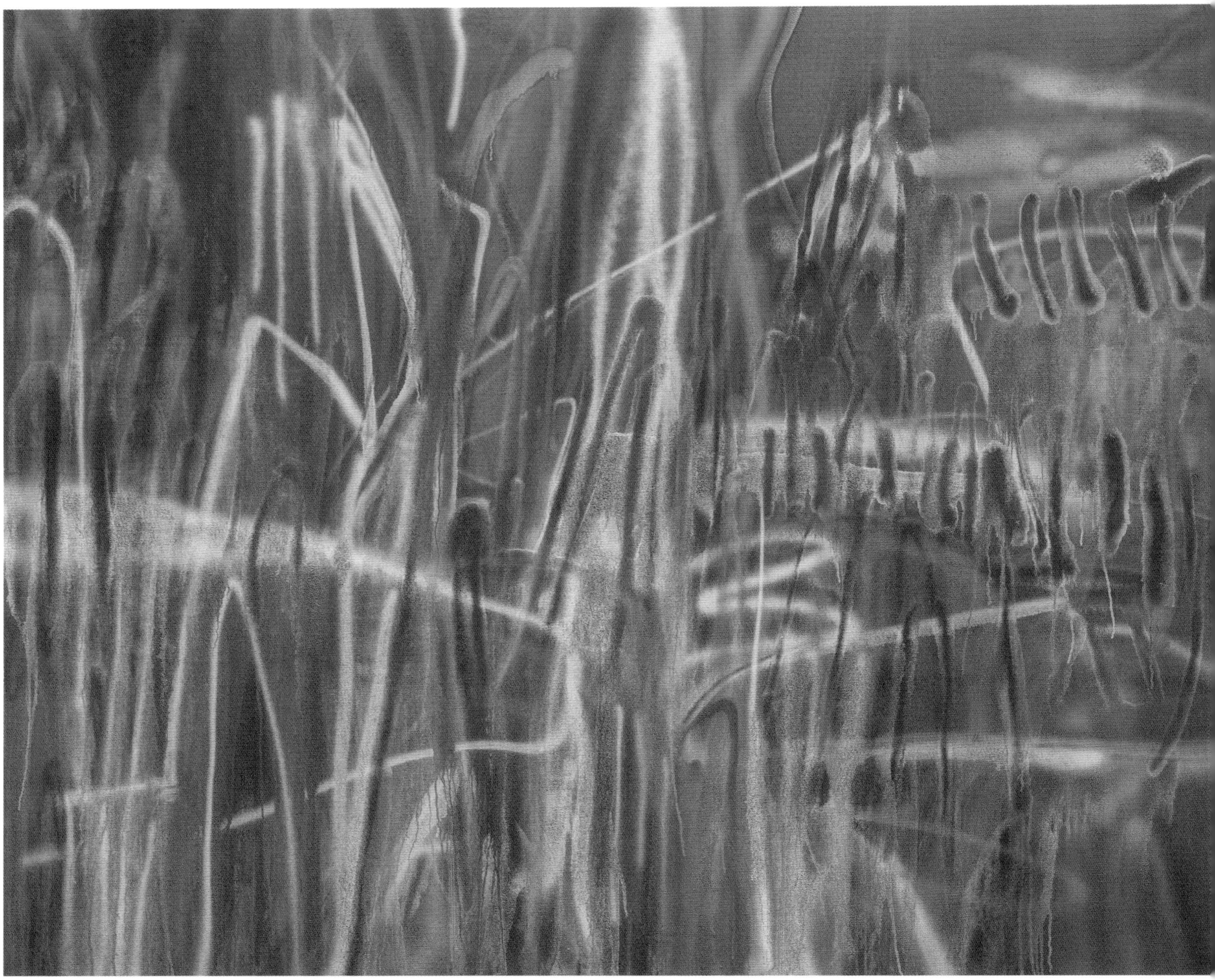

Untitled (171118) 2018 Oil on canvas 190 × 240 cm Chemnitz

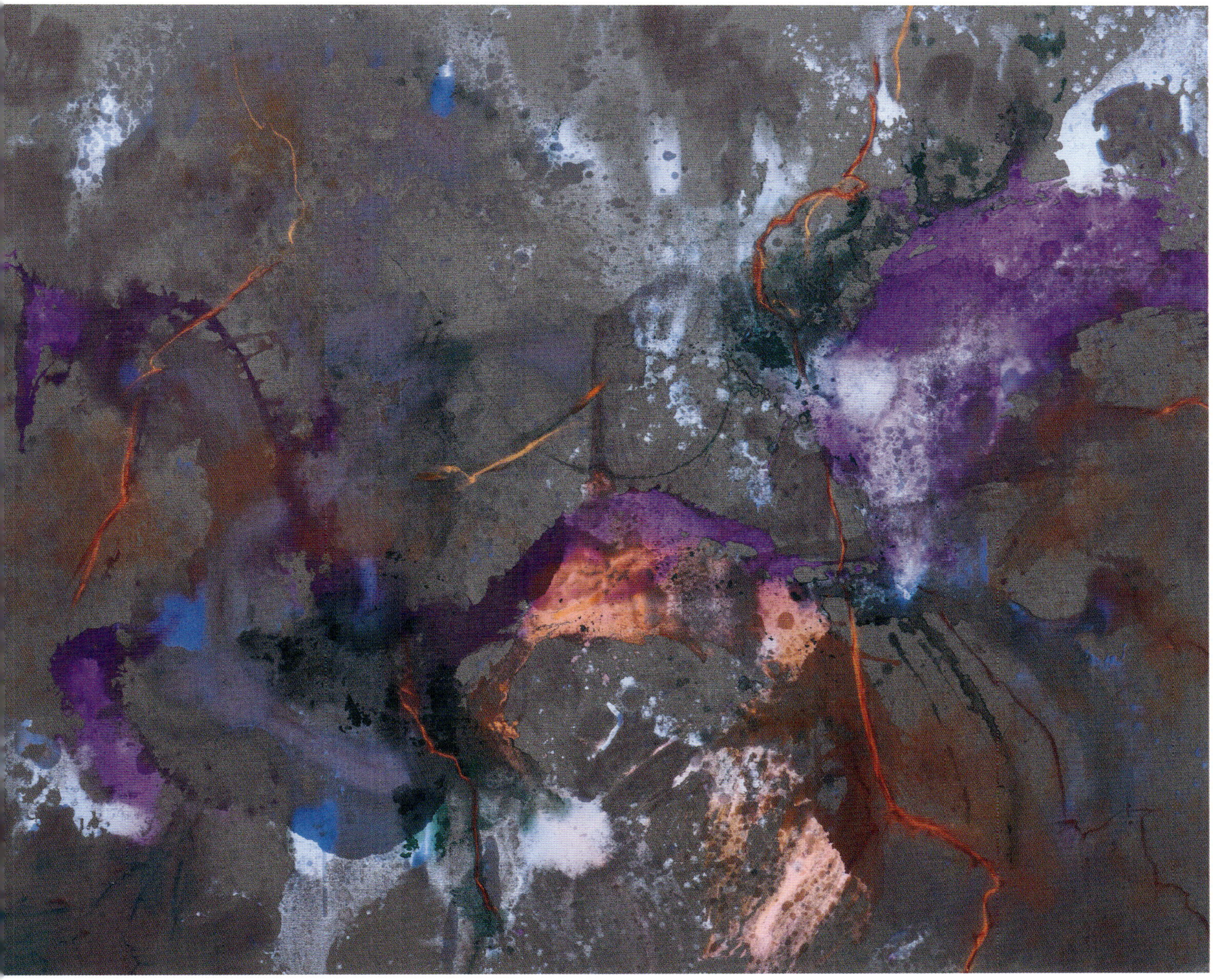

Untitled (130319) 2019 Oil on canvas 190 × 240 cm Wiesbaden

Franziska Holstein

History, painted

The fact that painters deal with painting is, on the one hand, a truism. Franziska Holstein is concerned not with all the famous forms of her challenge, but with the underlying wealth of painterly possibilities. It was so even in her early representational pictures: even here the different ways of representing the whole can be found – not yet systematically – but initially as a casual painterly exercise in what would be possible, picture by picture.

Today, precisely this has become the overriding preoccupation. The world of objects has been eliminated for some time now. Systematic questions are processed: those of sequences, of the determination of the number of attempts. The process moves forward thus: acrylic paint is applied to the paper, layer upon layer, until the picture carrier is no longer visible. Hundreds of pictures we cannot see are produced, are overpainted because they were not the final picture for the moment. Holstein processes both sides all over with the same intensity. Then – when the work has already acquired a certain physical weightiness – the decision is taken: this is the one picture that is valid within the series, the picture that the artist places in relation to all her other works, the picture which can stand the test in its own right and within the overall picture of the series.

What remains visible of this concentrated pictorial effort? Unlike oil painting, here there is no shining through of the layers which lie underneath. Acrylic paint covers, seals, makes invisible. The result is a diversely monochrome picture that bears the traces of fingers, of the painting medium and the layering.

The overpainted pictures bulge forward into what is now visible, into the result. Like a quarry of our lives, only the artist herself is aware of them, because she has seen them, made them. But of course there is also something there which we, too, can sense: history. All in all, each of us can see the "coloured plane, that was not there before" (Samuel Beckett). —— *Klaus Gerrit Friese*

Franziska Holstein was born in 1978 in Leipzig and currently lives and works there

Hochschule für Grafik- und Buchkunst Leipzig, with Prof. Arno Rink, 2000–2005

Meisterschülerin with Prof. Neo Rauch, 2008

2019	Forum Kunst Rottweil (S)
	Kunstverein Bremerhaven (S)
	Franz Gertsch Museum, Burgdorf, Schweiz (G, C)
2018	Camera, Cluj, Rumania

franziskaholstein.de

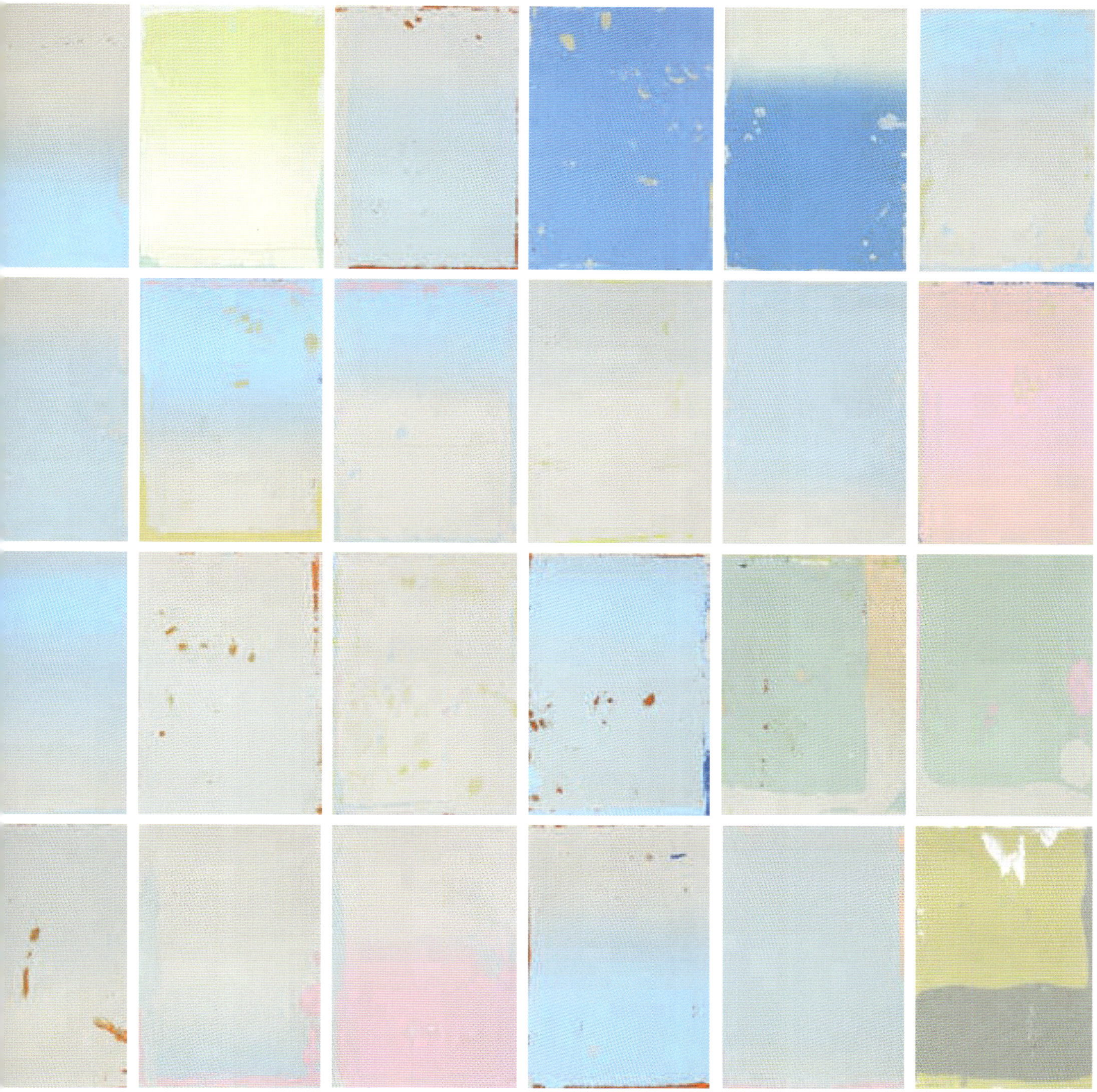

Untitled (32)
2019
Acrylic on paper, framed
32-part series, 42 × 29.7 cm, each, ca. 194 × 288 cm, total
Chemnitz

Untitled (1/32)
from 32-part series

2019

Acrylic on paper, framed

42 × 29.7 cm

Chemnitz

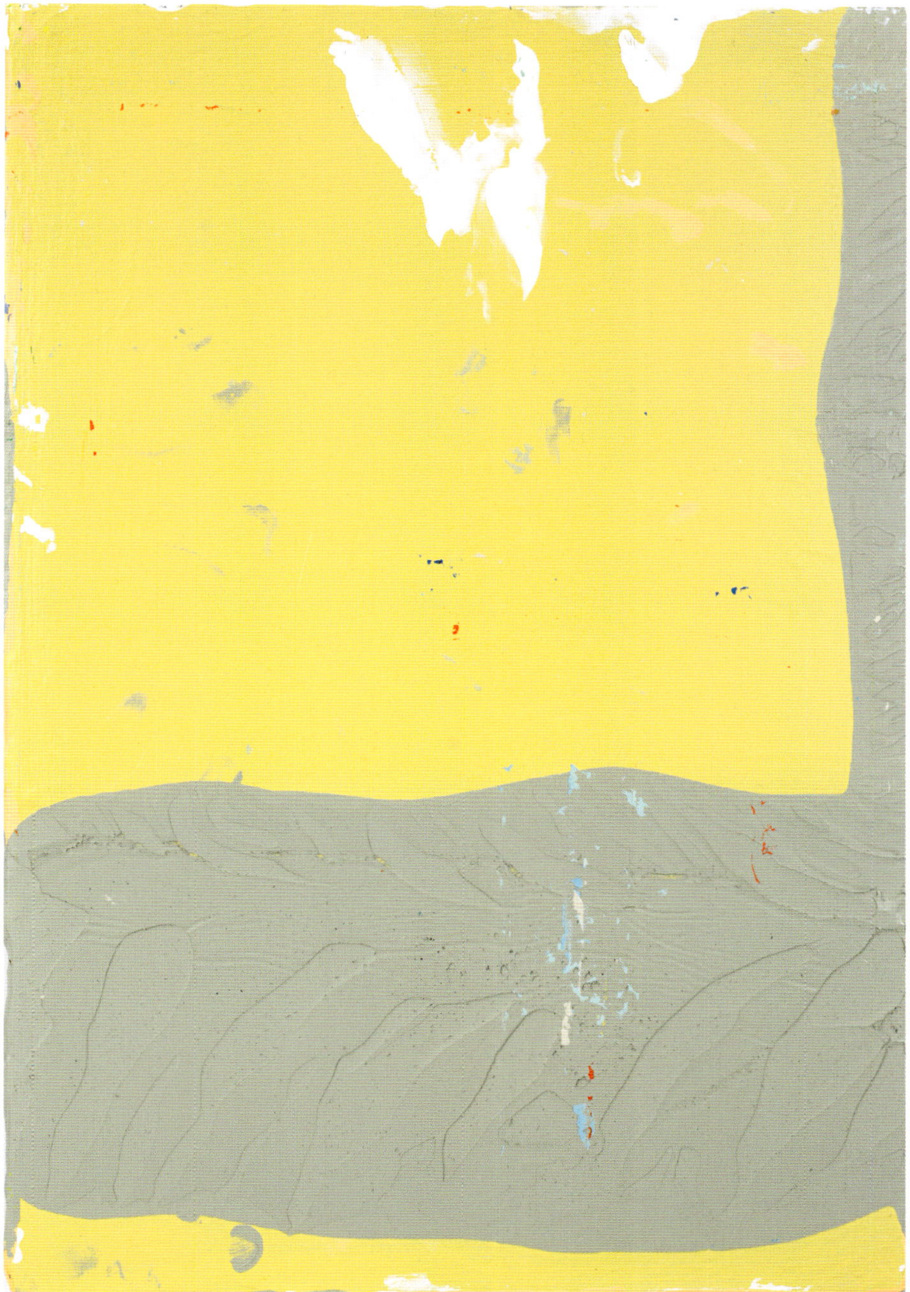

Untitled (32/32)
from 32-part series

2019

Acrylic on paper, framed

42 × 29.7 cm

Chemnitz

Aneta Kajzer

Aneta Kajzer was born in 1989 in Kattowitz (Poland) and currently lives and works in Berlin

Kunsthochschule Mainz, with Prof. Anne Berning, Prof. John Skoog and Prof. Shannon Bool, 2011–2017
Master's Degree with Prof. Anne Berning, 2017

2019 Aneta Kajzer, CONRADS Galerie, Düsseldorf (S)
They Catch Feelings, I Catch Bodies, Sim Smith, London (G)
2018 Out of Touch, Künstlerhaus Bethanien, Berlin (S)
ARCHIPELAGO -Goldrausch 2018, Reinbeckhallen, Berlin (G, C)

anetakajzer.de

March to a different drummer

The Cuban cha-cha-cha is characterised by the alternation of closed and open figures. At times the dancers are close together and the next moment they move apart again. Looking at the paintings of Aneta Kajzer we recognise a similar interplay. Her painting is not based on a pre-defined sequence of steps; rather, her technique seems to erase the boundaries between closed and open in much the same way as the cha-cha-cha. While the dance steps in Kajzer's works vary, the beginning is always the same. In an intuitive process she starts to fill the canvas with rapid strokes of colour and then gradually feels her way towards her subject by means of those first movements. Her paintings are not subject to a preconceived idea; each brushstroke is initiated by the previous one.
One, two, cha-cha-cha. This movement is always a reaction to what Aneta Kajzer finds in the picture space. While some of the brushstrokes she places arouse concrete associations, which the artist then develops into figures, in other cases she paints over the original area several times until it has been completely negated and a new picture space arises. Her technique blurs the boundaries between abstraction and figuration and questions the traditional conventions of painting. The subjects behave similarly and never claim an interpretation for themselves, but are rather characterised by the interaction of opposites. Kajzer's pictures dance between seriousness and humour, between trite concepts of beauty and the courage to create ugliness. She shows us figures whose limbs are deformed or who defy gender classification. Her works elude normative picture concepts, raise questions about the world in which we live, and show us its abysses and absurdities.
Aneta Kajzer's painting always follows its own rhythm, remains on the beat and ultimately proves that it is sometimes rewarding to march to a different drummer. —— *Carina Bukuts*

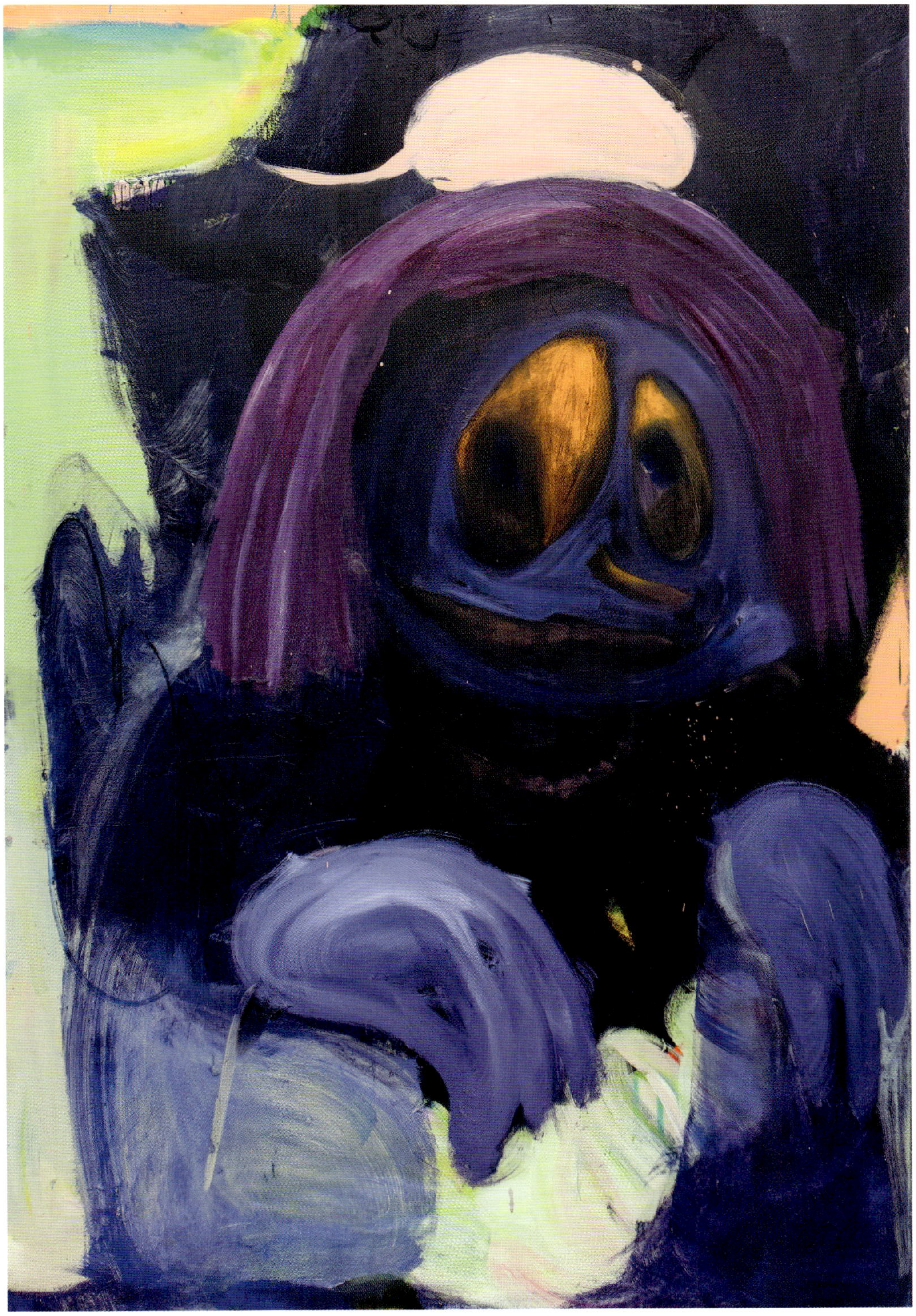

Out of the Dark 2018 Oil on canvas 200 × 140 cm Chemnitz

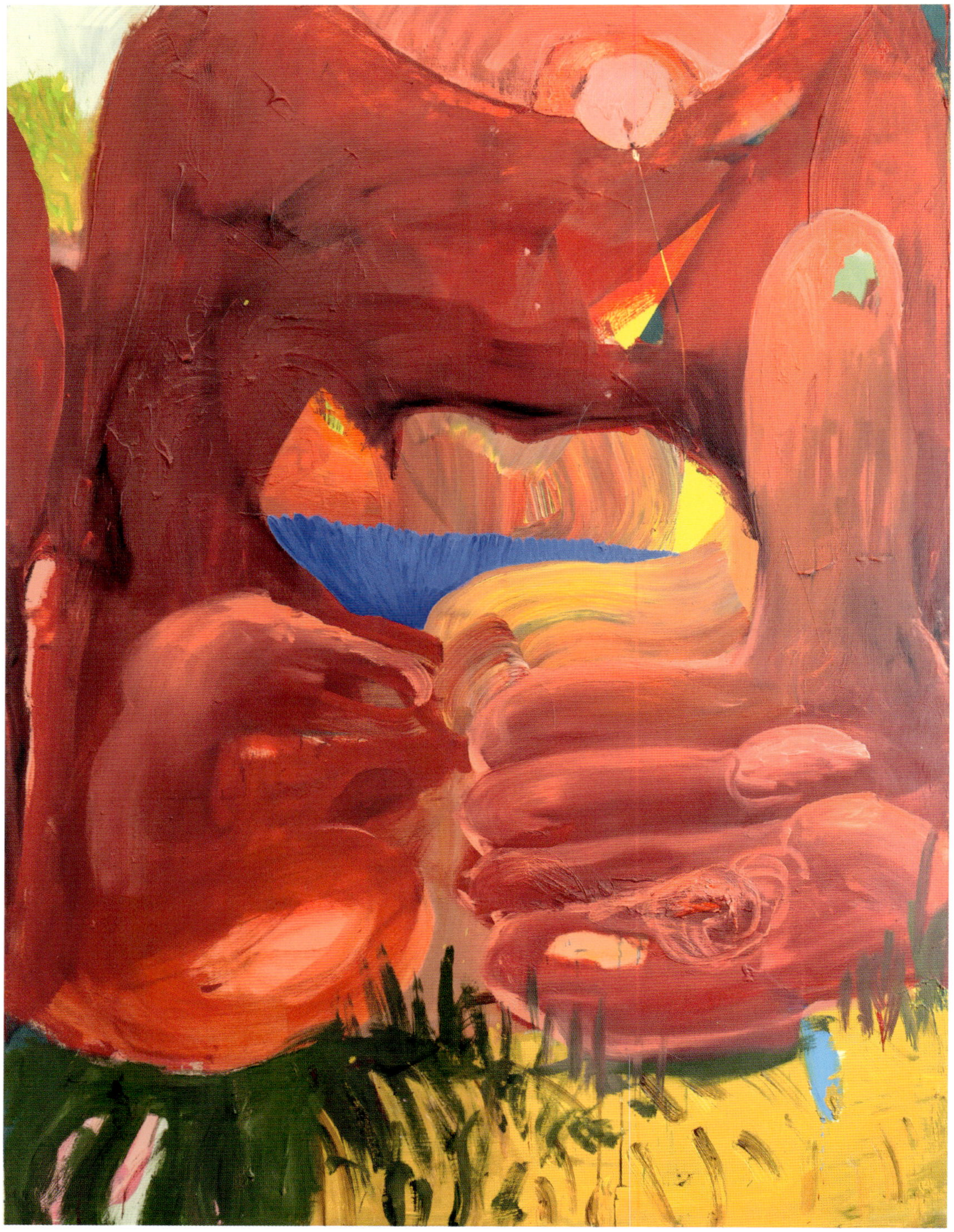

Thumbs Up 2018 Oil and acrylic on canvas 200 × 150 cm Wiesbaden

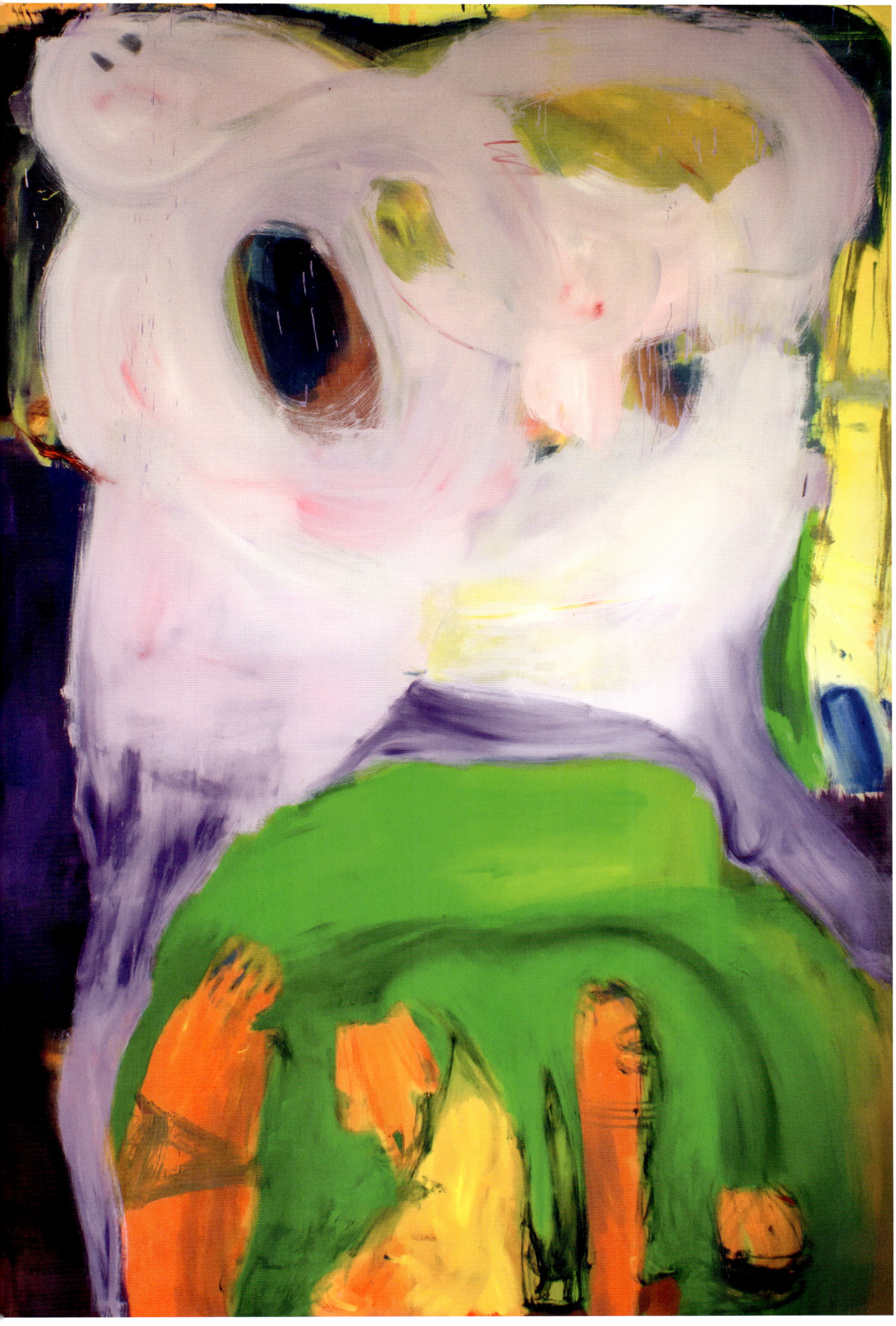

AI Taking Over 2019 Oil and acrylic on canvas 300 × 200 cm Bonn

Sumi Kim

Sumi Kim's pictures arise, to some extent, before the viewer's eyes. They contain a lot of white, with lines and long, broader stripes crossing the surface. We can feel the progress and the hesitancy, the momentum and the fragility, this act of feeling one's way – in similarities and interconnections, sometimes closer-meshed, sometimes pulled loosely apart. Here and there surfaces appear which are also moving, that change direction and encounter other sections. On one occasion, a dark-green bundle of energy looms up – before dissolving towards the bottom right and becoming very delicate. The white is the very opposite of the lines and areas, penetrating their darkness or swallowing them up like a fog. There are echoes of Far Eastern thought patterns and codes of behaviour in the activity of the white, in this drawing-related painting, this focus on transition.

That is the touching thing about Sumi Kim's pictures: everything is in a process of becoming; there is no conclusion. Nothing is confirmed – for example by a clarified form or a determining rule. We can sense the thoughtfulness, the hesitancy, the vulnerability of every action. And yet, the way these processes are kept open also demonstrates an absolute determination and insistence – namely on keeping everything in a state of becoming, on changing the route or stopping before something becomes set in stone – not falling victim to repetition. Sumi Kim does not repeat anything, produces no series. She creates only a small number of works, with long gaps in between.

With each new picture she approaches the painting process as if she were tackling it for the first time. Her painterly skill consists not least in her rejection of previously trodden paths. Sumi Kim moves with surprising confidence along the swaying tightrope of the painterly process. Only thus, in this unpredictability, can each picture lead the viewer into a movement which he or she will experience here for the very first time – and time and time again. —— *Erich Franz*

Sumi Kim was born in 1983 in South Korea and currently lives and works in Cologne

Konkuk Universität, South Korea, 2002–2008

Kunstakademie Münster with Prof. Daniele Buetti, 2009–2016

2019 Ida Gerhardi-Förderpreis, Städtische Galerie Lüdenscheid (G)

2018 unplugged, Schloss Ringenberg, Hamminkeln (G)

sumikim.com

Untitled 2016 Oil on canvas 200 × 145 cm Wiesbaden

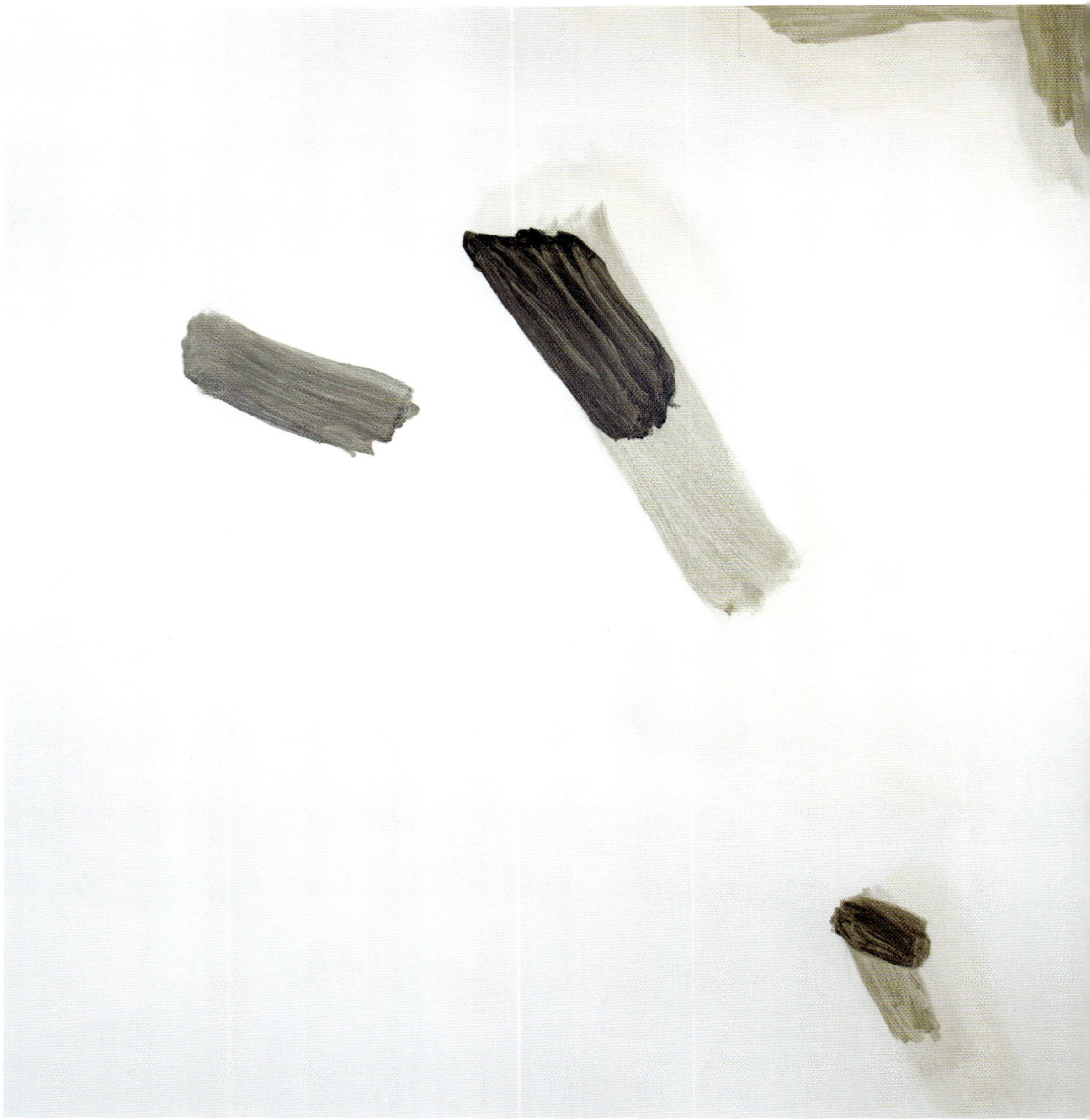

Untitled 2018 Oil on canvas 150 × 150 cm Chemnitz

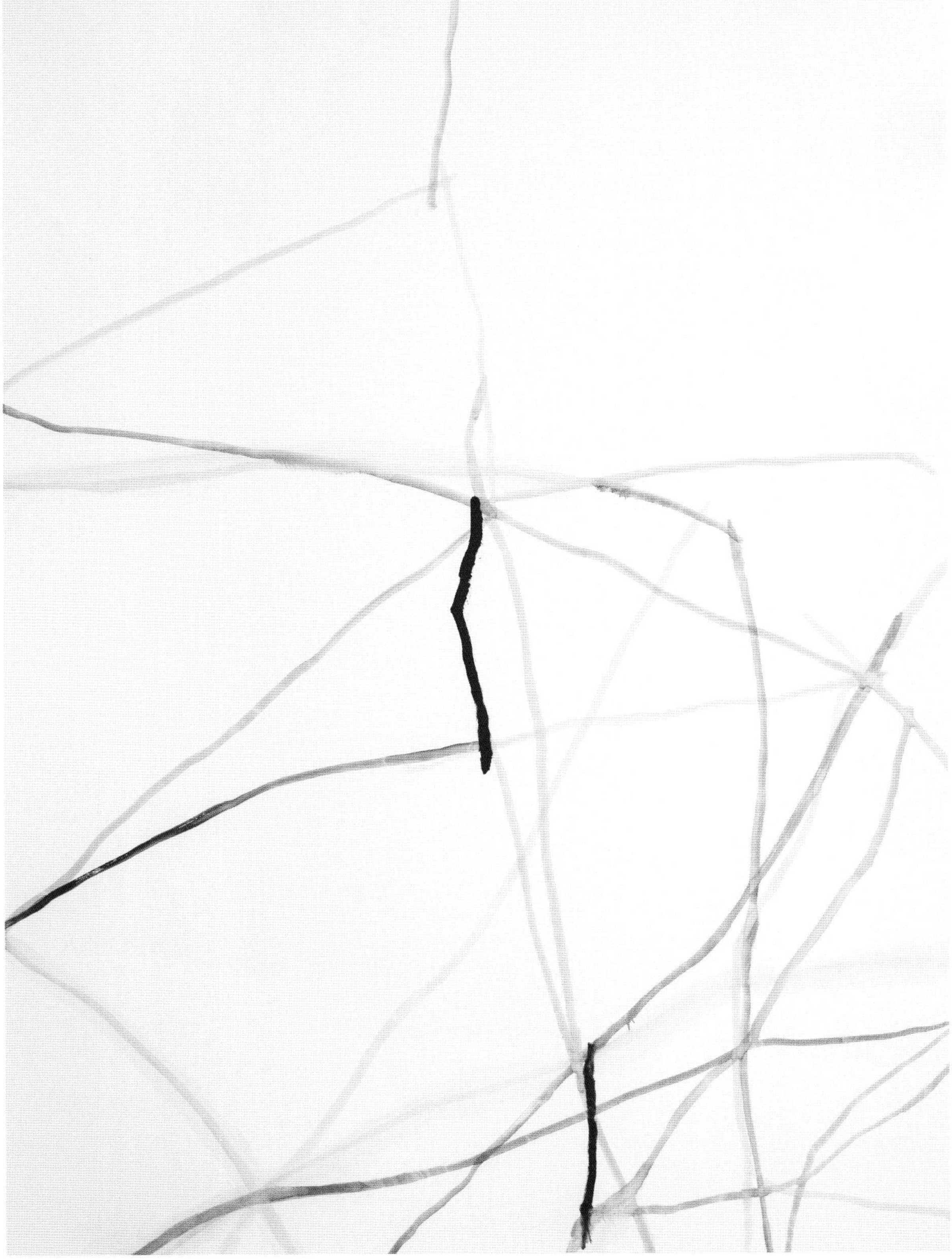

Untitled 2018 Oil on canvas 200 × 150 cm Bonn

Maximilian Kirmse

Intermezzo

He is sitting once more on his office chair in a familiar pose: in one hand he is holding a book of sudokus, and he is propping himself up on the other. A broad face with regular features covered by a large amount of dark-brown hair, green eyes, cheap nickel glasses frame, critical gaze. An attractive, white, heterosexual man with an East German background. He submitted himself extensively to the trials and tribulations of the art academies of the Federal Republic, but that will not be allowed to come between us just now.
At the moment we are both taking a break; in a minute he will come back to me. I am hanging on a whitewashed wall under a fluorescent light and am slightly bored. Well, inasmuch as something which is not yet finished can actually experience boredom.
Our story goes back a lot further than this. Initially, I was an image in his head, a fleeting thought. It could have been at a techno party. Pale, sweaty bodies pushing themselves away from droning basses and into steel cabins. Most of them come like pilgrims with battered PET bottles to stock up with the precious water, to refresh their stupor. He is there too; he goes to the tap and holds a glass underneath. Slowly the transparent liquid dribbles into the glass, it's as easy as that. But perhaps it was at his home, in the bathroom (of course the children's teeth are brushed twice daily). Water in the glass, mouth open, brush, spit out, rinse. Water from the tap in Germany, as if it could never dry up.
But to return to me; I am not finished yet. Just a single idea is not enough.
He finally drags himself away from his sudoku and eats a Snickers. Then he comes over to me and starts.
Very carefully: dabdab. Gently rubs at the paint, five colours together. A critical gaze.
Another Snickers.
Like a draughtsman he opens up two strips of white; that feels good too, a few little edges. Another paintbrush.
No solvent,
dabdab,
I awaken from delicately woven clouds of colour and ...
... then I am here.
I'm fine. —— *Fid. Fischer*

Maximilian Kirmse was born in 1986 in Berlin and currently lives and works there

Kunstakademie Düsseldorf, Akademiebrief with Prof. Andreas Schulze, 2014

Hochschule für Grafik und Buchkunst Leipzig, Meisterschüler with Prof. Astrid Klein, 2017

2019 Amazoni, Philipp Haverkampf Galerie, Berlin (S)
2018 interzoni, Nino Mier Gallery, Los Angeles (S)
2017 Groupshow, Galerie Tobias Naehring, Leipzig (G)
Bülow Ecke Steinmetz, Real Positive, Cologne (S)

maximiliankirmse.de

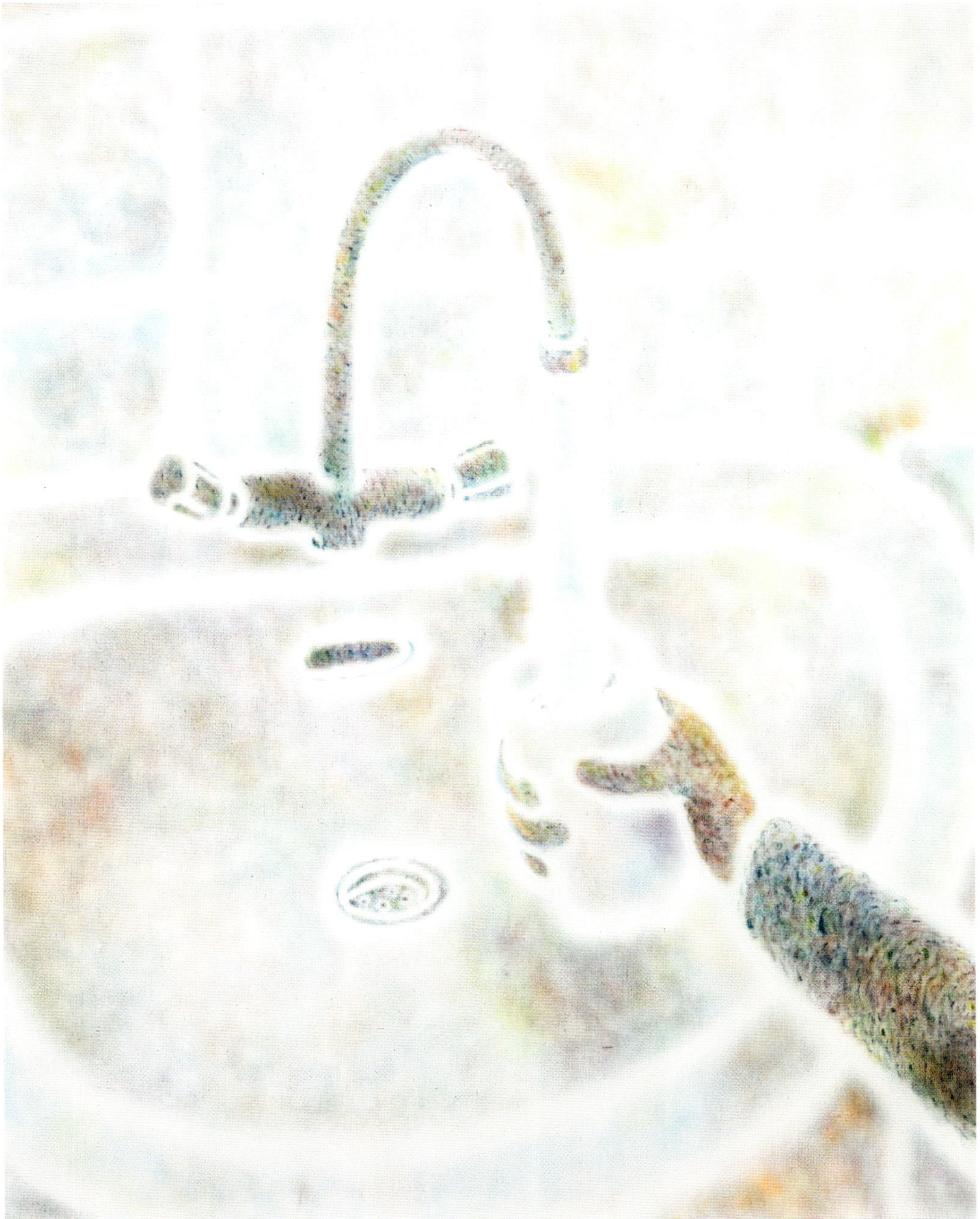

G.O.W. 2017 Oil on canvas 160 × 130 cm Bonn

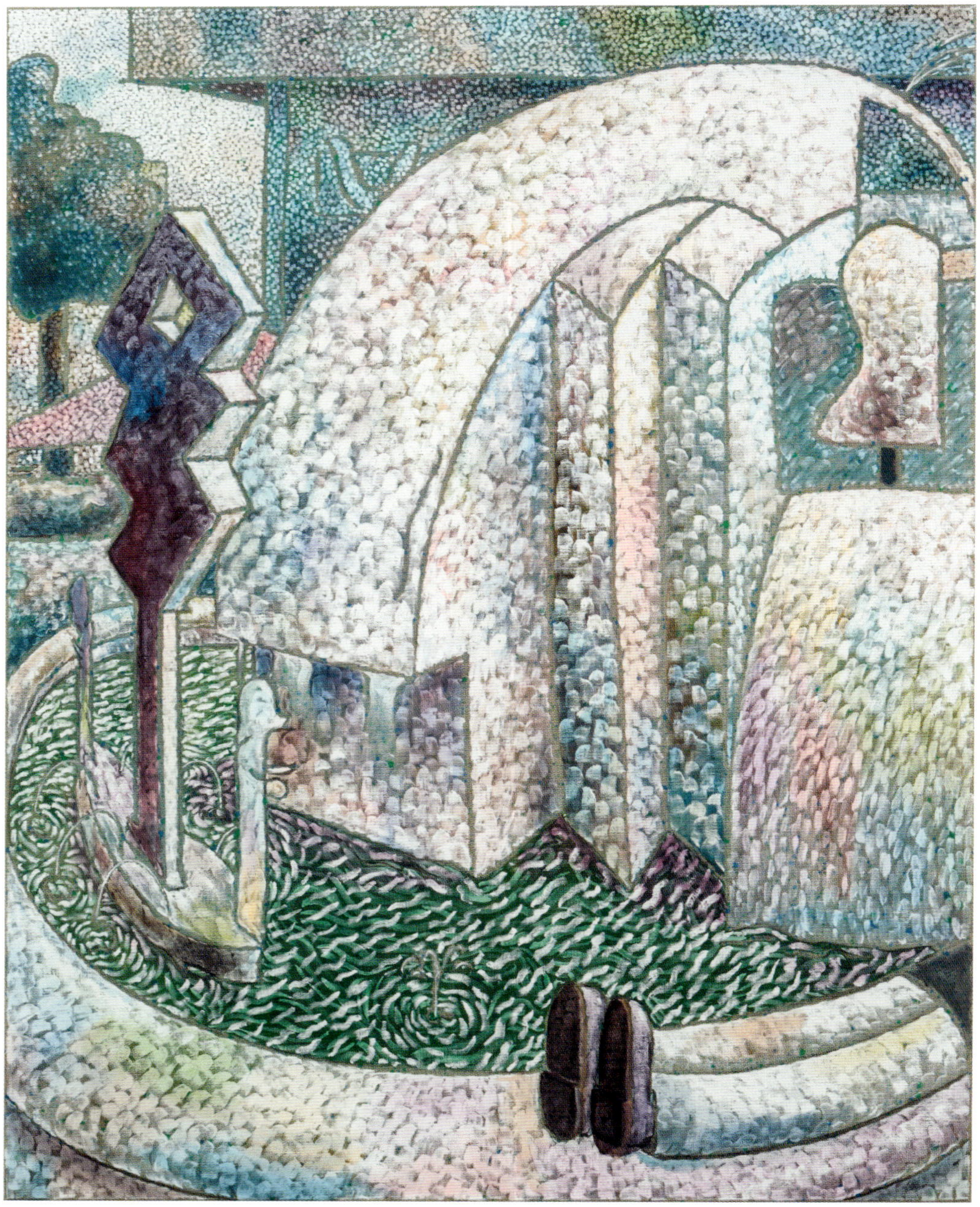

am Brunnen

2019

Oil on canvas

160 × 130 cm

Wiesbaden

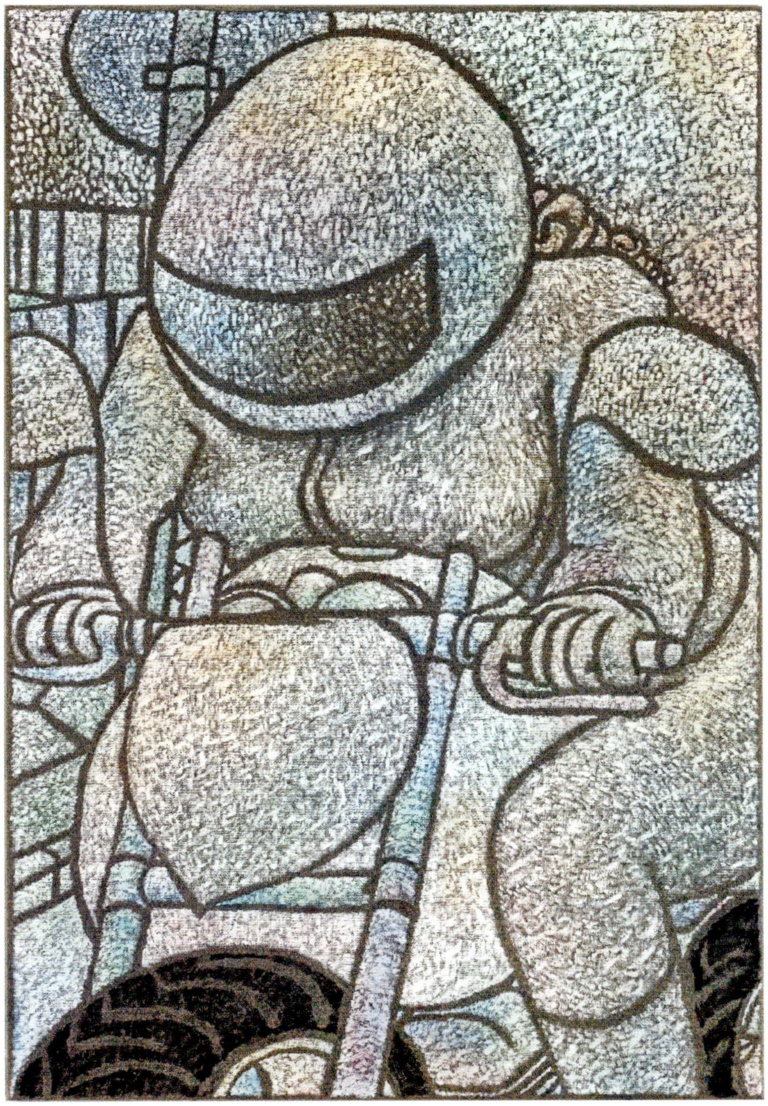

M.W.B. 2017 Oil on canvas 65 × 45 cm Chemnitz

Li-Wen Kuo

Veil

In front of the entrance to the Cappella Sansevero in Naples there is a queue of visitors waiting to see two marble statues dating from the eighteenth century. What the supine body of the dead Christ and the standing figure of a naked woman representing Chastity have in common is the fact that they are both covered by a thin veil. The veil draped over the bodies is also of marble, but it looks so deceptively real that we are tempted to take hold of it in order to reveal the bodies. It is good that the stubborn material resists this desire in the very moment of temptation. The veils cling so closely to the bodies that they emphasise the somehow attractive forms rather than obscuring them. At the same time, they demonstrate the mercy which consists in preserving them from the intrusive gaze, saving them – indeed, lovingly protecting them. Because the dissecting human eye has always wanted to uncover and penetrate; veils reveal this urge and imply that the folds harbour the necessary consolation of concealment.
Li-Wen Kuo's mysterious paintings take up this theme and translate the masterly working of the stone into an equally masterly, precise and careful processing of the canvas with oil paint. Her brushstrokes obey a grammar whose rules we can learn through patient observation. The edgy lines striving diagonally upwards return to form mountain peaks, and the semi-elliptical stripes sink downwards, obeying the laws of gravity, bringing movement to the rigidness of the straight lines. The brushstrokes of different widths and thickness are piled up layer upon layer. We do not know what they conceal, only that they do so. We are all the more grateful for this patient hand which allows us to slip under the protective veil for the duration of our viewing, to hover across the restless white surface and from there to observe the world with another, transformed perspective. —— *Chiara Caradonna*

Li-Wen Kuo was born in 1980 in Viernheim and currently lives and works in Frankfurt a. M. and Copenhagen

Staatliche Akademie der Bildenden Künste Karlsruhe, Diploma, 2013, Meisterschülerin with Prof. Gustav Kluge and Prof. Marcel van Eeden, 2014

2018 exchanging realities, Evelyn Drewes Galerie, Hamburg (with Alex Feuerstein) (S)

2017 Abweichungen, Nordheimer Scheune, Nordheim (S)

Nordbecken-Festival, Karlsruhe (G)

liwenkuo.com

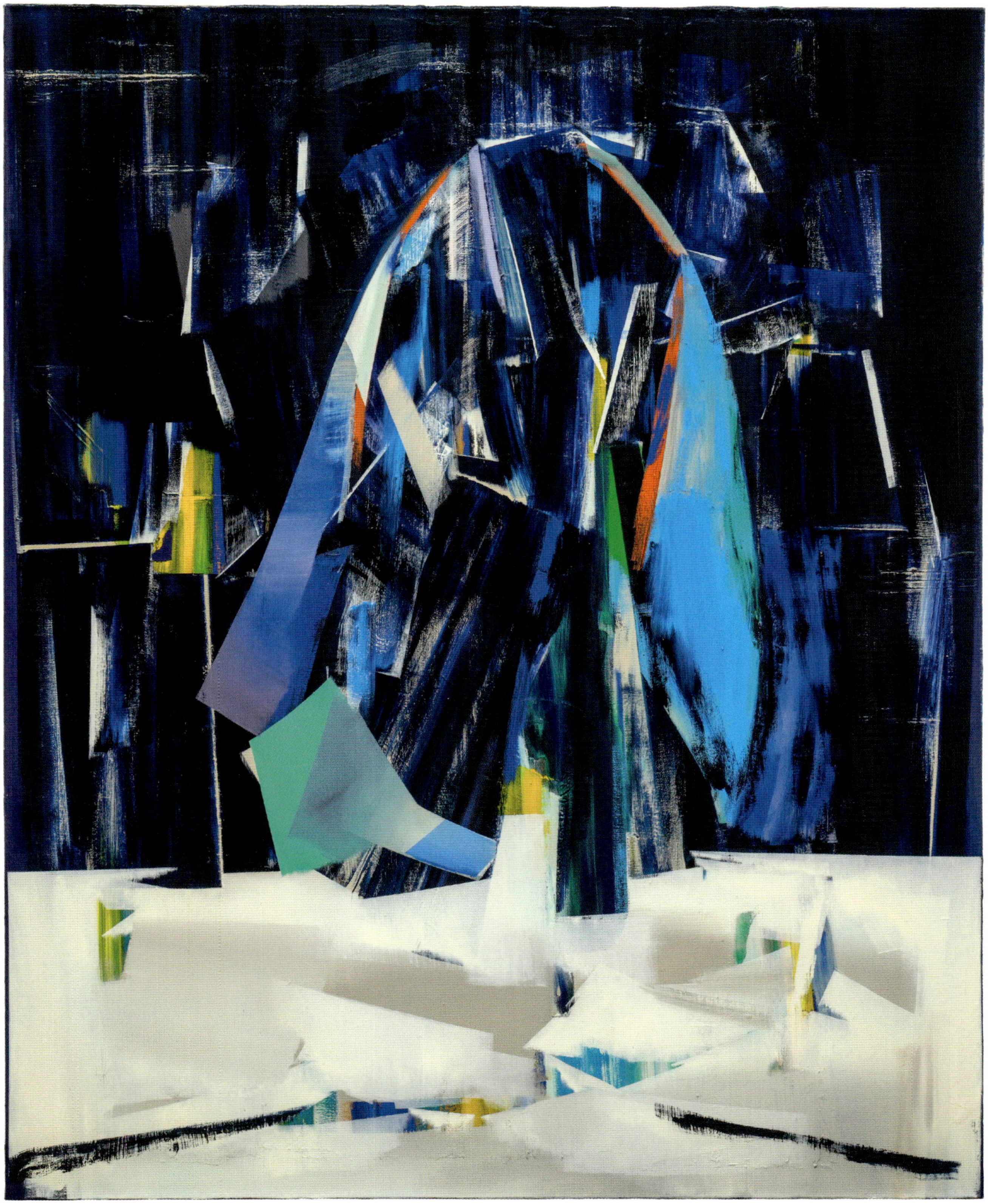

In einem dunklen Wort 2019 Oil on canvas 200 × 165 cm Wiesbaden

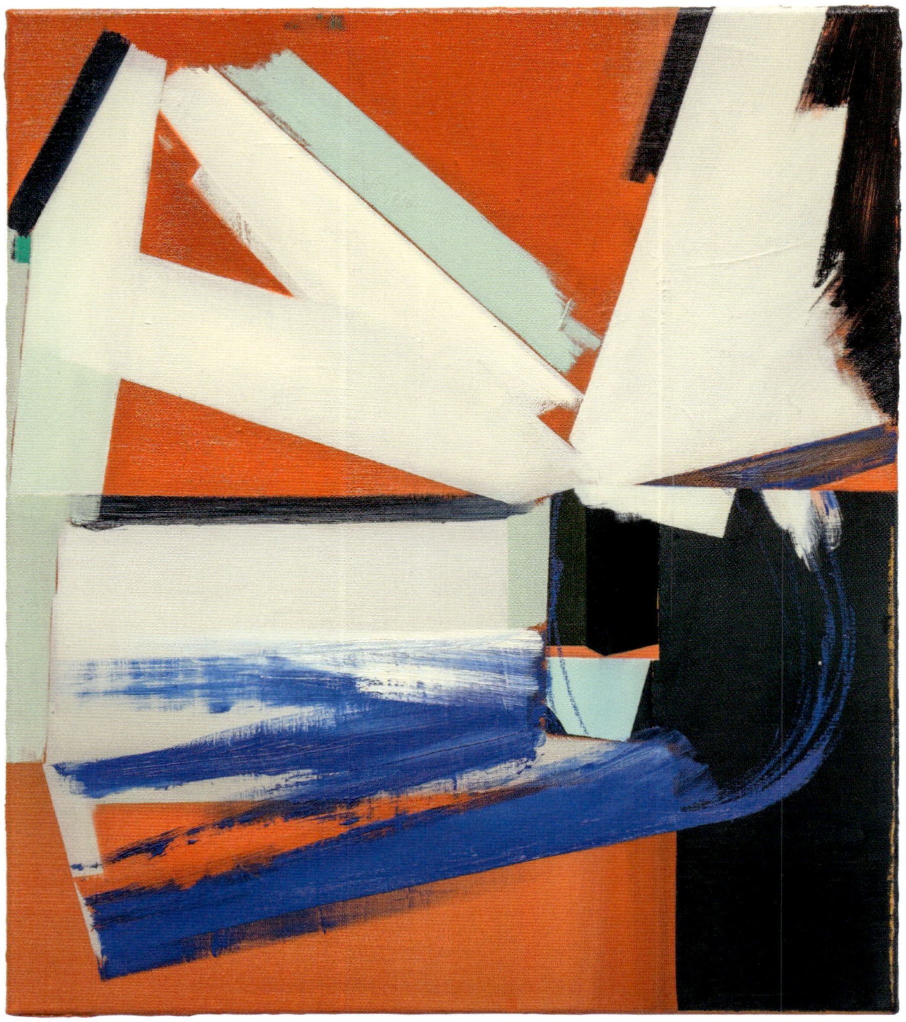

Wilde Ontologie 2018/19 Oil on canvas 73 × 65 cm Chemnitz

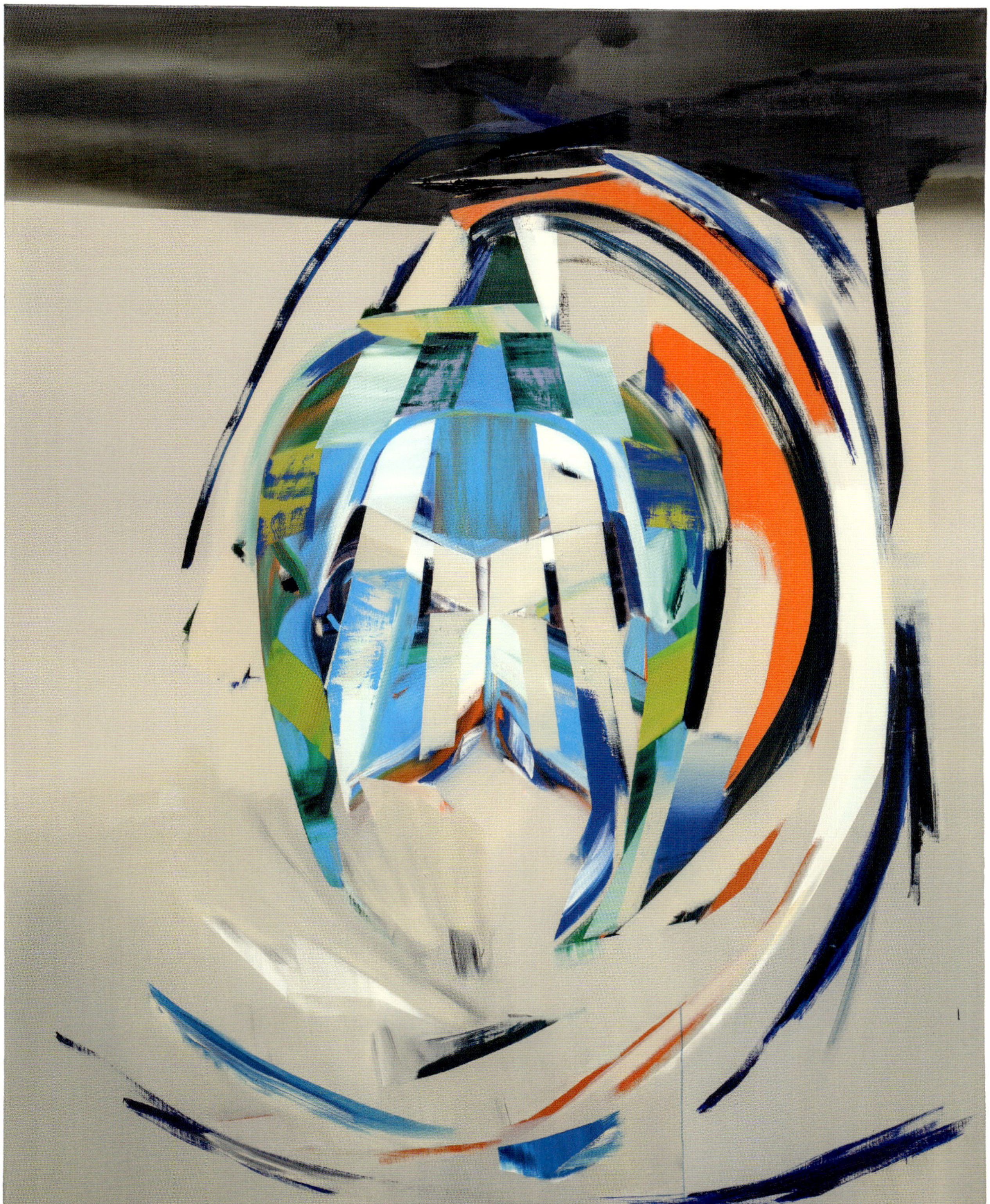

Häutung 2019 Oil on canvas 200 × 160 cm Bonn

David Lehmann

David Lehmann was born in 1987 in Luckau and currently lives and works in Cottbus

Universität der Künste Berlin, 2009–2014
Meisterschüler with Prof. Valérie Favre, 2014

2018 Losito Kunstpreis 2018, Stiftung Starke, Berlin (G)

2017 Capriccio-Kunstpreis des Haus am Kleistpark 2017, Haus am Kleistpark, Berlin (G)

2016 BRANDENBURGISCHE KUNST-PREISTRÄGER, Vertretung des Landes Brandenburg bei der EU, Brussels (G)

Menschen sind Teufel und leben im Kino, Kunstmuseum Dieselkraftwerk, Cottbus (S)

david-lehmann.de

Ambivalences

David Lehmann's painting is never just painting, because his pictures are always and very explicitly pervaded by discourses on painting, its history and its narratives as well as its content and technical possibilities. Lehmann's paintings are rich in colours and forms, evincing both profound seriousness and delicate, light-footed wit; in them, he devotes himself in to an extensive but never arbitrary range of topics, for which he skilfully uses different forms of expression and painting techniques. With a practised hand, he employs the traditional painting techniques of the old masters; they outdo themselves with superimpositions, only to be dismantled at the same time. In this way David Lehmann creates an exciting painting which also always flirts gently – in a calculated manner – with the idea of potential failure. He interweaves classical subjects and myths of art (history), especially painting, with current socio-political and contemporary subjects and their cultural frameworks. In the resulting pictorial worlds, the boundaries between (supposedly) individual and collective narratives of reality and fiction are intentionally blurred and mixed. David Lehmann fosters and breaks with projections of authenticity, with which art and in particular painters and painting are frequently confronted, by adding a substantial pinch of (self-)irony within a single brushstroke, so to speak. Thus, for example, one of his recurring subjects is the painter as male subject who knows the ropes with regard to the artistic and social principles of seduction, has mastered them but also distrusts them. Also informed by the knowledge of the legendary, deceptive and in some ways outdated aspects of the myth of the virile figure of the artist, Lehmann lets his supposed alter ego gaze out at the world from the canvas (or vice versa). Designed sometimes as omniscient and sometimes as a doubter, but always as a bon-vivant, this imaginary figure never reveals the hard, serious work of the painter when he is painting. —— *Ulrike Kremeier*

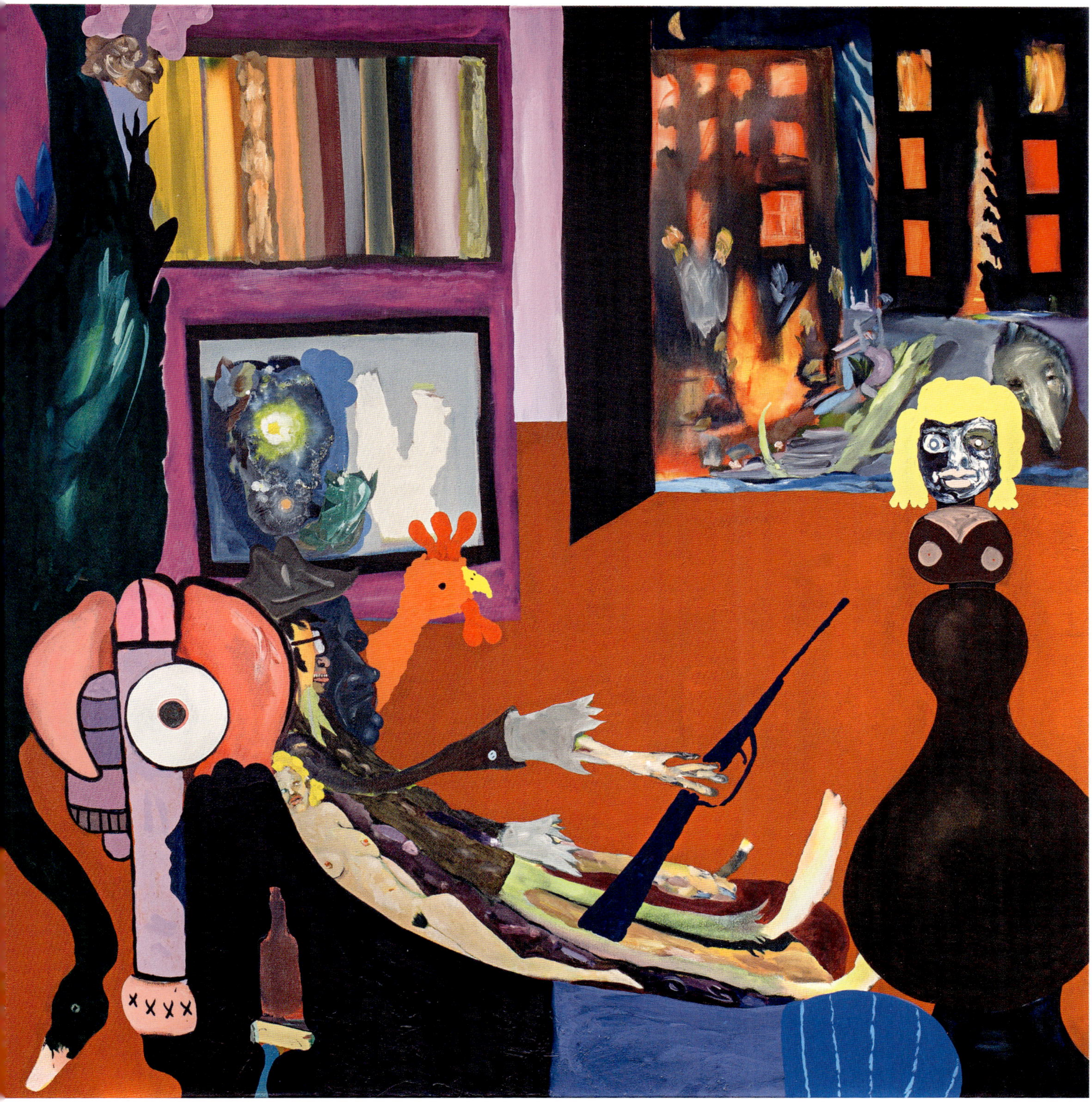

Piano Nobile

2019

Gouache, resin, egg tempera, dispersion paint and copper oxidation

190 × 190 cm

Chemnitz

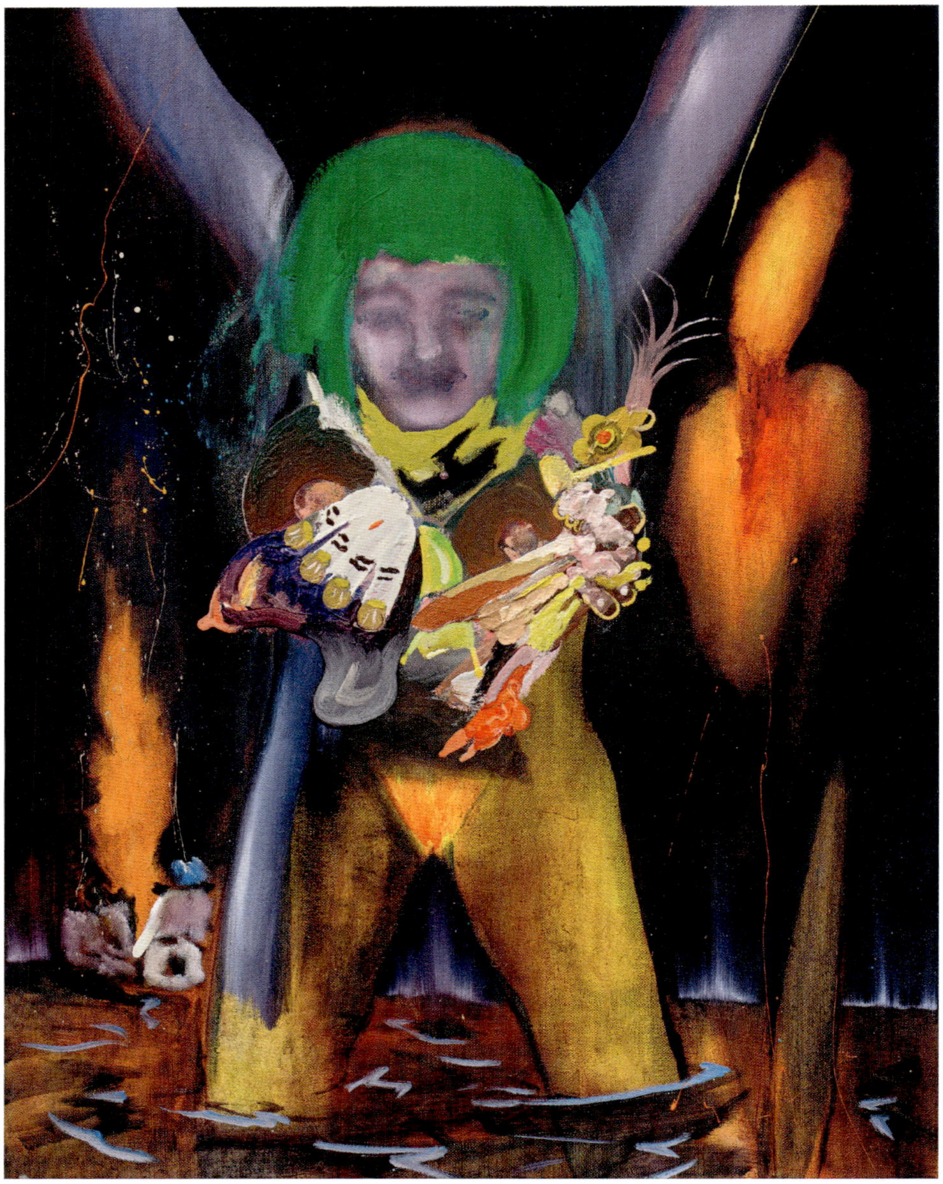

Borderline 2018 Gouache, resin and oil on canvas 100 × 80 cm Bonn

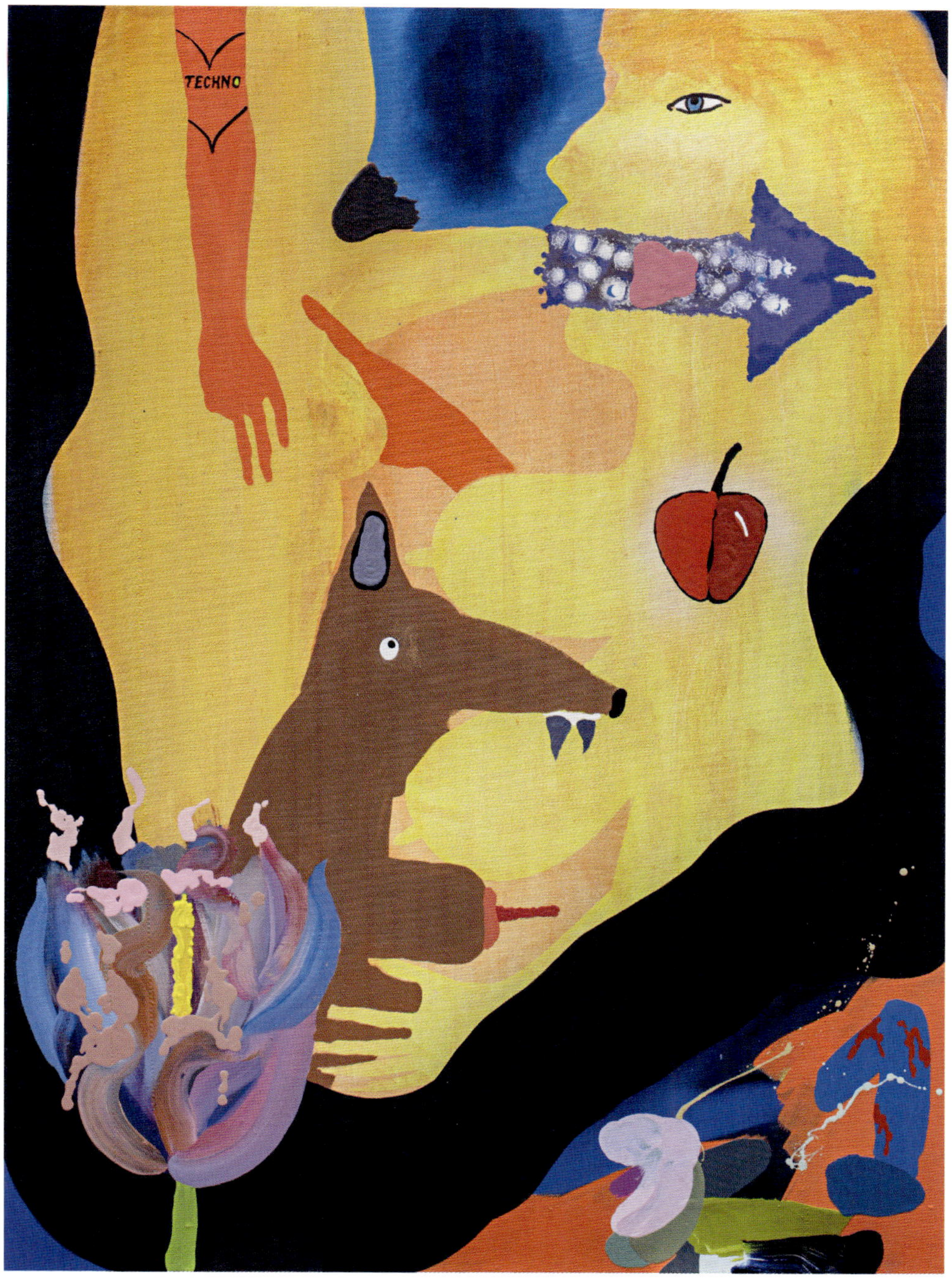

Soul Power

2019

Gouache, resin, dispersion paint, copper oxidation, spray paint and oil on canvas

120 × 90 cm

Wiesbaden

Benedikt Leonhardt

The gaze wanders slowly and cautiously from the edge of one picture to the next, then loses itself once more in the depths of a world of colour which seems to extend to infinity. Only at second glance do the forms, traces and scratches on the surface of the paint reveal their presence.
Benedikt Leonhardt produces atmospheric abstractions of a unique kind, characterised by object-related aspects of the digital pictorial world and their colourful surface. The pictorial techniques prompt in the artist fleeting visual impulses which he translates into concrete painting by means of gestural-intuitive actions and formal-aesthetic insight.
Leonhardt does not distinguish between what it is, what it represents, and how it was created. We experience colour not only optically, but also in its complete materiality. His works show the process of painting, the creation of colour and its effect. The semi-transparent areas of colour, layered on top of each other, are alternately subjected to vertical and horizontal gestures. The temporal process of the treatment culminates in countless layers and three-dimensional structures which result from scraping, smudging and constructing. It is not simply a matter of the translation of calculated coincidence or the development of defectiveness through the application of various textures, but rather that during the act of painting Leonhardt stands in an intrinsic and intensive discourse with the canvas, so that he makes the emancipation of the picture visible.
His works are projections of his pattern or perception and his reaction to the moods within the space. Through his work Benedikt Leonhardt ensures an increased observation of abstract painting as an art form and demands at the same time a new sensibility that takes place within the recipient. And he demonstrates simultaneously a direct and fascinating treatment of colour, surface, volume and space.
—— *Defne Kizilöz*

Benedikt Leonhardt was born in 1984 in Leipzig and currently lives and works there

Hochschule für Grafik und Buchkunst, Diploma, 2014
Meisterschüler with Prof. Astrid Klein, 2016

2017 LUX, 12. Kunstpreis der Leipziger Volkszeitung, Museum der bildenden Künste Leipzig (S)
19 Positionen – 11. Absolventenausstellung der Künstlerförderung des Cusanuswerks, UG im Folkwang, Museum Folkwang, Essen (G)
Win/Win – Die Ankäufe der Kulturstiftung des Freistaates Sachsen 2017, Halle 14, Leipzig (G)
Livid, Galerie FeldbuschWiesnerRudolph, Berlin (S)

benediktleonhardt.net

Untitled (CCD-MR/VD-CYD-1) 2019 Oil, acrylic, vinyl paint, tape and spackle on canvas 240 × 172.5 cm Chemnitz

Untitled (PSM-CB-V/2/2)
2018
Oil, acrylic, vinyl paint, tape and spackle on canvas
68.7 × 51.6 cm
Bonn

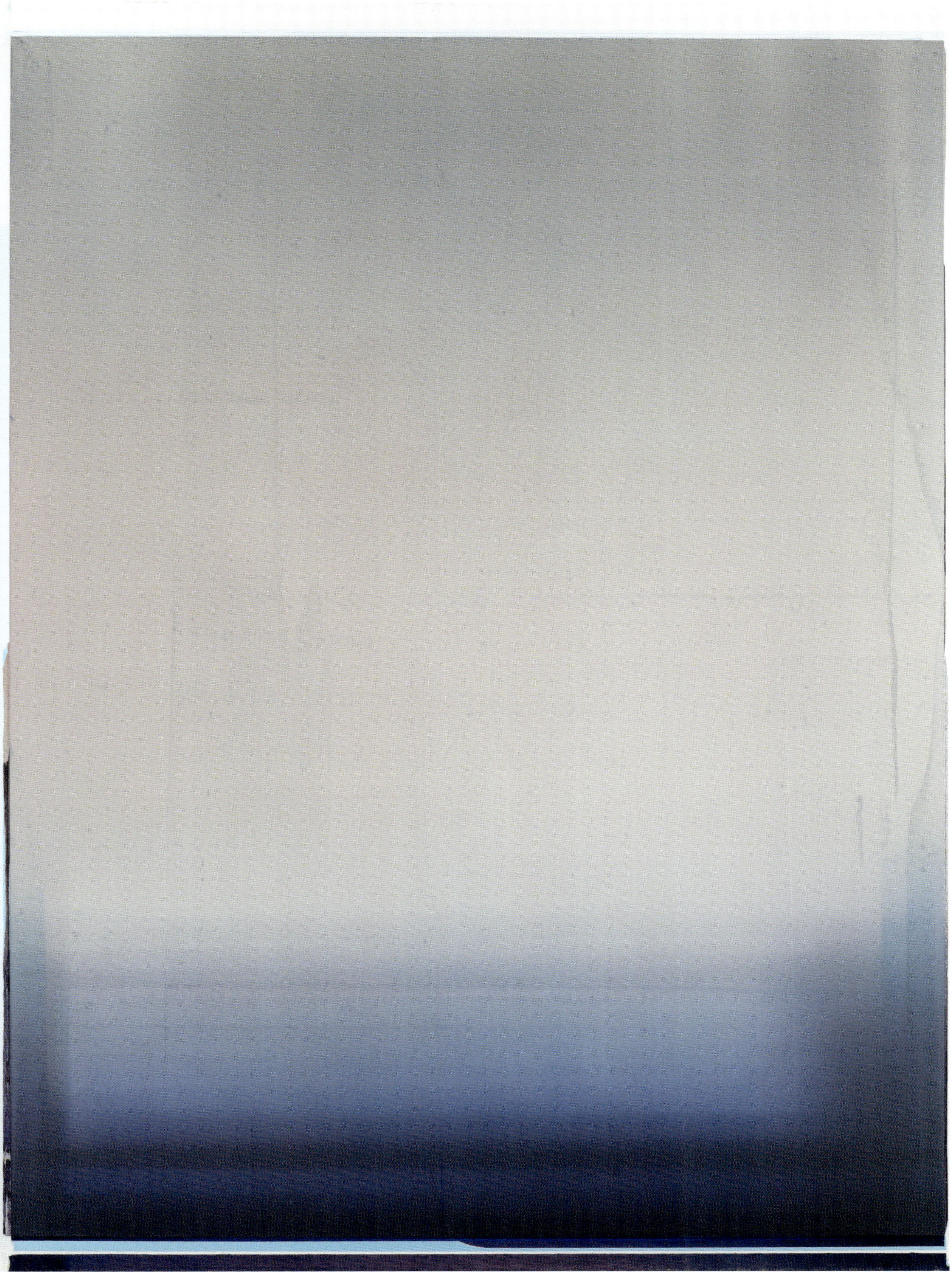

Untitled (V-PCB-RB-NM)

2019

Acrylic, vinyl paint, tape and spackle on canvas

220 × 170 cm

Wiesbaden

Florian Meisenberg

Loops of overtraded melodic repetitions and vocal-less junctions, inducing infinite murals of sociopathic collisions.
Long prolonged, coma-less, set-less theorems: allegorically seducing the intimations of collusion; falling into an arrangement of unpredictable blasts.

Towards the infinite sphere of awoken symbols and trustworthy lust.
Schemes and diagrams overstrain the loyalty of imagery and so the perception in pragmatic trust.
Sign me up,
Locate me down,
Punch me through,
and prod me in any irrational vow...

Dislocated assemblage – shared systematics, loaded into an affirmative scene;
Jump in-between the frivolous sequences of gentle landscapes:
delude the source path – introduce shared lust.
—— *Anna K.E.*

Florian Meisenberg was born in 1980 in Berlin and currently lives and works in New York City

Kunstakademie Düsseldorf Meisterschüler with Prof. Peter Doig

2019 TBA, curated by Monika Čejková, Berlinskej Model, Prague (S)

Complimentary Blue, curated by Milena Mercer, Kunstpalais Erlangen, with Anna K.E. (S, C)

2017 Myths of the Marble, curated by Alex Klein and Milena Hoegsberg, ICA Philadephia & Henie Onstad Kunstsenter, Oslo (G, C)

2016 ICH, Neue Formen des Selbstportraits, curated by Martina Weinhart, Schirn Kunsthalle, Frankfurt a. M. (G, C)

100untitledworksinmillaluminum.org

bombmagazine.org/florian-meisenberg-by-peter-rostovsky

florianmeisenberg.com

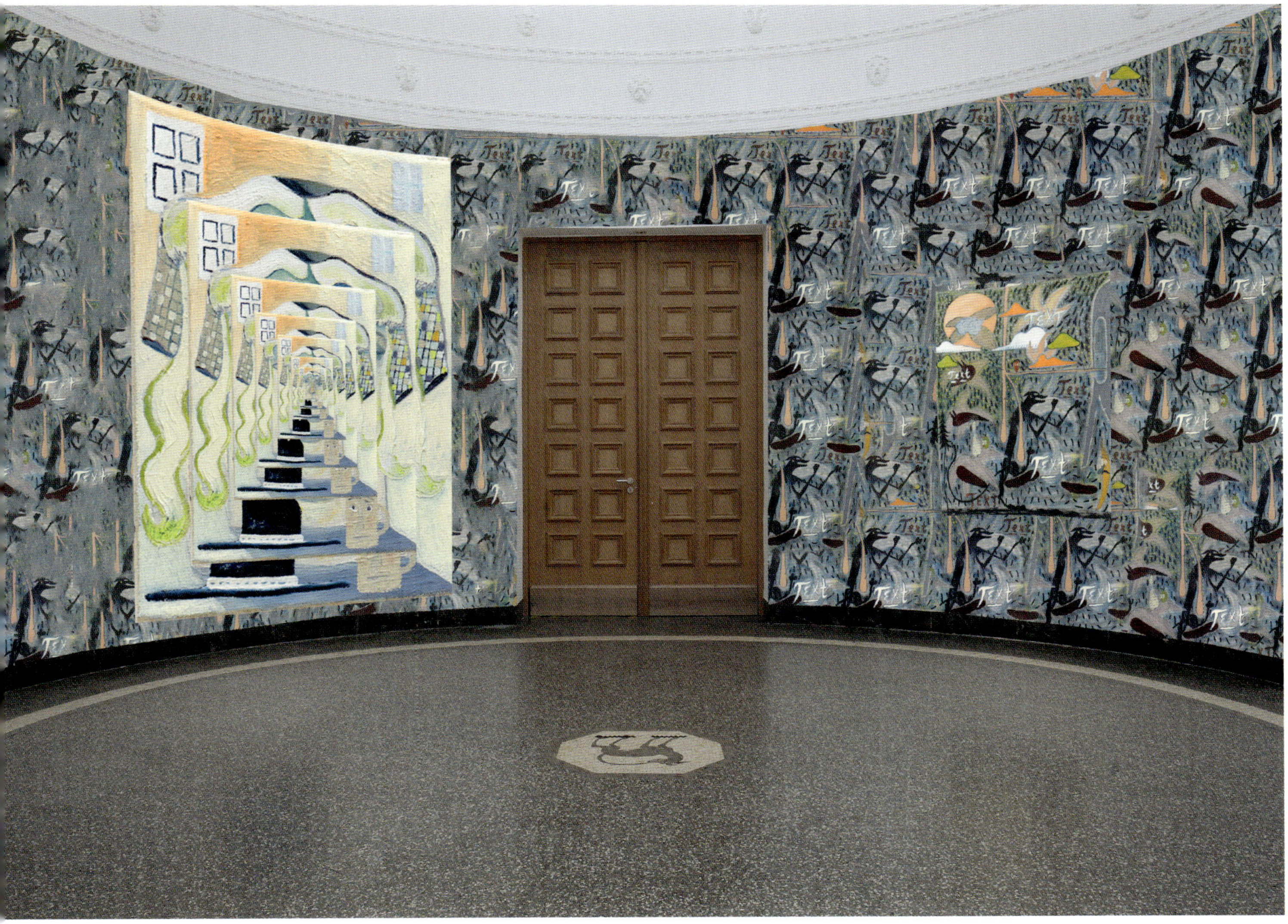

Reichwald (History of this Moment)
Day 5: 8 mm
Installation view at Museum Wiesbaden
(simulation)

2018

Oil, oil stick, airbrush and glass dust on linen
Oil on canvas

153 × 122 cm
28 × 20.5 cm

Forgery & Copyright (Arbeitslose Autoren & Unschuldige Hunde) | 2019 | Airbrush and oil on canvas | 183 × 147 cm | Bonn
Speaking Sanskrit with a German Accent (Chapter II Ordering Food) | | Ink and oil on canvas | 193 × 162 cm |

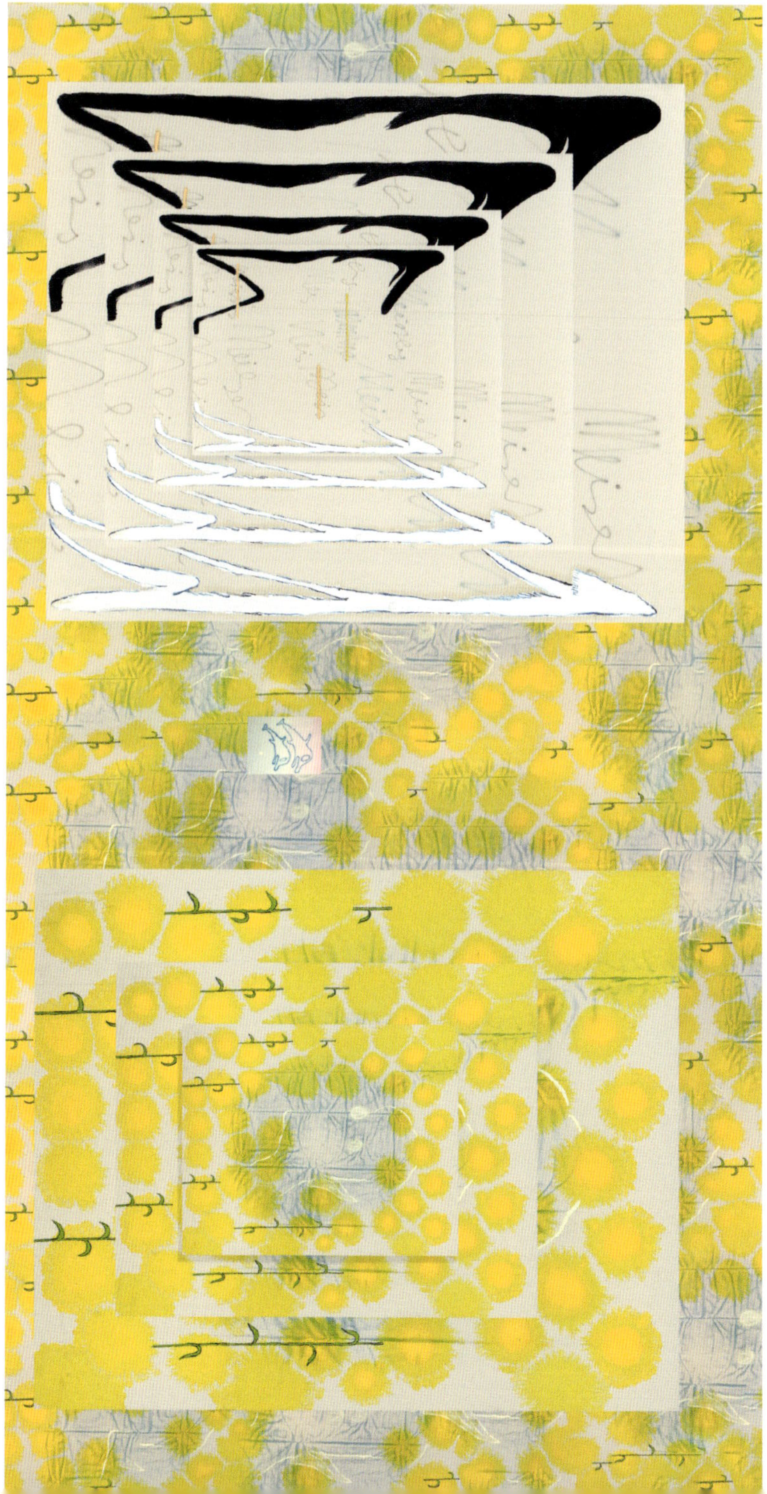

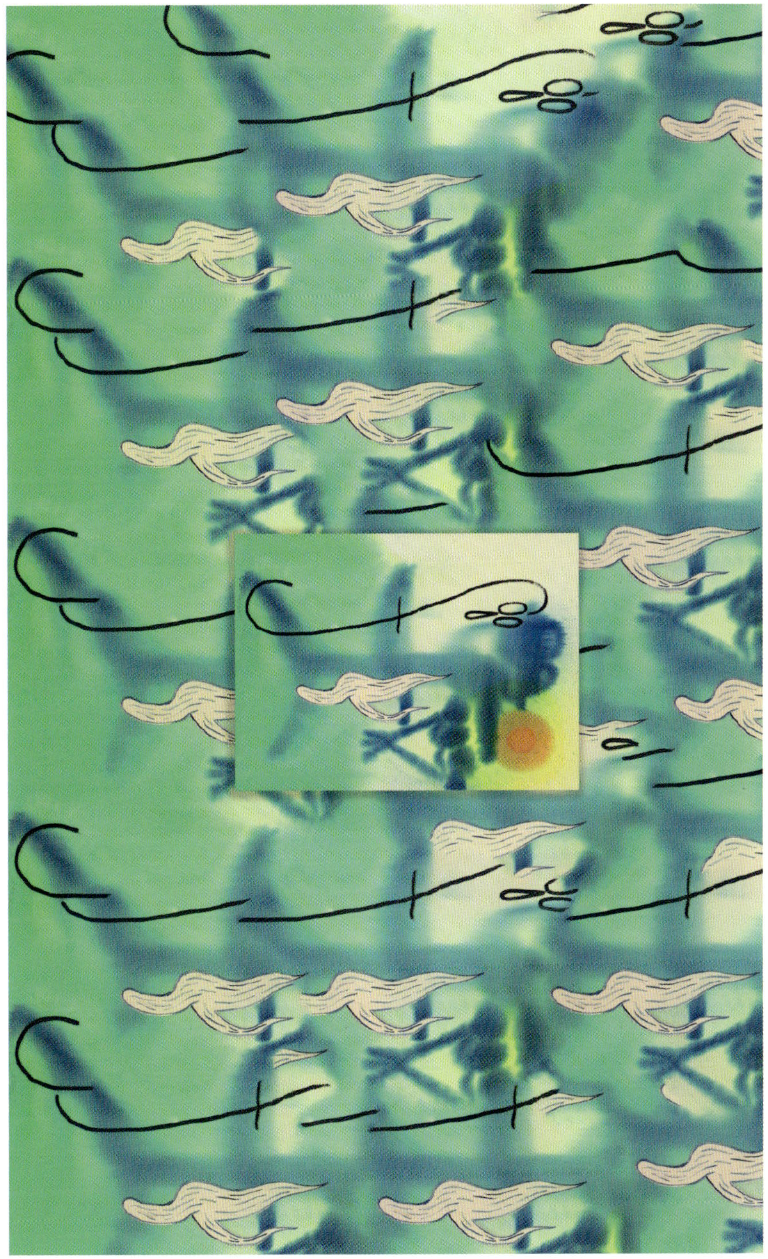

From the series:
Speaking Sanskrit with a German Accent
(Chapter VII Vocalizing)
2019
Ink and oil on canvas
102 × 77 cm
Chemnitz

Monika Michalko

Dark coloured

The painting of Monika Michalko contains fluid transitions between representational and abstract, figuration and ornamentation. Her pictures are characterised by a contrasting and intense colourfulness, which is quietly presented and often contains a hint of the torrid. She heightens the colours with shades that may be dark or grubbily faded and makes them glow. Together with the supposedly naive, folkloristic element, the origins for this lie in her biography as well as the region from which she comes: Michalko was born in what is now the Czech Republic and from an early stage used aspects of the local folk art as a source of inspiration in her work.
More recent influences derive from another part of the world: until March 2019, Michalko lived for a year in Sri Lanka. There the colourful painting of façades, doors and vehicles as well as colourful clothing form part of everyday culture. "In some places I had the impression I was walking through my own pictures", observed the artist in conversation. "The colours and the architecture of the temples and cities became engraved into my head and my heart." Many subjects and titles bear witness to this: *Colombo, Rayagiriya side* and *My own shop* (all 2018) are city scenes that interweave the architecture and rampant tropical flora in complex layers, repeatedly interrupted by written characters.
Borella (2018), at first sight completely abstract, is also named for a district of Colombo. The composition consists of superimposed coloured shapes and is designed like a picture-within-a-picture. Although nothing specifically representational has been depicted, nonetheless the colours of the city, the brightly coloured doors, walls and façades flow together as if to create a distillation of the artist's perception. The graduated forms also play in abstract manner with the impression of lettering.
On the way to far east (2017) also refers to oriental travel experiences. The complex structure consciously keeps figurative and abstract moments in suspense. Small, colourful patches of colour, from garish to grubby, border the picture like a frame. The elements of the inner zone are partly abstract, partly readable in a representational manner and often both at the same time. Piles of bottles, dishes and circular shapes are transformed into abstract figures – a cast, as it were, that Michalko positions in a pale, restless environment.
A picture must never be too beautiful and never perfect in order to reveal its innate power – and so a latently chaotic vibrancy dominates here and leads the composition into the open.
—— *Jens Asthoff*

Monika Michalko was born in 1982 in Sokolov (Czech Republic) and currently lives and works in Berlin
Hochschule für bildende Künste Hamburg with Prof. Norbert Schwontkowski, 2009

2019 Im Garten der Dichter, Produzentengalerie Hamburg (G)
2018 Veylon, Galerie Maïa Muller, Paris (S)
In the tropics the hair feels different, Galerie Franzkowiak, Berlin (with Jan Michalko) (G)
2017 1000 Sterne, kuratiert von F. Bornstück, Galerie Michael Andersen, Copenhagen (G)

salon.io/monika-michalko

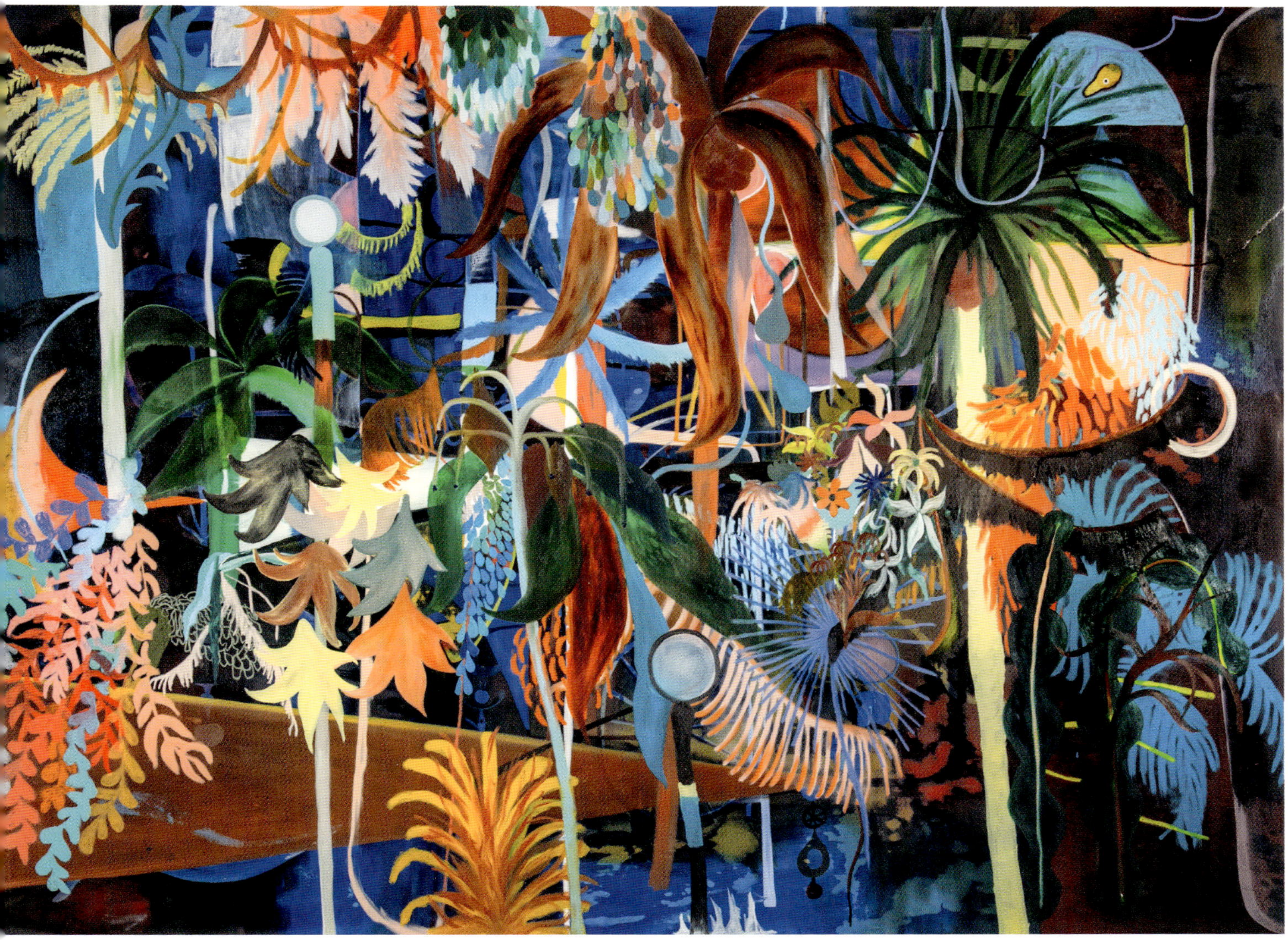

Colombo 2018 Oil on canvas 200 × 280 cm Wiesbaden

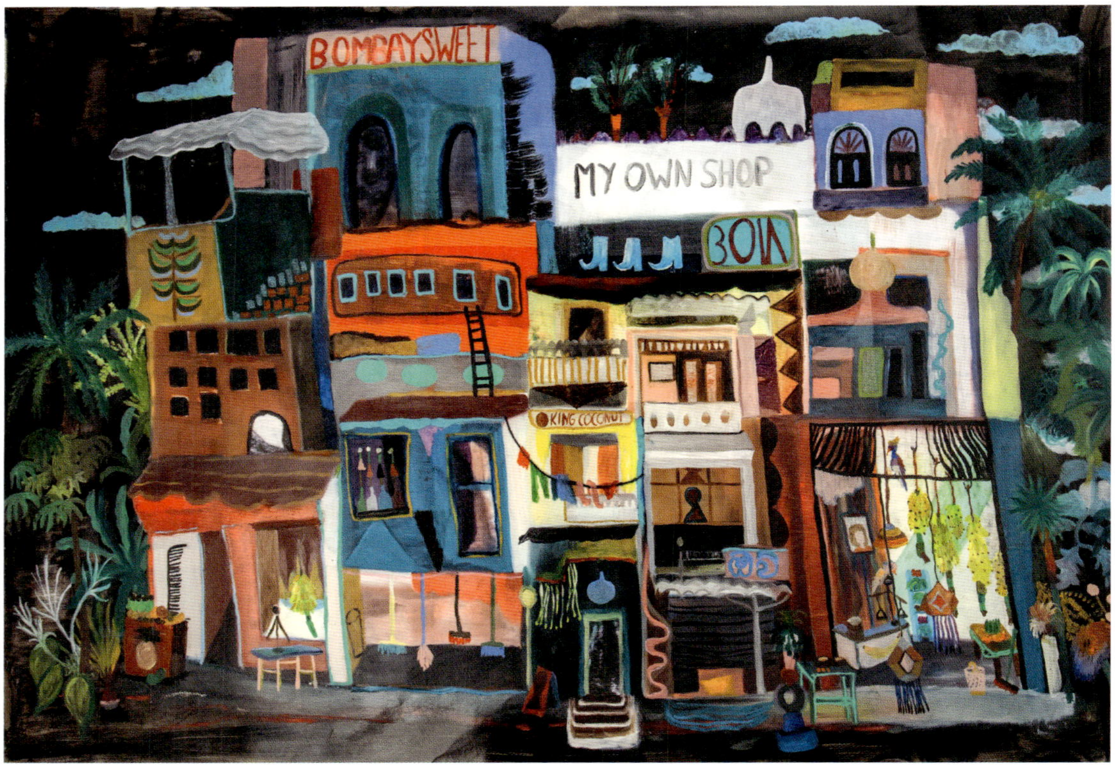

My own shop 2018 Oil on paper 105 × 157 cm Chemnitz

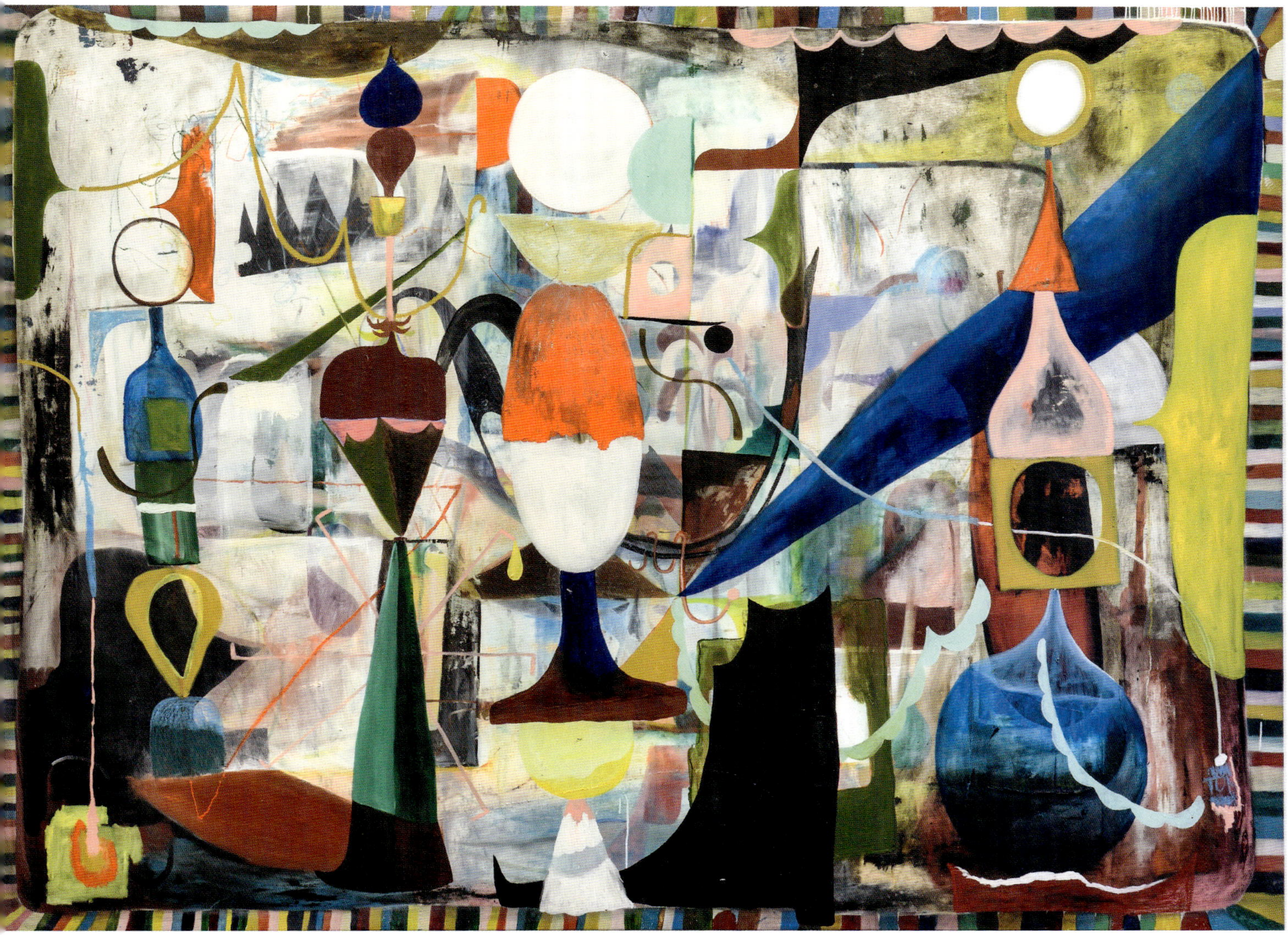

On the way to far east

2018

Oil on canvas

200 × 280 cm

Bonn

Hannes Michanek

Looking across country

It is hard to say what the predominant climate is in the landscapes which Hannes Michanek paints. It seems to have become rough in these environments. In which regions do these trees and plants grow, and where are these creatures heading for as they stride away into the picture, quite in the manner of the Romantic Age? Perhaps the landscapes and their inhabitants have experienced dangerous phenomena – strange weather – or something man-made, as if animated in a computer game. And then, suddenly, there are vast expanses and views of the sky. Tranquillity returns to the scene. The birds settle back onto their perches (or what is left of them) and all the things that exist in the world step to the fore as colour imperative – for a moment my "Where-am-I?" search recedes into the background, because now things are non-representational.
That makes me think of the question: What exactly is it that makes a landscape? When do we understand all the individual blades of grass as steppe, the stones beneath our feet as mountain cliffs? When do the individual branches of the trees form a forest, and when does the sky become an expanse? When will all the individual elements, the seething mass, become the great whole which makes a landscape, and when do we experience a landscape as "beautiful"? The Swiss sociologist and planning theorist Lucius Burckhardt recognised this connection and answered the questions with the prompt observation: "Landscapes are born in the mind."
I realise: the familiar points of view that I am used to adopt as an observer when standing in front of the representation of a landscape will be of no use to me when I study the pictures of Hannes Michanek. He takes delight in cutting through the countless details vertically, turning them upside down, dissecting them into their individual components and then reassembling them in an abstract picture context. And I, the viewer, am actually put in the position of imagining quite different landscapes from any that I have ever seen before on this planet.
Today is 15 May 2019, and it is 11.34 pm at night. What will most certainly reappear tomorrow, when I open my laptop, is the desert landscape which a computer firm supplied as a screen saver (I have no idea where the picture comes from, or in which country the desert actually exists). – It is not important, because now I have gained images in my mind's eye of the landscapes of Hannes Michanek! —— *Judith Hopf*

Hannes Michanek was born in 1979 in Sweden and currently lives and works in Frankfurt a.M.

2018 Honey Bear, Galerie Parisa Kind, Frankfurt a.M. (S)

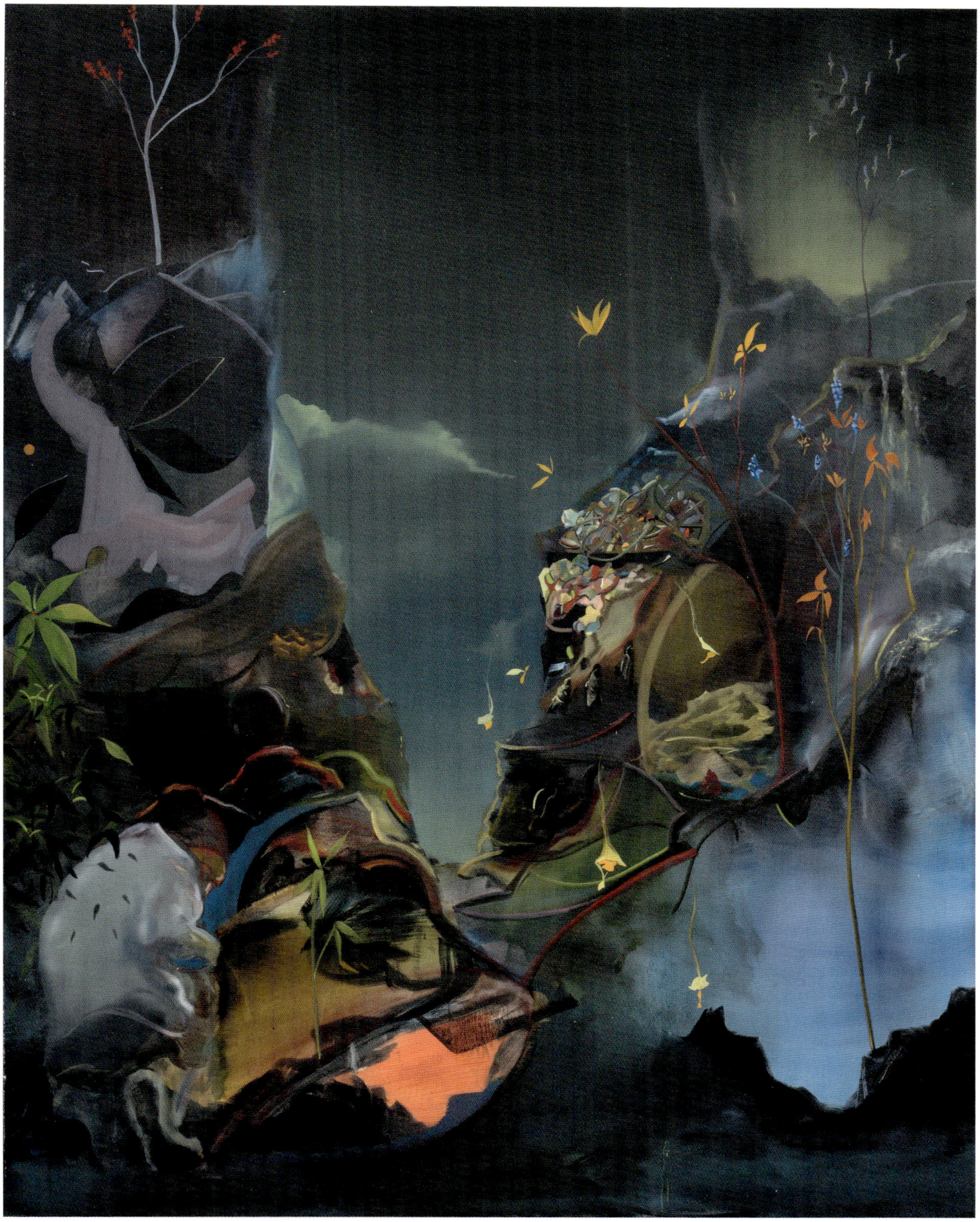

Digging funnels, beyond things ahead. 2018 Oil on canvas 230 × 190 cm Wiesbaden

All these things what happened and more, quantum with physics at an endless war. Bugs move, fruit flies. Hollow bones.

2019 Oil on canvas 190 × 230 cm Bonn

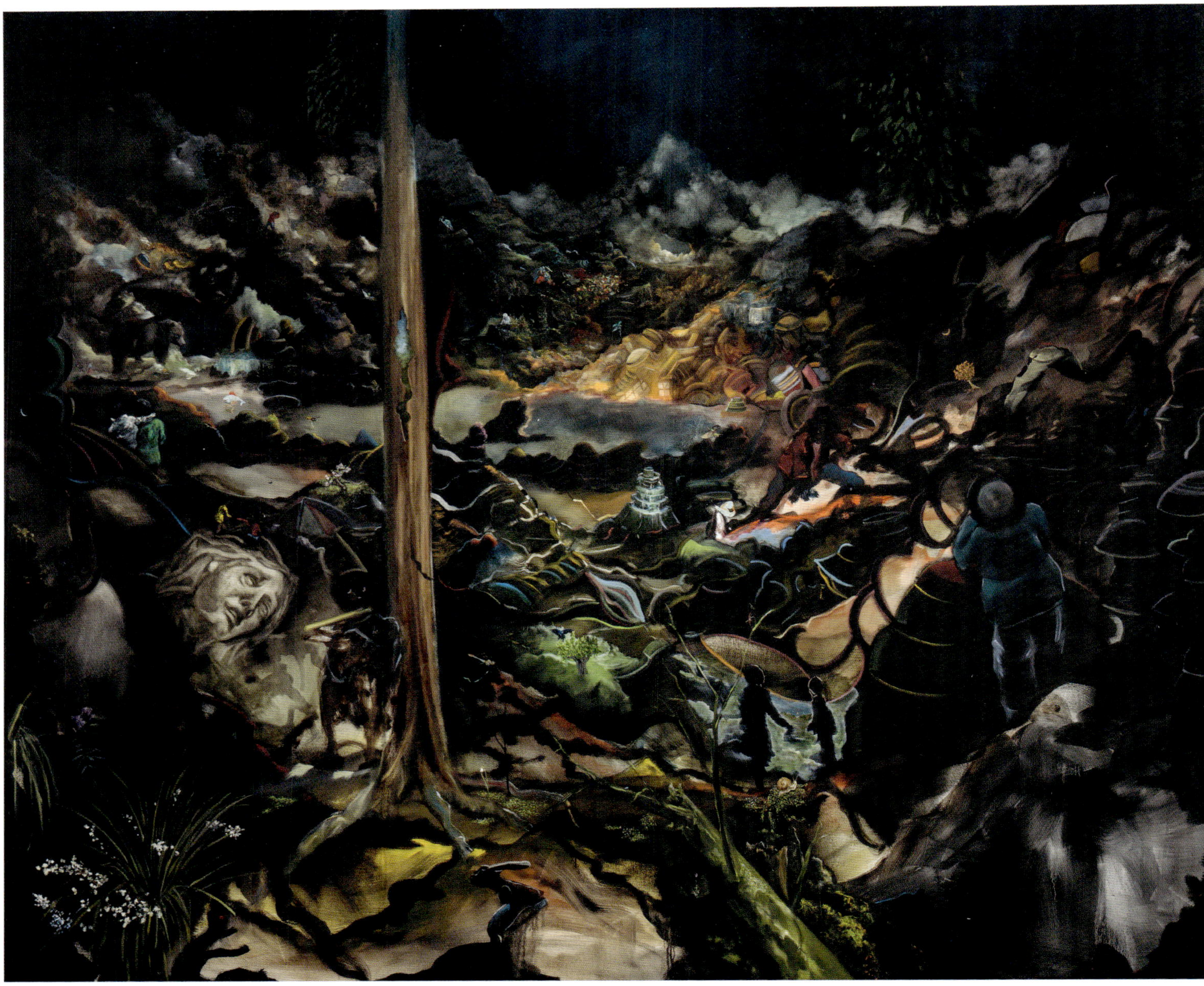

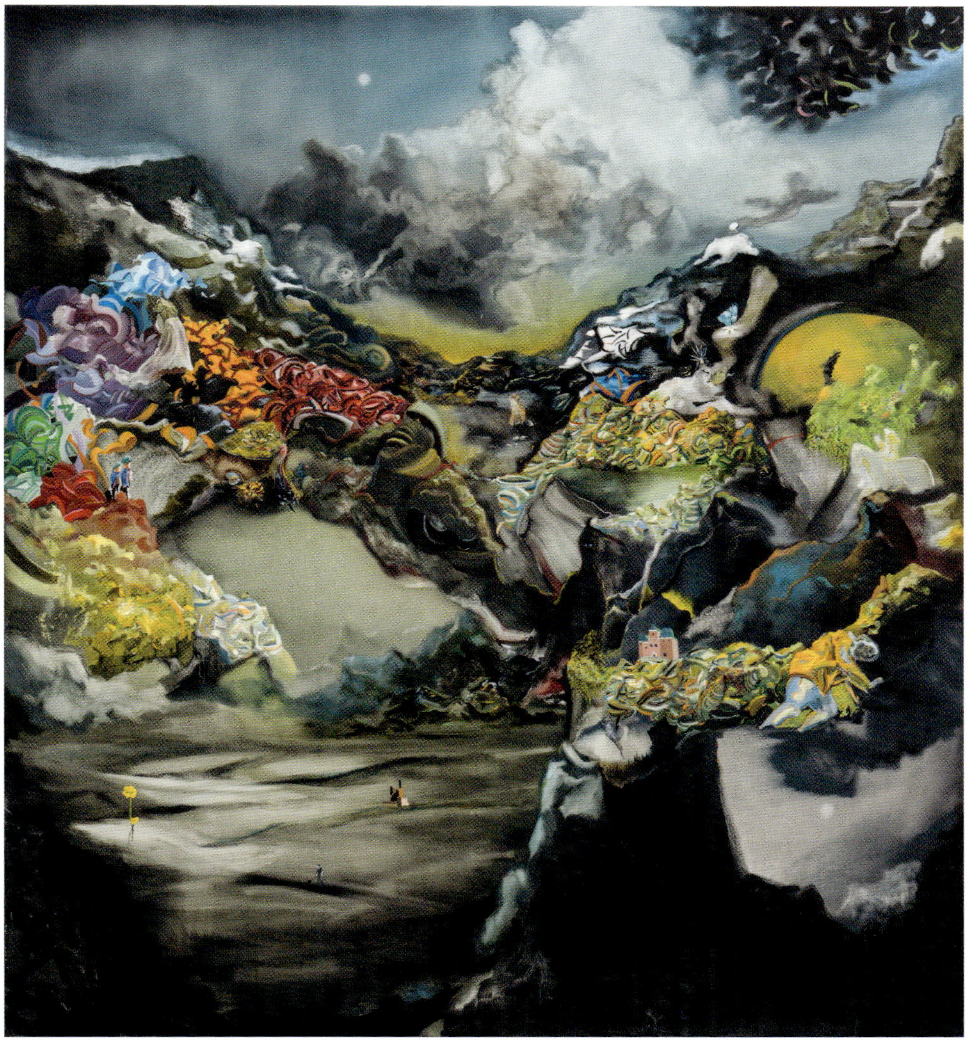

Pearl. How awful-(y) kind. Thought the fox of sky. Day in and day out, looking down on a daily life.

2019

Oil on canvas

160 × 150 cm

Chemnitz

Simon Modersohn

An upturned flower pot lies on one of those gabion walls constructed of stones and metal that are currently so incredibly fashionable. The perfectly trimmed box tree to one side has evidently toppled head first to the ground. Perhaps out of frustration at its unnatural surroundings? *Selbstmord* (Suicide), the title of this painting by Simon Modersohn, encourages this speculation.
Modersohn trained with Werner Büttner at the University of Fine Arts (HfbK) in Hamburg. His figurative oil paintings combine a restrained objectivity with surreal, narrative elements. He often seeks the unfathomable in everyday trivialities. The atmospheric density of his imagery is heightened on a verbal, often humorous level by means of pithy titles. Thus a formally somewhat reduced picture showing an empty cage for a small animal with drinking equipment attached to the upper bars has been given the laconic title *Durststrecke* (Hard Times) (2018).
Recurring subjects in Modersohn's paintings are detached family homes in the country with mysteriously lit windows. These unspectacular buildings are mostly surrounded by meticulously manicured gardens enhanced by accessories that can be bought in any do-it-yourself store. Heat sources such as home saunas or working lights appear regularly in his pictures and lend them an irresistible ambivalence. Simon Modersohn seeks a way to achieve intellectual depth and truthfulness in the representation of complex interconnections in our lives through painting. The narrative develops only during the painting process. His concern lies not least in the interplay of changing perspectives and angles. The scenes he thinks up dispense with people, and yet there are traces of previous human activity which pervade the pictures in a subtle manner. His pictures develop their enormous density and equilibrium in the carefully balanced tension field between presence and absence, coincidence and remembrance, tragedy and comedy, big-city experiences and country life.
—— *Nicole Büsing and Heiko Klaas*

Simon Modersohn was born in 1991 in Ottersberg and currently lives and works in Hamburg
Hochschule für bildende Künste Hamburg with Prof. Gregor Hildebrandt and Prof. Werner Büttner, 2011–2019

2018 sommer.frische.kunst, Bad Gastein (G)
2017 salondergegenwart, Hamburg (G)
2016 Innercircle, Elektrohaus Hamburg (G)
2015 AUA! Auf und Ab, Westwerk Hamburg (G)

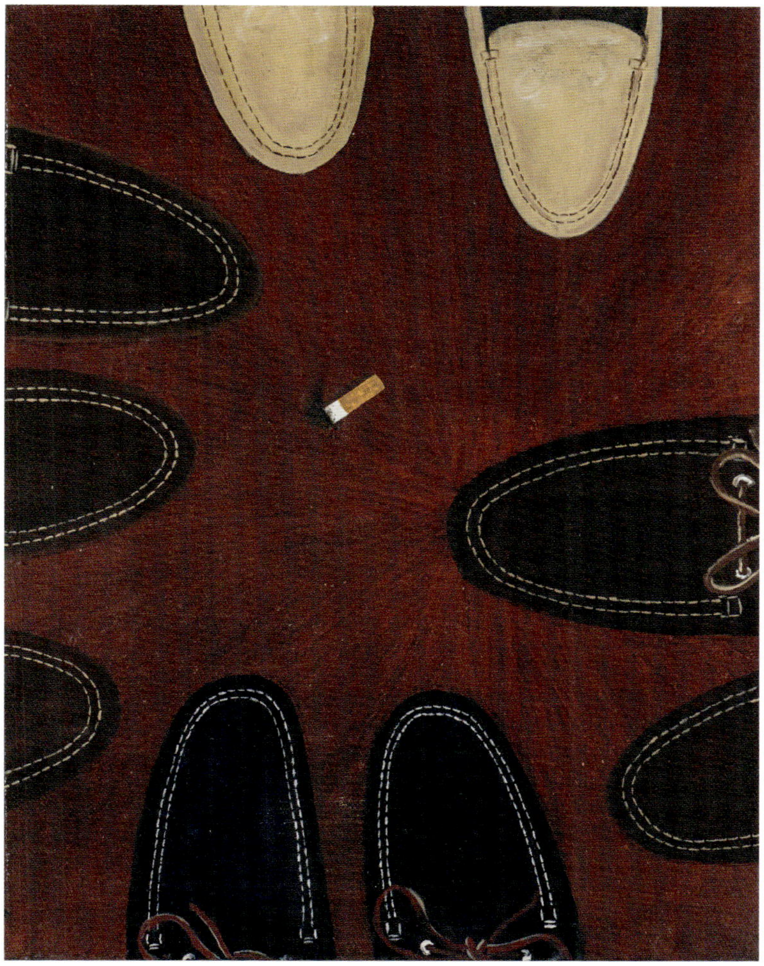

Club zur Vahr 2015 Oil on canvas 50 × 40 cm Bonn

Durststrecke 2018 Oil on canvas 80 × 140 cm Chemnitz

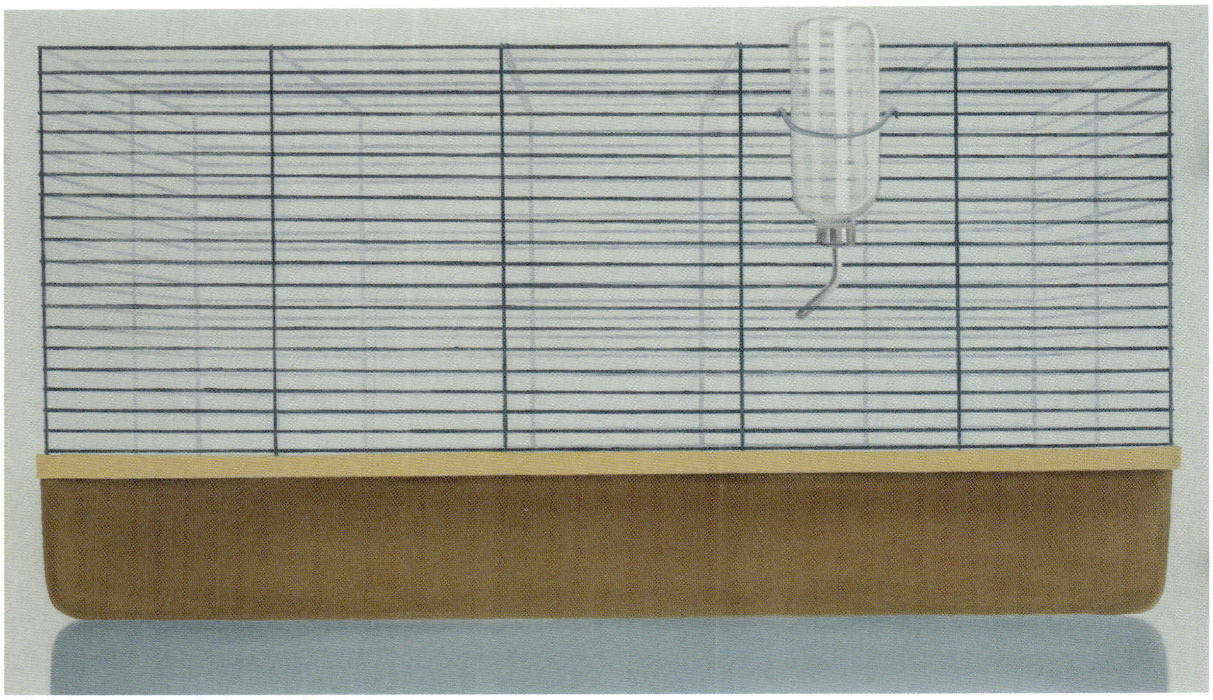

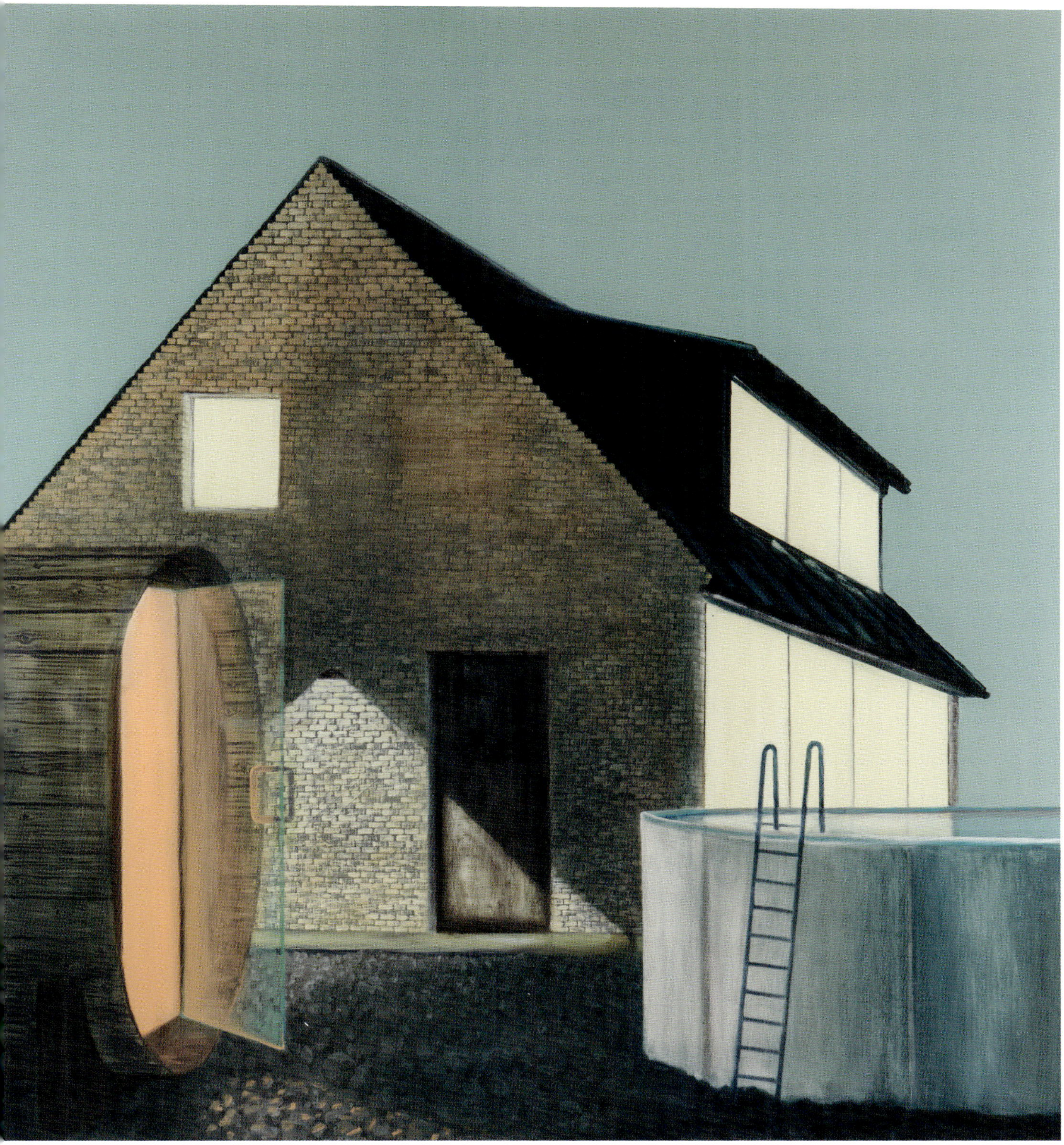

Round Up 2018 Oil on canvas 190 × 180 cm Wiesbaden

Bastian Muhr

Since studying in Leipzig, Bastian Muhr has presented works both in the form of paintings and large-format drawings. The artist develops the latter not only on paper, but also in the form of ephemeral floor works which he creates as extensive linear textures using white chalk. In his oil paintings, too, which are usually executed in monochrome and in black, the line recurs as a central pictorial tool as well as the specific element in a fabric-like structure. In fact, it is as such that Muhr constructs his pictures successively. The basis is formed by the brushstroke, which continues to remain visible after the painting process has been concluded. He develops forms by means of the interplay of numerous lines executed with the paintbrush; the latter remain planar despite the plasticity of the paint application. His pictures are the result of the interaction between control and spontaneity, as can be seen in the lively, albeit controlled brushwork with which the forms are created. The forms which Bastian Muhr creates in this way occasionally occur in fragmented form; many are rounded on several sides and linked together. They contrast clearly with the neutral background of the white priming of the canvas. This effect is enhanced by the gentle relief of the paint application. The colour and shape modules developed by Muhr which occupy the canvas or the paper remain abstract despite their representational echoes. They reveal themselves to be concrete manifestations of a process of pictorial development which is the true subject of his painting.

Muhr's monochrome oil paintings on paper also demonstrate that the primary graphic impulse which determines his brushwork leads step by step to a concentration, indeed a modelling, of painterly textures. Here, even more clearly than in the large paintings, ornamental and labyrinthine aspects are in evidence. The changes in direction which the brushstrokes undergo are particularly obvious and are indicated by tight "curves". The neutral whiteness of the paper, which shines through in many places as a result of the thin application of the paint, reveals here that its purpose is to serve as a resonance chamber for the painterly process.

—— *Andreas Schalhorn*

Bastian Muhr was born in 1981 in Braunschweig and currently lives and works in Leipzig

Hochschule für Grafik und Buchkunst Leipzig, Diploma of Fine Arts, 2010

2019 In bester Gesellschaft, Kupferstichkabinett, Staatlichen Museen zu Berlin (G)

2018 Kante, Museum der Bildenden Künste, Leipzig (S)

Über das Geistige in der Kunst, Deutsche Gesellschaft für christliche Kunst, Munich (G)

2017 Schwarzbunt, Galerie Jochen Hempel, Leipzig (S)

bastianmuhr.de

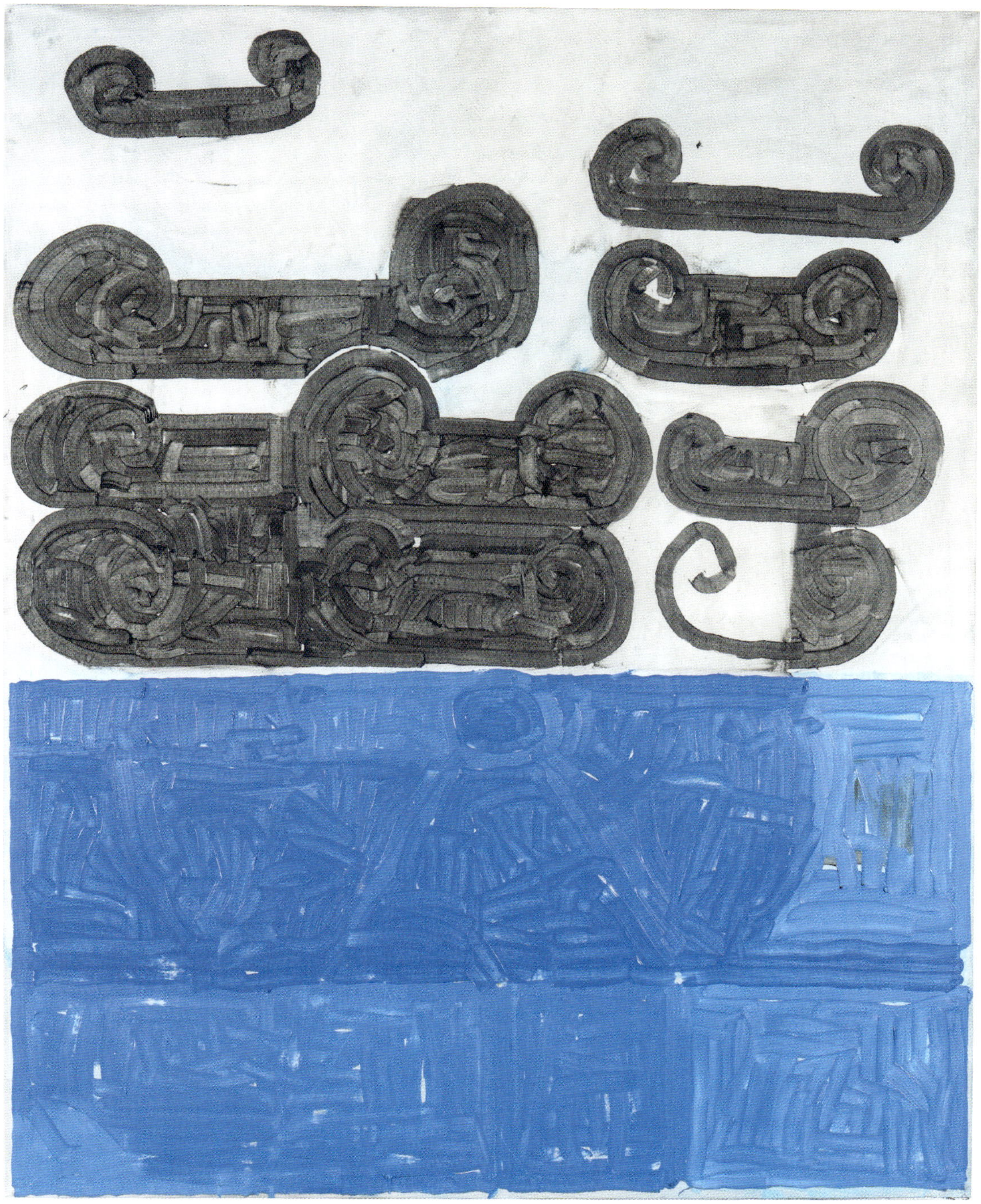

Zwenkau 2019 Oil on cotton 170 × 140 cm Wiesbaden

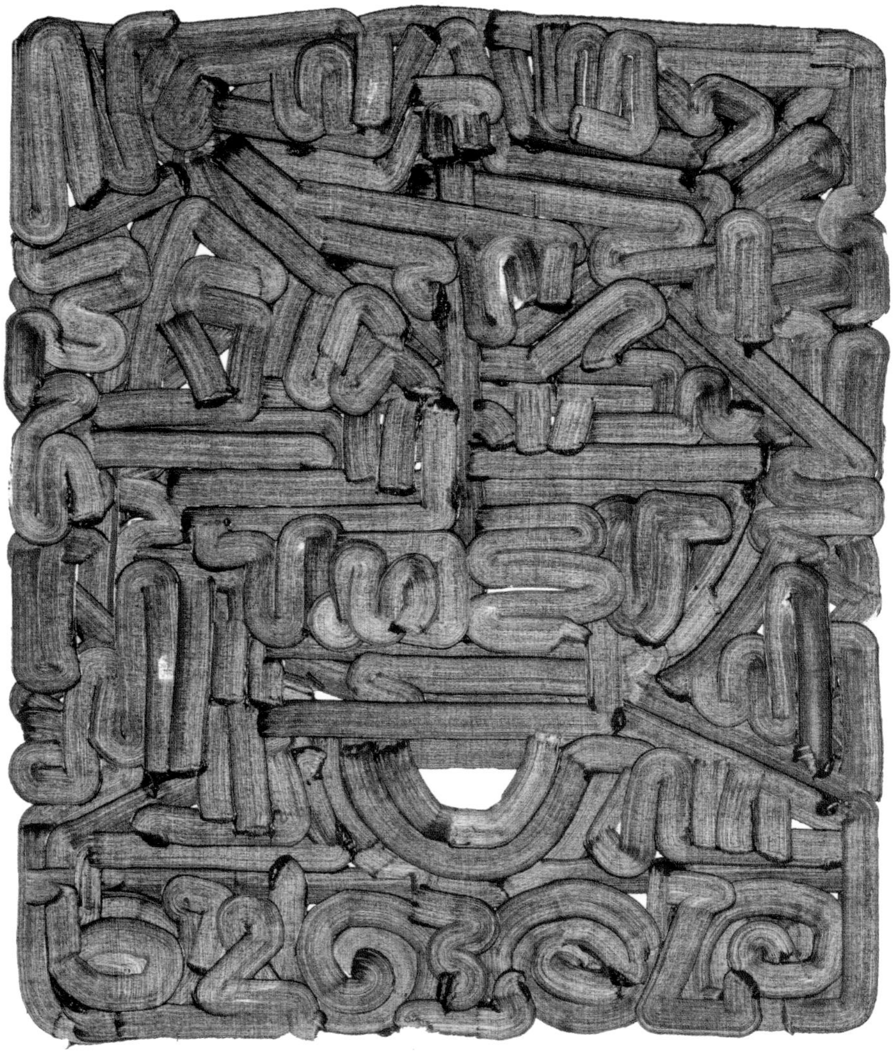

Untitled
part of 24-piece series

2018

Oil on paper, framed

70 cm × 60 cm, each,
220 × 500 cm, total

Bonn

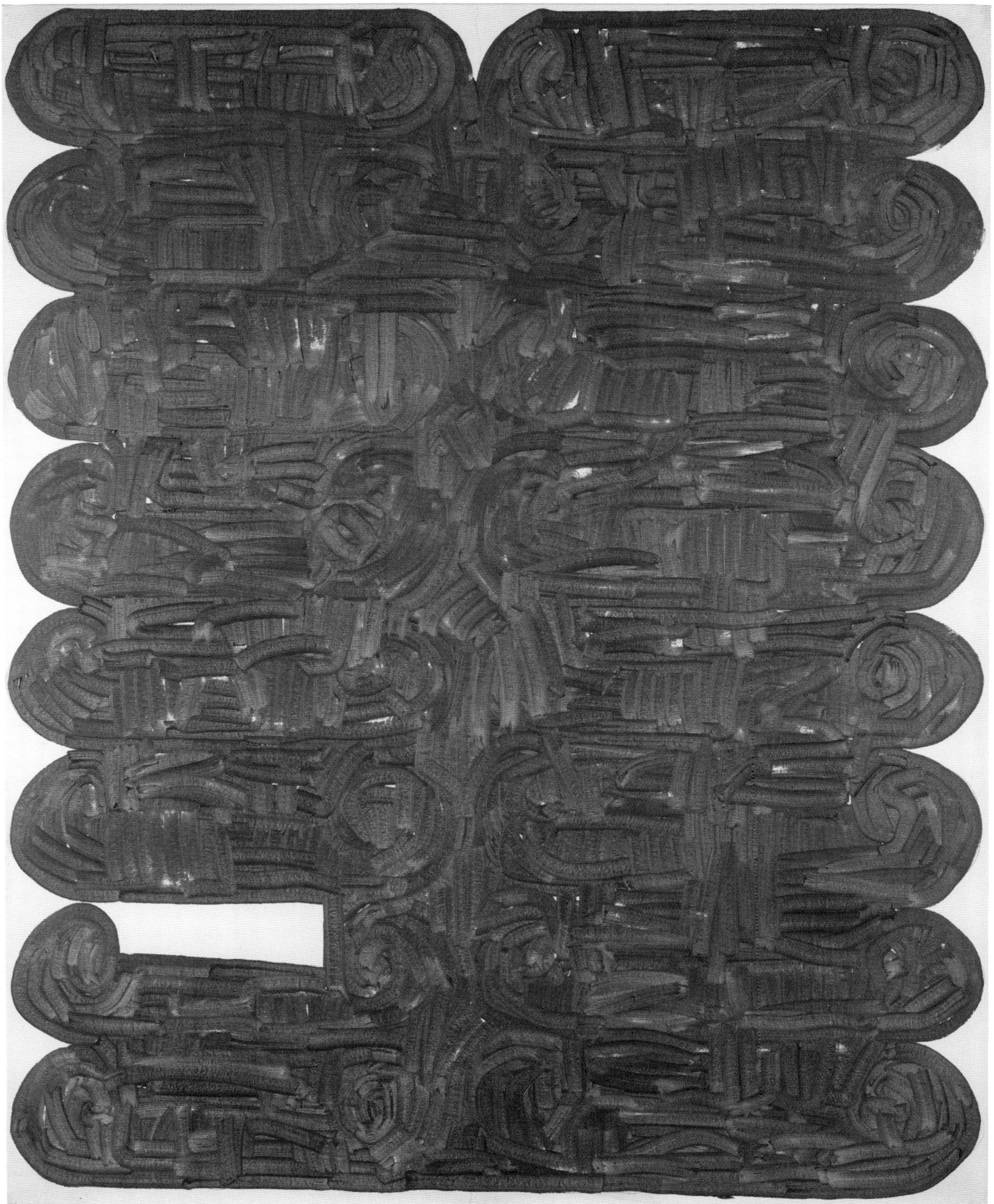

Untitled 2019 Oil on cotton 170 × 140 cm Chemnitz

Anna Nero

I am interested in the objects around me – their nature, their materiality, their functionality, their context and also their "essence". I find myself thinking about the question of when paint becomes an object or space and when it remains in its role as a material and/or a pictorial medium. In my work, painterly gestures, lines and areas are more than mere tools – they themselves are both content and subject. In my pictures blotches, bulges and lines often take on lives of their own, flirt with each other, negotiate or repel each other. They form agglomerations and groups and thereby offer possible narratives and contexts.
I work with different forms of painting and possibilities of representation. When generating my pictures I follow certain parameters which I have developed for myself over the past years. My process mostly begins with rigorous geometric constructions such as orthogonal grids, bars, patterns, frames, shelves. As a next step there follow gestures and areas which are positioned somewhat playfully and intuitively, and which either become attached to the underlying system or which disrupt or subvert it.
Since my father is a commercial artist I came into contact with design and digital image-processing programs at an early age, which certainly influenced my present work. I do not plan my works in advance on the computer. But because I build things up like a collage layer by layer, as I described above, they acquire an aura like the digital layers of an image. I find it fascinating to assemble forms of representation, surfaces and materiality which seem to be difficult to unite. I deal with art history in a similar manner, in that I quote and sample modern positions from the fields of abstract and Constructivist art, Concrete painting and Pop Art in my work. —— *Anna Nero*

Anna Nero was born in 1988 in Moscow (Russia) and currently lives and works in Frankfurt a. M. and Leipzig

Hochschule für Grafik und Buchkunst Leipzig, Diploma, 2015, Meisterschülerin 2017

2019 Two Truths, Galerie Kramer, Bremen (S)
CONTROL, Kunstraum Ortloff, Leipzig (S)

2018 Utility Violence, Galerie Oel Früh, Hamburg (S)
Masters of None, Myanm/art, Yangon (Myanmar) (G)

annanero.de

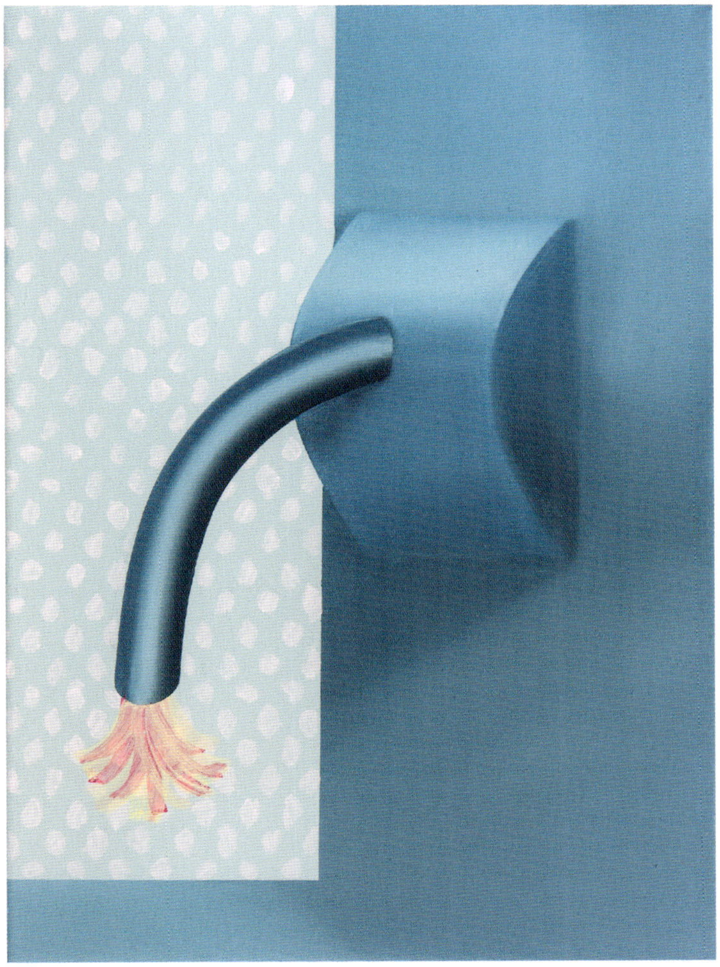

Jetlag (mit Happy End) 2019 Oil and acrylic on canvas 40 × 30 cm Chemnitz

Useful Things | 2018 | Oil, acrylic, colour paste and ink on canvas | 40 × 30 cm | Bonn

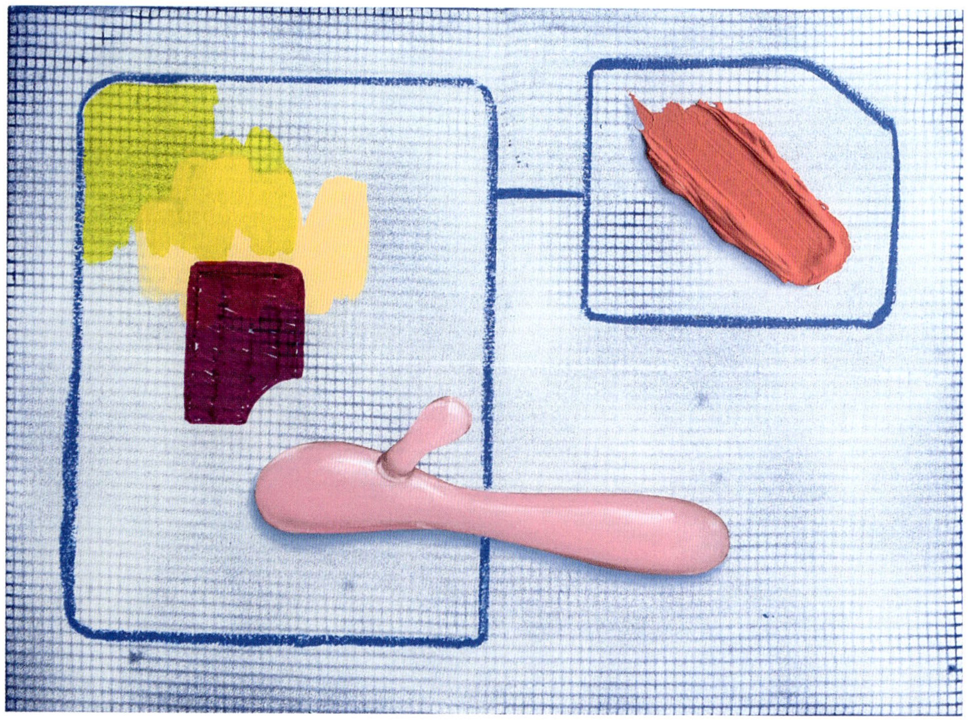

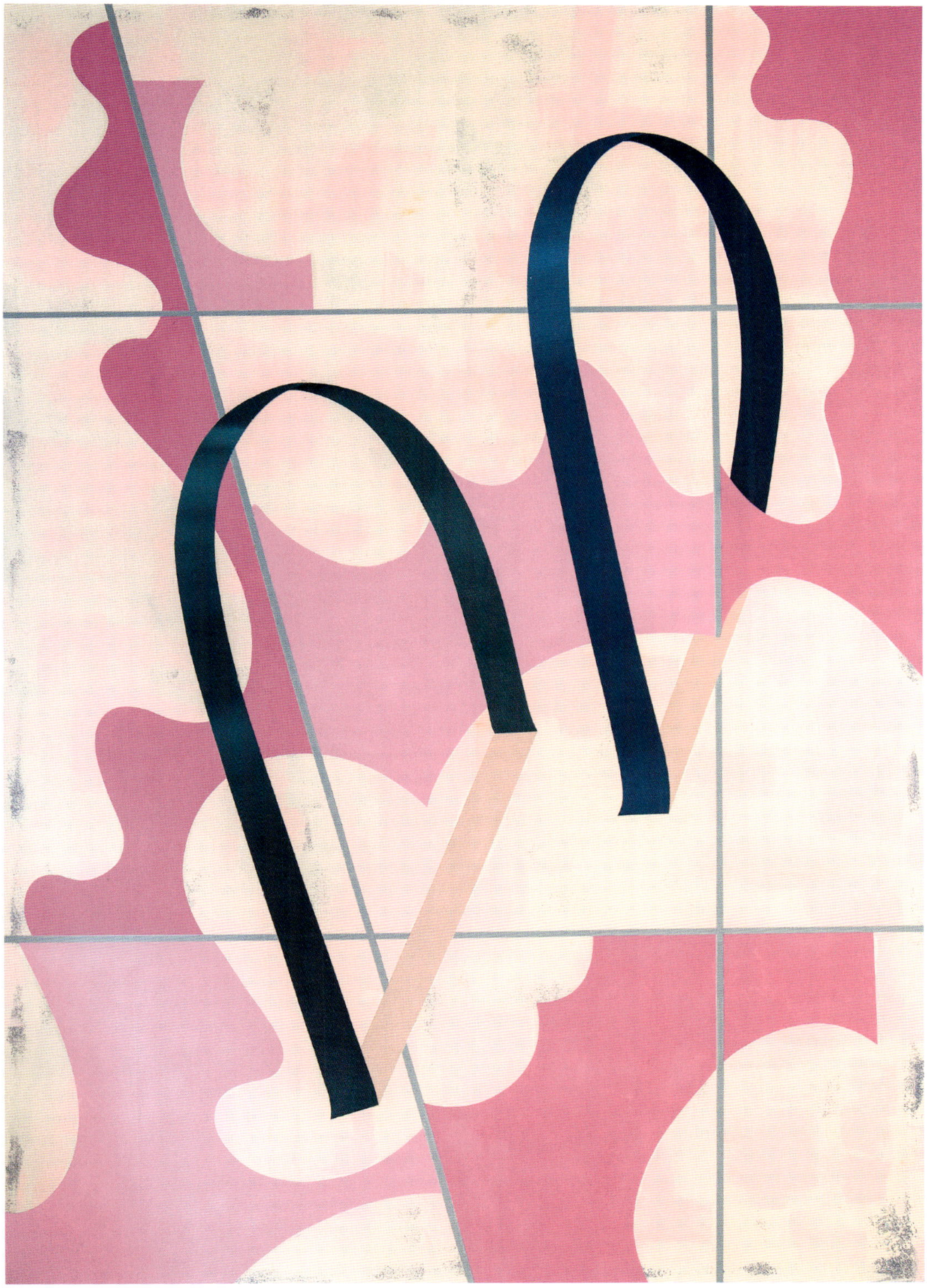

We belong 2gether 2018 Oil and acrylic on canvas 180 × 130 cm Wiesbaden

Moritz Neuhoff

Moritz Neuhoff explores a broad spectrum of abstract painting in his large-format pictures. As in an experimental laboratory, he implements very varied approaches to coloured material and interconnects them in curious constellations. This happens in a masterful, detached manner. In their urge for movement, the impulses of a body, the brilliance of a painterly hand, the impetuousness of an emotional character appear to build up the pictorial world, but at the same time there is a worldly-wise intellect at work, which constructs mysterious control systems, so that viewers will ask themselves whether the lively painterly existence has not been generated by a complex machine instead of being formed by human hand. What seems from a distance to be a massive outburst of coloured material, can be seen at close quarters to be shallow, barely more than a delicate colouring of the canvas. It transpires that all haptic elements are an illusion of complex patterns of shadows and light which have penetrated the canvas almost intangibly. In this back and forth of optical illusions, the viewer becomes uncertain of his own powers of sight. The apparently haptic painting is transformed into a virtual event which refers back to media experiences of the last decade and processes them pictorially. Not only the colour values and hues of the paints, but also the light and space become intangible or indeterminate. The painterly movements with their multilayered overlapping and changing levels, the iridescent roaming light and the indefinable flickering colours create a pictorial event which seems like the appearance of an alien cosmos, of which we do not know in which dimensions it extends. —— *Rolf Hengesbach*

Moritz Neuhoff was born in 1987 in Osnabrück and currently lives and works in Berlin

Kunstakademie Münster, Meisterschüler with Prof. Cornelius Völker 2016

2019 apparent magnitude, Museum gegenstandfreier Kunst, Otterndorf (S)

2018 schön schrecklich schön, Pavillon am Milchhof, Berlin (G)

2017 current status, Hengesbach Gallery, Wuppertal (S)

good news, KunstVerein Ahlen e.V. (G)

moritzneuhoff.de

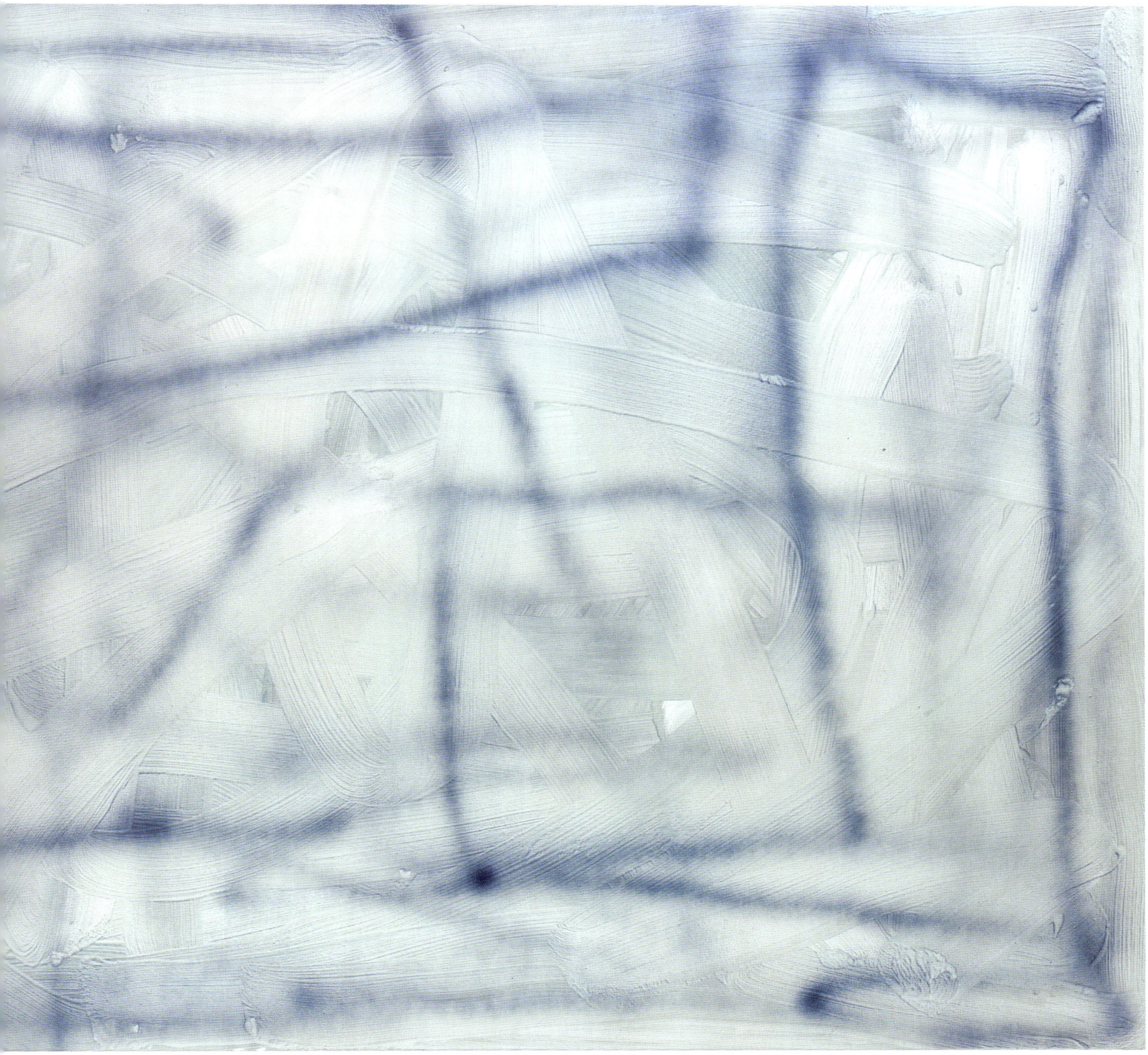

Plexus 2019 Acrylic on canvas 200 × 300 cm Chemnitz

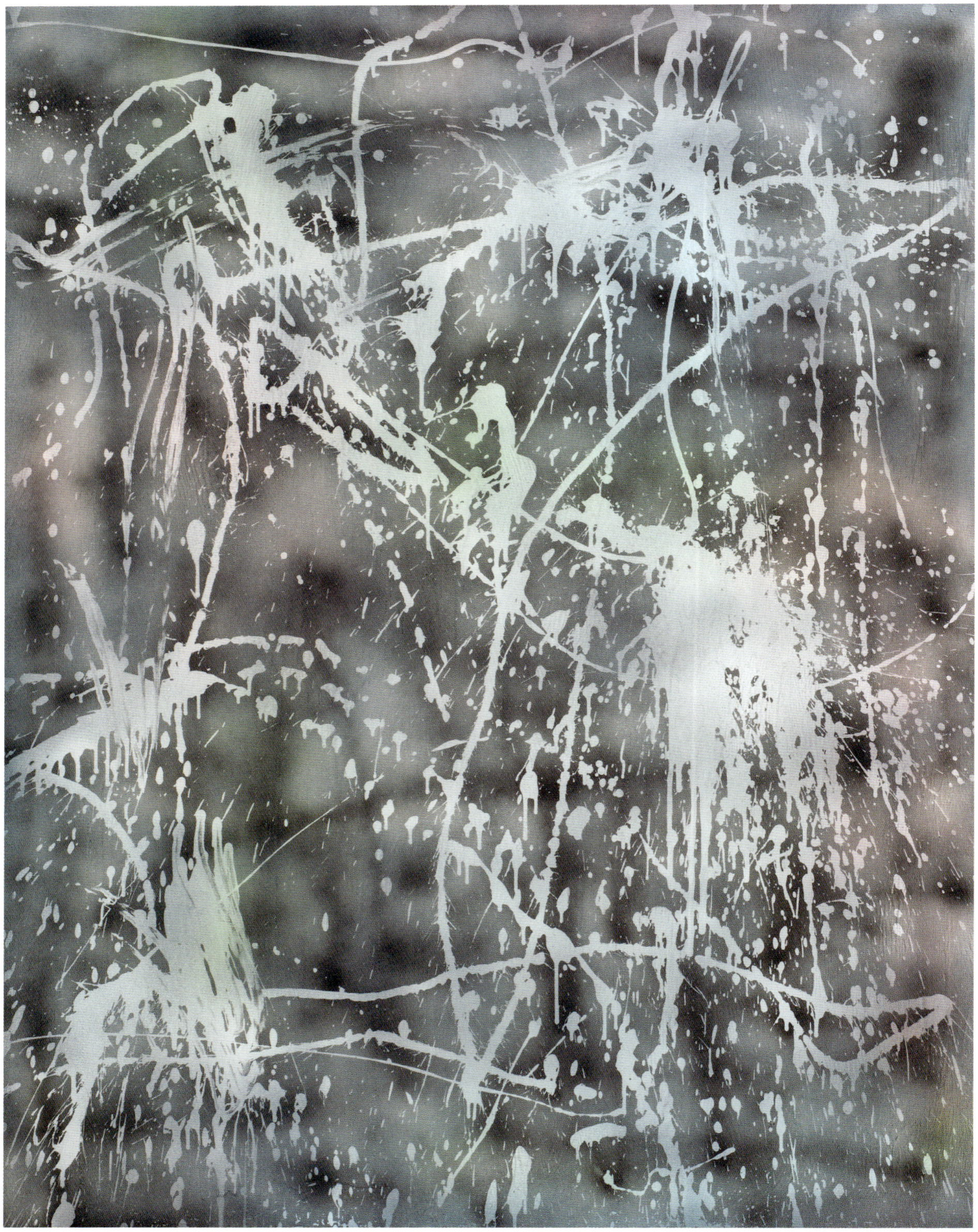

dash 2018 Acrylic on canvas 250 × 200 cm Wiesbaden

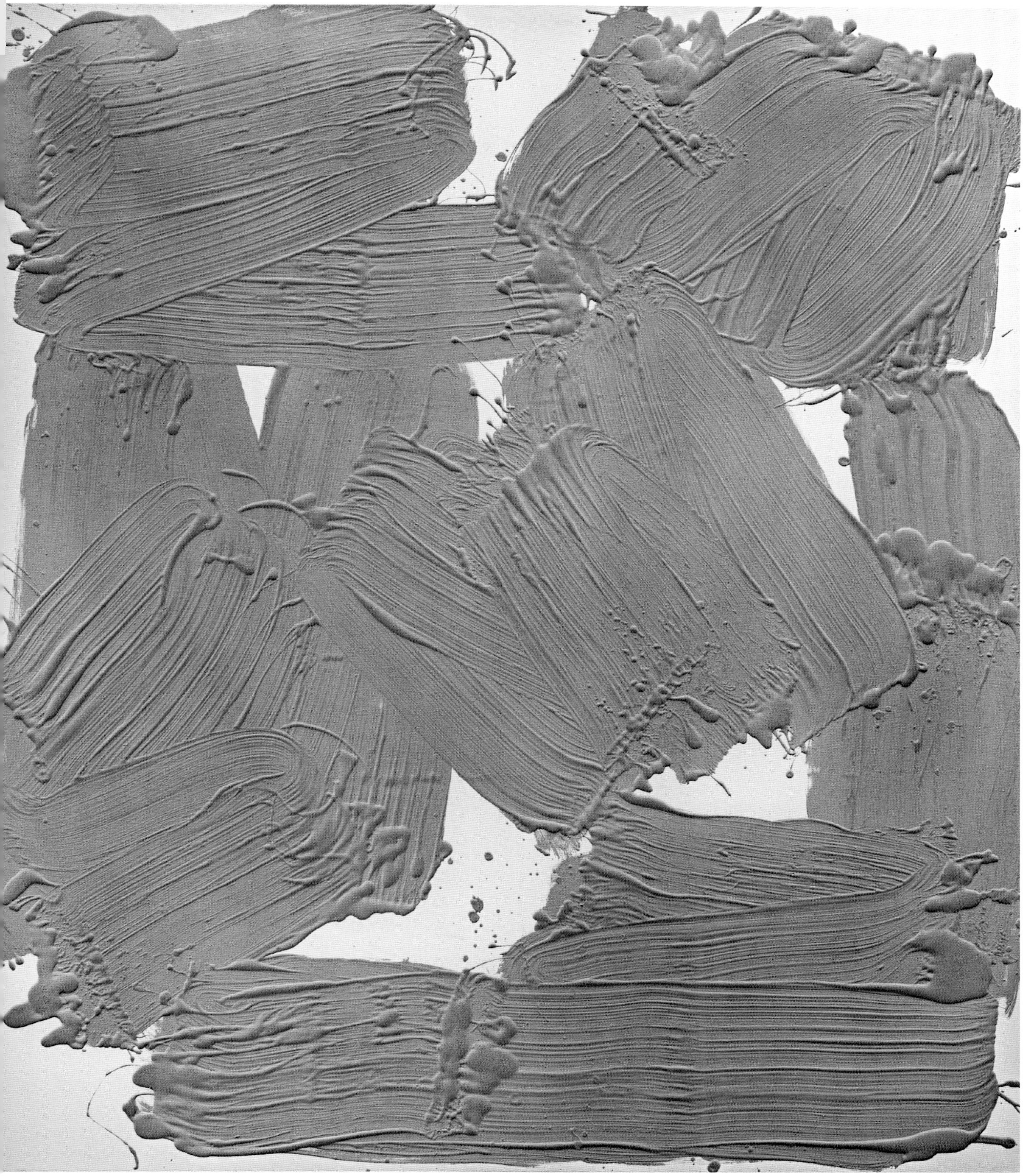

brushstrokes (gray) 2019 Acrylic on canvas 280 × 250 cm Bonn

Vera Palme

Vera Palme paints in an abstract manner, we think at first. While works that are being exhibited in Bonn and Chemnitz were produced not very long ago, the paintings on canvas that are being shown in Wiesbaden are completely new. And they show something recognisable: containers with flowers in them. Perhaps it is necessary to see precisely these "new" works in order to look at earlier canvases by Palme and to realise that there was always something there, be it only a quotation, a reference, artistic mimicry. Abstract painting is still one of the forms of contemporary art that apparently remains "more difficult" to communicate. And unlike the tradition of developing the one true painting style, Vera Palme's approach is more expansive. She explores, is restless, refuses to be limited to a single style, resists being forced into a specific canvas format. With regard to the colours of her works it is similar; dull tones and an earthy palette dominate her individual works.

And then there are these moments which are different. Moments which transform a surface into a landscape, a relief into a frame, a shadow into an accent. Palme's canvases may seem classical at first sight, may recall a painting style of past times, but they use this moment to teach us a lesson, to make us look more carefully. The works from the series *The Owner* are dominated by dark colours: with deep shades of brown applied thickly or "smokily filtered", they work with contours and hint at frame elements as if they were attempting to record something or even pin it down, while in fact they are concealing the picture. The earlier works by Vera Palme from the year 2017 appear lighter and at the same time considerably more abstract. They seem to be moving in all directions at the same time, even though there are painterly attempts to limit this movement, to choreograph it. And now we see on the canvas these containers with flowers, all of which were produced in 2019. Here the artist's signature also becomes a visible part of the subject. "Palme" becomes a message, but the message remains abstract.

—— *Fabian Schöneich*

Vera Palme was born in 1983 in Frankfurt a. M. and currently lives and works there

Städelschule Frankfurt a. M. with Prof. Judith Hopf, 2017

2019 Die Marmory Show IV – Erratic Resistance, Deborah Schamoni, Munich (G)

2018 A rat, Swimming Pool, Sofia (S)

Colt Jonner's Desecration of Descent, Büro BDP, Berlin (with Elif Saydam) (S)

Towards A New Nepotism, Etablissement d'en Face, Brussels (G)

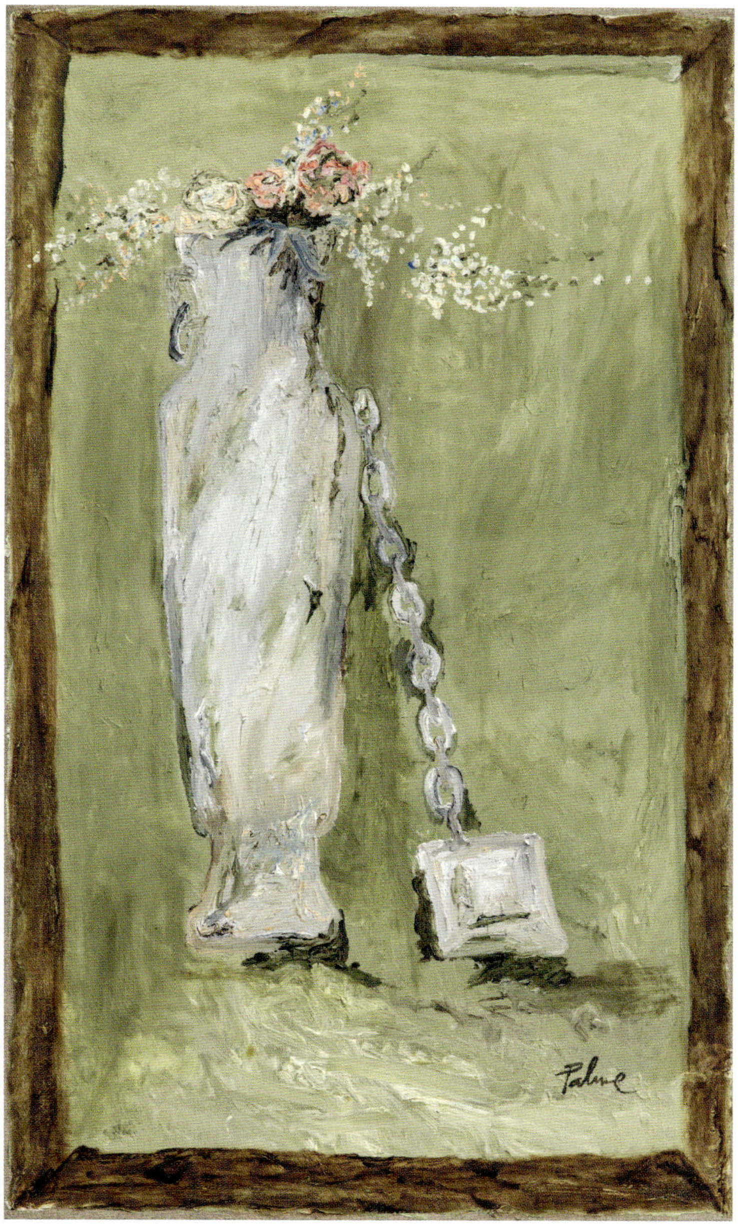

Still Life (II) 2019 Oil on burlap 95 × 55 cm Wiesbaden

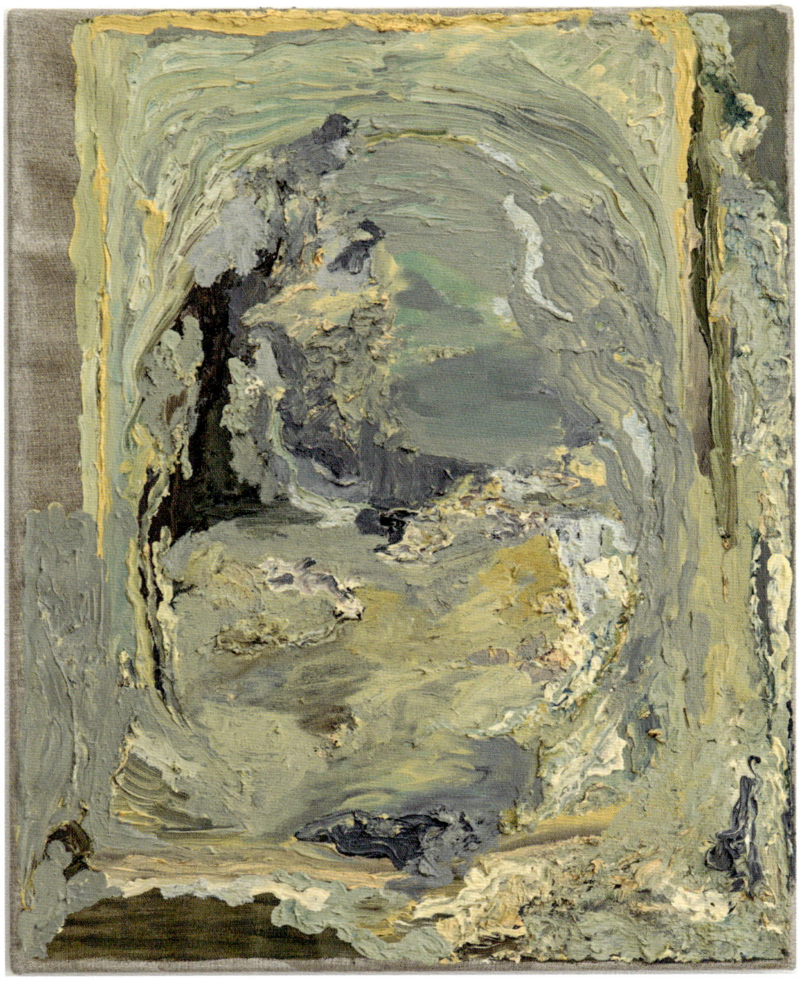

politics 2017 Oil on burlap 55 × 45 cm Chemnitz

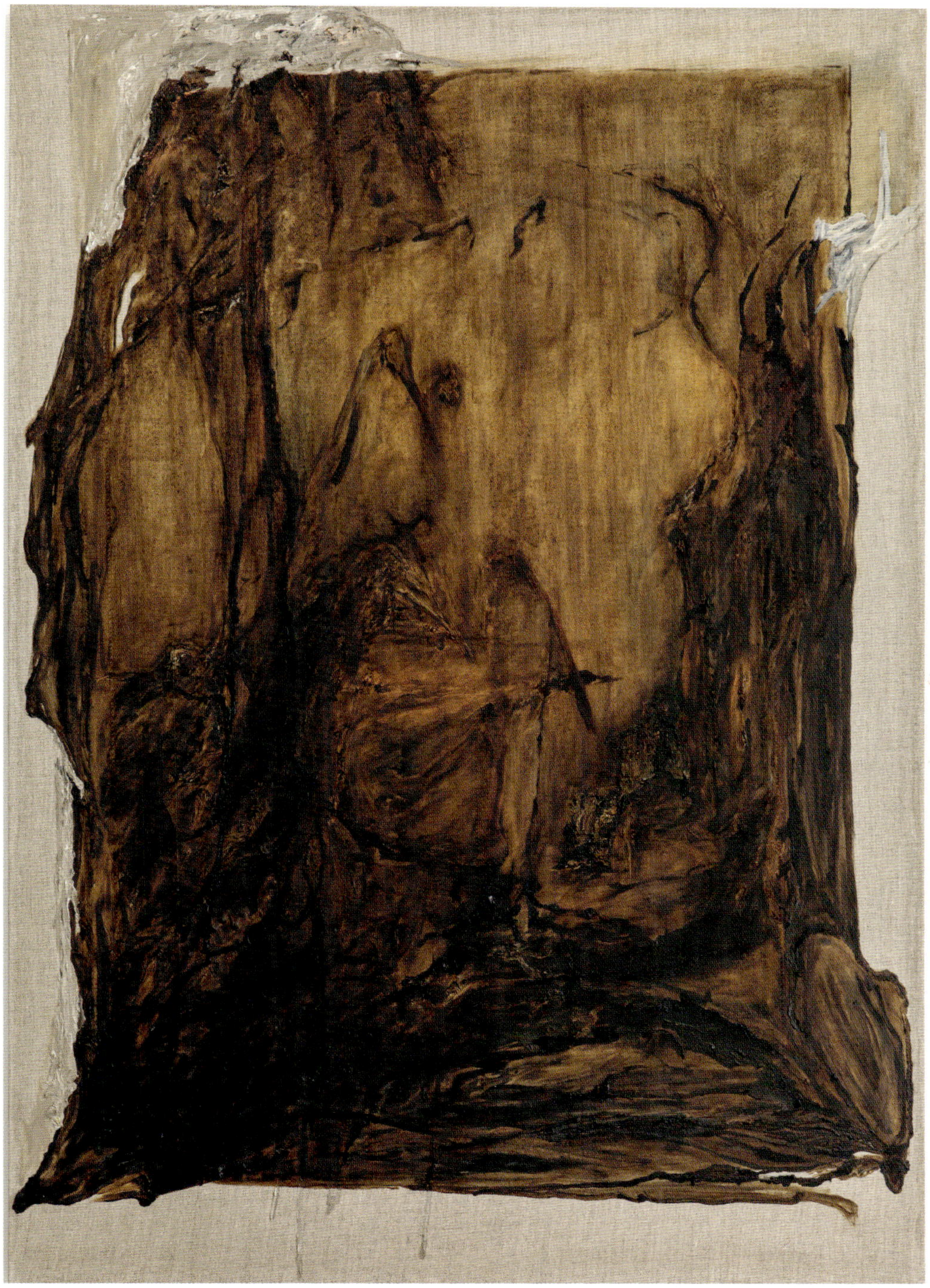

The Owner 2018 Oil on burlap 140 × 100 cm Bonn

Alexander Pröpster

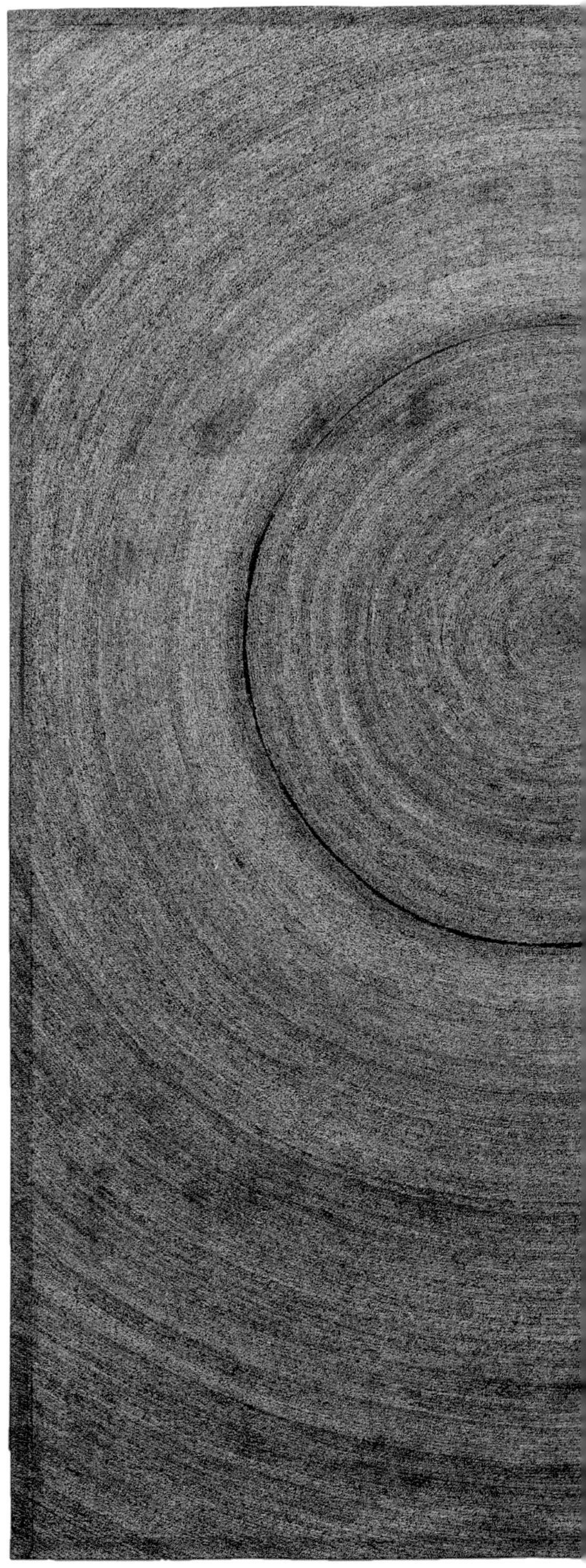

23 April
A woman is standing on the other side of the road. Since I have been here she has stood on the steps leading down to the suburban train like a large white rock. She is holding a sheaf of magazines under her arm. We exchange a look from time to time. Her eyes are calm and clear. I have never seen her talking to anyone, and whenever someone greets her she simply smiles back briefly. Today she didn't arrive until almost noon. She has dressed up and is wearing a red velvet dress. She came over and asked me why I was standing on the bridge. I explained. And then she introduced herself. I. told me that she stands here for 30 hours every week, not like the other Jehovah's Witnesses, who do 60 hours on duty. She simply couldn't manage that any more. I nodded. Then she went back to her steps again.
24 April
I. has the day off. But she has come all the same in order to bring me some chocolate eggs. She stood in front of me, beaming, and blinked against the bright sunlight. Then she handed over her gift and said with stoic gentleness, as if she had not spoken a single word for years: "Carry on – doing it!" I was deeply impressed and asked if I could paint her.
25 April
I. looks sad. The others have forbidden her to let me paint her. That afternoon two men in dark suits appeared. They made it clear to me that I should leave I. in peace and that they didn't want me to make fun of her. That was not at all how I had seen it. I looked across at I. and felt incredibly sorry for her.
The tone of the two men had been decidedly sharp at first, but then it suddenly changed. They knew why I was standing on the bridge. They wanted to tell the congregation about it and they invited me to attend their meeting that afternoon. In any case, there were about 15 people in the room. I was relieved that I. was among them. She stood there the way she always stood, and looked at me unmoved.
The whole thing was strange and I no longer knew whether I should feel sorry for her and her composure ... —— *Alexander Pröpster*

Alexander Pröpster was born in 1983 in Amberg and currently lives and works in Hamburg
Hochschule für Bildende Kunst Hamburg, Master of Fine Arts, 2016

2018 Straight, Crooked, Shaped – über die Linie, Galerie Marstall Ahrensburg (G)
Krawall im All, Künstlerhaus Meatzel, Hamburg (G)
2017 salondergegenwart, Hamburg (G)
7 Walks in the Woods, Gesellschaft für zeitgenössische Konzepte (Kunstverein Kiel), Struxdorf (G)

alexander-proepster.com

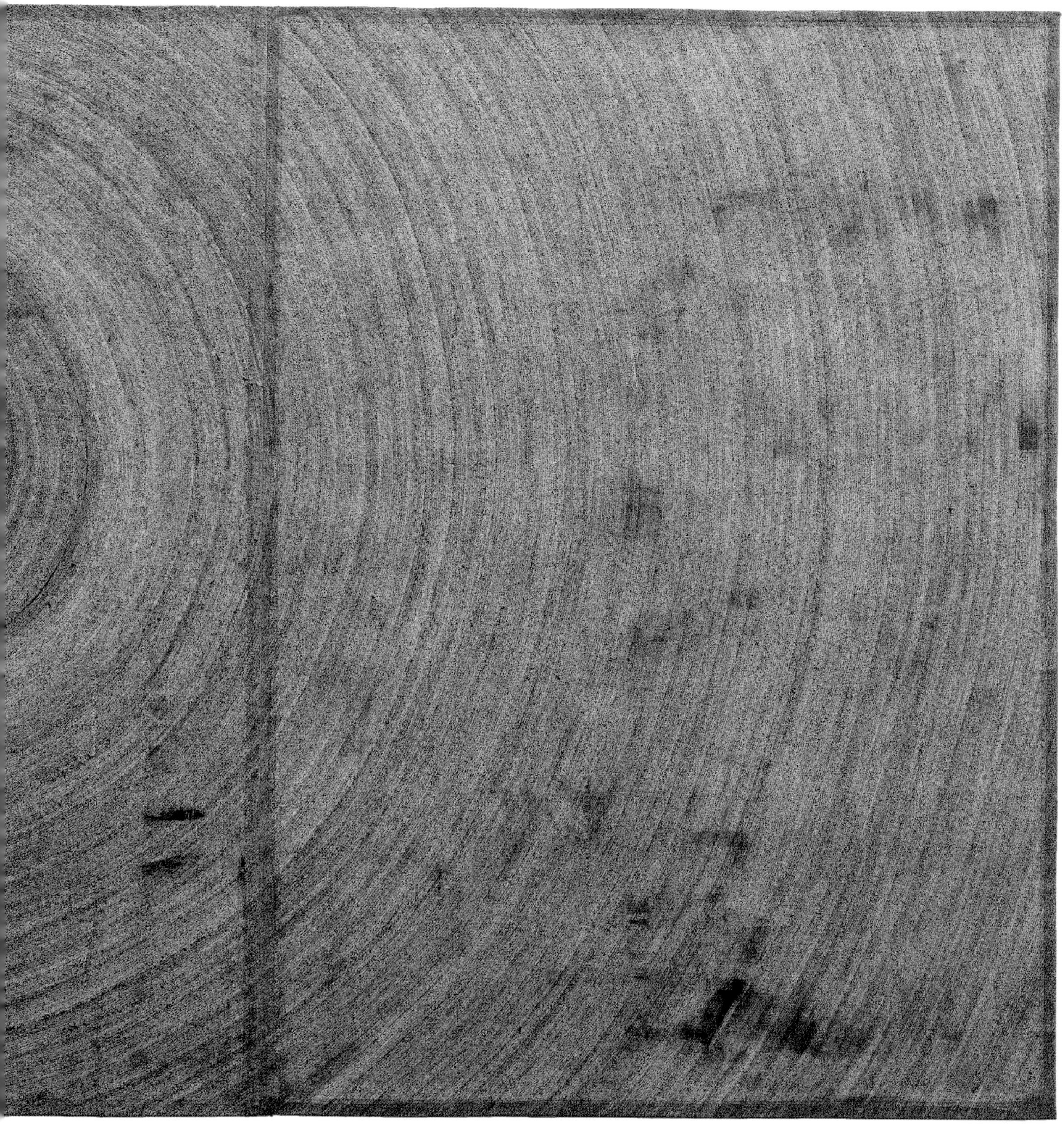

Holzwegbeschreibung (Nr. 510) 2018 Oil on paper 210 × 300 cm Wiesbaden

üt oder jüt (Nr. 451) 2016 Oil on paper 100 × 70 cm Bonn

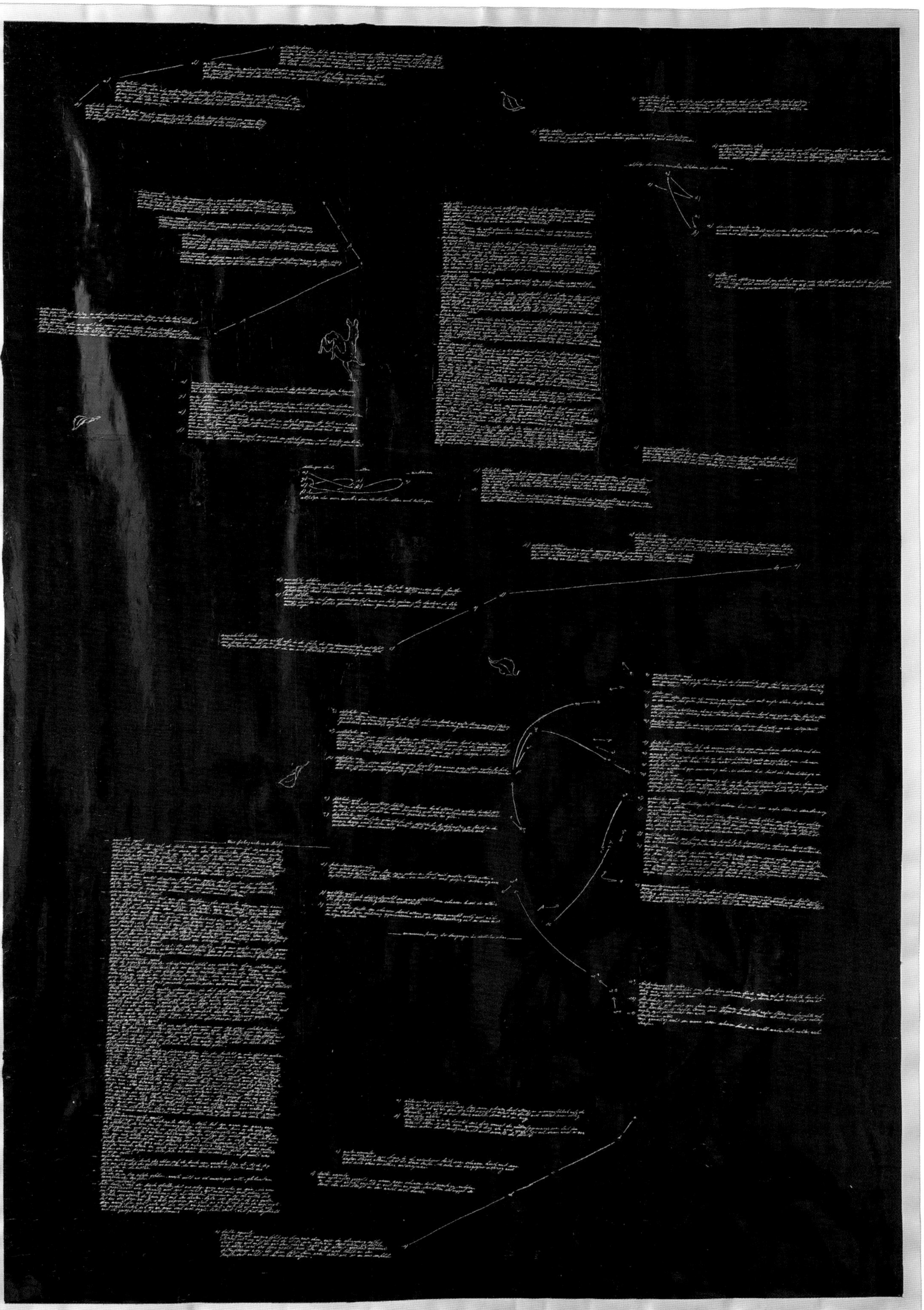

Holzwegbeschreibung (Nr. 512) 2019 Oil on paper 210 × 150 cm Chemnitz

Franziska Reinbothe

The black square has slipped out of the frame. It is hanging there "loosely", bulging and curling. There is no doubt about it: here it is a matter of all or nothing – as is always the case with Franziska Reinbothe.
Initially, it's a question, quite literally, of the whole object "picture": paint, canvas, stretcher frame. Painted canvases are unclamped again entirely or in part, folded over, stitched, gathered, or even cut right out of the frame and rolled up. Stretcher frames are exposed, broken, sawn up and the entire picture is simply folded up. Reinbothe reveals what can be seen at the backs of the paintings, their innermost anatomy. But as if that were too much exposure, she withdraws from the inquisitive gaze (sometimes more, sometimes less) the thing that normally forms the principal element of a picture – the front of the canvas, on which the painting is executed.
And yet that is quite evidently precisely what this is about: painting. Franziska Reinbothe experiments with paint as a material by a process of trial and error. She mixes masses of colour together like an alchemist and applies them to the canvas. Here, too, she is prepared to resort to any means available. Just at the point when the painting would presumably be complete, she simply continues in a kind of delaying moment, giving the body of the picture a new form by destroying the panel picture. Here, too, it is a case of do or die, because the process is a highly risky one: just a bit too much or too little would destroy the work. The artist revels in the experimental game which is always also a questioning of the material and the painting as such and which is characterised by apparent contradictions. And so it stands to reason that above all the works in which Reinbothe distances herself the farthest from traditional painting, by stretching transparent fabrics over stretcher frames like coloured glazes, are the ones that most closely resemble traditional panel pictures. Each of her works not only poses a question about the picture, but at the same time suggests a possible answer. Each one necessitates a change of perspective and is thus also an expansion of the possibilities of painting and perception.
—— *Kim Behm*

Franziska Reinbothe was born in 1980 in Berlin and currently lives and works in Leipzig

Hochschule für Grafik und Buchkunst Leipzig
Meisterschüler with Prof. Ingo Meller, 2013

2019 bei genauer Betrachtung, Kunstverein Lüneburg (S, C)
redefine relief, Kunstverein Schwerin (G)

2018 Kräfte messen, Museum Wilhelm Morgner, Soest (S, C)
Backstage – The rear Side, Galerie Mehdi Chouakri, Berlin, Galerie Thomas Rehbein, Cologne and Gallery Sofie Van de Velde, Antwerp (G)

franziska-reinbothe.de

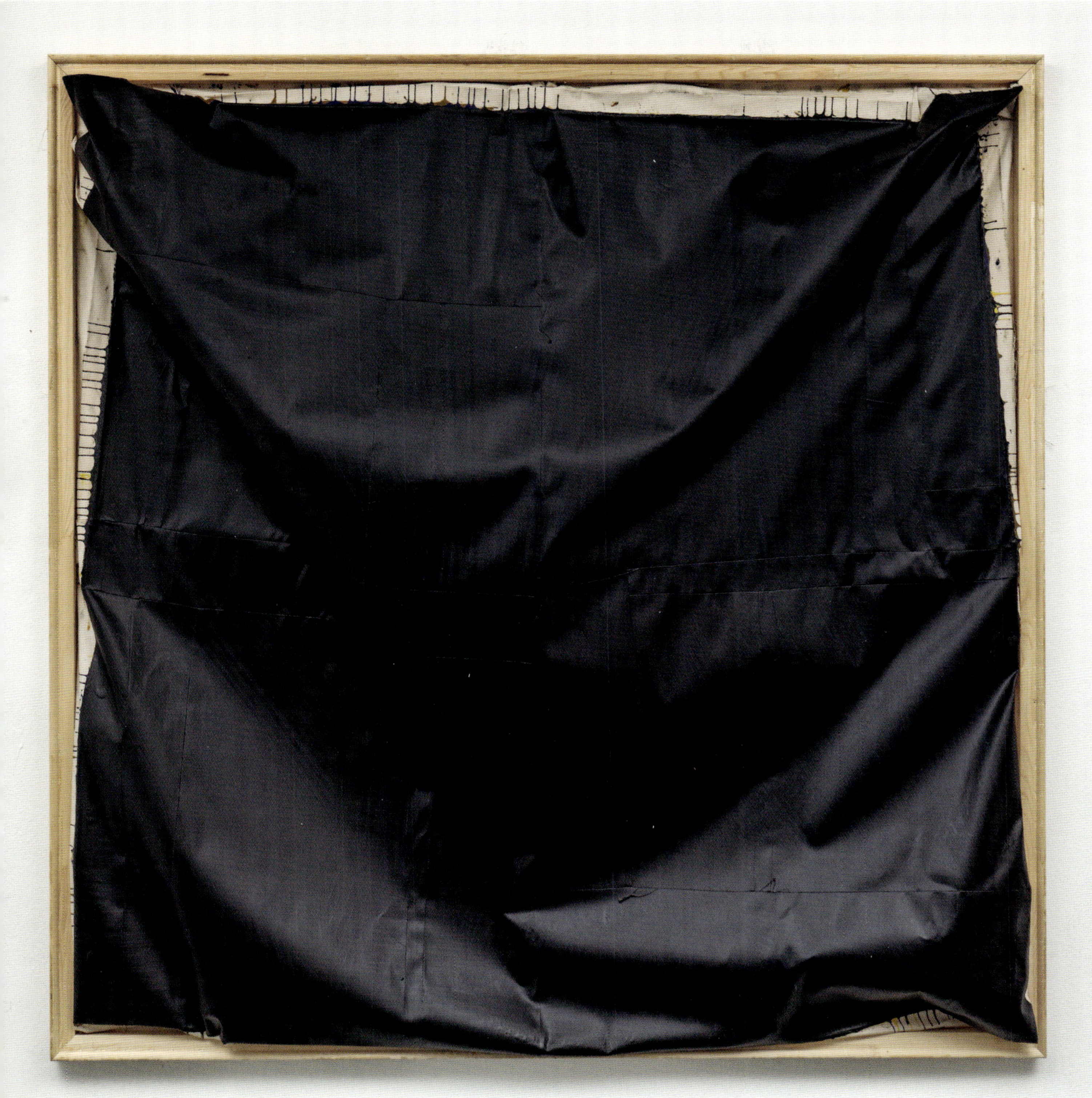

Schwarz, in legerer Haltung 2014 Acrylic on canvas, yarn ca. 180 × 180 × 20 cm Chemnitz

Untitled

2016

Acrylic on canvas

80 × 60 cm

Bonn

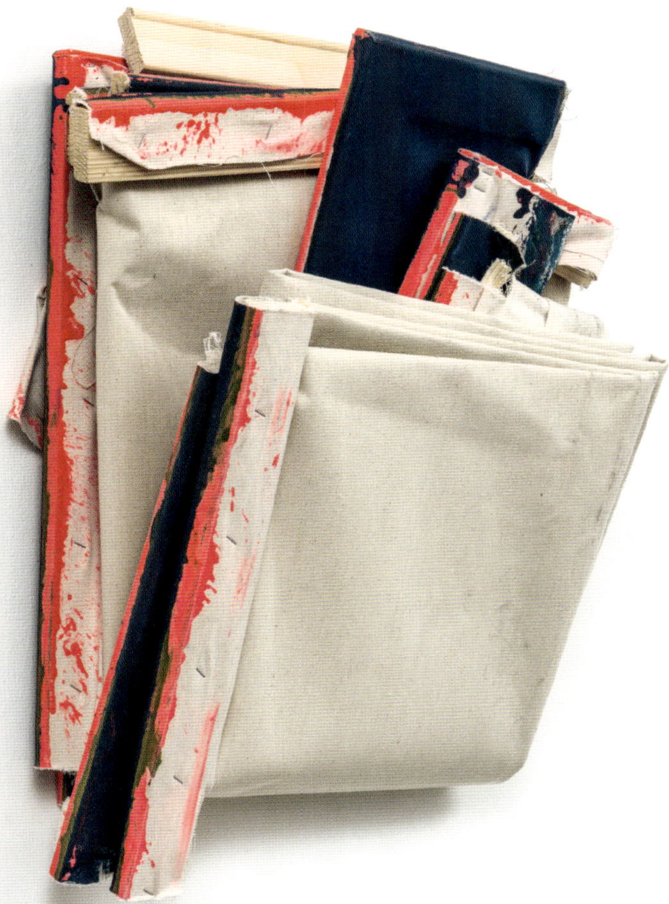

Untitled

2016/2018

Acrylic and forestry marker on canvas

ca. 58 × 44 × 18 cm

Wiesbaden

Daniel Rossi

The power of the material

Layers lie exposed; the depth draws us into the picture; energies build up at transition points. Daniel Rossi's painting finds its focal points at thresholds. It is based in the material and exposes it at the same time. It keeps the zone between fabric and form elastic. The contouring can be read in the setup and the dismantling. Colours enter into flexible relationships as organoid forms. Matter acts in the picture space not as a rigid substance, but as a field of relations full of tensions. Figure and ground lie on the same level of the material and change their position in the tactile eye of the viewer. The manual space and the optical space elide.
The painter relinquishes part of the authorship to the material. Assembling, dismantling, re-assembling – in the transformation of the material the elements remain a fragment and yet strive towards a figurative unity. Rossi acts as a non-authorial presence between a self-organisation of the material, the fluid entity of the work and the fantasies of the viewer. In this exchange, figurations appear which are engraved into the gestures of the picturesque and the memory of the viewer. Pure presence releases representations.
Figuration and abstraction, material action and the artist's hand, fragment and unit, composition and deconstruction, material as medium, subject and object – various painting dialogues are included in the layers of Rossi's pictures, which strive in format towards the dissolution of boundaries. The Italian artist is filled with pictorial traditions and activates them subliminally in autonomous painting. His pictures are rooted in the empirical. His industrial material is saturated with society. His painting is filled with tradition and yet entirely topical. Simultaneity and the afterlife of the pictures replace a modernistic development concept. Daniel Rossi's art proclaims the power of the real, which includes being, knowledge and consciousness. —— *Rainer Beßling*

Daniel Rossi was born in 1985 in Vicenza (Italy) and currently lives and works in Bremen

Hochschule für Künste Bremen with Prof. Stephan Baumkoetter and Prof. Martina Klein, Master of Fine Arts, 2010–2017

Akademie der bildenen Künste Wien with Prof. Erwin Bohatsch, 2015

2019 So wie wir sind, Museum Weserburg, Bremen (G)

2018 Casa Odahara & Rossi, Galerie für Gegenwartskunst, Bremen (G)

Entangled Tales, Rupert, Vilnius (G)

2017 TRUNK, Kunstverein Lüneburg (G)

danielrossi.net

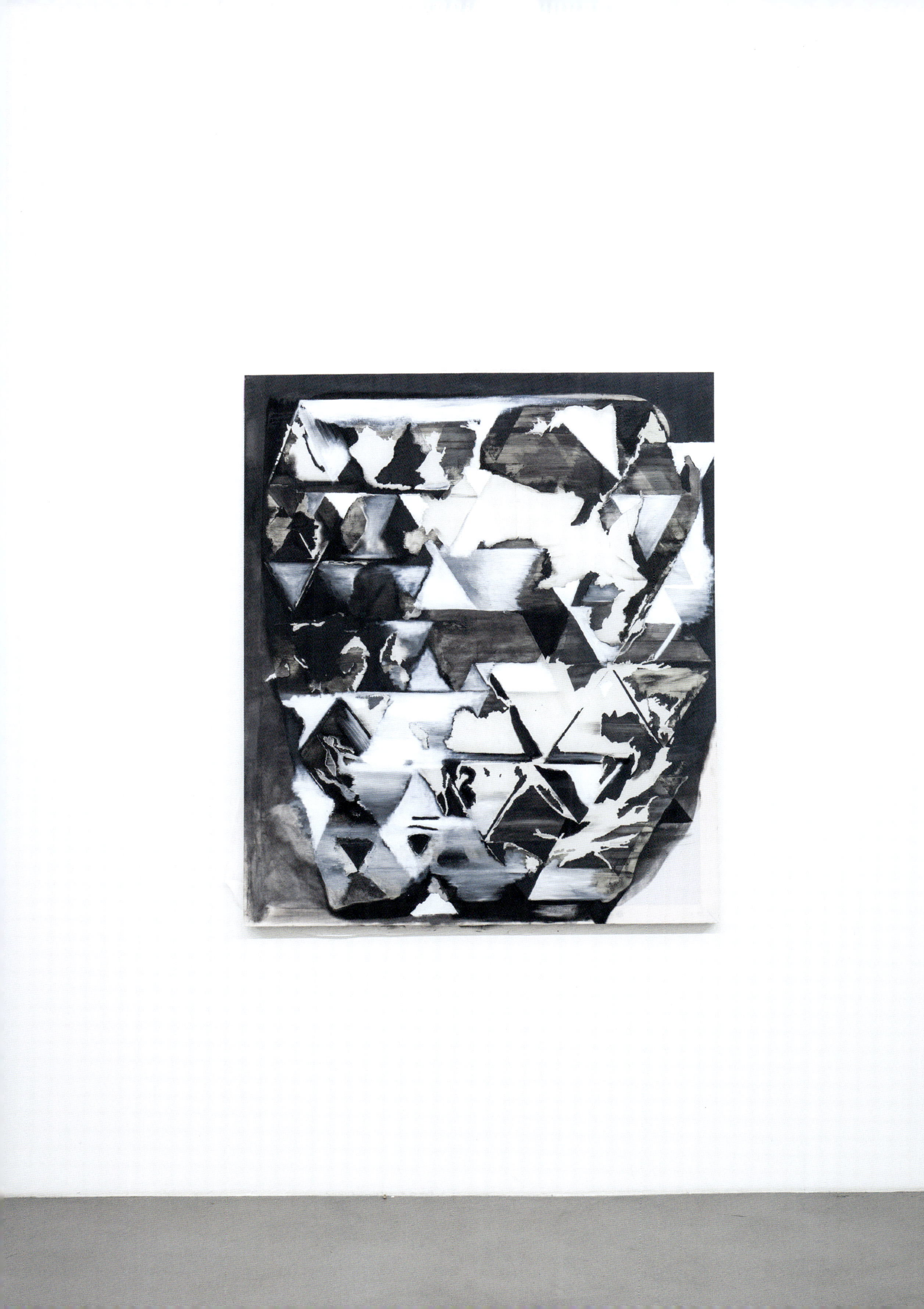

Untitled (Reversed) 2018 Acrylic and oil on polyester 140 × 120 cm Wiesbaden

Untitled (Caritas) 2017 Acrylic, oil, latex and lacquer on polyester 111 × 111 cm Bonn

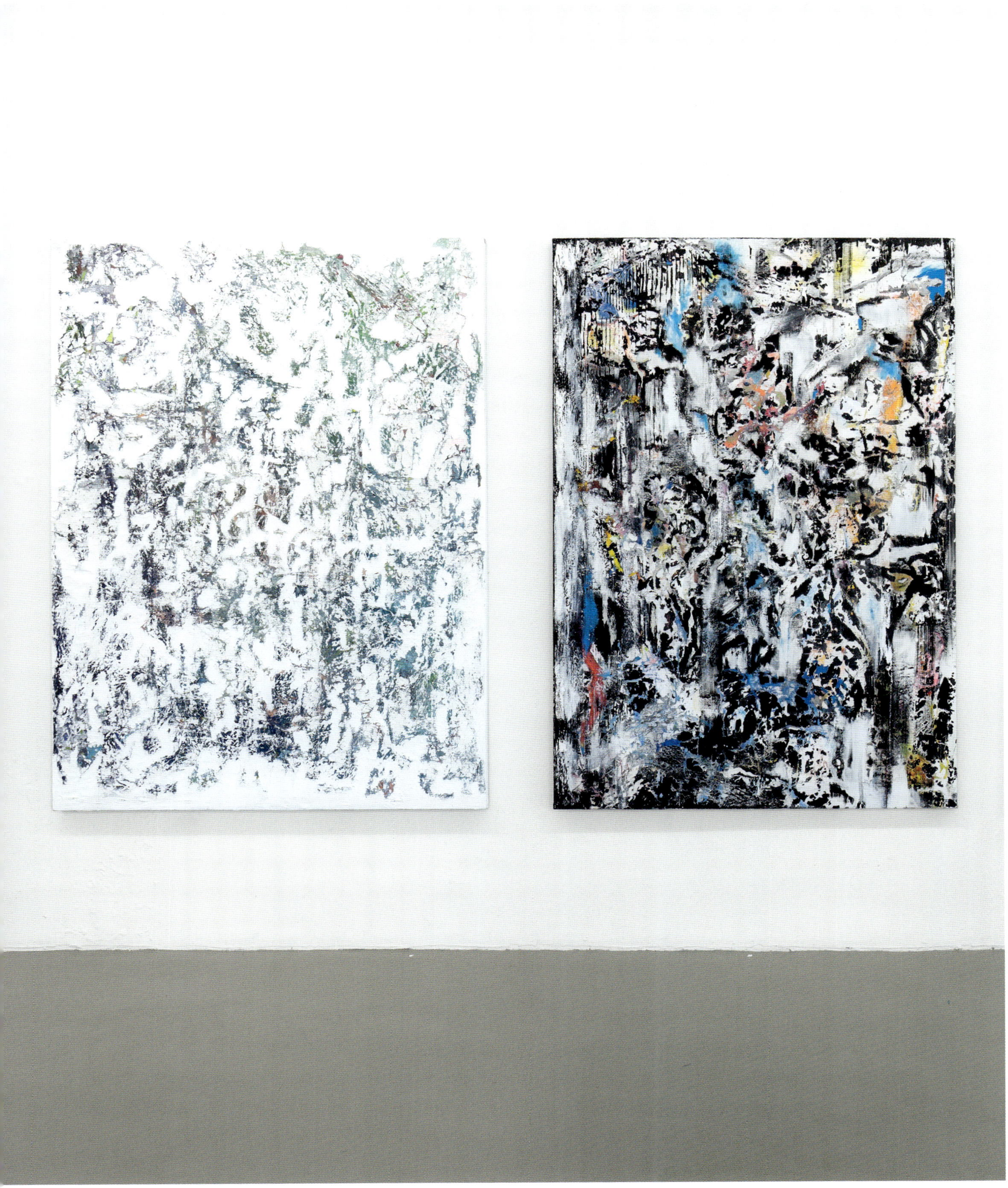

Untitled (Destruction, Creation) 2018 Acrylic, oil and lacquer on wool 205 × 160 cm Chemnitz
2017 210 × 147 cm

Markus Saile

Fluff on retina

The works of Markus Saile suggest a change of medium with regard to painting. The line has become a trace. Paint has become turpentine. Painting has become unstable because turpentine, used to thin oil paint, has separated it from its undercoat, allowing it to slide, slip, fly across the smooth surface. The effect penetrates the eye and could have its counterpart there: fluff on retina. Moments of seeing which have nothing real and nothing unreal before them, but rather an indescribably fleeting, material something which appears to be very close. The formats vary, are frequently small, often eye images, with only the larger ones as body images. Sometimes they act contrary to the idea of good picture proportions in painting, with shapes that are almost square or nearly DIN format.
There is a chalk ground which creates a perpetually slippery surface. And at the same time this smooth surface produces a background radiance. In line with the observation that new media change the view of the old ones and also of the present-day production and further development of these old ones as well, the paintings of Markus Saile can additionally be understood as a production of screens. They show subjects of paintings which are to a certain extent dried-out moments of states. They are frozen, as it were, and toy at the same time with the reference to film and its close-up, the close focusing. The chalk ground is an old medium which now brings a present-day mediality into Saile's paintings. This chalk ground always shines through and every streak or form which Saile produces today appears against it as if on an operating table, in a microscope or also in a detail of a painting that refuses to decide whether it aims to be abstract or not. —— *Susanne Titz*

Markus Saile was born in 1981 in Stuttgart and currently lives and works in Cologne

Braunschweig University of Art
Meisterschüler with Prof. Frances Scholz, 2011

2019 STRABAG Artaward International, STRABAG Kunstforum, Vienna (G)
Köln um halb acht, Temporary Gallery, Cologne (G)

2018 face my boost by your ShotSpotter, Hardspace, Basel (G)

2017 time is the longest distance, Galerie Nathalie Halgand, Vienna, with Talisa Lallai (S)

markussaile.de

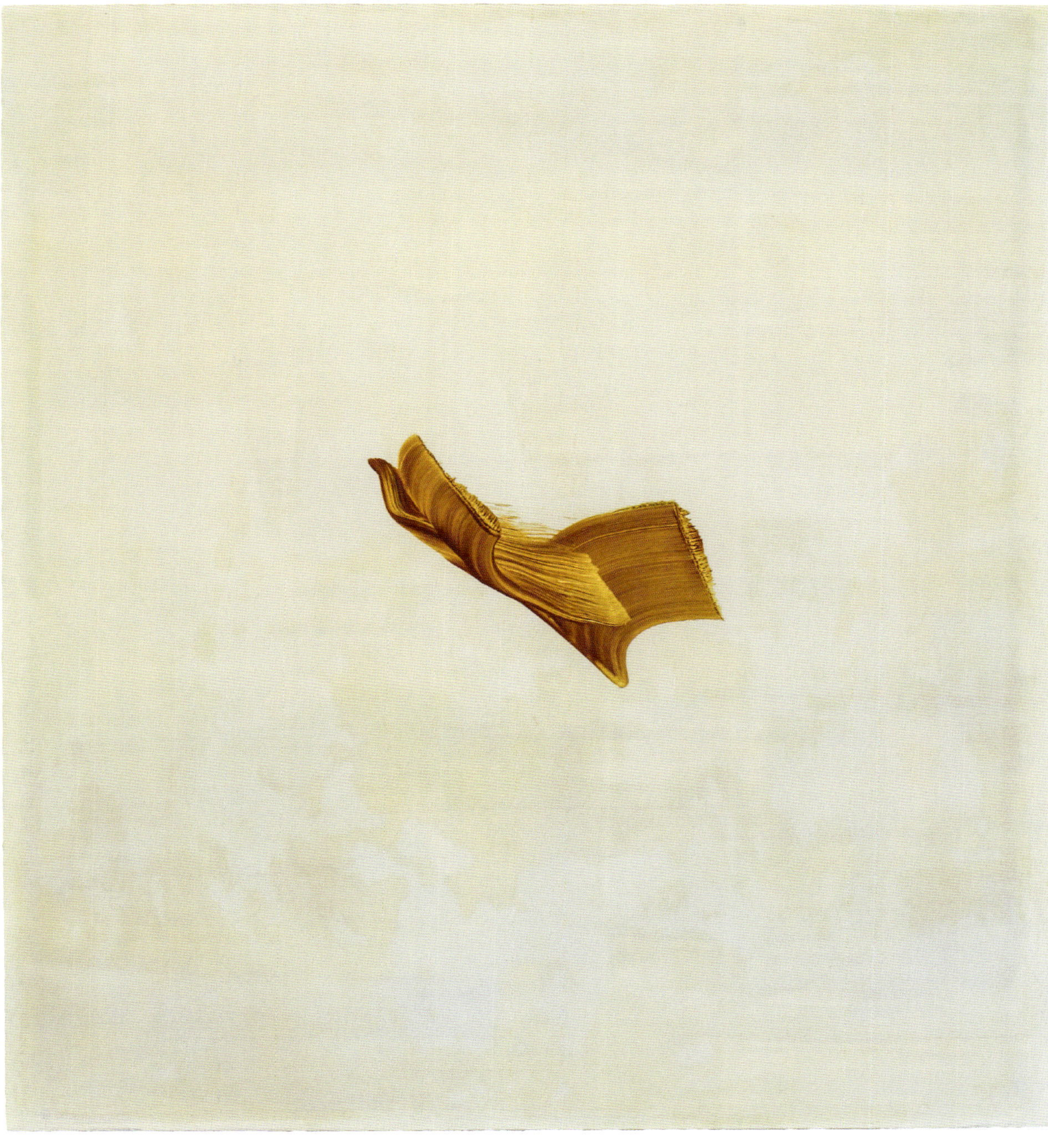

Untitled 2019 Oil on wood 81 × 76 cm Bonn

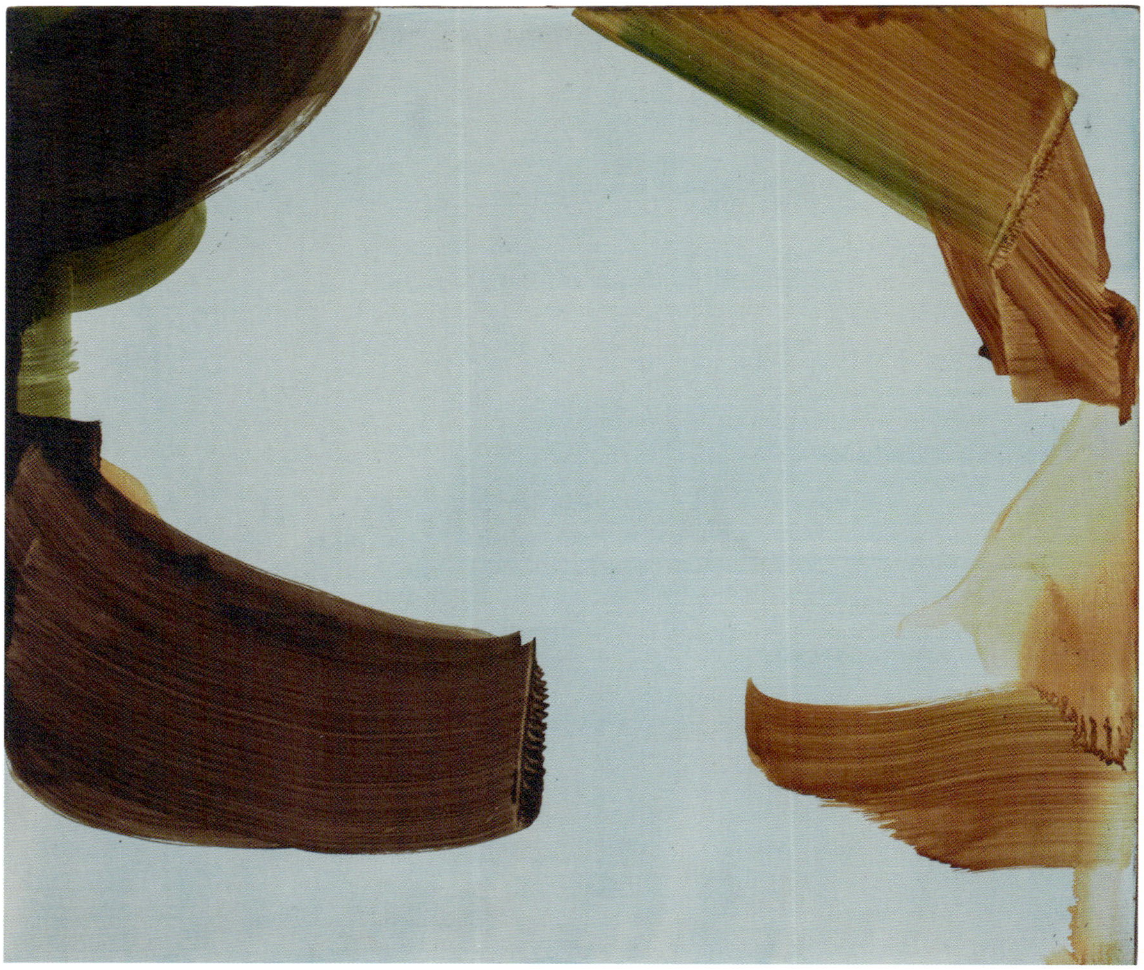

Untitled 2018 Oil on wood 33 × 39 cm Chemnitz

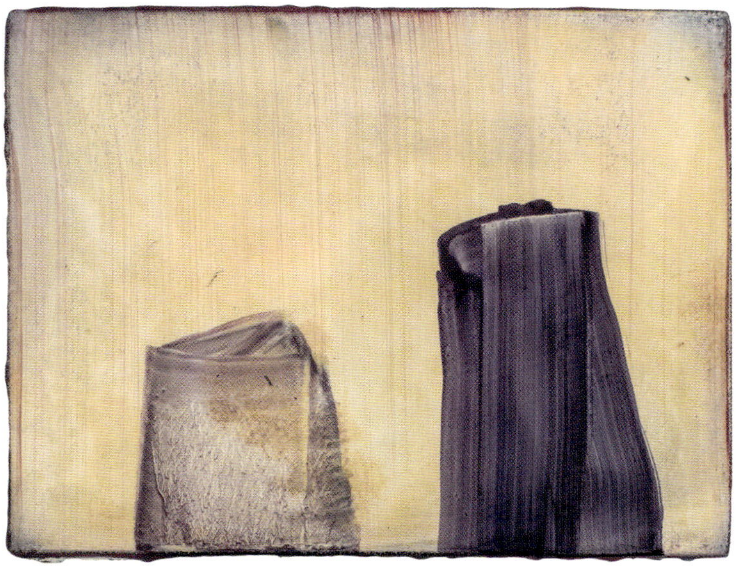

Untitled   2019   Oil on wood   17 × 23 cm   Wiesbaden

Moritz Schleime

Painting – stirred and shaken

Moritz Schleime preserves his memories of childhood in a small collection of photographs which he has given the titles *Kinderzimmer Ost* (Child's Room East) and *Kinderzimmer West* (Child's Room West). As a small child, his smile reveals how he loved to play, while as a teenager he can be seen rehearsing his performance as a rock star. In 1991 Nirvana released the hymn *Smells Like Teen Spirit.* Moritz Schleime was thirteen years old and very receptive.
In April of this year, the literary supplements were full of reports on Nirvana and the Grunge Sound in commemoration of the 25th anniversary of the death of the singer Kurt Cobain. The raw Seattle Sound, characterised not by artificial studio technology but by the resonance of a garage space, found its battle cry in Grunge, which means "grubby", no less.
During 2018, Moritz Schleime worked on a group of works showing painters in their studios. The floors are covered with the remains of viscous paint, which probably make a noise approximating to the enunciation of the word "Grunge" with every step. The painters portrayed by Schleime resemble Captain Sparrow from the film series *Pirates of the Caribbean*, but they have sacrificed his stand-up creativity. Here they look either pensive or mesmerised, always screened off and yet in danger of falling asleep in front of the canvas. But then they are surprised by the way that paintbrush and paint develop their own dynamic, recalling the sorcerer's apprentice who fails to tame the powers he has conjured up and turns away in despair, as if the sleep of reason had transformed the artist himself into a monster. Since Schleime always adds a judicious pinch of humour as a binding agent, the comic aspect outweighs the tragedy. The artist in his studio decorates his work on canvas with a chorus of voices and leaves a colourful array of pictures which paper the walls of the room – although he really seems to be searching for the firm outline of the pure figure.
Moritz Schleime gives his pictures exotic-sounding titles. They are the names of cocktails, descriptions of mixed drinks in which the alcohol is combined with the variety of a fruit basket and the world of herbs. And as a special tonic the extended family of cocktails includes vodka with beef bouillon – a plain, powerful statement. —— *Hans-Werner Schmidt*

Moritz Schleime was born in 1978 in Berlin and currently lives and works in Berlin and Leipzig

Weißensee Kunsthochschule Berlin, Diploma and Meisterschüler with Prof. Hanns Schimansky and Prof. Werner Liebmann in Painting and Fine Art, 2004

2018 Royal Bermuda Yachtclub, Laden für Nichts, Leipzig (S)

Salon Hansa, Johann König Berlin, St. Agnes, Berlin (G)

Mother and sun, Rosenhang Museum, Weilburg, with Cornelia Schleime (S)

2016 The Virgin Suicides, Jarmuschek & Partner, Berlin (S)

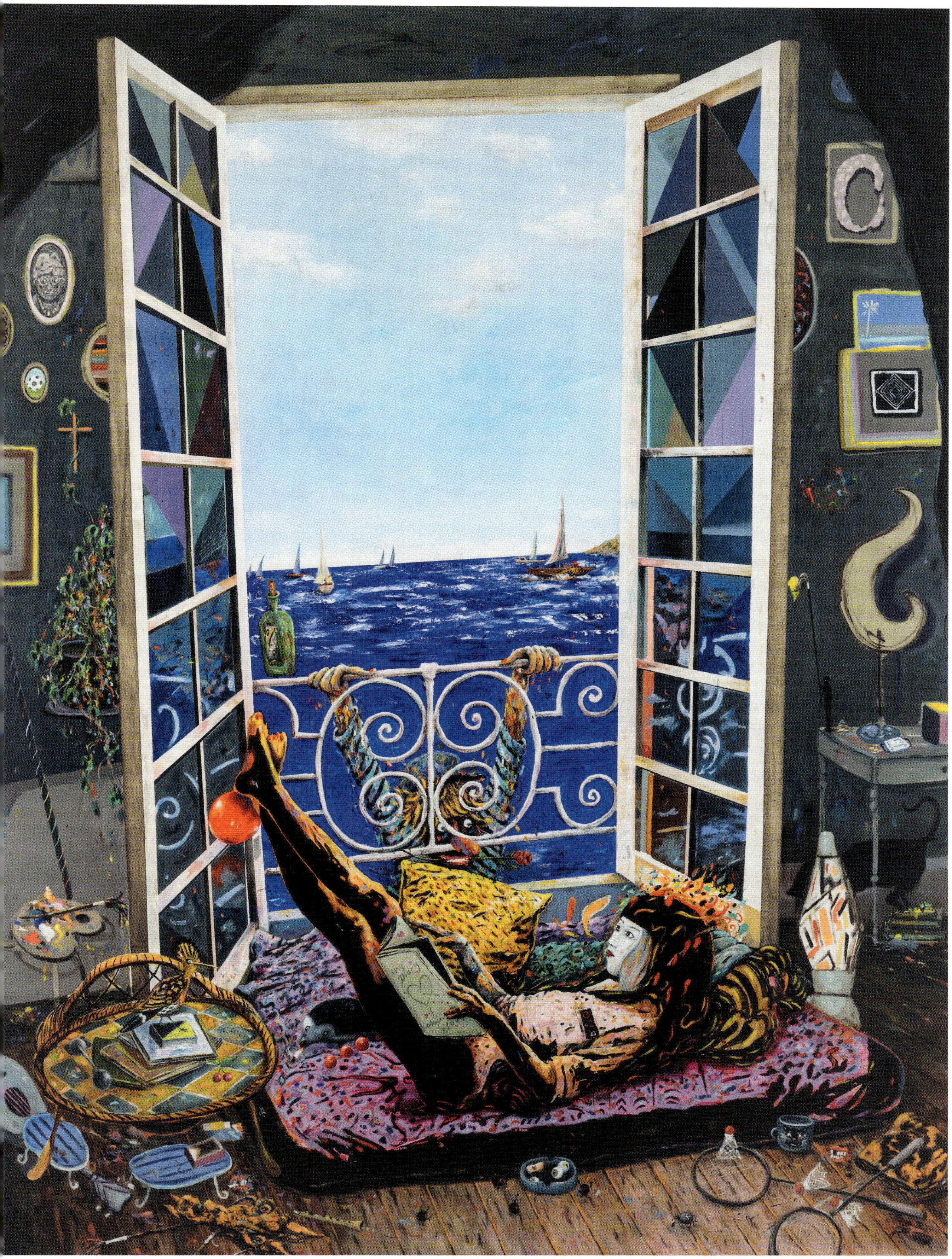

Keine Pizza auf Ibiza (The Diary) 2018 Oil on canvas 250 × 190 cm Wiesbaden

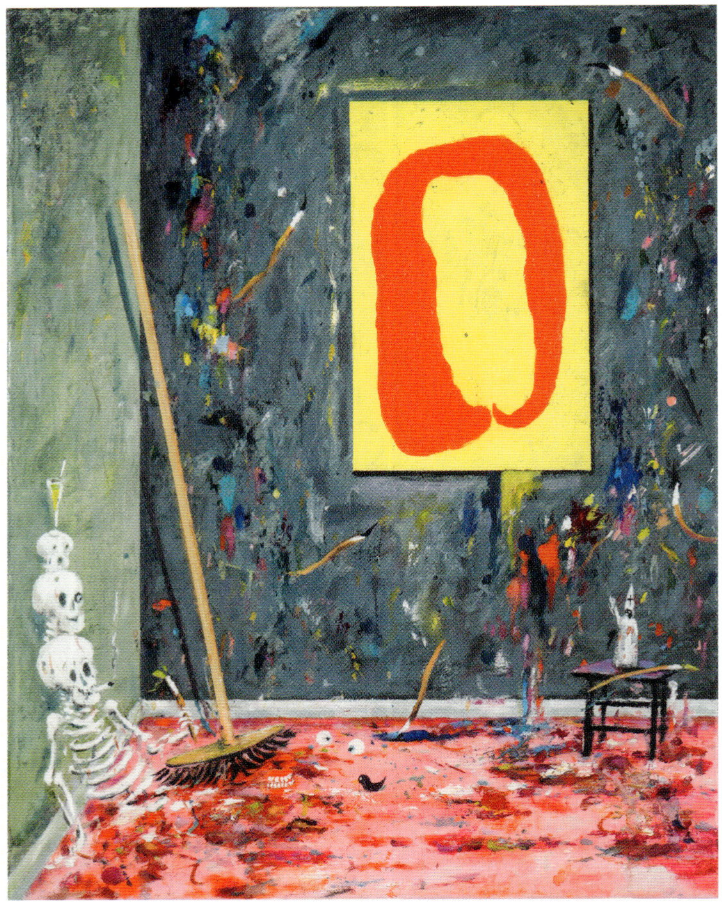

Painters Corner XI

2019

Oil on canvas

50 × 40 cm

Bonn

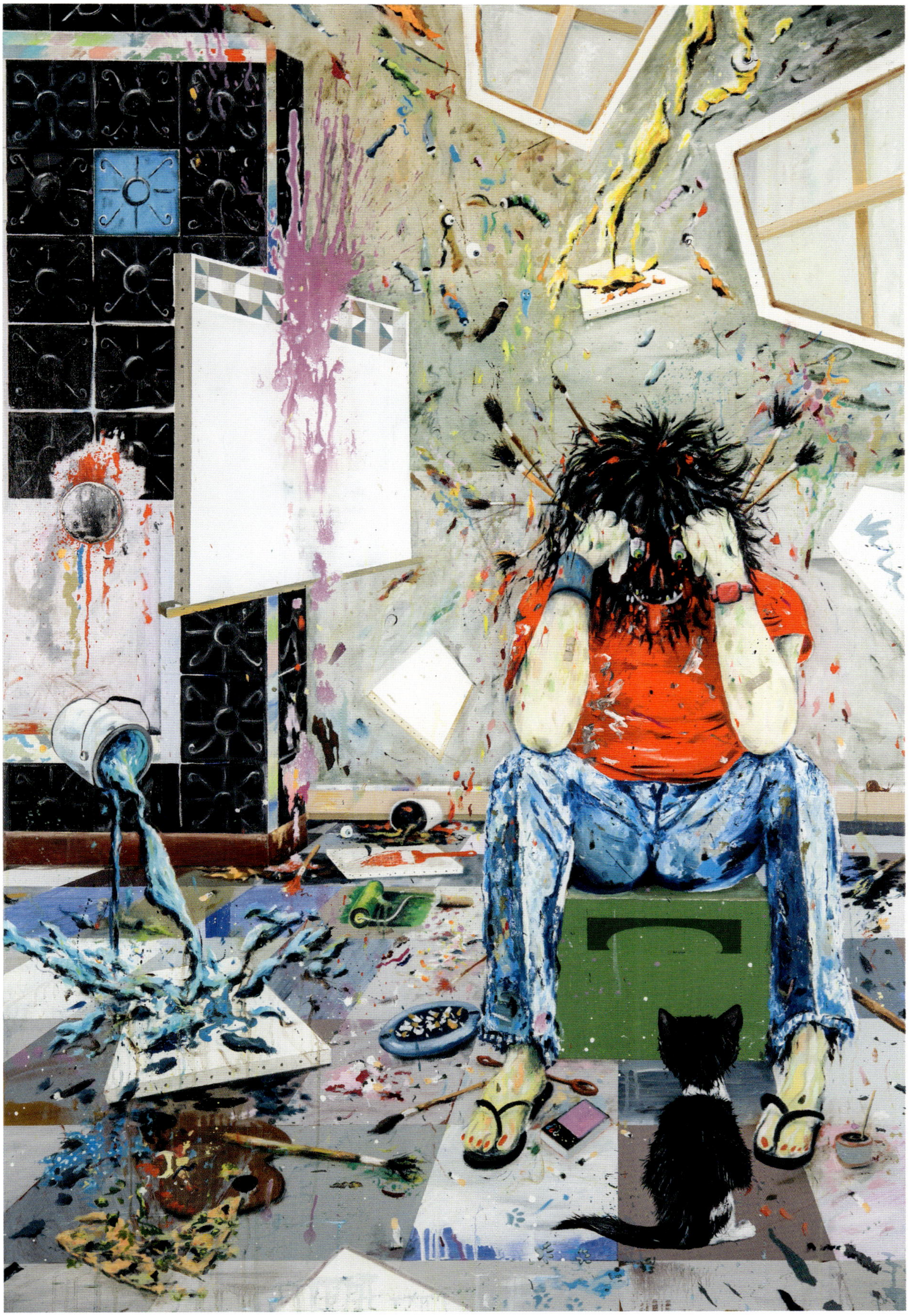

Lazyland (den Arsch voll Angst) 2018 Oil on canvas 180 × 125 cm Chemnitz

Jana Schröder

Spontacts – Kinkrustations – Kadlites

Painting is the result of a dialogue of colour and surface on a background. The colour spreads out until it encounters another area of colour or the edge of the picture carrier. The edges are points of tension and friction which can vary from flowing into each other and gently touching to sharp, hard boundaries. A line is a long, narrow area with relatively small dimensions but a maximal expansion along its length. The line as a reduced area is always the start of a drawing, reduces the painting to the same. These observations apply in particular to Jana Schröder's painting.
Spontacts are characterised by the strong light and dark contrast of the blue lines on a white surface and are clearly an analogy to a free drawing which acquires significance through the format and brushstroke and thus becomes a statement. In *Kinkrustations,* the line solidifies to become a relief and stands out largely – albeit not as regards colour – from the depths of the midnight blue surface. The greatest possible contrast of line to surface is thus consistently continued through the materiality. The endless depths of the colour blue are limited only by the format of the picture, but in thought and feeling extend far beyond these boundaries.
The affirmation of the colour yellow determines Schröder's most recent series *Kadlites.* Against the energetic attraction of the homogenous yellow surface, the lines assert themselves like dark, vocal traces. The graphite lines, which here consolidate to form a grid structure – towards the second painting surface, away from the drawing – dominate the dynamic of the pictures. Whereby it is also a question of a promise – the assumption which lies behind the depth of the lines, broken by the expanse of the light background, which forces its way involuntarily into the foreground. Inexhaustible, the tension field that arises through the liveliness of the lines together with the self-assurance of the prominent yellow is experienced repeatedly when viewing the pictures. —— *Anna Friedel*

Jana Schröder was born in 1983 in Brilon and currently lives and works in Düsseldorf

Kunstakademie Düsseldorf with Prof. Albert Oehlen, 2009

2019 Kadlites RS6-17, T293, Rome (S)
Kadlites, Nino Mier Gallery, Los Angeles (S)

2018 Kadlites and Kinkrustations, Natalia Hug, Cologne (S)

2017 Spontacts and Kinkrustations, Kunstverein Reutlingen (S)

janaschroeder.com

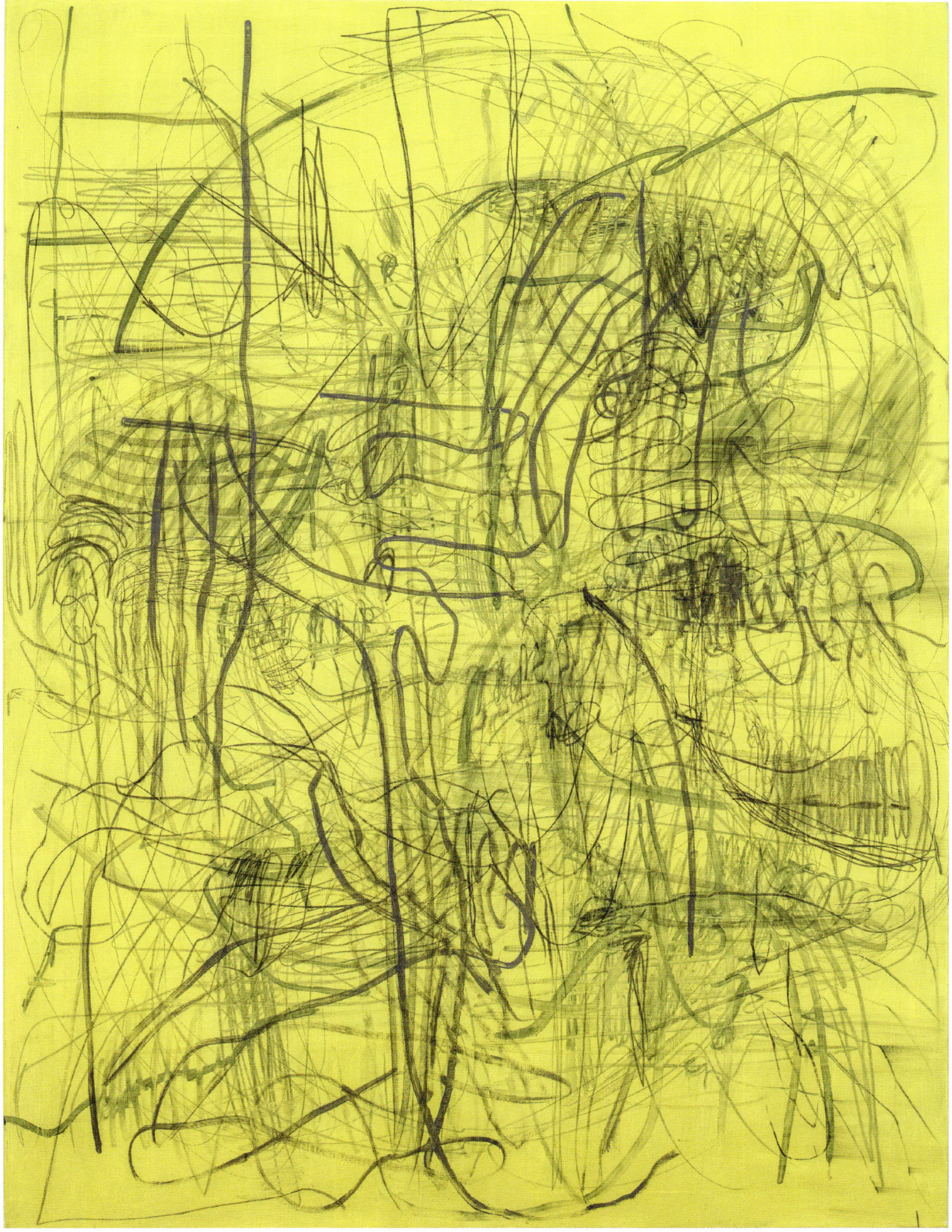

Kadlites M5 2017 Acrylic, graphite, and pencil and oil on canvas 200 × 155 cm Chemnitz

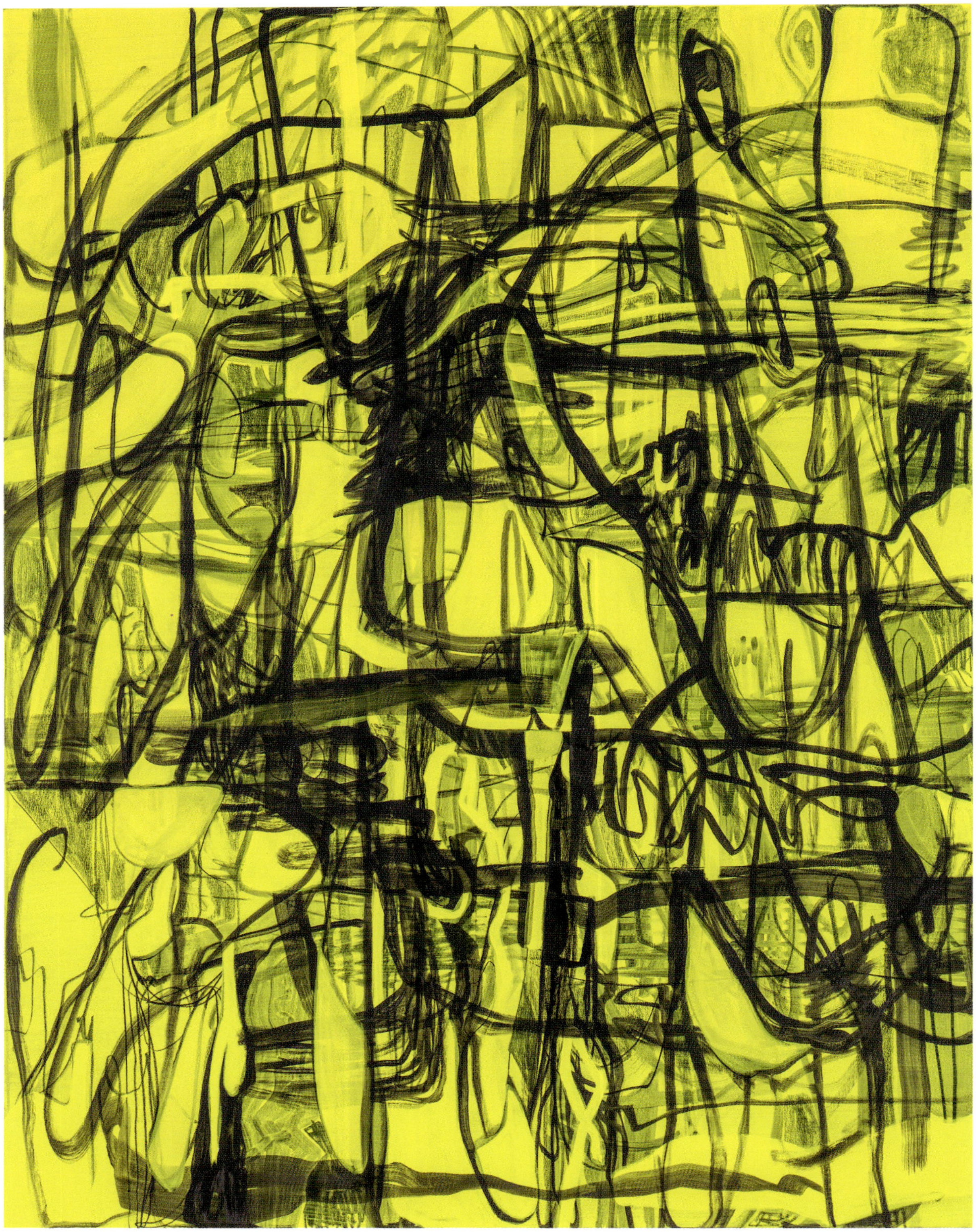

Kadlites M11 2018 Acrylic and graphite on canvas 200 × 160 cm Wiesbaden

Kinkrustation PB10 2017 Papier-mâché, acrylic and oil on canvas 240 × 200 cm Bonn

Daniel Schubert

The wind blows gently. The fabric does not move, but we can still feel it with our eyes. It comes and goes to envelop all things, the wind of light. Observing its actions seems logical and yet remote. When thoughts pause for a moment and the blessing of outward calm is added as well, it could well happen that our eyes glimpse not only his late works.

The colours lie on the surface of things – the colours are in the air. It is not entirely clear where they come from. Surface and air belong together and yet are so different. It is an offer of the colours and an offer of these pictures: to see both together. On the surface, the givens: stretcher frame, canvas, paints; in the air the coming and going – transitions and progressions, gestures and attrition, radiation and atmosphere.

The pictures look large as they face each other. They can still be carried alone. Then, on the wall, they open up expanses. Their spaces have been freed of many elements. Much can therefore come. With some, time it is already there: out of the centre, into the centre or beyond the centre. In some places, consolidations can be heard and then fall silent again. They have space for that and find support in the tranquil light of the picture. Which of its many names does Japanese have available for this blue-grey?

Painting takes note of what is already there and belongs to it: the structure of the stretcher frame, the texture of fabric and bubble wrap, the consistency of priming and painting media. Something lights up in and with them that is neither picture nor thing. Instead of a representation, emergence becomes visible. A different colour set could achieve it too, but differently, and that can be seen just a few paces further on. Insights into the early work of visibility open up together.

And hence, every picture revolves around the beginning of what could be there. Something was there and will perhaps be again. For the moment what exactly it's about remains open. In this peace and generosity, the beauty of the colours unfolds.

—— *Thomas Schlereth*

Daniel Schubert was born in 1984 in Viersen and currently lives and works in Düsseldorf

Kunstakademie Düsseldorf, Meisterschüler with Prof. Herbert Brandl, 2010

Akademiebrief with Eberhard Havekost, 2012

2018 Totem, Atelier Schloss Jägerhof, Düsseldorf, with David Benedikt Wirth (S)

2017 A Four Hand Piano Piece, Gerhard Hofland, Amsterdam (S)

Freimütig, Galerie Gebr. Lehmann, Dresden (G)

We call it work / Opere Scelte, Turin (G)

danielschubert.eu

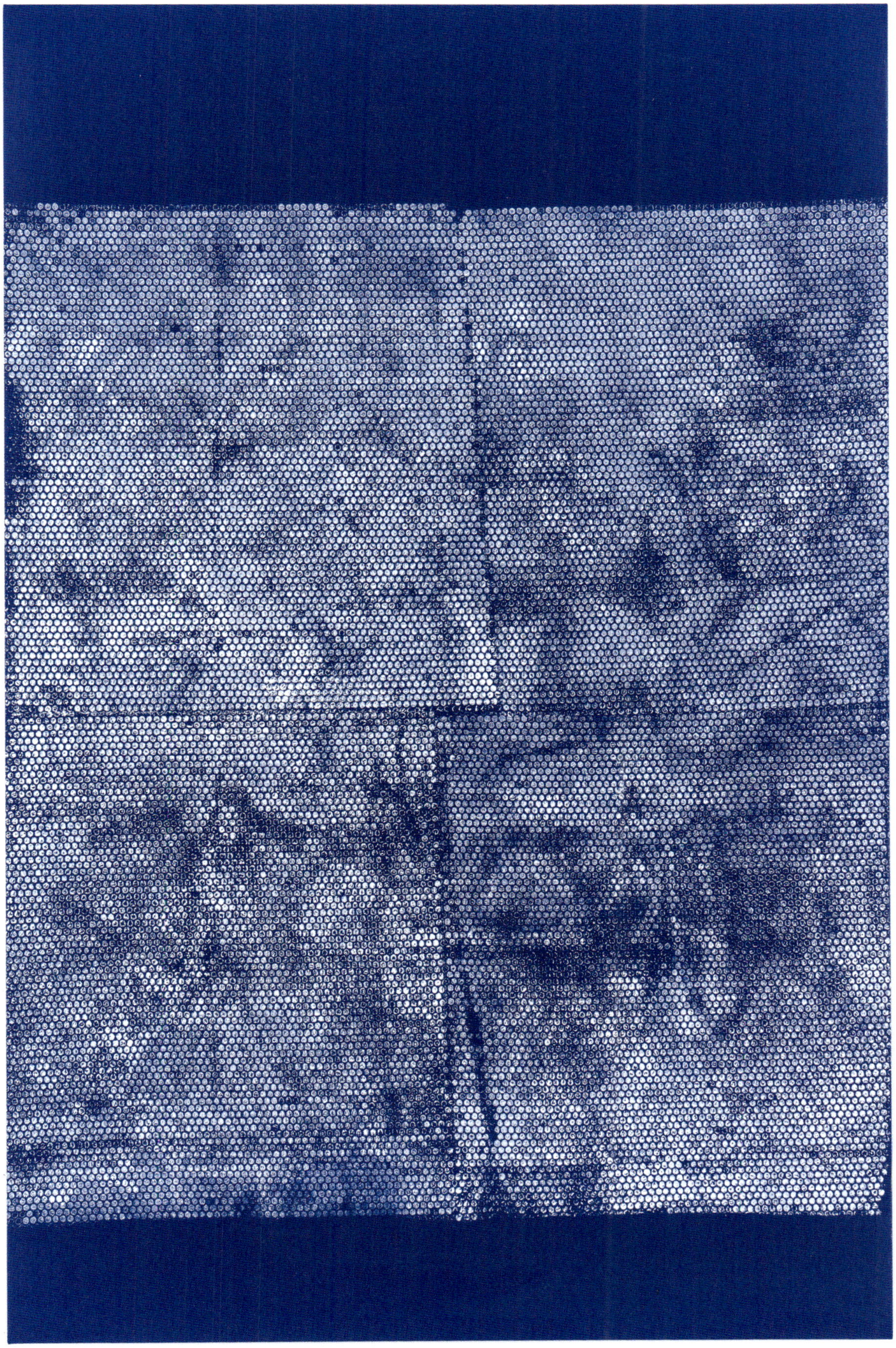

Untitled 20 – aus der Nivea-Serie 2019 Acrylic on blue fabric 220 × 147.5 cm Bonn

Untitled 25 – aus der Shimmer-Serie 2018 Acrylic on canvas 170 × 115 cm Chemnitz

Untitled 2017 Stretcher, canvas, acrylic, distemper dimensions variable, ca. 115 × 170 cm Wiesbaden

Kristina Schuldt

Something or somebody is always on the move in the pictures of Kristina Schuldt. People – mostly women – body parts, hair, plants. She works with a repertoire of forms and styles that recalls something that she has seen, but she does not betray whether it was a picture from the Internet, a photo from a magazine, a situation on the street or a figure from an illustrated volume about classic Modernism or Cubism, for all these sources find their way in parts into Schuldt's painting. The movement and energy which is concealed in her work results not only from the flowing body forms, the powerful, tube-shaped legs and hands surrounded by virulent whirls of colour, but also from a principle employed in painting since Modernism: the multiple perspective. In her more recent pictures Schuldt positions fragments side by side as if she were zooming into the picture and then out again. She splinters the surface into fuzzy details which consist entirely of abstract colour gradients. Or she places parts that belong together in different places on the canvas, as in a puzzle that has got mixed up. Or like the square pictures on the online platform Instagram which we have become accustomed to seeing nowadays, as in Schuldt's *Einkaufswagen eine Treppe herabsteigend* (Shopping Trolley Descending A Staircase). Distributed across twelve squares, each one painted from a different viewpoint, in fact the steps seem to whirl downwards. Referring back to Marcel Duchamp, whose *Nude Descending a Staircase* served to record a movement sequence in a single picture, Kristina Schuldt makes an attempt to capture the movement in the superordinate sense: the changes of a social state and the circulation of pictures via the Internet, but also movements in the form of political protests, such as the mobilisation of masses or groups, which she has recently been observing with a certain unrest, but also fascination.
—— *Leonie Pfennig*

Kristina Schuldt was born in 1982 in Moscow and currently lives and works in Leipzig

Hochschule für Grafik und Buchkunst Leipzig, 2002–2004
Fachklasse für Malerei und Grafik with Prof. Annette Schröter and Prof. Sighard Gille, 2004–2008
Fachklasse für Malerei und Grafik with Prof. Neo Rauch, 2008–2009
Diplom 2009, Meisterschülerin 2012

2019 DAS KOLLEGIUM, Grafikstiftung Neo Rauch Aschersleben (G)
Meisterstück! Hauptwerke aus der Sammlung der Sparkasse Leipzig, Zitadelle Spandau, Berlin (G)
Collection Reloaded, G2 Kunsthalle, Leipzig (G)
Die Schönheit kann ebenso gut aus der Hölle stammen wie aus dem Himmel, Städtische Galerie im Alten Feuerhaus, Bad Reichenhall (G)

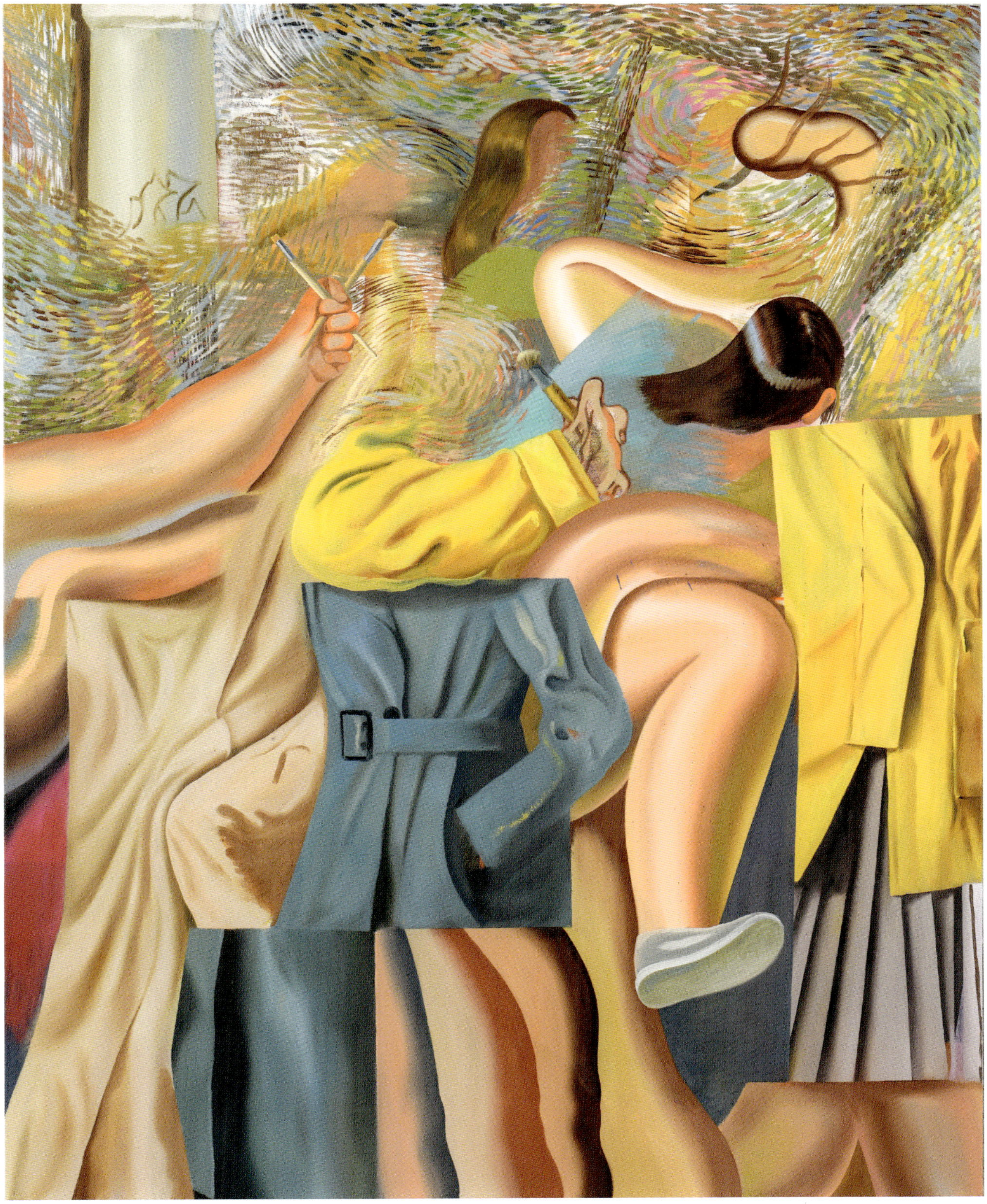

Nebelwand 2018 Oil and egg tempera on canvas 220 × 180 cm Wiesbaden

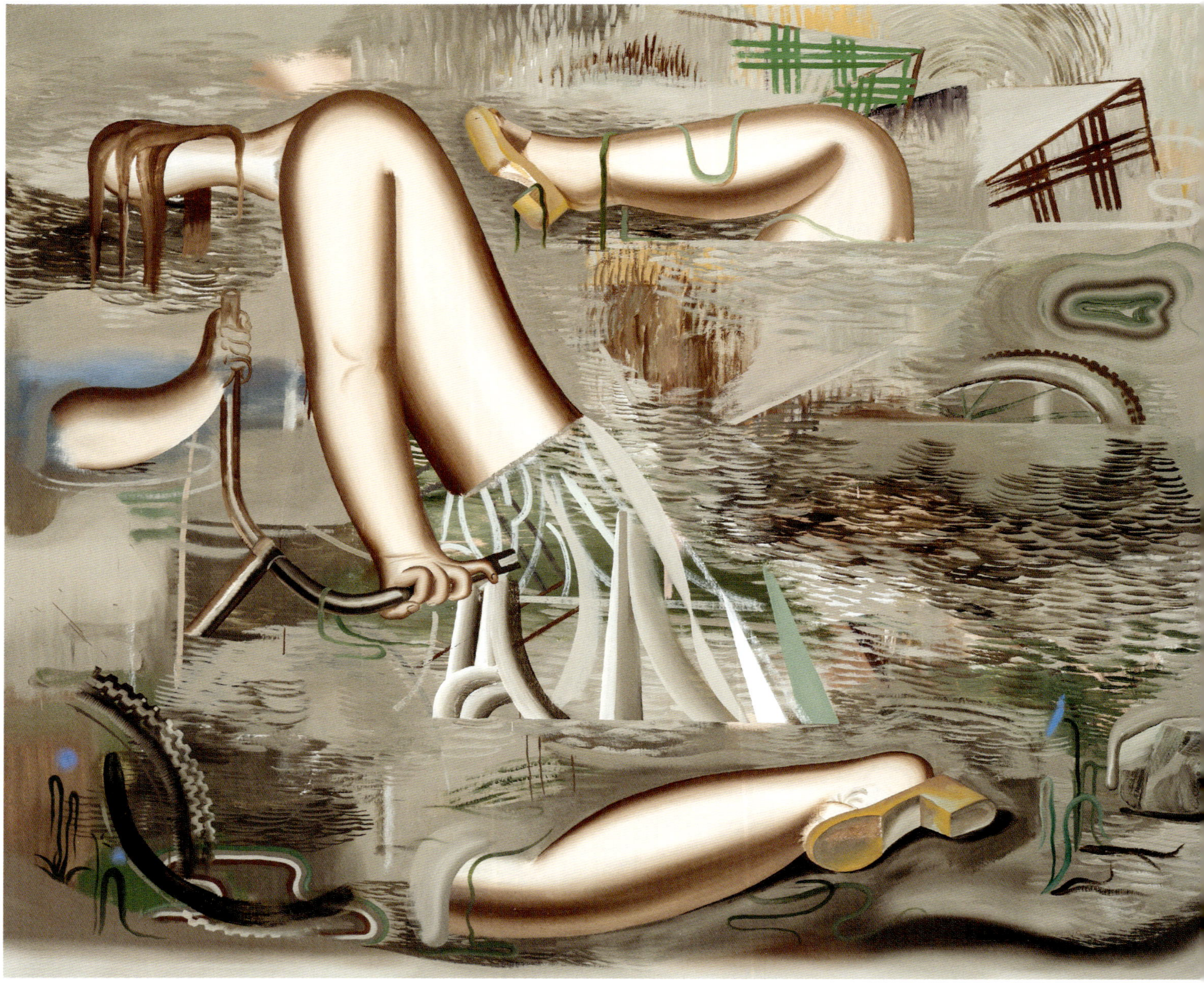

reverse

2016

Oil and egg tempera on canvas

170 × 210 cm

Bonn

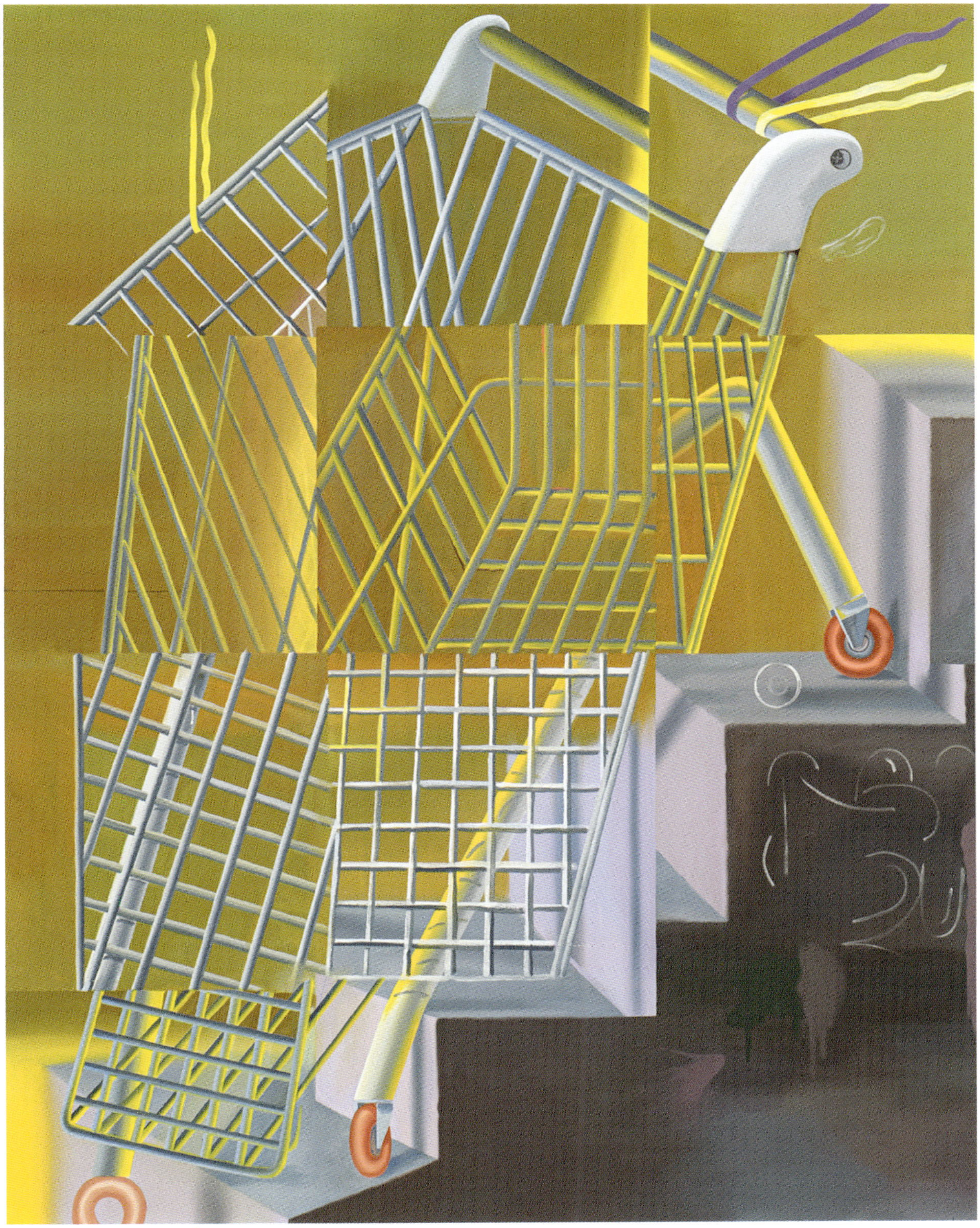

Einkaufswagen eine Treppe herabsteigend

2017

Oil and egg tempera on canvas

210 × 170 cm

Chemnitz

Alicia Viebrock

Viebrock's pictures remind us of the Informel painting of the post-war period, while their motifs are rooted in nature. They do not succumb to the beauty of the floral, however, but show an abstraction which appears to conjure up a new, natural force of its own, capturing the way it flows, grows, twines and bursts without surrendering to an idealised romantic symbolism.
At first sight, the painting of Alicia Viebrock seems like a euphoric gesture which has been translated into a form. Tempo and dynamics play an important part – they depend on the viscosity of the coloured China ink which captures fleeting structures. At times it is applied rapidly, at others thickly, with brushstrokes that are sharp-edged and generous or finely smoothed out. Chance and control, rejection and inclusion form part of a painting process which concentrates on the colour and gives it space. However, the painting does not lose itself in its calligraphic or lyrical lightness, because the gravitational pull of the canvas plays an important role. It permits a growth process, not only from the bottom upwards, but also out of its own pictorial centres. These main areas of focus within the picture are not always physically tangible; the depth of their look and feel arises through layerings, concentration and places where the flow of paint seems to pause for a moment. And yet, despite all this energy, none of the pictures suffers from a loss of concentration. If we stand quite close, they do not dissipate but reveal more colour formations in which particles swirl and surfaces crumble and break up. The fine details which were submerged can appear like the fringes of a scarf, like combed paint or cryptically playful signatures which reveal flashes of Alicia Viebrock's closeness to the picture and give her painterly self-image a form.
—— *Marina Rüdiger*

Alicia Viebrock was born in 1986 in Munich and currently lives and works in Cologne

Kunstakademie Düsseldorf with Prof. Herbert Brandl, 2009–2017, Meisterschülerin, 2013

2018 New Acquisitions, Rubell Family Collection, Miami (G)
calories, FILIALE, Frankfurt a. M. (S)
Nightfly, Galerie Heinz Holtmann, Cologne (S)
salondergegenwart, Hamburg (G)

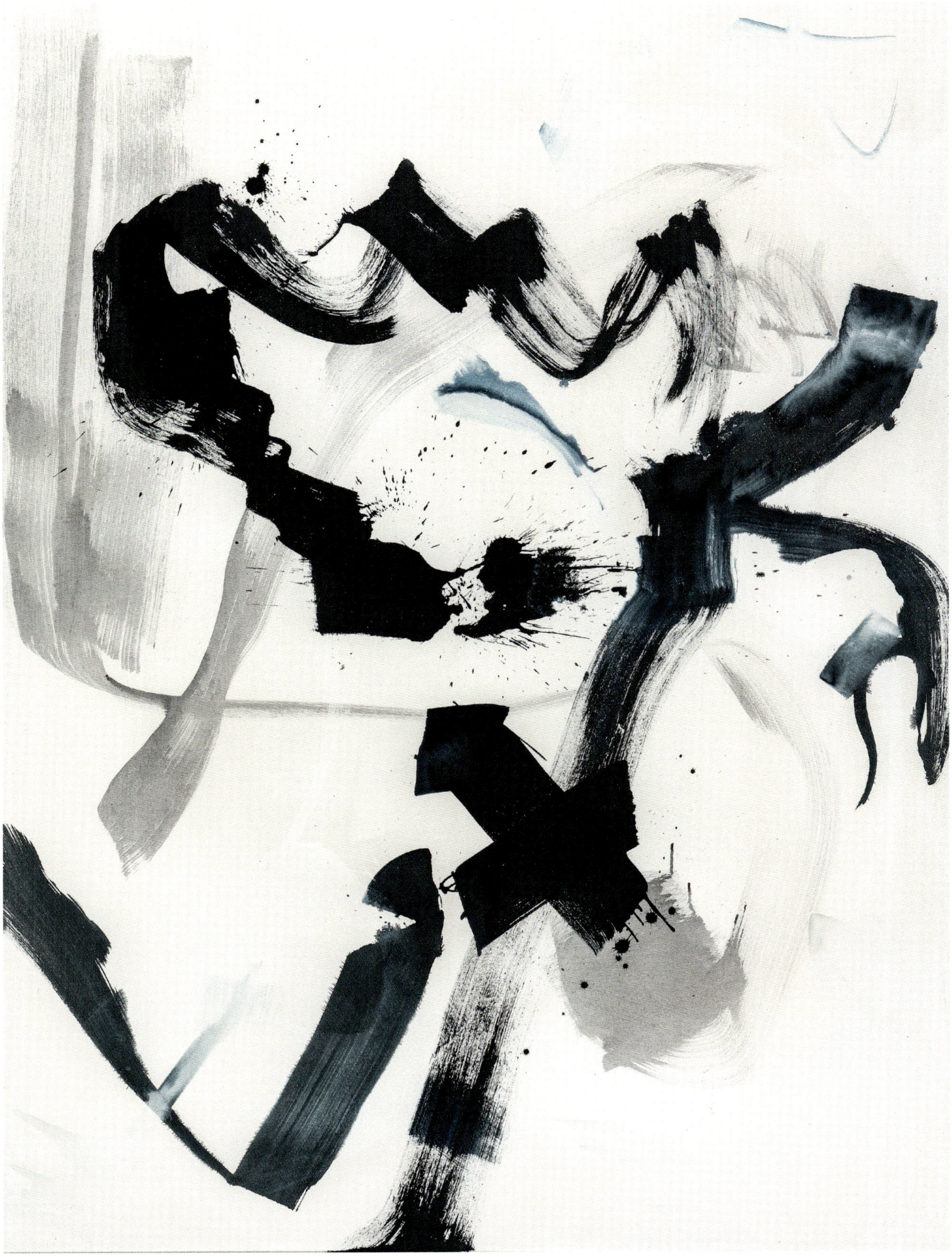

Untitled 2019 Ink, acrylic and medium on canvas 210 × 160 cm Bonn

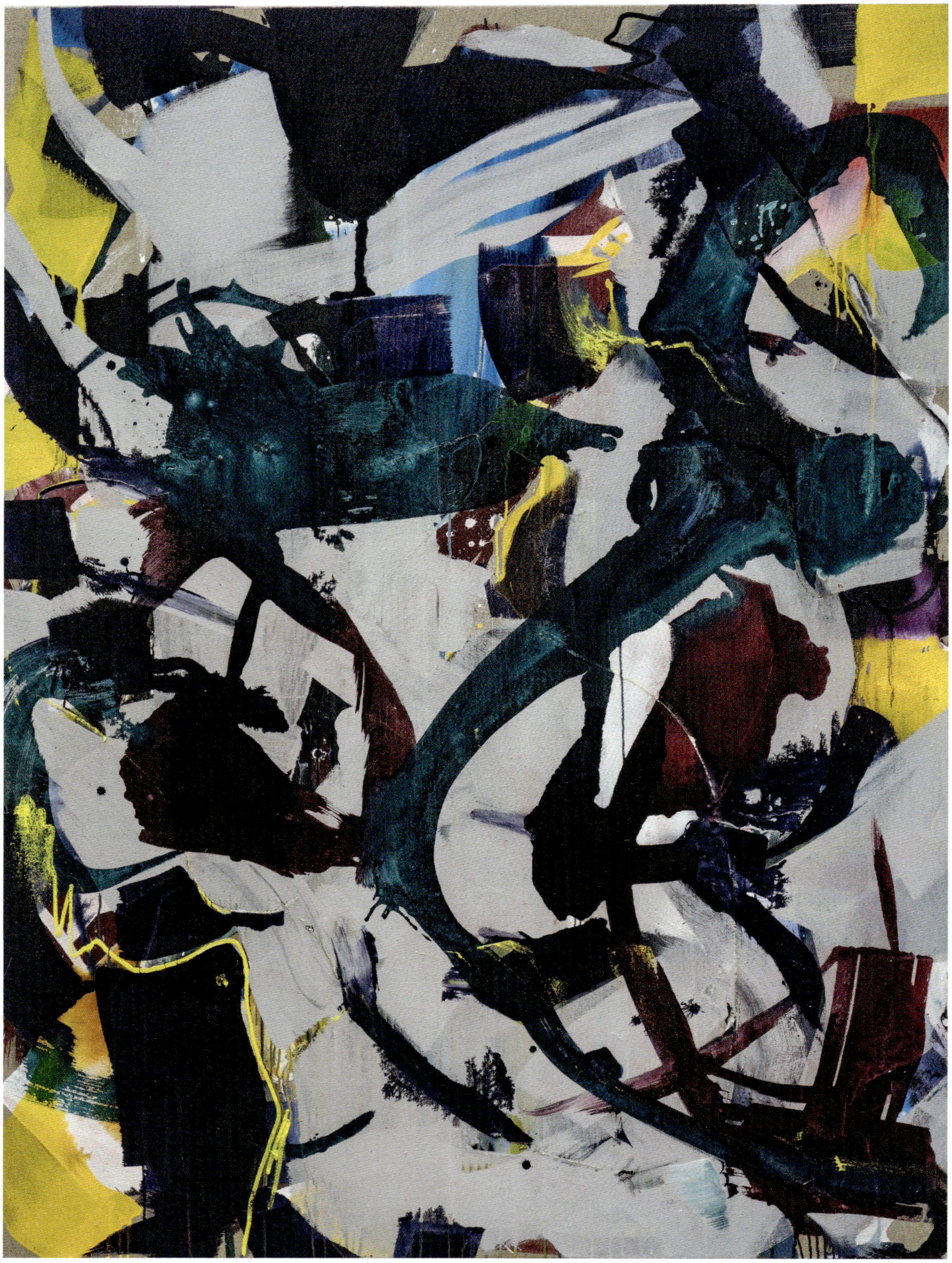

Untitled 2019 Ink, acrylic, oil and medium on canvas 190 × 150 cm Chemnitz

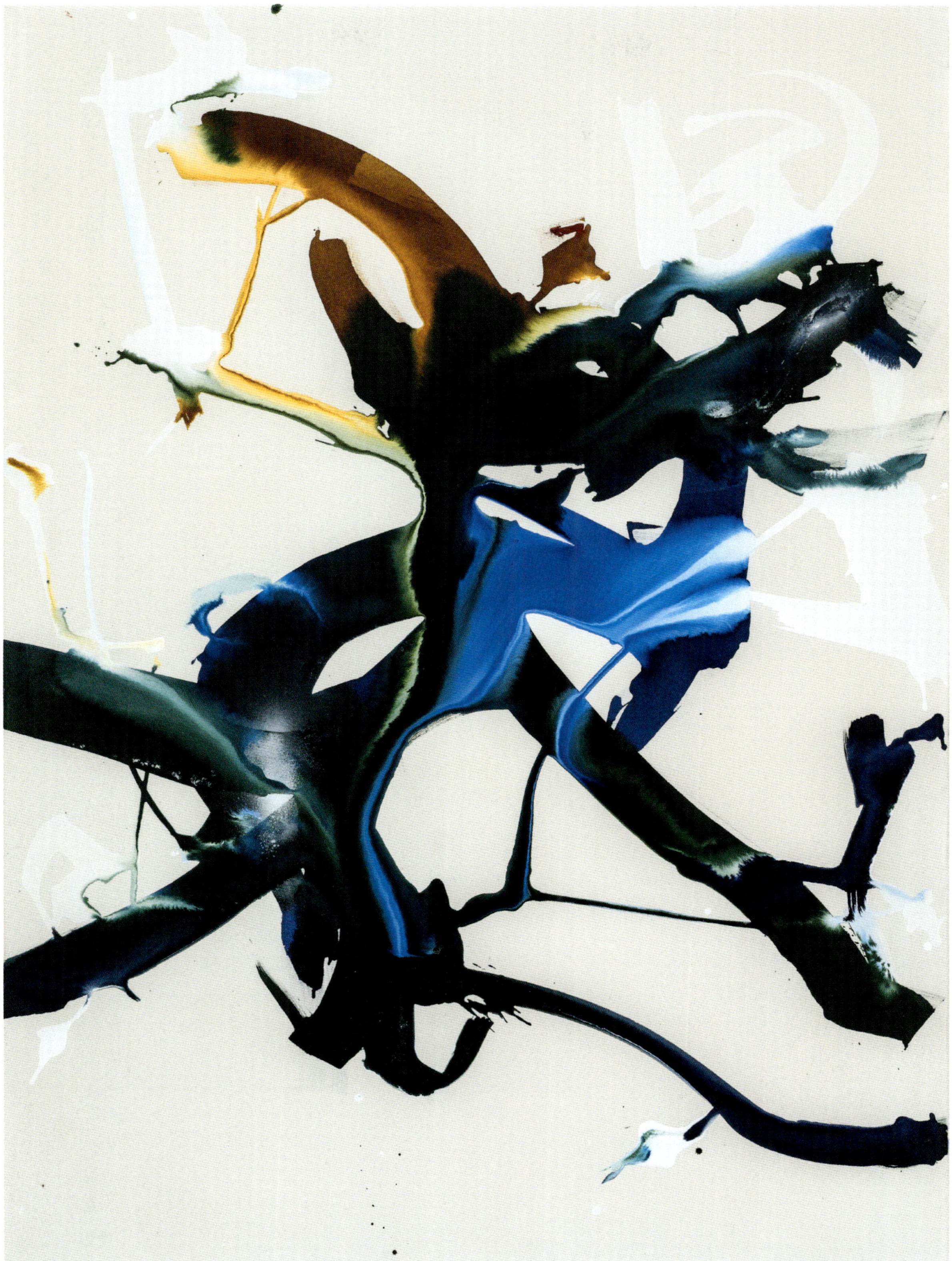

Portal

2018

Ink, acrylic and spray paint,
medium on canvas

190 × 150 cm

Wiesbaden

Stefan Vogel

Stefan Vogel combines drawing, writing and forms to create a dense whole. His language pictures are marked by the influence of concrete poetry. In his wall paintings, which often consist of several parts, and in his space-filling installations he interweaves organic and artificial elements to create fragile interrelated webs. He locates the paths and the hills and valleys of the terrain to be marked out like a cartographer. The pictures that arise in this way are reminiscent of wastelands. Vogel himself labels them "Gebrache" (Broken Spaces), thereby heightening the vulnerable state of the hiatus, the sense of incompleteness. Something has been shut down – but unrest is brewing within! Chaos and order, like suffering and thriving, arise from the same possibilities. Only time and logic change, repeatedly and yet again. The specific aesthetics of material and colour in his works are based on the use of everyday objects, natural substances and construction materials. With the rhythmical repetition of important elements of form, colour and substance, decay and chance inspire the anarchy of things and words. On the one hand, proliferation – and on the other, structure, concentration and reduction. With the help of this complementary principle, Vogel works on a visual equivalent of complex relationships. His works can thus be read as projection surfaces for insoluble conflicts of inner sensitivities, recurring mechanisms in social or familiar constellations and interpersonal communications behaviour.

—— *Anka Ziefer*

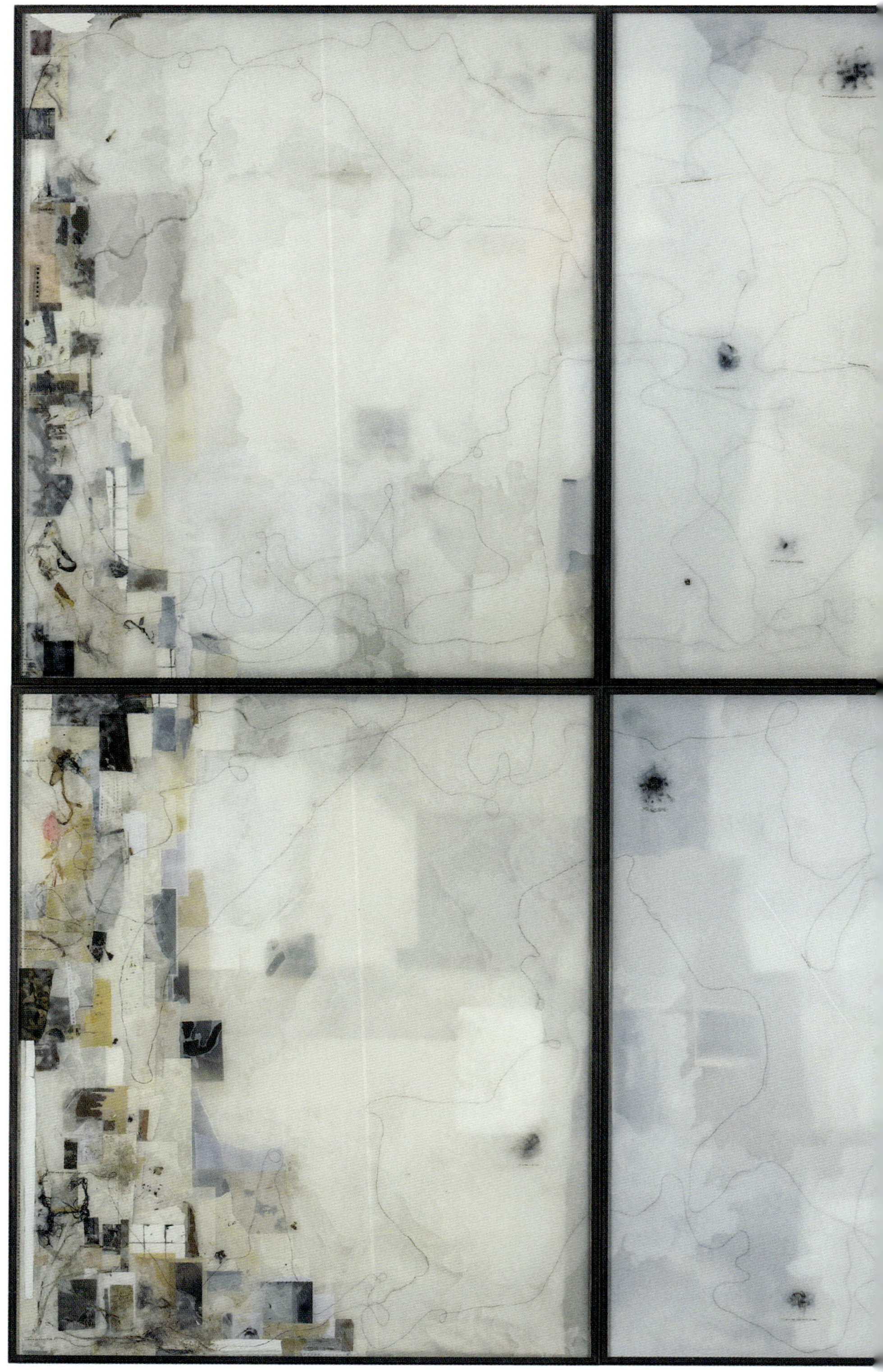

Stefan Vogelwas born in 1981 in Fürth and currently lives and works in Leipzig and Berlin
Hochschule für bildende Künste Hamburg, 2004–2012

2019 Wege zur Welt, G2 Kunsthalle, Leipzig (G)
bis hierhin ging's noch gut – Archiv Massiv, Baumwollspinnerei Leipzig (G)
Relief II, Kunstverein Schwerin (G)
bis der Kopf den Geist aufgibt, Galerie Schönewald, Düsseldorf (S)

stefanvogel.info

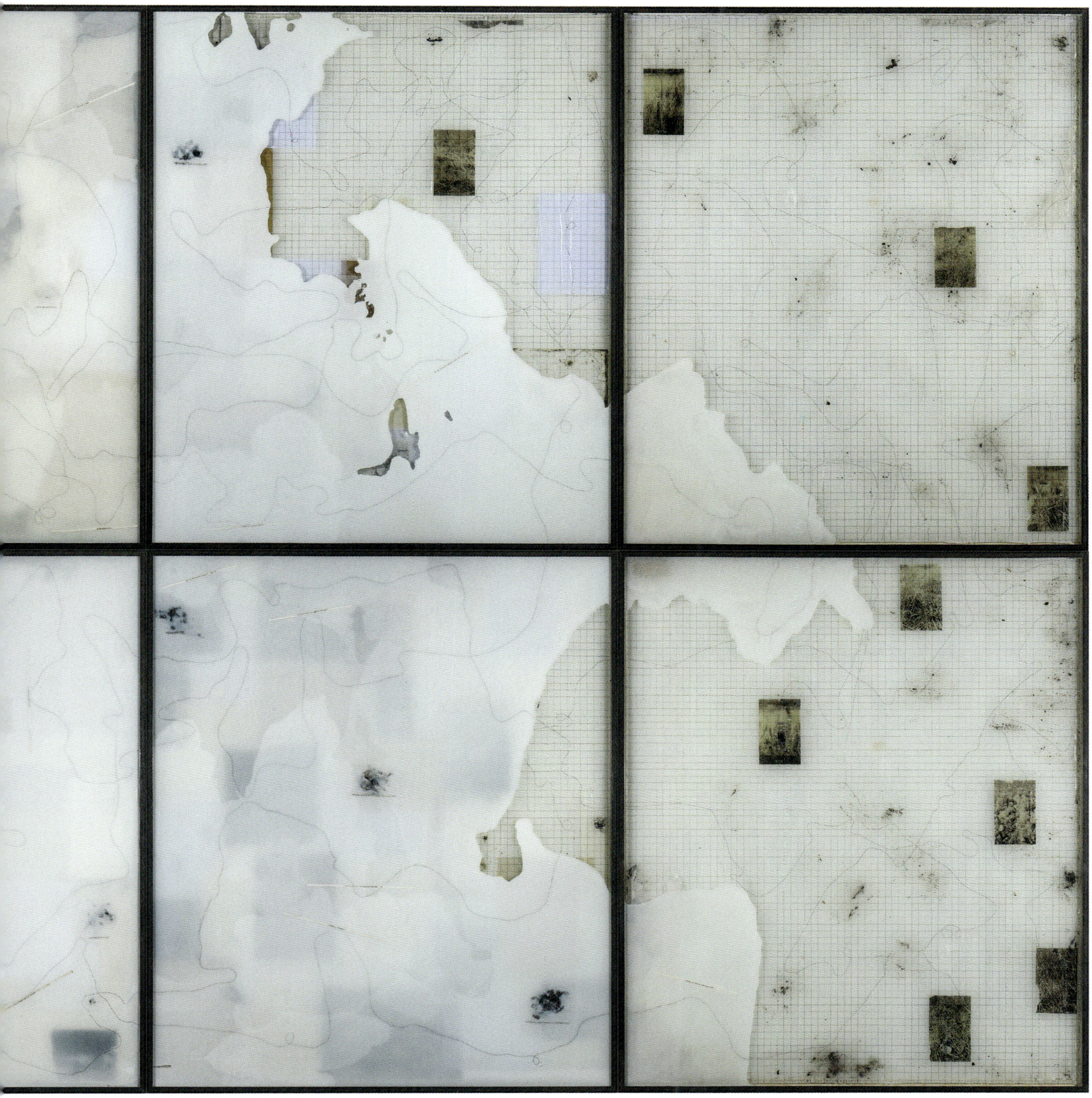

Gebrache

2017

Paraffin, paper, threads, plastic, dirt, dust, metal, acrylic, lacquer, silicone, staples and typewriter on glass

320 × 560 cm

Chemnitz

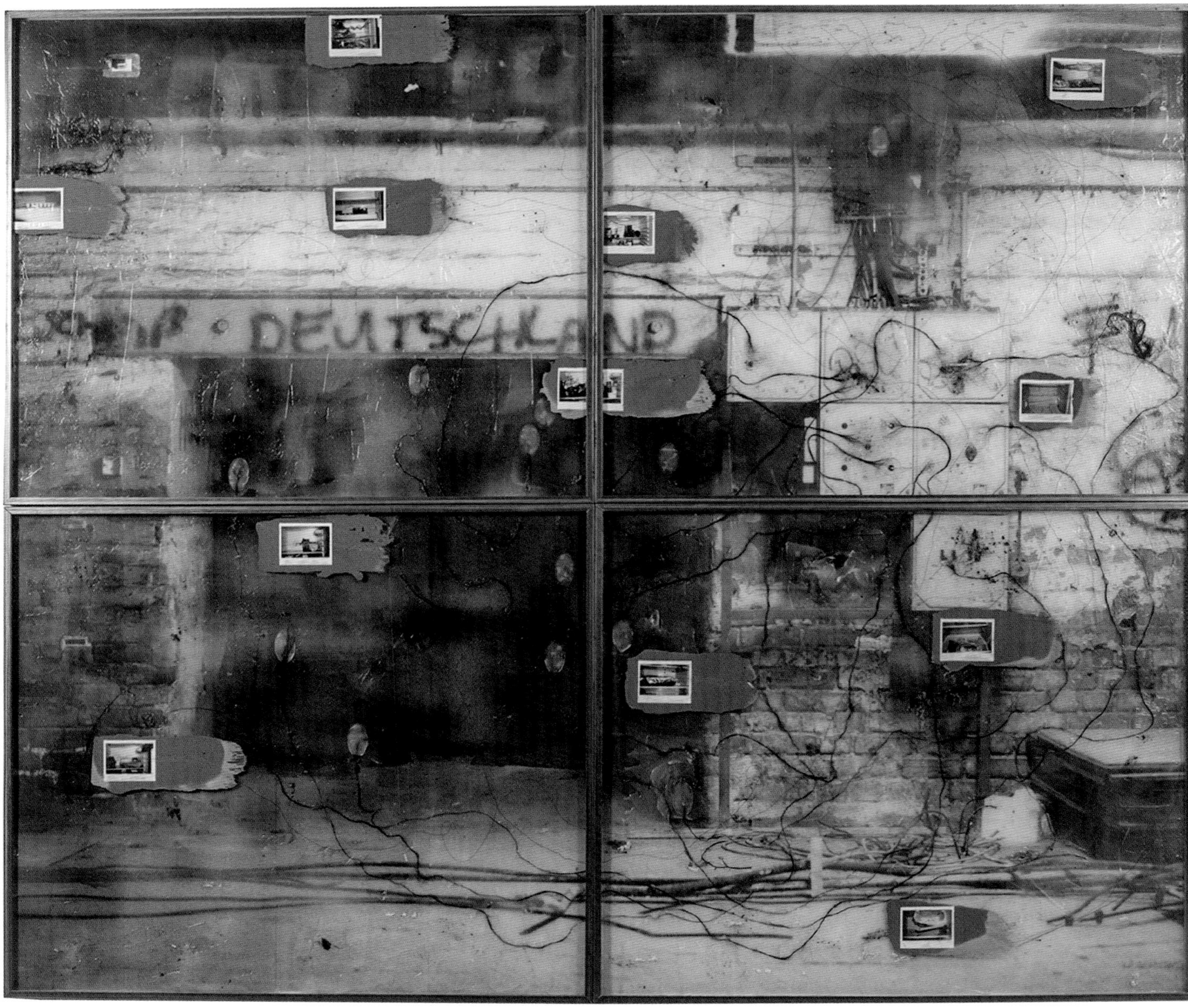

Salbe

2018

Quadripartite, paraffin, paper, copies, concrete, Polaroids, wire, hair, threads, typewriter, staple gun, plaster, blistering ointment, dirt on glass

200 × 240 cm

Bonn

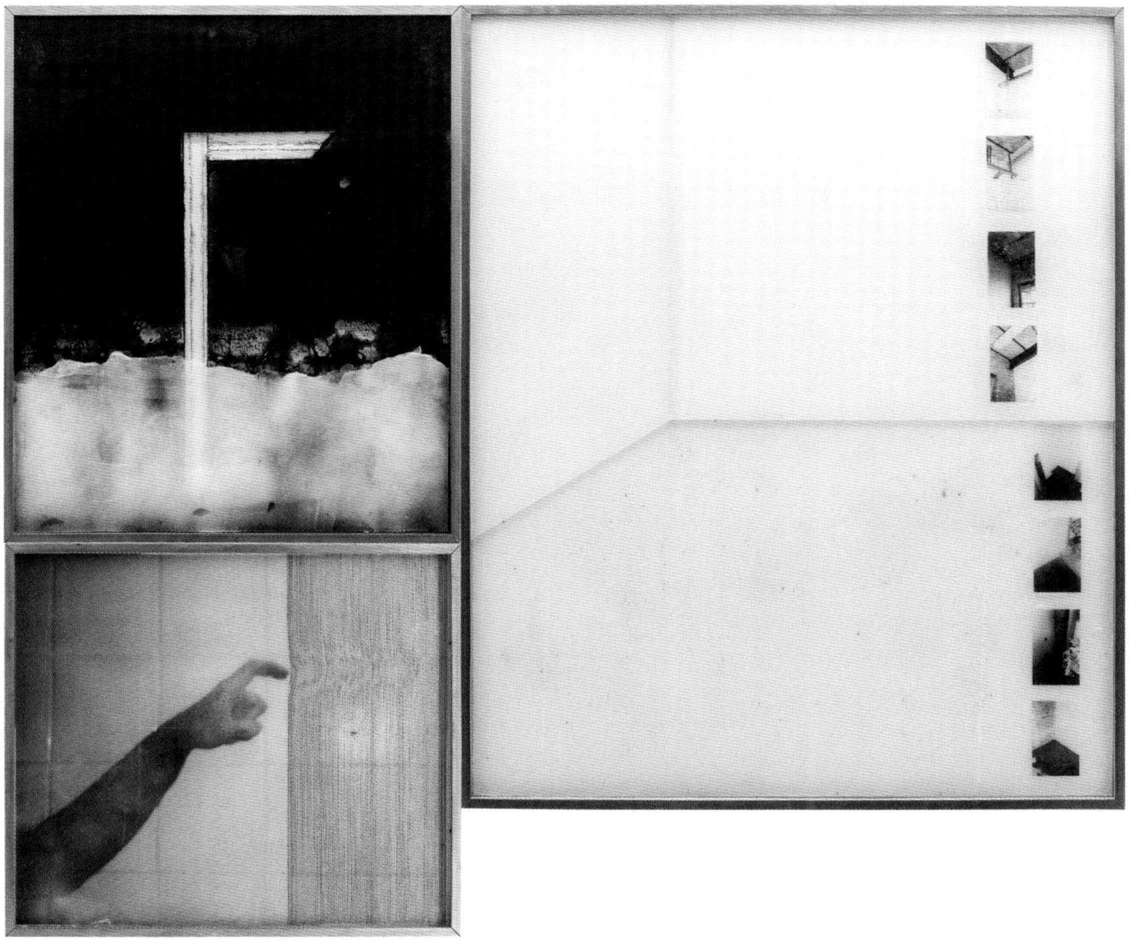

Der rechte Winkel, der gekrümmte Zeigefinger und die ewige Baustelle

2017

Paraffin, threads, stain, copies, dirt on glass

140 × 170 cm

Wiesbaden

Jonas Weichsel

Jonas Weichsel was born in 1982 in Darmstadt and currently lives and works in Frankfurt a. M.

Kunsthochschule Mainz with Prof. Anne Berning, 2004–2009

Kunstakademie Düsseldorf with Prof. Tomma Abts, 2010–2011

Städelschule Frankfurt a. M. with Prof. Judith Hopf, 2009–2012 Meisterschüler

2018 Echo Box, Galerie Thomas Schulte, Berlin (S)

Parcours, Josef Albers Museum Quadrat, Bottrop (S, C)

Social Facades, MMK Museum, Museum für Moderne Kunst, Frankfurt a. M. (G, C)

2016 Jonas Weichsel, Museum Wiesbaden, Wiesbaden (S, C)

If Modernist art were to challenge its media-specific identities radically (Clement Greenberg), then the postmodern arts would be governed by spatial and intermedial opening (Umberto Eco). The fact that the ambivalence of modern and postmodern theory can be systematically updated for contemporary questions of media aesthetics is demonstrated by the complex pictorial logic which Jonas Weichsel has developed by following the lines of painterly tradition.

For example, if we study his *TC-Bilder* (Two-Colour Pictures), a series which encompasses some forty individual works to date and which builds directly on a two-colour composition, then it can be seen that Weichsel extends the aesthetic picture experience in the tension field of formal and visual differences by means of the systematic questioning of painting as a medium. But he does not simply split the painterly into formalistic particularism. On the contrary: what appears to be taking place within the frame is the contemporary search for the semantic field of the picture, which lies between digital automation, subjective gesture and scientific theory. Weichsel's series, freed from the traces of the creation process, are the results of processes of excessive repetition and flat hierarchies of the media, in which electronics and the painterly techniques of the old masters stand equally empowered and unresolved side by side. Thus the transparent brushstrokes let us read which ones determine the structure of the *TC-Bilder* and which are not executed by the artist's hand but by a specially designed piece of apparatus that draws the extra-broad paintbrush across the surface of the picture, like an automated print head. When it comes to layering, it can be seen that Weichsel also uses acrylic paint as a material for modelling, in order to counter the dissonant colour tones of light and shade as well as reflective effects.

Only step by step does it become possible to take in the complex structure of the relationships in which composition, pictorial space and colour values behave towards each other in an aesthetic process of seeing. Finally, the pictures negotiate a virtual perceptive situation for the redefinition of a picture theory for the present day. —— *Vivien Trommer*

United Europe Flag (A) 2019 Acrylic screen print on canvas 72 × 104 × 1.3 cm Bonn

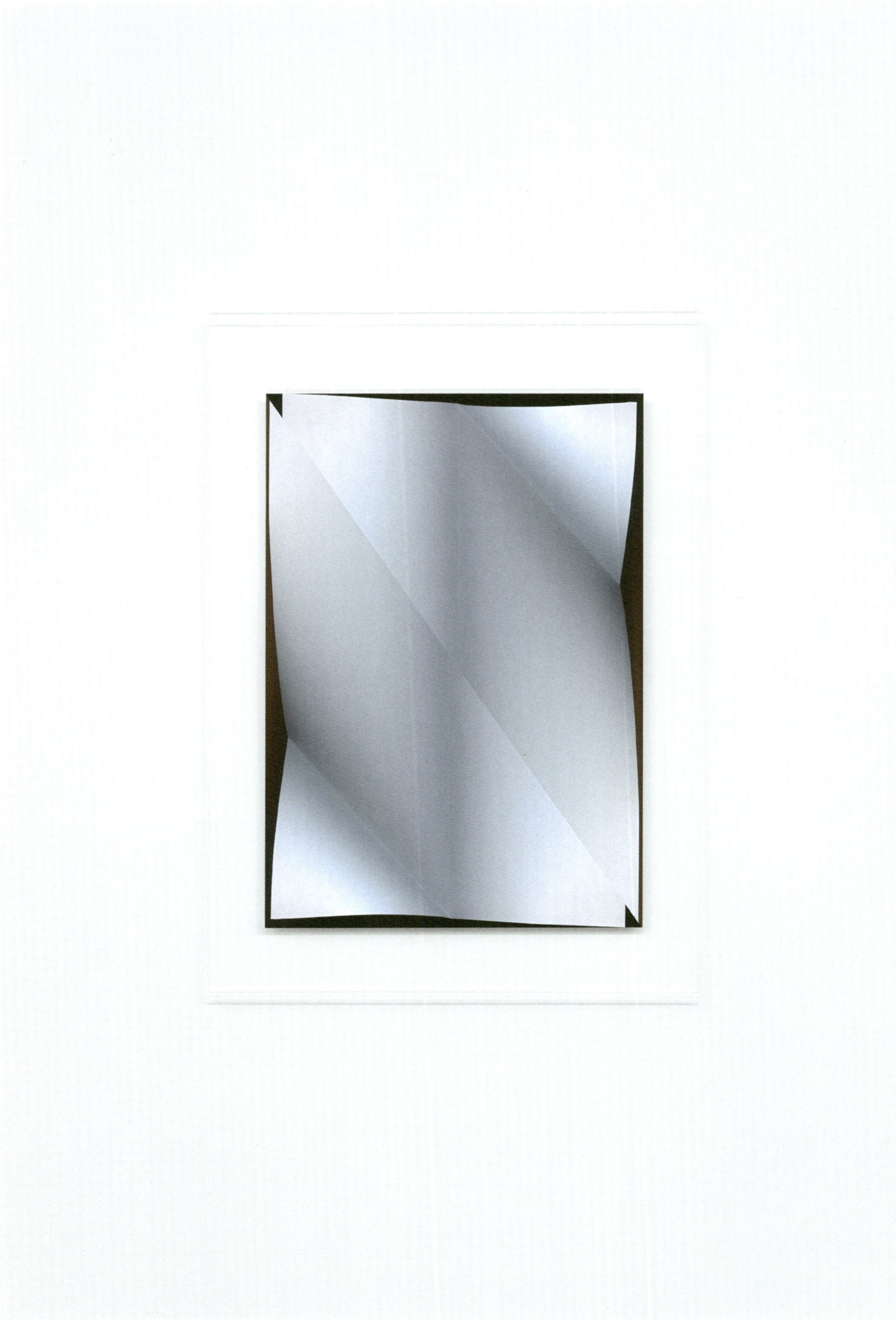

Glass Penny
2019
Oil and UV printing on glass
49 × 34 × 0.8 cm
Wiesbaden

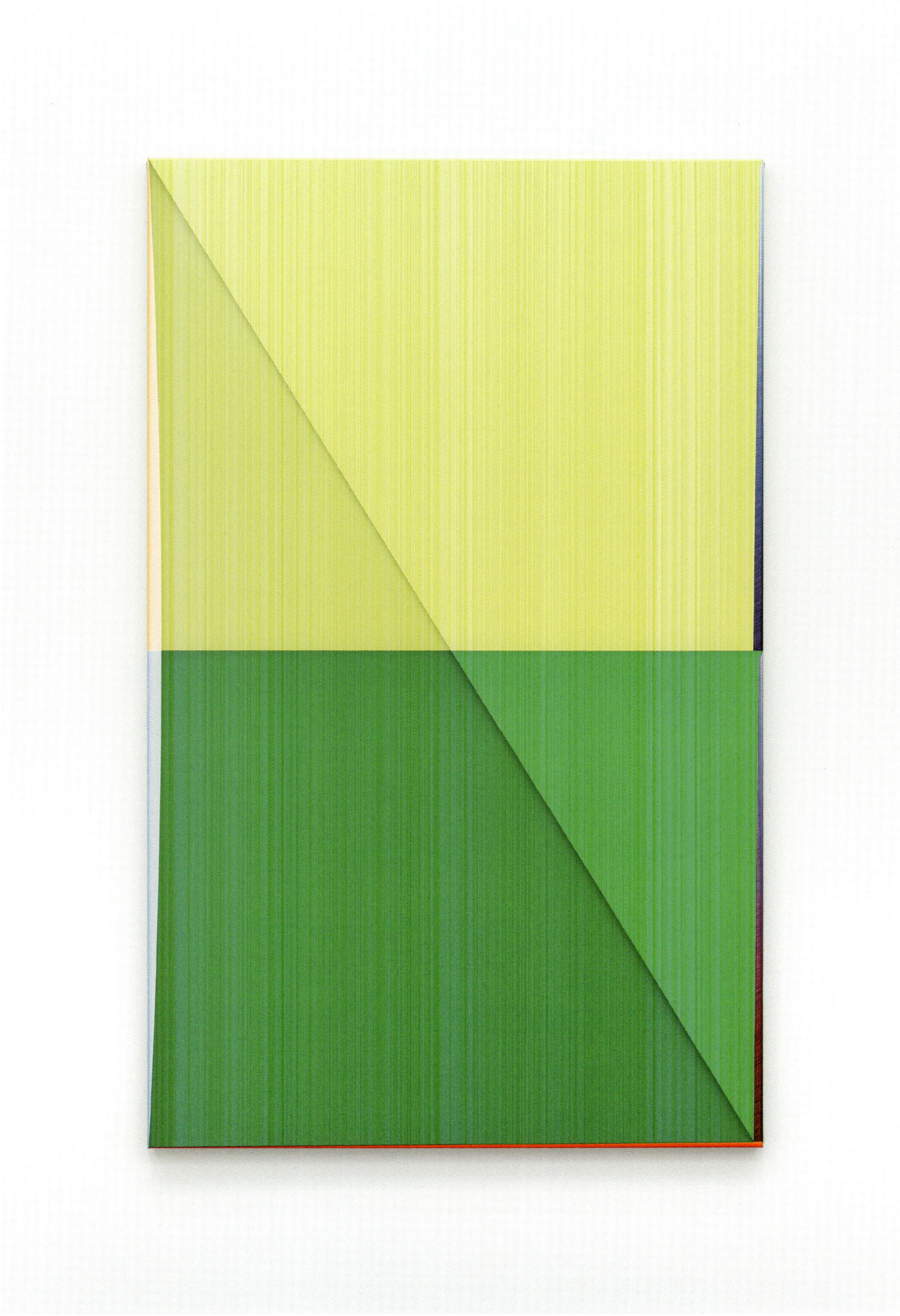

TC Dia (W) Hansagelb/Heliogrün 2019 Oil and acrylic on canvas 76 × 47.5 × 1.5 cm Chemnitz

Tristan Wilczek

Tristan Wilczek was born in 1989 in Lüdenscheid and currently lives and works in Düsseldorf

Kunstakademie Düsseldorf with Prof. Herbert Brandl, 2010–2017 Meisterschüler

2019 Markus Lüttgen, Düsseldorf (S)

2018 Klassentreffen (works from the collection of W. & G. Schürmann), MUMOK, Vienna (G)

2017 Markus Lüttgen, Cologne (S)

2016 ICIL, Markus Lüttgen, Cologne (G)

markusluettgen.de/tristan-wilczek

The works of Tristan Wilczek rephrase the question regarding the possibilities of painting today in order to ask a more fundamental one. They take as their subject the status and relationship of character, picture and space. The individual motifs, symbols and surfaces already positively advertise their pictorial or symbolic character and permit even smaller pictorial connections to question the procedures for the attribution of meaning or the assignation of significance, the removal and emptying of meaning. Above all, however, these visual elements and pictorial contexts are embedded in complex visual systems that mostly make use of the logic of technical drawings, in which they are placed in relationships that are sometimes causal, sometimes paradoxical, and sometimes come to nothing. The relationship between these different layers remains open. If the pictures appear on the one hand to formulate the rules by which they were generated and hence a fundamental precedence of linguistic and knowledge disposition, then they seem to be on the other the results of such rules of generation and to insist on the independence of the aesthetic field with rules and criteria which are valid only here.
Tristan Wilczek's works show themselves in this openness as an artistic practice. Painting here is not an artistic genre which aims to seal itself off hermetically from the viewer and extort a solitary and unilateral effort in deciphering the work in the classical manner of work aesthetics. Painting is instead a communicative act, in which the picture presents itself in an open relationship to its opposite number by creating a space into which it transports its viewers beyond the motivic and physical space. And so when its own status *as* a picture is questioned *with* the picture, the question does not remain a self-referential one within the realms of the aesthetic; imagery and perception are questioned equally within their political-normative dimensions as they encroach on the picture concerned. And so its references extend over and beyond its own space.
—— *Sebastian Hammerschmidt*

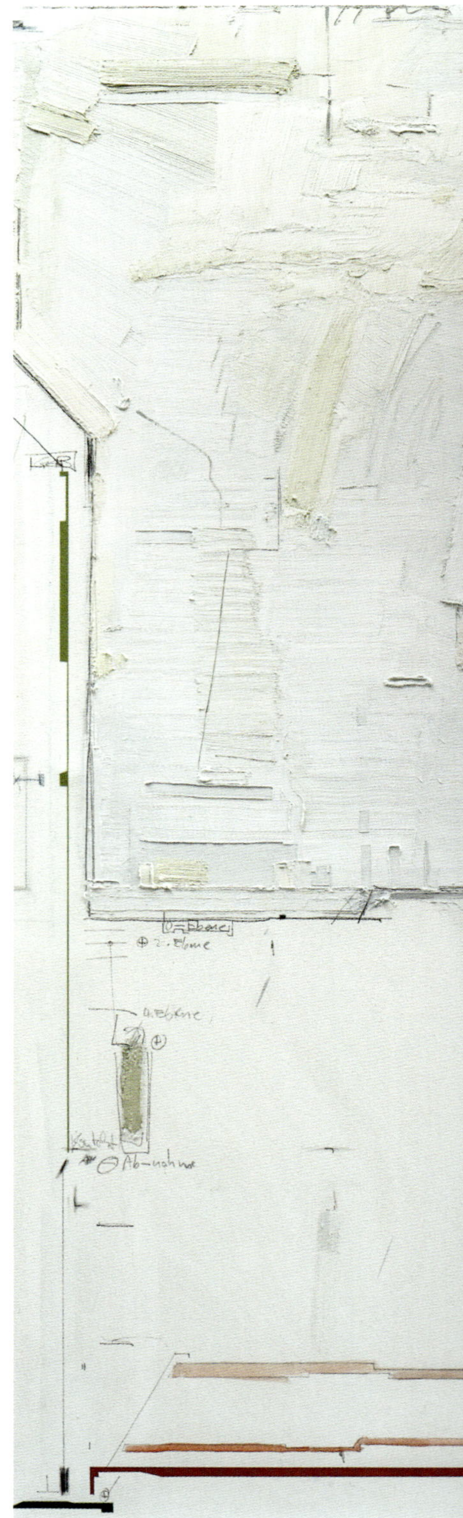

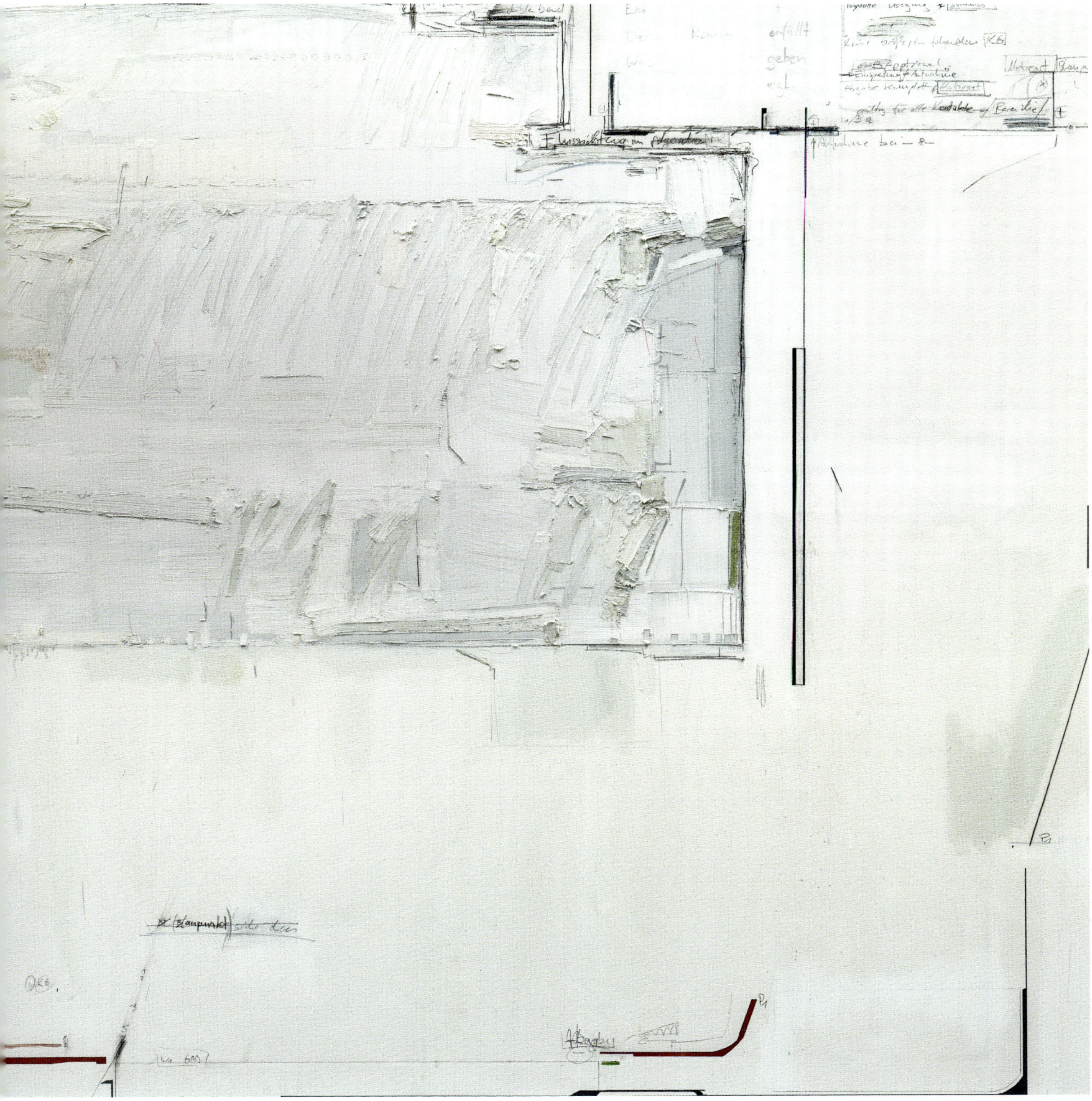

Untitled (Blaupunkt) 2019 Acrylic, oil and graphite on canvas 180 × 240 cm Bonn

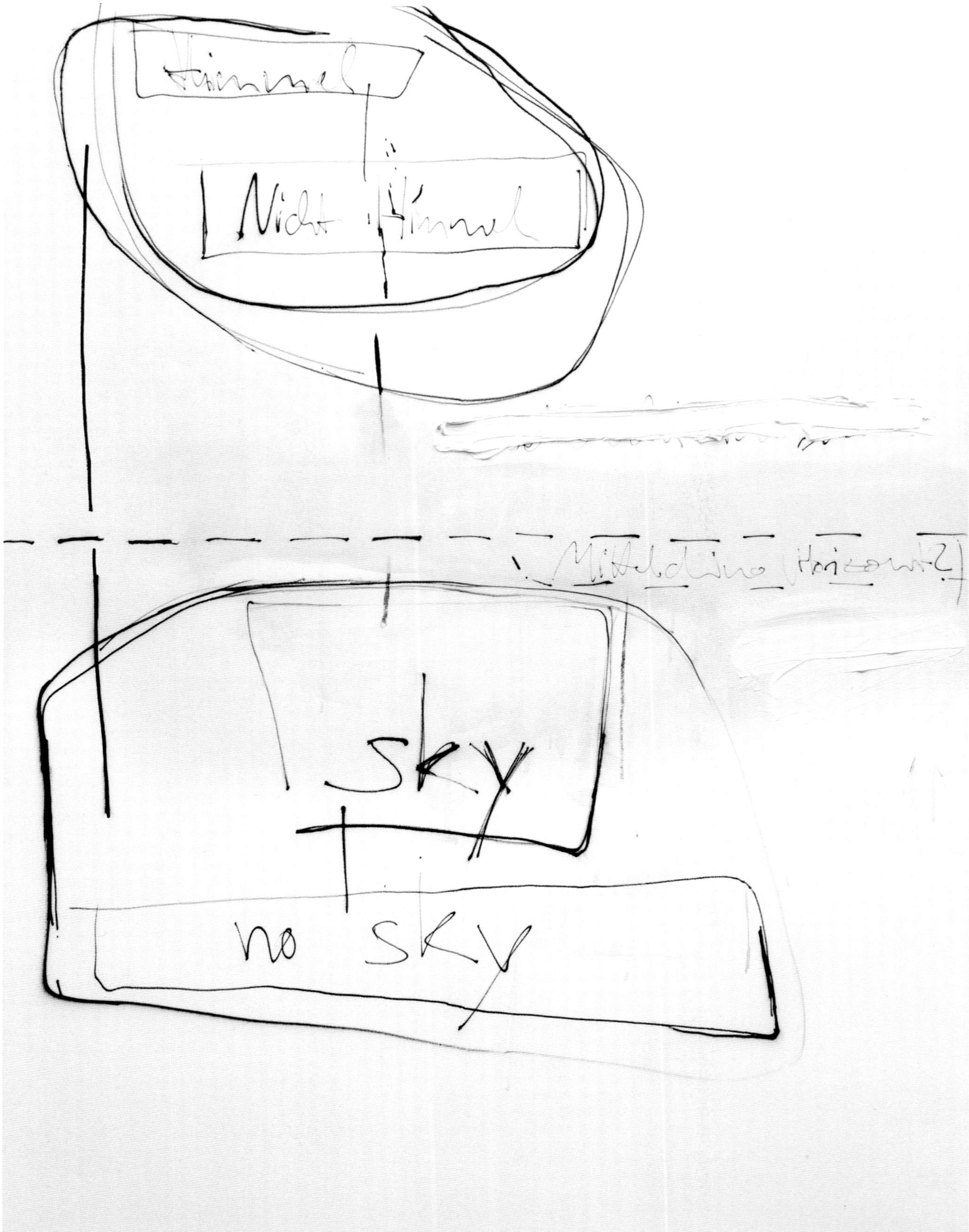

Untitled (Instabile Landschaft) 2017 Oil and acrylic on canvas 140 × 110 cm Chemnitz

Untitled (die leeren Zeichen 3) 2019 Acrylic, oil and graphite on canvas 140 × 105 cm Wiesbaden

Franz Ackermann

Painting can conquer a room, but not necessarily.

Painting can hurl illusion to the ground of hard facts, but not necessarily.

Painting may be a light or become one, but can refrain from being one.

Painting has a body and sometimes a good figure as well.

Lyotard speaks of Karel Appel's paintings as an offering...

"The younger you are, the more you can claim. The older you become, the more you need to prove."

This was the answer Markus Lüppertz gave to my insistent questions regarding his offering.

That was more than thirty years ago...

The matter of painting is entirely unexplored until now. In contrast to the black hole, of which at least we now have a photo.

Painting as an offering I gladly accept, both as an observer as well as a practitioner. This morning it was irreplaceable. Now too. Painting NOW and tomorrow as well, quite certainly.

Julia Apitzsch-Haack

Green arsenic smeared on an egg-white cloth,
Crushed strawberries! Come, let us feast our eyes.
(Ezra Pound, "L'Art")

"Painting simply looks like shit in the first ten years!", said a member of the jury with both empathy and approval during the jurying for an art scholarship about the hard struggle of young students. A struggle that in spite of centuries of cumulative art history that stare back at you unmercifully from the white canvas. Still, again and again, it brings forth a new, unbelievably important, fresh, formal-aesthetic, cheeky, painful, poetic, political, revolutionary, observant, quiet, astounding condensing of reality, finds an artistic form that vibrates. Don't stop! Keep on fighting! And, flabbergasted, we're emptying another Coke with Frank O'Hara.

Stephan Baumkötter

Of course, there is no such thing as painting, only an infinite number of paintings. Painting is interesting when it is a specific medium that displays in the painting its own idiosyncratic material and historical conditions in the process of painting. Painting shows this by way of painting, not by means of a narrative via painting. Painting displays its peculiar and unique dual character by being both appearance and material (object) at the same time. And its form of appearance is based on the contradiction between the simultaneous corporeality and the immateriality of the painting. The visibility of the body is suspended in painting and the surface of the painting touches the body in front of it. Painting exists through this contradiction. For this reason, painting is neither an old nor a new medium, but a specific one. Painting has always understood that it had no desire to be mixed up with that which is not painting. Painting is its own vernacular. Therefore, it also lies. Painting has already gone through its own history. It has worked its way through a mountain of history and has come out on the other side. Therefore, painting has no problem. Only for those who paint.

Pia Fries

Now is the moment when a decision is being made.

The decision as to what painting needs, what needs to be done.

Now is the moment when something is given to painting and simultaneously something is taken away.

In every area of the painting a decision might be made.

The idea for the decision involves its own material, its own form and colour.

Now is the moment when all decisions made become visible.

Visibility is a long chain through which the painting evolved and through it turned into what it is now.

Rolf Bier

The process of painting has always been synthetic through and through: from the first positioning, it leads to a completely self-contained entity in which no detail is dispensable – an image. This unity of the image is opposed to our own constantly roving, limitless perception. The image, even as it reveals its process of creation, is suspended in time and design in more than one sense: what hangs on the wall as an image belongs to our world as much as it is another world. This dimension, which is as philosophical as it is spiritual, belongs in a fundamental way to the experience of painting as to no other medium and it may be presented again and again in surprisingly economic ways.

Anne-Marie Bonnet

What and how painters create from and with paint continues to surprise. The specific, almost alchemical condensing of room and space. All previous paintings reverberate in the new paintings, but they keep reinventing the colours and juxtapose all technical and digital promises with the traces of painterly approaches that define our presence in the here and now, while transporting us at the same time.

Katharina Grosse

There is a lack of empathy for the openness of the world – in all of us.
So our questions are always: How do I get away from what has always been known to me as my knowledge? How do I reach a site that is unattainable for me, unknown to me?

The haptic picture summons up empathy as no other picture with a homogeneous surface does.
Paintings compress emotions and cause vehement agitation. Paintings can disturb us to such an extent, positively or negatively, that we develop the wish to change something. Immediately and repeatedly.

This is how radical empathy arises.

It is always possible to also view and experience reality differently. Not only there where I show it. Everywhere. Always. Here. Now.
Painting brings to light a prototype of possible realities that we otherwise don't see. Imagination is a physical capability. The painted picture is haptic, multilayered; it is a time-cluster and stimulates the entire bodily intelligence.

Martin Germann

Perhaps it will be painting after all that will survive everything – how it and its weighty history will interact with the currency of an artistic reality that hasn't been evolving in clearly delineated chronological "isms" for quite a while – not to be confused with the post-modern dogma of simultaneity. In the meantime, digitisation came along, too, which added new interpretative layers and challenges to painting and our Western art history is practically cross-examined from the other side by equitable concepts on what art and its roles might be. And how, ironically, painting of all things will now be in a position to react to these situations basically as a global *pars pro toto* of the arts, will be exciting. However, in the end let's not forget that it is always the artists who are the champions, not painting.

Paule Hammer

1997 – I had just learned that I had been accepted to study painting – I had a dispute with my boyfriend in a hostel room in New York. (My friend had emigrated to the USA several years earlier and had just started his IT career.) He said painting hadn't much longer to live, digital imaging processes were much superior to it on many levels and developing quickly.

I don't remember what I responded then.

Today I would say that painting is a physical matter. It is about bodies, material, a state of aggregation and space. Like football. Which will not be replaced by its digital form either (although certainly be influenced by it).

Kaspar König

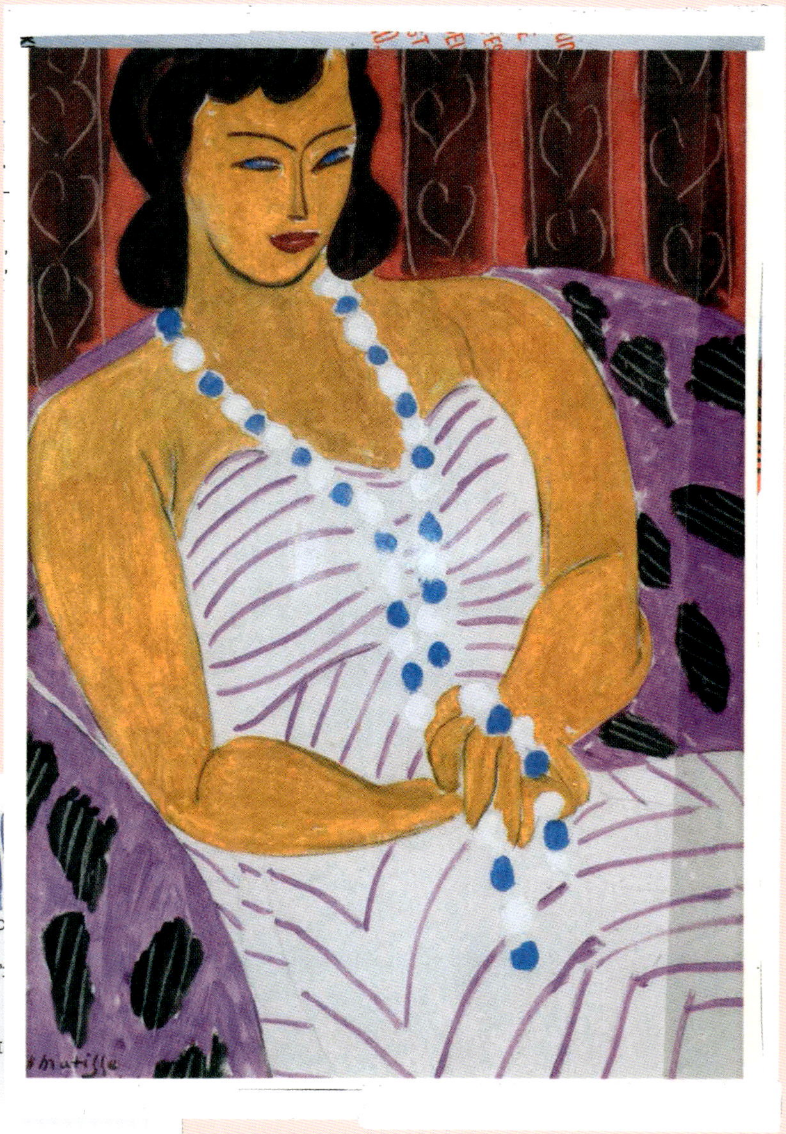

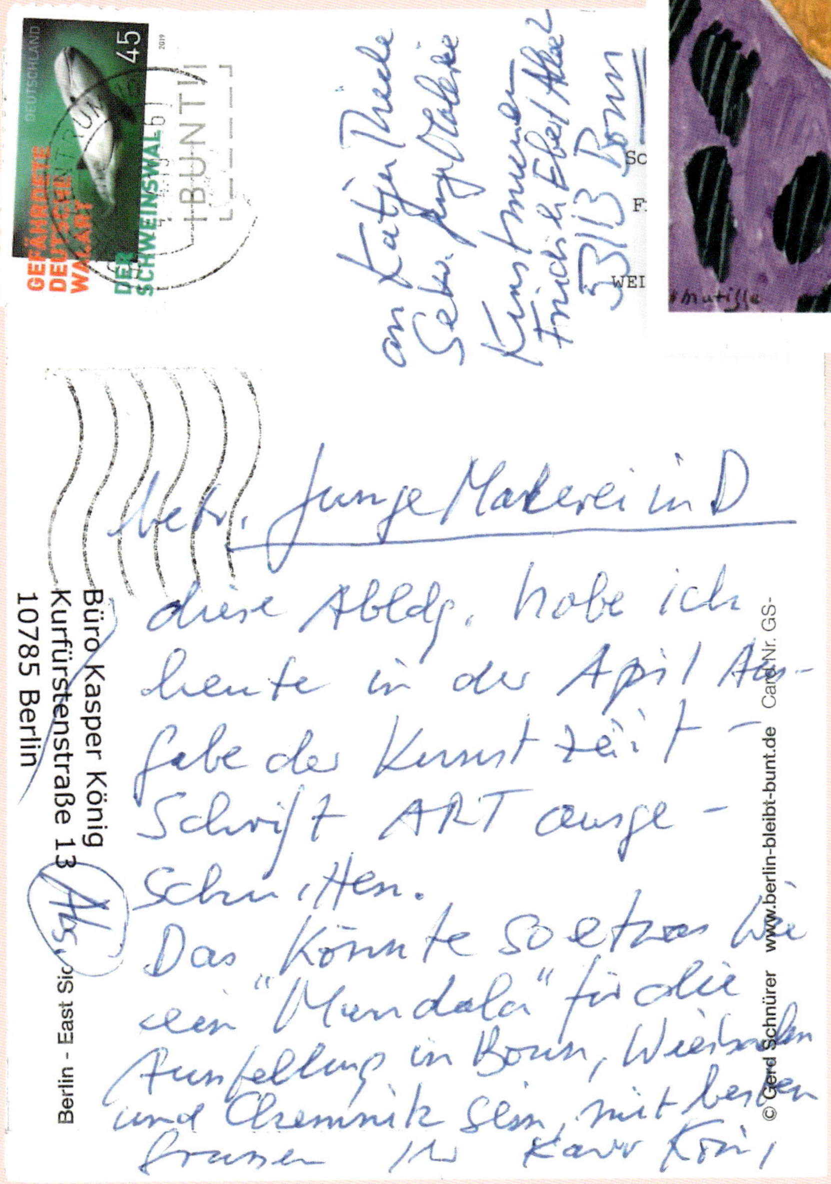

Betr.: Junge Malerei in D

diese Abbldg. habe ich heute in der April Ausgabe der Kunstzeitschrift ART ausgeschnitten.
Das könnte so etwas wie ein "Mandala" für die Ausstellung in Bonn, Wiesbaden und Chemnitz sein, mit besten Grüssen Ihr Kasper König

Kunstmuseum
Friedrich-Ebert-Allee 2
53113 Bonn

Büro Kasper König
Kurfürstenstraße 13
10785 Berlin

Berlin - East Side

© Gerd Schnürer www.berlin-bleibt-bunt.de Card Nr. GS-

Michael Jäger

Of Margins and Presence, or: A Lump of Gold

Superimposed and visible. Bearing the silence of the paintings. Being a reflection. Mirror. The nuances of the colours. To visualise. Not having appeared this way before. Being a painting. From the previous. Blue. Believing one's eyes. Discovering passion, rejecting, allowing and pursuing. Paintings as a stage. The colours of the participants. Orange. Material of the colour, forming the colour. The form, the how of the matter, the what of the matter, of the form. Connecting substance and idea. Sum plus balance. Strength and content. The remembering of sites, of sound, of taste, of elevations and valleys. Violet. Wonder, the added value of the experience gained from seeing. When a piece of wood turns into a chair. Conscious. Black. Taking responsibility. Red. The idea of the works. Subjectivity. The images as reservoirs of sites and memories. White. Utopia and pathos. Green. Opportunity and the place in-between, painting. Objectivity. *Begriffslexikon zur zeitgenössischen Kunst* [Dictionary of Terms in Contemporary Art]. Observing, parting, participating, letting go, inventing, expanding. Subconscious. Arriving at a point of certainty. Repeat. The righting of the painting. Yellow. Seeing a counterpart. Presence. What is happening there? In the end, it's still a lump of gold!

Martin Köttering

It is significant that "painting" is not listed as a separate entry in the *Begriffslexikon zur zeitgenössischen Kunst* [Dictionary of Terms in Contemporary Art]. Nonetheless, as president of an art university, I am aware that the topicality of this classic medium that has been the foundation of the artistic tradition is undisputed: every walk around my own institution confronts me with fifty painterly positions. Young artists continue to love painting, they work on it, trying to test their limits and bringing forth relevant clarifications through it. Contemporary painting that is represented in Hamburg by personalities as diverse as Werner Büttner, Jutta Koether, Anselm Reyle and Jorinde Voigt, is no matter of *l'art pour l'art* in the best sense of the word, but strives for a sober and open discourse with the present world – also in view of its sovereign ignorance of its great tradition.

Hans-Joachim Kreilbohm

For years on end we had to listen to the dictum about the end of painting. Then suddenly, the triumphal march of painting was announced, re-emerging from the ashes again like a phoenix. Frequently, the discourse on painting isn't conducted with the matter-of-fact attitude and deliberateness that it deserves . For some, painting is a commodity, conforming with the market and held in low esteem as a medium, while others still continue to see it as a royal discipline and the one and only true genre. Therefore, the exhibition project, *Now! Painting in Germany Today* offers an opportunity to restart the discourse on painting and also to treat it with greater objectivity.

Ingo Meller

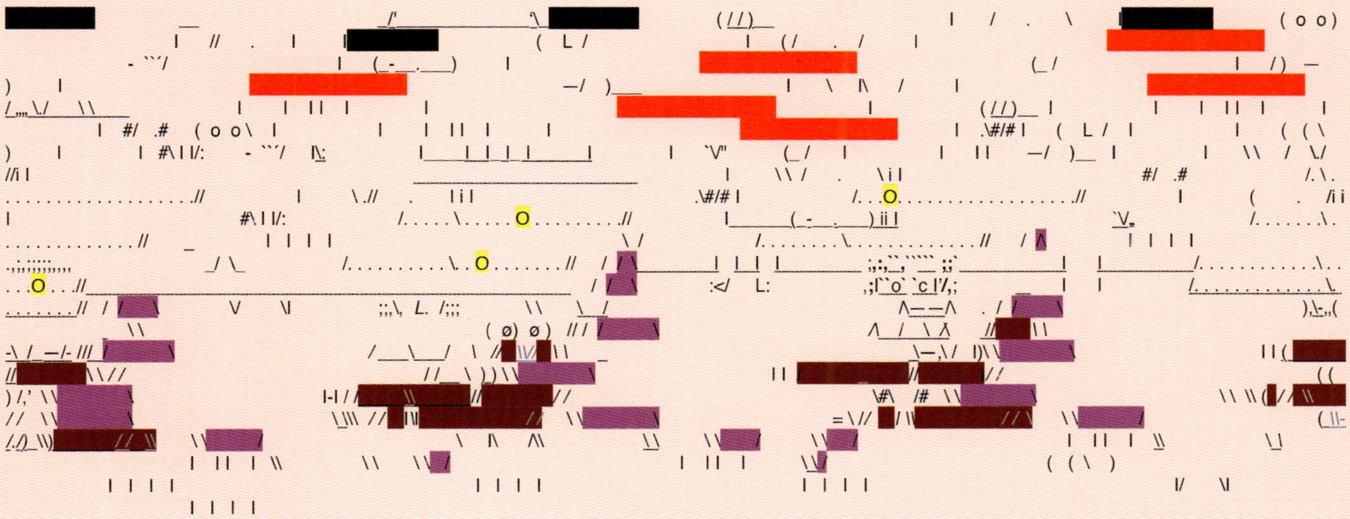

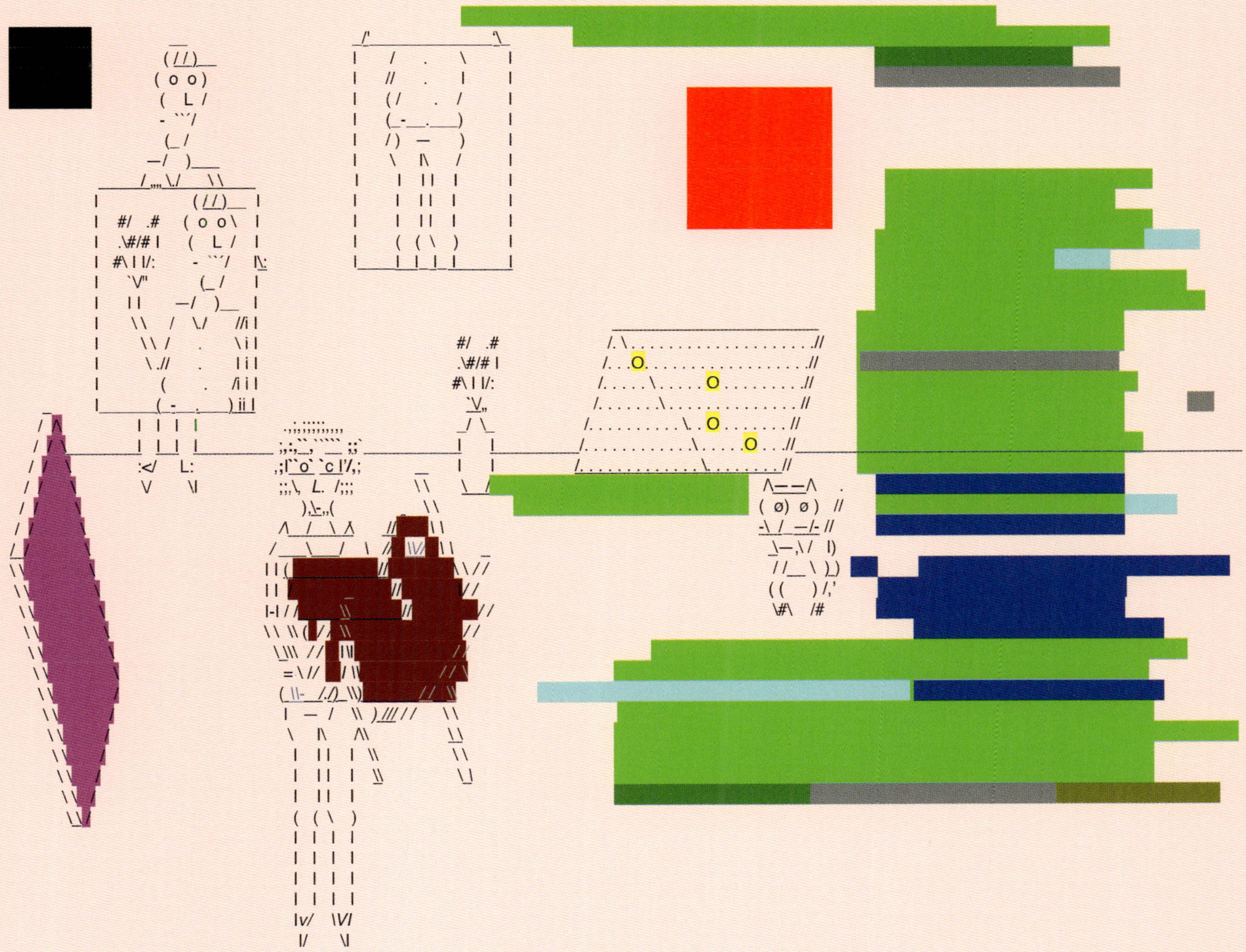

Klaus Merkel

Painting as an argument, a structural model, concept and craft, and painting as caught within the tension of repetition and idea; painting as a frame of reference of idiosyncratic paintings that in model-like fashion mutate into other paintings; repainted, they are building blocks for additional paintings that grow into a progressive system with the passing of time. My paintings follow a syntax or grammar, they are frequently dependent on the installation in space. In the operational field of painting, a showroom can literally be staged or deal with entirely different questions such as reproduction, catalogue and archive. On the other hand, paintings are nothing but canvasses that wish to inform about ideas on availability, the copy, and the migration of images, as well as to comment on, arrange and stage. Theory derived from practice and reflexion on the modalities of the presentation of painting are at the core of my pictorial concept.

Hartmut Neumann

Painting isn't a means to an end, to me it is an inner necessity to articulate my view of the world. Artists look at the world and find their imagery in the process. Even today, painting still exerts a strong emotional force. It should utilise its entire range reflectively to the highest degree.

A gradual transformation of simple but complex ideas as well, it takes place in the process of painting into paintings of lasting insights.

Painting is a concentrate of emotions. Sometimes one drop is sufficient!

Albert Oehlen

I am prepared to refute every statement on painting, provided I haven't done so already. Including, and especially, my own. I am asking all female colleagues to refrain from submitting statements.

Felix Ruhöfer

If the dictum is true that art after 1960 is conceptual, then it has been a minefield since then for young artistic careers. And yet, the artistic practice articulates still today – as a reflexional field of the self, as the assassin of teleological strands of development, as social commentary and as a negation of a merely imagined two-dimensional pictorial space – timeless and fundamental questions to ourselves and our present situation. As several positions in painting make clear, the minefield of painting can be crossed without dying in the process or, worse, becoming boring in the process.

Thomas Rehbein

Painting, the royal class...

All theories about painting become void the moment one sits in front of a canvas. The tools are boundless, provided one has studied painting's history so one can gauge one's own position.

Going deeper, as "the essential is invisible to the eyes" (Antoine de Saint-Exupéry) and will remain so.

Paint does not mean the panel painting, and the panel painting, in turn, is not painting.

"The precondition for understanding modern painting is the awareness that it is not the components of the material that create a painting; rather, the art of painting is determined by the painted quality of the paint within the framework of its objectness." (Joseph Marioni)

Painting means to reorder and re-evaluate marks and to be aware of the essential difference between painting with paint and drawing with coloured material.

The paint itself is an emotional object.

Thomas Scheibitz

Short note on painting, 2019 and later

To me, painting is one of the most unbiased ways to confront art. Doing so, one can seriously and disrespectfully look at up to 5,000 years of the past and/or equally deal with tomorrow's newspaper. It all remains the way it is. – The experience of the artist must be able to stand the test of theory. Regulations such as language, irony, chance and the private cosmos are probably an artist's driving force for which there will not or cannot exist an exact description. An idea and a work of art keep art, and thus painting, alive. Everything else is nothing but speculation.

Annette Schröter

IN SPITE OF IT ALL!
A plea for the house, the cow or the gesture in the painting

There is no area in painting where you can embarrass yourself as much as in figuration. "Why is that so?" – you might ask now or feel like contradicting me.

On the one hand, there is the knapsack of art history full to bursting, which contains first and foremost the oldest medium, namely painting. All of us *figurative artists* have shouldered this bag and keep dragging it through our artistic daily life groaning, whether we like to or not. This knapsack happens to be filled 90% (seen over the decades) with representational figurative motifs: landscapes, images of people, animals and objects surrounding us, called still lifes. In other words: the competition from the depths of art history – the more recent one as well – is immense and if one happens to be wide awake, there is hardly any ignoring it.

Something entirely different might lead to embarrassing imagery, something that stands in our way – with legs apart, hands on hips – that is the INTENTIONAL content that underlies every figurative painting. It knows how to thwart a generous and ambivalent view of the world surrounding us. Whatever one wishes to express, it should, to begin with, speak ONLY the language of painting – without a message, sympathy, aversion, or whatever. That's what makes it doubly complicated. You agree with me, don't you? In addition, the demand for a contemporary mode of expression is always put forward. This may impede, restrict and give rise to doubts. Similar to a fly that circles a light source in the studio incessantly, this expectation is constantly present. Do contemporary and highly topical not also mean that this visual vocabulary – exactly because it's hypermodern (occasionally it also gets hyped up and quickly finds numerous copycats) it seems outmoded faster, fallen out of time than other forms of expression? And, thus, fall prey to the verdict of UNCOOL?

So much on the specific side effects of figurative painting. Paint, turpentine, water, brushes and palette knife, sponge, canvas or paper make up the rest. Distance toward one's own work, toward one's own activities – as much as this is even possible – is of great advantage. Not to be forgotten: a fair amount of self-exploitation in the profane daily life that makes this profession possible for most painters. All of these are necessary to experience the few happy moments in front of one's own paintings.

Peter Tollens

"Colours contain secret properties about harmony or contrast. Properties that produce effects on their own that cannot be expressed through any other medium." (J.W. von Goethe).

Painting is not dead. Painting is still alive.

It is important how we paint. Looking at the history of mankind we recognise: painting has been around longer than the baking of bread, hard to believe, even longer than the brewing of beer. Since the first paintings, the fundamental conditions for painting have not changed very much. Then as now, we apply on a more or less even plane a pigment bound by a medium by hand or with a tool and organise it.

Reflexion and absorption disperse the light, creating an image in our brain.

We recognise colours and forms, an image that imitates nature or illustrates it or, parallel to nature, is so self-evident that it is almost nature itself. We have changed the materials we used, the medium in which the pigments are bound, the forms and the materials of the supports, we changed the function of painting and the mission of painting. It was and still is important how we handle materials, how we interrelate them each other, how we correlate them to the world. If painters today find their authentic way of perception, which truly requires time and attention, we might be lucky to add another aspect to the history of painting, to shift an aspect or perhaps to take away an aspect.

Cornelius Völker

Artists need to be courageous.

Corinne Wasmuht

No other medium seems to be as polarising as painting. The most abstruse discussions are carried out on its back. The spectrum of the buzz words in their wake range from "commodity" to Mount Olympus. Painting is dead! Long live painting!

It seems that as if 90% of all applicants to art academies continue to apply with paintings and drawings. Painting is, as it were, the gateway drug to the arts. It occurred to me that painting is almost automatically equated with art, like a Pavlovian reflex. Written texts, on the other hand, are not considered literature, neither are photos, music and objects generally seen as art. Most paintings, however, are basically not art but frequent repetitions of already existing paintings.

In addition, I am astounded again and again with how little innovation, how derivatively this basically versatile medium is treated. I am all the more thrilled about the rare diamonds that are sparkling amidst the mainstream dross.

Rupert Walser

The world of painting, as the world of art as a whole, is a bit like the Wild West. Both the one in the films and the real one. While there is a difference between the two, both are real. That's what it is still like today: there exists a genuine world of painting, of art ... and another one in the media. The latter is the one that is almost exclusively known and taken for real – and therefore becomes "reality". So: there are cowboys and Indians – okay, basically Indians and cowboys. And land surveyors, trappers, gold prospectors, claim stakers, villains, sheriffs ... and gunslingers who even perform in a circus, travel the world, with gorgeous female assistants and even a real savage.

And then there are the great, wise, white men in faraway big cities who "pay" for all that and take responsibility for it and for that reason make the laws as well. Or they carry out scholarly research, write books, make films about it... Later on, everything ends up in a museum and is history.

There are barely any Indians left – ah well, on reservations. (Oh, and I forgot, the saloons earlier – very important that – they are still around, too, in droves, huge!)

Now more and more women appear on the "scene" – that gives you hope. Perhaps they are the new Indians.

Catalogue of Exhibited Works

Mona Ardeleanu

Bonn

Fade 2019/I, 2019
Oil on canvas,
100 × 80 cm
Private collection, Nuremberg

Fade 2019/IV, 2019
Oil on canvas,
80 × 100 cm
Courtesy Galerie Thomas Fuchs,
private collection

Kuro 2018/IV, 2018
Oil on canvas,
140 × 120 cm
Courtesy Galerie Thomas Fuchs,
private collection, northern Germany

Kuro 2019/I, 2019
Oil on canvas,
140 × 120 cm
Courtesy Galerie Thomas Fuchs,
private collection, Stuttgart

Chemnitz

Fade 2019/II, 2019
Oil on canvas,
100 × 80 cm
Courtesy Galerie Thomas Fuchs,
TRUMPF GmbH + Co. KG

Kuro 2018/II, 2018
Oil on canvas,
140 × 120 cm
Courtesy Galerie Thomas Fuchs

Pliss 2019/I+II, 2019
Oil on canvas, diptych,
70 × 50 cm, each
Courtesy Galerie Thomas Fuchs,
private loan, southern Germany

The Bow 2018/I, 2018
Oil on canvas,
100 × 80 cm
Courtesy Galerie Thomas Fuchs,
private collection, Germany

Wiesbaden

Fade 2019/III, 2019
Oil on canvas,
100 × 80 cm
Courtesy Galerie Thomas Fuchs,
TRUMPF GmbH + Co. KG

Kuro 2018/III, 2018
Oil on canvas,
140 × 120 cm
Courtesy Galerie Thomas Fuchs,
private collection, northern Germany

Kuro 2019/II, 2019
Oil on canvas,
140 × 120 cm
Courtesy Galerie Thomas Fuchs,
private loan, southern Germany

Schnürungen 2019/III, 2019
Oil on canvas,
50 × 40 cm
Courtesy Galerie Thomas Fuchs,
private collection

Israel Aten

Bonn

OTBP, 2019
Synthetic polymer, silver foil,
graphite, pastel, spray paint on canvas,
240 × 160 cm
Courtesy of the artist

Untitled, 2019
Synthetic polymer, spray paint on canvas,
240 × 160 cm
Courtesy of the artist

Interior Dark Brain, 2017
Synthetic polymer, oil stick,
spray paint on canvas,
270 × 190 cm
Courtesy of the artist

Untitled, 2019
Synthetic polymer, silver foil,
graphite, pastel, oil stick,
spray paint on canvas,
290 × 195 cm
Courtesy of the artist

Chemnitz

M31, 2019
Synthetic polymer, pastel,
spray paint on canvas,
240 × 165 cm
Courtesy of the artist

Untitled, 2018
Synthetic polymer, silver foil,
graphite, pastel, spray paint on canvas,
240 × 170 cm
Courtesy of the artist

Evolution Rush, 2019
Synthetic polymer, silver foil, graphite,
pastel, spray paint on canvas,
240 × 160 cm
Courtesy of the artist and Natalia Hug Gallery

Wiesbaden

Flickering Silver Smile, 2019
Synthetic polymer, silver foil,
graphite, spray paint on canvas,
240 × 165 cm
Courtesy of the artist

TG 1 r8, 2019
Synthetic polymer, spray paint on canvas,
240 × 165 cm
Courtesy of the artist

Deathground, 2019
Synthetic polymer, silver foil,
graphite, pastel, spray paint on canvas,
270 × 165 cm
Courtesy of the artist

Paula Baader

Bonn

Fabric Shop, 2018
Mixed media on canvas,
152.5 × 213.5 cm
Courtesy of the artist

Leighton House, 2017
Acrylic on canvas,
167.5 × 152.5 cm
Courtesy of the artist

Frank's Cafe, 2016
Acrylic on canvas,
170 × 150 cm
Courtesy of the artist

Chemnitz

Two Temple Place I+II, 2019
Mixed Media on canvas,
170 × 150 cm
Courtesy of the artist

Greenwich Park, 2018
Acrylic on canvas,
152.5 × 213.5 cm
Courtesy of the artist

Wiesbaden

Tavor 1.0, 2019
Mixed media on canvas,
150 × 220 cm
Courtesy of the artist

King Henry's Mound, 2016
Acrylic on canvas,
152.5 × 213.5 cm
Courtesy of the artist

Lydia Balke

Bonn

Her Fading. My Stumbling. Our Collapse.
(Hibernation Battlefield I), 2017
Oil on muslin,
230 × 160 cm
Courtesy of the artist

A Stained Mattress. Two Frozen Bodies. One
Shattered Life. (Hibernation Battlefield II), 2017
Oil on muslin,
230 × 160 cm
Courtesy of the artist

But What If We Need One Second of Sleep?
(Hibernation Battlefield III and IV), 2018
Oil on muslin, two-parts,
110 × 160 cm, each
Courtesy of the artist

Chemnitz

There Are Too Many Words for Damage.
(Psychosis 1), 2019
Oil, acrylic on muslin,
200 × 140 cm
Courtesy of the artist

Everything That's Left.
And Everything That Isn't Right.
(Psychosis 2), 2019

Oil, acrylic on muslin,
200 × 140 cm
Courtesy of the artist

Nach Scheiße kommt Tod, 2017
Oil on muslin,
160 × 110 cm
Courtesy of the artist

Wiesbaden

Le Corps Sans Organes, 2016
Oil on muslin,
160 × 110 cm
Courtesy of the artist

The Misconception of One Morning
(to Become a Fucking Frozen Life), 2017
Oil on muslin,
160 × 110 cm
Courtesy of the artist

X, 2018
Oil on muslin,
160 × 110 cm
Courtesy of the artist

Cornelia Baltes

Bonn

Semm, 2019
Acrylic on canvas,
140 × 100 cm
Courtesy of the artist, Galleri Nicolai Wallner, Copenhagen

Colm, 2019
Acrylic on canvas,
190 × 140 cm
Courtesy of the artist, Galleri Nicolai Wallner, Copenhagen

Olgh, 2019
Acrylic on canvas,
210 × 150 cm
Courtesy of the artist, Galleri Nicolai Wallner, Copenhagen

Chemnitz

Clak, 2019
Acrylic on canvas,
190 × 140 cm
Courtesy of the artist, Galleri Nicolai Wallner, Copenhagen

Ferl, 2019
Acrylic on canvas,
190 × 140 cm
Courtesy of the artist, Galleri Nicolai Wallner, Copenhagen

Loel, 2019
Acrylic on canvas,
190 × 140 cm
Courtesy of the artist, Galleri Nicolai Wallner, Copenhagen

Wiesbaden

Takk, 2019
Acrylic and oil stick on canvas,
140 × 100 cm
Courtesy of the artist, Galleri Nicolai Wallner, Copenhagen

Immi, 2019
Acrylic on canvas,
190 × 140 cm
Courtesy of the artist, Galleri Nicolai Wallner, Copenhagen

Remu, 2019
Acrylic and oil stick on canvas,
210 × 150 cm
Courtesy of the artist, Galleri Nicolai Wallner, Copenhagen

Jagoda Bednarsky

Bonn

Medela Symphony, 2019
Oil, oil pastels, acrylic and charcoal on canvas,
220 × 190 cm
Courtesy of the artist,
Philipp Pflug Contemporary, Frankfurt a.M.

Shadowland, 2019
Oil, gouache, acrylic and spray paint on canvas,
220 × 190 cm
Courtesy of the artist,
Philipp Pflug Contemporary, Frankfurt a.M.

Chemnitz

J. BEDNARSKY, 2019
Oil, gouache on book object, screen print, wood,
102 × 72.5 × 9 cm
Courtesy of the artist,
Philipp Pflug Contemporary, Frankfurt a.M.

VOLUME 1, 2019
Oil, gouache on book object, screen print, wood,
102 × 72.5 × 9 cm
Courtesy of the artist,
Philipp Pflug Contemporary, Frankfurt a.M.

OPTIX (Temperature), 2018
Oil and spray paint on canvas,
150 × 110 cm
Courtesy of the artist,
Philipp Pflug Contemporary, Frankfurt a.M.

Wiesbaden

Wenn es zu Boden fällt, ist es ein Ei, 2018
Oil, oil pastels, acrylic, charcoal and spray paint on canvas,
220 × 190 cm
Courtesy of the artist,
Philipp Pflug Contemporary, Frankfurt a.M.

WELLNESS (Milk & Honey), 2019
Oil, acrylic, gouache and pastel on canvas,
220 × 190 cm
Courtesy of the artist,
Philipp Pflug Contemporary, Frankfurt a.M.

Viola Bittl

Bonn

Untitled II, 2019
Oil on canvas,
190 × 200 cm
Courtesy of the artist

Untitled I, 2019
Oil on canvas,
190 × 150 cm
Courtesy of the artist

Untitled XII, 2018
Oil on canvas,
160 × 180 cm
Courtesy of the artist

Chemnitz

Untitled V, 2017
Oil on canvas,
180 × 160 cm
Courtesy of the artist

Untitled I, 2018
Oil on canvas,
96 × 96 cm
Courtesy of the artist

Untitled XI, 2016
Oil on canvas,
89 × 76 cm
Courtesy of the artist

Wiesbaden

Untitled XI, 2018
Oil on canvas,
180 × 160 cm
Courtesy of the artist

Untitled VIII, 2016
Oil on canvas,
90 × 140 cm
Courtesy of the artist

Untitled II, 2018
Oil on canvas,
70 × 60 cm
Courtesy of the artist

Untitled V, 2018
Oil on canvas,
68 × 55 cm
Private collection, Frankfurt a.M.

Peppi Bottrop

Bonn

sw prog, 2019
Graphite, bronze pigment and charcoal on canvas,
310 × 380 cm
Courtesy Studio Bottrop

FFP, 2019
Graphite, bronze pigment and charcoal on canvas,
310 × 380 cm
Courtesy Studio Bottrop

Pol S. N., 2019
Graphite, bronze pigment and
charcoal on canvas,
410 × 290 cm
Courtesy Studio Bottrop

Chemnitz

infi scope, 2019
Graphite, copper pigment and
charcoal on canvas,
310 × 280 cm
Courtesy Studio Bottrop

dis phen, 2019
Graphite, copper pigment and
charcoal on canvas,
310 × 280 cm
Courtesy Galerie Gerhardsen Gerner

kadom surs, 2019
Graphite, copper pigment and
charcoal on canvas,
310 × 280 cm
Courtesy Galerie Gerhardsen Gerner

Wiesbaden

perp Eff, 2019
Graphite, aluminium pigment and
charcoal on canvas,
310 × 380 cm
Courtesy Gallery Marc LeBlanc

inef s.c., 2019
Graphite, aluminium pigment and
charcoal on canvas,
310 × 380 cm
Courtesy Gallery Marc LeBlanc

Andreas Breunig

Bonn

Hi >°< LoRes No. 60, 2019
Oil, graphite and charcoal on canvas,
210 × 260 cm
Courtesy Friedrichs Collection

Hi >°< LoRes No. 24, 2018
Oil, graphite and charcoal on canvas,
210 × 145 cm
Courtesy Nino Mier Collection

Hi >°< LoRes No. 56, 2019
Oil, graphite and charcoal on canvas,
210 × 170 cm
Courtesy Nino Mier Collection

Chemnitz

Hi >°< LoRes No. 61, 2019
Oil, graphite and charcoal on canvas,
210 × 170 cm
Courtesy of the artist,
Alexander Warhus Art Advisory/Cologne

Hi >°< LoRes No. 70, 2019
Oil, graphite and charcoal on canvas,
210 × 260 cm
Courtesy of the artist, Nino Mier Gallery/LA

Hi >°< LoRes No. 66, 2019
Oil, graphite and charcoal on canvas,
210 × 140 cm
Courtesy of the artist, Nino Mier Gallery/LA

Wiesbaden

Hi >°< LoRes No. 62, 2019
Oil, graphite and charcoal on canvas,
210 × 170 cm
Courtesy of the artist, Nino Mier Gallery/LA

Hi >°< LoRes No. 71, 2019
Oil, graphite and charcoal on canvas,
210 × 140 cm
Courtesy of the artist & Alexander
Warhus Art Advisory/Cologne

Hi >°< LoRes No. 72, 2019
Oil, graphite and charcoal on canvas,
210 × 140 cm
Courtesy of the artist, Nino Mier Gallery/LA

Paul Czerlitzki

Bonn

Delay, 2019
Acrylic on canvas, folding chairs,
ca. 255 × 190 × 50 cm, total
Courtesy of the artist, Galerie annex14

Delay, 2019
Acrylic on canvas, folding chairs,
ca. 255 × 190 × 50 cm, total
Courtesy of the artist, Galerie annex14

Chemnitz

Untitled, 2011–2019
Acrylic on canvas,
210 × 190 cm
Courtesy of the artist, Galerie Laurent Godin

Untitled, 2011–2019
Acrylic on canvas,
210 × 190 cm
Courtesy of the artist, Galerie Laurent Godin

Untitled, 2011–2019
Acrylic on canvas,
210 × 190 cm
Courtesy of the artist, Galerie Laurent Godin

Wiesbaden

Untitled, 2011
Acrylic on canvas,
210 × 190 cm
Courtesy of the artist, Konrad Fischer Galerie

Untitled, 2011–2019
Acrylic on canvas,
210 × 190 cm
Courtesy of the artist, Konrad Fischer Galerie

Benjamin Dittrich

Bonn

Devo. (2), 2018
Lacquer on canvas,
180 × 110 cm
Courtesy of the artist

Kamb., 2017
Lacquer on canvas,
165 × 115 cm
Courtesy of the artist

Karb., 2018
Lacquer on canvas,
200 × 140 cm
Courtesy of the artist

SUS-01, 2018
Lacquer on canvas,
180 × 120 cm
Courtesy of the artist

Chemnitz

DHE3, 2017
Lacquer on canvas,
50 × 35 cm
Courtesy of the artist

KEN35-SW, 2016
Lacquer on canvas,
84 × 60 cm
Courtesy of the artist

KEN55-SW, 2016
Lacquer on canvas,
84 × 60 cm
Courtesy of the artist

Sedimentgesteine, 2019
Lacquer on canvas,
170 × 110 cm
Courtesy of the artist

Trias, 2019
Lacquer on canvas,
125 × 80 cm
Courtesy of the artist

Wiesbaden

Ordovizium (2), 2019
Lacquer on canvas,
180 × 110 cm
Courtesy of the artist

SUE3, 2017
Lacquer on canvas,
115 × 80 cm
Courtesy of the artist

SUE4, 2017
Lacquer on canvas,
70 × 50 cm
Courtesy of the artist

Jens Einhorn

Bonn

Auf Dem Heimweg, 2019
Oil, acrylic, polyester, collage on canvas,
200 × 150 cm
Courtesy of the artist

Tag Ohne Schatten, 2019
Acrylic, linen, muslin, canvas, cotton,
collage on canvas,
220 × 180 cm
Courtesy of the artist

Tag Am Fenster, 2019
Acrylic, oil, canvas, mesh material,
collage on canvas,
200 × 150 cm
Courtesy of the artist

Chemnitz

Benzin Und Kartoffelchips, 2019
Cotton, muslin, linen, canvas, oil, acrylic, ink, gesso, mesh material, glue, collage on canvas,
200 × 150 cm
Courtesy of the artist

Einen Schritt Weiter, 2019
Mesh material, polyester fabric, oil, acrylics, gesso, glue, collage on canvas,
200 × 150 cm
Courtesy of the artist

Kaugummiwelt, 2019
Linen, muslin, cotton, polyester fabric, mesh material, oil, acrylic, gesso, glue, collage on canvas,
200 × 150 cm
Private collection

Wiesbaden

Auf Der Treppe Vor Dem Haus, 2019
Acrylic, oil, ink, gesso, cotton, linen polyester fabric, mesh material, glue, collage on canvas,
200 × 150 cm
Courtesy of the artist

Straße Der Jugend, 2019
Oil, acrylic, polyester fabric, gesso, glue, collage on canvas,
200 × 150 cm
Courtesy of the artist

Wir Starren Löcher In Die Wand, 2019
Oil, acrylic, spray paint, linen, muslin, cotton, glue, collage on canvas,
200 × 150 cm
Courtesy of the artist

Jenny Forster

Bonn

Gestirn_I, 2018
Mixed media on paper laid on wood,
180 × 120 cm
Courtesy of the artist

Gestirn_IV, 2018
Mixed media on paper laid on wood,
180 × 120 cm
Courtesy of the artist

Gestirn_V, 2018
Mixed media on paper laid on wood,
180 × 120 cm
Courtesy of the artist

Chemnitz

Paravent_I, 2016
Mixed media on paper laid on wood,
180 × 120 cm
Courtesy of the artist

Paravent_II, 2016
Mixed media on paper laid on wood,
180 × 120 cm
Courtesy of the artist

Paravent_III, 2016
Mixed media on paper laid on wood,
180 × 120 cm
Courtesy of the artist

Wiesbaden

Gestirn_VII, 2019
Mixed media on paper laid on wood,
180 × 120 cm
Courtesy of the artist

Port, 2017/18
Mixed media on paper laid on wood,
180 × 120 cm
Courtesy of the artist

Pyrit, 2016
Mixed media on paper laid on wood,
180 × 120 cm
Courtesy of the artist

Pius Fox

Bonn

Aufgewirbelt, 2015
Oil on glass,
40 × 30 cm
Courtesy of the artist

Diesseits des Meeres, 2019
Oil and egg tempera on canvas,
150 × 110 cm
Courtesy of the artist, CONRADS Düsseldorf

Tagesreste, 2019
Oil and egg tempera on canvas,
150 × 110 cm
Courtesy of the artist, CONRADS Düsseldorf

Die andere Seite des Mondes, 2019
Oil and egg tempera on canvas,
90 × 60 cm
Courtesy of the artist, CONRADS Düsseldorf

Raumdurchquerung, 2018
Oil and egg tempera on canvas,
200 × 150 cm
private collection, Hamburg,
CONRADS Düsseldorf

Untitled, 2016
Oil on glass,
40 × 30 cm
Courtesy of the artist

Ping Pong, 2019
Egg tempera and oil on paper,
28 × 20 cm
Courtesy of the artist

Tanoki und das Vogelnest, 2019
Egg tempera on paper,
24.5 × 17 cm
Courtesy of the artist

Ausblick, 2017
Crayon on paper,
25 × 17.2 cm
Courtesy of the artist

Dach, 2017
Crayon on paper,
23.8 × 17.2 cm
Courtesy of the artist

Wasserglas, 2019
Oil and egg tempera on canvas,
90 × 80 cm
Courtesy of the artist,
CONRADS Düsseldorf

Chemnitz

Burgtheater, 2017
Crayon and watercolour on paper,
24 × 18 cm
Courtesy of the artist

Berge über Berge, 2019
Egg tempera and oil on paper,
28 × 20 cm
Courtesy of the artist,
CONRADS Düsseldorf

Türschwelle, 2019
Egg tempera and oil on paper,
24 × 18 cm
Courtesy of the artist

Etappen, 2018
Gouache and egg tempera on paper,
28 × 20 cm
Courtesy of the artist,
Galerie Martin Mertens

Das Versprechen, 2019
Oil and egg tempera on paper laid on aluminium,
28 × 20 cm
Courtesy of the artist,
Galerie Martin Mertens

Fensterfall, 2018
Acrylic and egg tempera on paper,
44 × 32 cm
Courtesy of the artist,
Galerie Martin Mertens

Wiesbaden

Blick in den Flur, 2018
Oil on paper,
24 × 17 cm
Courtesy of the artist

Der Raum der Koralle, 2018
Oil on canvas, 33 × 24 cm
Courtesy of the artist

Ha Ha, 2017
Crayon and oil pastel on paper,
25 × 17 cm
Courtesy of the artist

Pyramid Song, 2019
Egg tempera and oil on paper,
24 × 17 cm
Courtesy of the artist,
Galerie Martin Mertens

Maya, 2019
Egg tempera and oil on paper,
24 × 18 cm
Courtesy of the artist,
Galerie Martin Mertens

Max Frintrop

Bonn

Untitled (Das Geld der Bienen ist der Honigsaft), 2019
Ink, acrylic, pigments on canvas,
290 × 205 cm
Courtesy of the artist,
Berthold Pott Gallery

Untitled (Aphex Twin), 2019
Ink, acrylic, pigments on canvas,
220 × 170 cm
Courtesy of the artist,
Berthold Pott Gallery

Untitled (Immer Nein), 2018
Ink, acrylic, pigments on canvas,
200 × 300 cm
Courtesy Kunstmuseum Bonn,
donation from Berthold Pott Gallery, 2019

Chemnitz

Untitled (Literatur nervt), 2019
Ink, acrylic, pigments on canvas,
170 × 220 cm
Courtesy of the artist,
Berthold Pott Gallery

Untitled (Controlled Opposition), 2019
Ink, acrylic, pigments on canvas,
220 × 170 cm
Courtesy of the artist,
Berthold Pott Gallery

Untitled (Spandau), 2019
Ink, acrylic, pigments on canvas,
220 × 170 cm
Courtesy of the artist,
Berthold Pott Gallery

Wiesbaden

Untitled (know more games), 2019
Ink, acrylic, pigments on canvas,
290 × 205 cm
Courtesy of the artist,
Berthold Pott Gallery

Untitled
(auf Dornen schlief ich wie auf Flaum), 2019
Ink, acrylic, pigments on canvas,
290 × 205 cm
Courtesy of the artist,
Berthold Pott Gallery

Untitled (Dizzy), 2019
Ink, acrylic, pigments on canvas,
200 × 150 cm
Courtesy of the artist,
Berthold Pott Gallery

Sabrina Fritsch

Bonn

Nyx, 2018
Oil, acrylic on jute,
280 × 200 cm
Courtesy of the artist,
VAN HORN, Düsseldorf

Aer, 2018
Oil, acrylic on jute,
280 × 200 cm
Courtesy of the artist,
VAN HORN, Düsseldorf

Var, 2018
Oil, acrylic on jute,
280 × 200 cm
Courtesy of the artist,
VAN HORN, Düsseldorf

Nut, 2019
Oil, acrylic on jute,
280 × 200 cm
Courtesy of the artist,
VAN HORN, Düsseldorf

Chemnitz

pBuYrRl, 2019
Oil, acrylic on burlap, laid on cotton,
95 × 70 cm
Courtesy of the artist,
VAN HORN, Düsseldorf

play II, 2018
Acrylic, ink on canvas,
180 × 130 cm
Courtesy of the artist,
VAN HORN, Düsseldorf

BIYIRIB, 2019
Oil, acrylic on cotton,
280 × 200 cm
Joanna and Karsten Pradel, Düsseldorf

play I, 2018
Acrylic, ink on cotton,
180 × 130 cm
Courtesy of the artist,
VAN HORN, Düsseldorf

Wiesbaden

sItIaIhI, 2019
Acrylic on canvas,
280 × 200 cm
Courtesy of the artist,
VAN HORN, Düsseldorf

kGnPiOt, 2019
Oil, acrylic on burlap, laid on cotton,
95 × 70 cm
Courtesy of the artist,
VAN HORN, Düsseldorf

wCiAlRdD, 2019
Oil, acrylic on jute,
220 × 160 cm
Courtesy of the artist,
VAN HORN, Düsseldorf

Ina Gerken

Bonn

Untitled (Efflorescent), 2019
Acrylic and Japan paper on polyester canvas,
130 × 100 cm
Courtesy of the artist,
Makasiini Contemporary

Untitled (This must be the place), 2019
Acrylic and Japan paper on polyester canvas,
200 × 300 cm
Courtesy of the artist, Achenbach Hagemeier

Untitled (Lady Bug), 2019
Acrylic and Japan paper on polyester canvas,
100 × 80 cm
Courtesy of the artist,
Makasiini Contemporary

Chemnitz

Untitled (Lying has to stop), 2018
Acrylic and Japan paper on polyester canvas,
100 × 80 cm
Courtesy of the artist, Achenbach Hagemeier

Untitled (It won't be me), 2019
Acrylic and Japan paper on polyester canvas,
180 × 240 cm
Courtesy of the artist, Achenbach Hagemeier

Untitled (After Laughter), 2019
Acrylic and Japan paper on polyester canvas,
180 × 150 cm
Courtesy of the artist, Achenbach Hagemeier

Wiesbaden

Untitled (W.B.), 2018
Acrylic and Japan paper on canvas,
100 × 80 cm
Courtesy of the artist, Achenbach Hagemeier

Untitled (Imitationen), 2019
Acrylic and Japan paper on polyester canvas,
180 × 150 cm
Courtesy of the artist,
Makasiini Contemporary

Untitled (We're through), 2019
Acrylic and Japan paper on polyester canvas,
180 × 240 cm
Courtesy of the artist,
Makasiini Contemporary

Fabian Ginsberg

Bonn

Untitled (Miele, Serie IN), 2018
Acrylic and lacquer on aluminium,
Plexiglass, wood,
190 × 96 × 6.5 cm
Courtesy of the artist

Untitled (Apple, Serie IN), 2018
Acrylic and lacquer on aluminium,
Plexiglass, wood,
190 × 96 × 6.5 cm
Courtesy of the artist

Untitled (outside, Serie IS), 2017/19
Digital print on paper laid on jute, lacquer,
acrylic, wood, Plexiglass,
191 × 95 × 8 cm
Courtesy of the artist

Chemnitz

Untitled (Ihr sollt Scheide werden, Serie IB),
2019
Digital print on paper laid on jute, lacquer,
acrylic, wood, Plexiglass,
134 × 140 × 8 cm
Courtesy of the artist

Untitled (Canon, Serie IN), 2018
Acrylic and lacquer on aluminium,
Plexiglass, wood,
190 × 96 × 6.5 cm
Courtesy of the artist

Untitled (Grundriss Städtische Galerie Villingen-Schwenningen, Serie R), 2018
Digital print on paper, Plexiglass, oil, wood, 58.1 × 42.2 × 4.1 cm
Courtesy of the artist

Untitled (Grundriss Kunstverein Zlin, Serie R), 2018
Digital print on paper, aluminium, foil, wood, 45.9 × 31.3 × 4.1 cm
Courtesy of the artist

Wiesbaden

Liste, 2019
Digital printon paper, aluminium, foil, wood, 43 × 28 × 4 cm
Courtesy of the artist

Untitled (Glock, Serie IN), 2018
Acrylic and lacquer on aluminium, Plexiglass, wood,
190 × 97 × 6.5 cm
Courtesy of the artist

Untitled (outside, Serie IS), 2017/19
Digital print on paper laid on jute, lacquer, acrylic, wood, Plexiglass,
134 × 136 × 8 cm
Courtesy of the artist

Gregor Gleiwitz

Bonn

02.05.2016, 2016
Oil on canvas,
269.1 × 191.3 cm
SETAREH

10.12.2018, 2018
Oil on canvas,
252 × 201 cm
SETAREH

27.02.2018, 2018
Oil on canvas,
246.2 × 194.9 cm
Private collection, Rhineland

Chemnitz

02.11.2017, 2017
Oil on canvas,
244.0 × 192.7 cm
SETAREH

05.12.2017, 2017
Oil on canvas,
240 × 190 cm
SETAREH

07.04.2018, 2018
Oil on canvas,
237.4 × 196.5 cm
Private collection

Wiesbaden

12.07.2017, 2017
Oil on canvas,
289 × 199 cm
SETAREH

18.01.2019, 2019
Oil on canvas,
265.5 × 199.9 cm
SETAREH

19.09.2018, 2018
Oil on canvas,
264.5 × 200 cm
SETAREH

Lukas Glinkowski

Bonn

Funny Games, 2018
Oil and glass paint, mirror tiles on wood construction, four-parts,
210 × 240 × 4 cm
Courtesy of the artist

Crosswords, 2019
Oil and glass paint, mirror tiles on wood construction, four-parts,
210 × 240 × 4 cm
Courtesy of the artist

Chemnitz

Stern, Luchlandschaft, Baum und einsamer Falter, 2017
Lacquer and spray paint, tiles on wood construction,
230 × 515 cm
Courtesy of the artist

87.6–107.8, 2019
Oil, glass and lacquer paint, mirror tiles on wood construction,
210 × 240 × 4 cm
Courtesy of the artist

Eau de toilette VI, 2018
Oil and glass paint, markers, tiles on wood construction,
60 × 50 × 3 cm
Courtesy of the artist

Wiesbaden

S 42/04, 2016
Lacquer and spray paint, tiles on wood construction,
120 × 120 cm
Courtesy of the artist

Margherita, 2019
Lacquer, markers, tiles on wood construction,
40 × 30 × 3 cm
Courtesy of the artist

Untitled, 2019
Lacquer and glass paint, mirror tiles on wood construction,
40 × 30 × 3 cm
Courtesy of the artist

Sebastian Gögel

Bonn

Leerer Raum, 2017
Oil on canvas,
150 × 200 cm
Courtesy of the artist, Laden für Nichts

Leumund, 2017
Oil on canvas,
270 × 190 cm
Courtesy of the artist, Laden für Nichts

Gehäuse, 2018
Oil on canvas,
130 × 100 cm
Courtesy of the artist, Laden für Nichts

Chemnitz

Elements, 2017
Oil on canvas,
130 × 110cm
Courtesy of the artist, Laden für Nichts

Spalt, 2019
Oil on canvas,
240 × 180 cm
Courtesy of the artist, Laden für Nichts

Versenkung, 2019
Oil on canvas,
240 × 180 cm
Courtesy of the artist, Laden für Nichts

Wiesbaden

Prepared, 2018/19
Oil on canvas,
170 × 130 cm
Courtesy of the artist, Laden für Nichts

Hyperchon, 2019
Oil on canvas,
200 × 150 cm
Courtesy of the artist, Laden für Nichts

Frucht, 2019
Oil on canvas,
24 × 30 cm
Courtesy of the artist, Laden für Nichts

Henriette Grahnert

Bonn

Stilläleiftäbel, 2017
Acrylic on canvas,
190 × 140 cm
Collection Hildebrand, Leipzig

My son my sun, 2017
Acrylic on canvas,
43 × 34 cm
Courtesy of the artist, Galerie Kleindienst, Leipzig

Doubleface, 2019
Acrylic on canvas,
150 × 120 cm
Courtesy of the artist, Galerie Kleindienst, Leipzig

Keeping secrets 6, 2016
Acrylic on canvas,
180 × 140 cm
Courtesy of the artist,
Galerie Kleindienst, Leipzig

Chemnitz

The cute ghost, 2017
Acrylic on canvas,
150 × 120cm
Private collection

The painters table, 2017
Acrylic on canvas,
190 × 140cm
Private property, Leipzig

Where the magic happens, 2017
Acrylic on canvas,
200 × 150 cm
Courtesy of the artist,
Galerie Kleindienst, Leipzig

Wiesbaden

A page of you I prefer to flip, 2017
Acrylic on canvas,
200 × 150 cm
Courtesy of the artist,
Galerie Kleindienst, Leipzig

X, 2017
Acrylic on canvas,
43 × 34 cm
Courtesy of the artist,
Galerie Kleindienst, Leipzig

The tricky thing with the right balance, 2017
Acrylic on canvas,
120 × 90 cm
Courtesy of the artist,
Galerie Kleindienst, Leipzig

Don't miss the magical moment, 2017
Acrylic on canvas,
170 × 127 cm
Courtesy of the artist,
Galerie Kleindienst, Leipzig

Dana Greiner

Bonn

preplex xv, 2019
Spray paint on acrylic glass,
125 × 85 cm
Courtesy of the artist

Untitled (tria balette), 2019
Acrylic media, epoxy resin, spray paint,
graphite on canvas,
180 × 135 cm
Courtesy of the artist

preplex xi, 2019
Spray paint, acrylic on acrylic glass,
125 × 85 cm
Courtesy of the artist

Chemnitz

walking and phalling, 2018
Acrylic media, epoxy resin, vinyl on canvas,
110 × 90 cm
Courtesy of the artist

preplex xiii, 2019
Spray paint on acrylic glass,
125 × 85 cm
Courtesy of the artist

preplex xvi, 2019
Spray paint on acrylic glass,
125 × 85 cm
Courtesy of the artist

Wiesbaden

Sanctuary, 2019
Pigment without binder on support,
ø 100 cm
Courtesy of the artist

Untitled (querelle), 2019
Acrylic media, oil, spray paint, lacquer, vinyl,
graphite, rope on wood laid on canvas,
180 × 135 cm
Courtesy of the artist

Untitled (struggle of strength), 2019
Acrylic media, epoxy resin, spray paint,
graphite, tape, ribbon trim,
angle section on canvas,
180 × 135 cm
Courtesy of the artist

Vivian Greven

Bonn

Ais, 2019
Oil and acrylic on canvas,
180 × 156 cm
Private collection, France

Leea, 2017
Oil on canvas,
120 × 110 cm
SETAREH

)(VI, 2018
Oil on canvas,
180 × 130 cm
Private collection Andorfer

Aort I, 2019
Oil and acrylic on canvas,
140 × 105 cm
J. and C. Sieglen Collection

Aort II, 2019
Oil and acrylic on canvas,
140 × 105 cm
Wolfgang Zäh, Munich Collection

Chemnitz

Grazie, 2017
Oil on canvas,
43 × 35 cm
Courtesy of the artist

Lamia, 2017
Oil on canvas,
43 × 32 cm
Dirk Kessler Collection

Unda I, 2018
Oil and acrylic on canvas,
60 × 60 cm
Holle Collection

Lamia IV, 2019
Oil and acrylic on canvas,
170 × 128 cm
Apel Collection

Wiesbaden

Area, 2018
Oil and acrylic on canvas,
180 × 120 cm
Private collection Ibing

Tru I, 2018
Oil and acrylic on canvas,
49 × 35 cm
Private collection Schmalbruch

Tru II, 2018
Oil and acrylic on canvas,
60 × 41 cm
Private collection Schmalbruch

Toulu Hassani

Bonn

Untitled, 2018
Oil on canvas,
46 × 34 cm
Ültzen/Westhoff Collection

Echelette, 2018
Epoxy resin, pigment, aluminium powder
and marble powder,
36 × 27.5 cm
Private collection

Untitled, 2019
Mechanical pencil and oil on canvas,
50 × 39 cm
Courtesy of the artist, Petra Rinck Galerie

Untitled, 2017
Nitro-frottage, oil on canvas,
50 × 39 cm
Ültzen/Westhoff Collection

Untitled, 2019
Polymer gypsum aluminium powder and
pigment, in two parts,
57 × 44 cm, each
Courtesy of the artist, Petra Rinck Galerie

Chemnitz

Untitled, 2019
Oil on canvas,
43 × 33 cm
Pit Hofmann, Frankfurt a. M.

Untitled, 2018
Mechanical pencil and oil on canvas,
50 × 39 cm
Private property

Untitled, 2016
Epoxy resin and pigment,
68 × 55 cm
Udo and Anette Brandhorst Collection

Untitled, 2017
Epoxy resin and pigment,
and aluminium powder,
43 × 31 cm
Courtesy of the artist, Petra Rinck Galerie

Wiesbaden

Untitled, 2017
Epoxy resin and pigment,
65.7 × 53 cm
Ültzen/Westhoff Collection

Untitled, 2018
Epoxy resin and pigment,
36 × 27.5 cm
Ültzen/Westhoff Collection

Untitled, 2019
Mechanical pencil and oil on canvas,
50 × 39 cm
Private collection

Untitled, 2018
Epoxy resin and pigment,
55 × 43 cm
Ültzen/Westhoff Collection

Sabrina Haunsperg

Bonn

Untitled (040319), 2019
Oil on canvas,
240 × 300 cm
Courtesy of the artist

Untitled (120319), 2019
Oil on canvas,
190 × 240 cm
Courtesy of the artist

Chemnitz

Untitled (270219), 2019
Oil on canvas,
90 × 110 cm
Courtesy of the artist

Untitled (171118), 2018
Oil on canvas,
190 × 240 cm
Courtesy of the artist

Untitled (140319), 2019
Oil on canvas,
90 × 110 cm
Courtesy of the artist

Wiesbaden

Untitled (130319), 2019
Oil and tempera on canvas,
190 × 240 cm
Courtesy of the artist

Untitled (151118), 2018
Oil and tempera on canvas,
120 × 150 cm
Courtesy of the artist

Untitled (221118), 2018
Oil on canvas,
200 × 240 cm
Courtesy of the artist

Franziska Holstein

Bonn

28 from Untitled (39),
Selection of 28 works from the
39-part series, framed, acrylic on paper,
65 × 50 cm, each, ca. 295 × 405 cm, total
Courtesy of the artist,
Galerie Klaus Gerrit Friese, Berlin,
Galerie ASPN, Leipzig, and private collections

Chemnitz

Untitled (32), 2019
32-part series, acrylic on paper, framed,
42 × 29.7 cm, each, ca. 195 × 290 cm total
Courtesy of the artist,
Galerie Klaus Gerrit Friese,
Berlin, and Galerie ASPN, Leipzig

Wiesbaden

Untitled (45), 2018
45-part series, acrylic on paper, framed,
42 × 29.7 cm, each, ca. 245 × 325 m, total
Courtesy of the artist,
Galerie Klaus Gerrit Friese,
Berlin, and Galerie ASPN, Leipzig

Aneta Kajzer

Bonn

AI Taking Over, 2019
Oil and acrylic on canvas,
300 × 200 cm
Courtesy of the artist,
CONRADS Düsseldorf

Riding for the Feeling, 2017
Oil and acrylic on canvas,
280 × 190 cm
Courtesy of the artist,
CONRADS Düsseldorf

Space Invaders, 2019
Oil and acrylic on canvas,
300 × 200 cm
Courtesy of the artist,
CONRADS Düsseldorf

Chemnitz

I've Got No Brain Baby, 2017
Oil and acrylic on canvas,
160 × 145 cm
Private collection, Berlin

Out of the Dark, 2018
Oil on canvas,
200 × 140 cm
Courtesy of the artist,
CONRADS Düsseldorf

Witching Hour, 2019
Oil and acrylic on canvas,
200 × 150 cm
Courtesy of the artist,
CONRADS Düsseldorf

Wiesbaden

Badman and Boy, 2019
Oil and acrylic on canvas,
280 × 200 cm
Courtesy of the artist,
CONRADS Düsseldorf

Master of Puppets, 2019
Oil and acrylic on canvas,
160 × 110 cm
Private collection, Seoul

Thumbs Up, 2018
Oil and acrylic on canvas,
200 × 150 cm
Courtesy of the artist,
CONRADS Düsseldorf

Sumi Kim

Bonn

Untitled, 2018
Oil on canvas,
200 × 150 cm
Courtesy of the artist

Untitled, 2016
Oil on canvas,
150 × 150 cm
Courtesy of the artist

Untitled, 2019
Oil on canvas,
150 × 150 cm
Courtesy of the artist

Chemnitz

Untitled, 2018
Oil on canvas,
150 × 150 cm
Courtesy of the artist

Untitled, 2015
Oil on canvas,
200 × 120 cm
Courtesy of the artist

Untitled, 2019
Oil on canvas,
150 × 150 cm
Courtesy of the artist

Wiesbaden

Untitled, 2016
Oil on canvas,
200 × 145 cm
Courtesy of the artist

Untitled, 2019
Oil on canvas,
150 × 150 cm
Courtesy of the artist

Untitled, 2019
Oil on canvas,
190 × 120 cm
Courtesy of the artist

Maximilian Kirmse

Bonn

G.O.W., 2017
Oil on canvas,
160 × 130 cm
Kunstfonds, Staatliche Kunstsammlungen Dresden, Förderankäufe der Kulturstiftung Sachsen [Art Fund, State Art Collections Dresden, acquisitions by the Saxon Culture Fund], 2018

N.B.S.II, 2018
Oil on canvas,
160 × 130 cm
Philipp Haverkampf Galerie,
private collection, Berlin

Untitled, 2018
Oil on canvas,
160 × 130 cm
Haus N Kiel collection / Athens

F.S., 2017
Oil on canvas,
160 × 130 cm
Loaned by the artist,
Philipp Haverkampf Galerie

Chemnitz

M.W.B., 2017
Oil on canvas,
65 × 45 cm
Heidi Specker Collection, Berlin

Verkehr 4, 2019
Oil on canvas,
130 × 160 cm
Breitkopf Collection, Berlin

G.F.B., 2016
Oil on canvas,
160 × 130 cm
Courtesy of the artist

P.I., 2016
Oil on canvas,
160 × 130 cm
Courtesy of the artist

Wiesbaden

Dinos, 2019
Oil on canvas,
160 × 190 cm
Courtesy of the artist

am Brunnen, 2019
Oil on canvas,
160 × 130 cm
Philipp Haverkampf Galerie,
Simonow Collection

L.P.D., 2016
Oil on canvas,
160 × 130 cm
Private collection

Li-Wen Kuo

Bonn

Pars pro Toto, 2019
Oil on canvas,
185 × 145 cm
Courtesy of the artist

Häutung, 2019
Oil on canvas,
200 × 160 cm
Courtesy of the artist

Vorzüge eines Hammers, 2019
Oil on canvas,
210 × 160 cm
Courtesy of the artist

Chemnitz

Universal Grammar, 2019
Oil on canvas,
145 × 125 cm
Courtesy of the artist

Wilde Ontologie, 2018/19
Oil on canvas,
73 × 65 cm
Courtesy of the artist

Séance, 2019
Oil on canvas,
170 × 130 cm
Courtesy of the artist

Wiesbaden

In einem dunklen Wort, 2019
Oil on canvas,
200 × 165 cm
Courtesy of the artist

Metanoia, 2019
Oil on canvas,
200 × 150 cm
Courtesy of the artist

Schlafwandel, 2017/19
Oil on canvas,
125 × 105 cm
Courtesy of the artist

David Lehmann

Bonn

Halbzeit, 2019
Triptych, gouache, resin, egg tempera,
dispersion paint, copper oxidation,
gold leaf and oil on canvas,
220 × 180 cm, each, 220 × 540 cm, total
Courtesy of the artist

Waste Land, 2014/15
Gouache, resin, egg tempera, dispersion paint,
copper oxidation and oil on canvas,
180 × 220 cm
Courtesy of the artist

Hedoné, 2018
Gouache, resin, dispersion paint and
oil on canvas,
50 × 70 cm
Courtesy of the artist

Borderline, 2018
Gouache, resin and oil on canvas,
100 × 80 cm
Courtesy of the artist

Chemnitz

Piano Nobile, 2019
Gouache, resin, egg tempera,
dispersion paint and copper oxidation,
190 × 190 cm
Courtesy of the artist

Teutoburger Würmer, 2015
Resin, egg tempera and oil on canvas,
80 × 70 cm
Courtesy of the artist

Palmyra Mon Amour, 2017/18
Resin, dispersion paint, paper and
oil on canvas,
80 × 70 cm
Courtesy of the artist

Wiesbaden

Soul Power, 2019
Gouache, resin, dispersion paint,
copper oxidation, spray paint and
oil on canvas,
120 × 90 cm
Courtesy of the artist

Dune, 2019
Gouache, resin, egg tempera, dispersion paint,
copper oxidation and oil on canvas,
100 × 70 cm
Courtesy of the artist

Showdown, 2018
Gouache, resin, spray paint and oil on canvas,
80 × 80 cm
Courtesy of the artist

Benedikt Leonhardt

Bonn

Untitled (PSM-CB-V/1/3), 2018
Oil, acrylic, vinyl paint, tape and
spackle on canvas,
200 × 150 cm
Courtesy of the artist,
Galerie Feldbusch Wiesner Rudolph

Untitled (PSM-CB-V/2/2), 2018
Oil, acrylic, vinyl paint, tape and
spackle on canvas,
68.7 × 51.6 cm
Courtesy of the artist, Galerie ASPN

Untitled (WF-I/PG-QM/QV-B-2), 2019
Acrylic, vinyl paint, tape and
spackle on canvas,
200 × 145 cm
Courtesy of the artist, Galerie ASPN

Chemnitz

Untitled (WF-G-QM/QV-AB-2), 2017
Acrylic, vinyl paint, tape and
spackle on canvas,
242 × 195 cm
Courtesy of the artist

Untitled (WF-AB-PB-COG), 2019
Acrylic, vinyl paint, tape and spackle on canvas,
230 × 170 cm
Courtesy of the artist,
Galerie Feldbusch Wiesner Rudolph

Untitled (CCD-MR/VD-CYD-1), 2019
Oil, acrylic, vinyl paint, tape and spackle on canvas,
240 × 172.5 cm
Courtesy of the artist,
Galerie Feldbusch Wiesner Rudolph

Wiesbaden

Untitled (WF-COG-PB), 2019
Acrylic, vinyl paint, tape and spackle on canvas,
65 × 48 cm
Courtesy of the artist,
Galerie Feldbusch Wiesner Rudolph

Untitled (MCB-R-MY-2), 2019
Acrylic, vinyl paint, tape and spackle on canvas,
230 × 180 cm
Courtesy of the artist,
Galerie Feldbusch Wiesner Rudolph

Untitled (V-PCB-RB-NM), 2019
Acrylic, vinyl paint, tape and spackle on canvas,
220 × 170 cm
Courtesy of the artist, Galerie ASPN

Florian Meisenberg

Bonn

Forgery & Copyright (Arbeitslose Autoren & Unschuldige Hunde), 2019
Airbrush and oil paint on canvas,
183 × 147 cm
Courtesy of the artist,
Avlskarl Gallery, Copenhagen

Speaking Sanskrit with a German Accent (Chapter II Ordering Food), 2019
Ink and oil paint on canvas,
193 × 162 cm
Courtesy of the artist,
Avlskarl Gallery, Copenhagen

From the series: Acting and aging (odorless journey), 2017
Oil paint and airbrush on canvas,
50 × 40 cm
Courtesy of the artist,
Avlskarl Gallery, Copenhagen

Chemnitz

From the series: Speaking Sanskrit with a German Accent (Chapter VII Vocalizing), 2019
Ink, oil paint on canvas,
102 × 77 cm
Courtesy of the artist, Wentrup, Berlin

Wiesbaden

Reichwald (History of this Moment), 2018
Oil, oil stick, airbrush and glass dust on linen,
153 × 122 cm
Courtesy of the artist, Wentrup, Berlin

Day 5: 8 mm, 2018
Oil paint on canvas,
28 × 20.5 cm
Courtesy of the artist, Wentrup, Berlin

Monika Michalko

Bonn

On the way to far east, 2018
Oil on canvas,
200 × 280 cm
Courtesy of the artist,
Galerie Maïa Muller

An intelligent woman is sometimes forced to be drunk to spend time with her fools, 2017
Oil on canvas,
180 × 180 cm
Courtesy of the artist,
Produzentengalerie Hamburg

You lost little girls, 2019
Oil on canvas,
40 × 30 cm
Courtesy of the artist,
Produzentengalerie Hamburg

Chemnitz

My own shop, 2018
Oil on paper,
105 × 157 cm
Courtesy of the artist,
Produzentengalerie Hamburg

Crawling through Pettah, 2018
Oil on canvas,
50 × 40 cm
Courtesy of the artist,
Produzentengalerie Hamburg

Aerger wird durch Denken ausgelöst, 2019
Oil on canvas,
40 × 30 cm
Courtesy of the artist,
Produzentengalerie Hamburg

Rayagiriya side, 2018
Oil on canvas,
59 × 50 cm
Courtesy of the artist,
Produzentengalerie Hamburg

Wiesbaden

Flowers for Maia, 2019
Oil on canvas,
90 × 60 cm
Courtesy of the artist,
Produzentengalerie Hamburg

Colombo, 2018
Oil on canvas,
200 × 280 cm
Courtesy of the artist,
Produzentengalerie Hamburg

Borella, 2018
Oil on canvas,
60 × 70 cm
Courtesy of the artist,
Galerie Maïa Muller

Hannes Michanek

Bonn

All These Things That Happened and More, Quantum with Physics at an Endless War. Bugs Move, Fruit Flies. Hollow Bones., 2019
Oil on canvas,
190 × 230 cm
Courtesy of the artist

Trees Have Been Big Part of the Kings and Queens Life. Little Part Took Kings and Queens., 2018
Oil on canvas,
250 × 190 cm
Courtesy of the artist

Greetlings., 2018
Oil on canvas,
120 × 190 cm
Courtesy of the artist

Chemnitz

Pearl.
How Awful-(ly) kind. Thought the Fox of Sky. Day in and Day Out, Looking Down on a Daily Life., 2019
Oil on canvas,
160 × 150 cm
Courtesy of the artist

Astronaut Level People Making Alien Deals., 2019
Oil on canvas,
100 × 85 cm
Courtesy of the artist

Dusk, 2016
Oil on canvas,
140 × 80 cm
Courtesy of the artist

Wiesbaden

Digging Funnels, Beyond Things Ahead., 2018
Oil on canvas,
230 × 190 cm.
Courtesy of the artist

There's a Restless Gust Troubling Around the Mountain., 2019
Oil on canvas,
160 × 160 cm
Courtesy of the artist

Simon Modersohn

Bonn

Club zur Vahr, 2015
Oil on canvas,
50 × 40cm
Courtesy of the artist, Galerie Åplus, Berlin

Feuerteufel, 2017
Oil on canvas,
75 × 135 cm
Courtesy of the artist, Galerie Åplus, Berlin

Generation Trockner, 2018
Oil on canvas,
160 × 110 cm
Courtesy of the artist, Galerie Åplus, Berlin

Chemnitz

Durststrecke, 2018
Oil on canvas,
80 × 140 cm
Courtesy of the artist, Galerie Åplus, Berlin

Kraftclub, 2019
Oil on canvas,
125 × 150cm
Courtesy of the artist, Galerie Åplus, Berlin

Selbstmord, 2018
Oil on canvas,
100 × 85cm
Courtesy of the artist, Galerie Åplus, Berlin

Wiesbaden

Deep in the woods, 2018
Oil on canvas,
55 × 46 cm
Courtesy of the artist, Galerie Åplus, Berlin

Round Up, 2018
Oil on canvas,
190 × 180 cm
Courtesy of the artist, Galerie Åplus, Berlin

Heckenschütze, 2019
Oil on canvas,
120 × 190 cm
Holle Collection

Bastian Muhr

Bonn

Untitled, 2018
24-part series, oil on paper, framed,
70 cm × 60 cm, each, ca. 220 × 500 cm, total
Courtesy of the artist,
Galerie Jochen Hempel

Chemnitz

Untitled, 2019
Oil on cotton,
170 × 140 cm
Courtesy of the artist,
Galerie Jochen Hempel

Untitled, 2019
Oil on cotton,
170 × 140 cm
Courtesy of the artist,
Galerie Jochen Hempel

Untitled, 2019
Oil on cotton,
170 × 140 cm
Courtesy of the artist,
Galerie Jochen Hempel

Untitled, 2019
Oil on cotton,
170 × 140 cm
Courtesy of the artist,
Galerie Jochen Hempel

Untitled, 2019
Oil on cotton,
170 × 140 cm
Courtesy of the artist,
Galerie Jochen Hempel

Wiesbaden

Zwenkau, 2019
Oil on cotton,
170 × 140 cm
Courtesy of the artist,
Galerie Jochen Hempel

Untitled, 2019
Oil on cotton,
170 × 140 cm
Courtesy of the artist,
Galerie Jochen Hempel

Untitled, 2018
Oil on canvas,
170 × 140 cm
Courtesy of the artist,
Galerie Jochen Hempel

Untitled, 2018
Oil on canvas,
170 × 140 cm
Courtesy of the artist,
Galerie Jochen Hempel

Anna Nero

Bonn

Asphalt, 2017
Oil, acrylic and colour paste on canvas,
180 × 130 cm
Courtesy of the artist

GAG, 2018
Oil and acrylic on canvas,
40 × 30 cm
Courtesy of the artist

Stillleben mit Kreisen, 2019
Oil and acrylic on canvas,
100 × 130 cm
Courtesy of the artist

Useful Things, 2018
Oil, acrylic, colour paste and ink on canvas,
40 × 30 cm
Courtesy of the artist

Chemnitz

Chick Flick, 2018
Oil, acrylic and colour paste on canvas,
180 × 130 cm
Courtesy of the artist

Edison, 2019
Oil and acrylic on canvas,
40 × 32 cm
Courtesy of the artist

Jetlag (mit Happy End), 2019
Oil and acrylic on canvas,
40 × 30 cm
Courtesy of the artist

Nightlife, 2017
Oil and acrylic on canvas,
180 × 150 cm
Courtesy of the artist

Wiesbaden

Reoccurring Annoyance, 2019
Oil, acrylic and marker on canvas,
180 × 130 cm
Courtesy of the artist

UFO, 2016
Oil and acrylic on canvas,
69 × 65 cm
Courtesy of the artist

We belong 2gether, 2018
Oil and acrylic on canvas,
180 × 130 cm
Courtesy of the artist

Moritz Neuhoff

Bonn

Splatter 2, 2019
Acrylic on canvas,
280 × 250 cm
Courtesy of the artist, Hengesbach Gallery

brushstrokes (gray), 2019
Acrylic on canvas,
280 × 250 cm
Courtesy of the artist, Hengesbach Gallery

Sulpur 2, 2019.
Acrylic on canvas,
280 × 250 cm
Courtesy of the artist, Hengesbach Gallery

Chemnitz

Plexus, 2019
Acrylic on canvas,
200 × 300 cm
Courtesy of the artist, Hengesbach Gallery

traces, 2017
Acrylic on canvas,
200 × 280 cm
Courtesy of the artist, Hengesbach Gallery

Wiesbaden

traces 2, 2017
Acrylic on canvas,
250 × 200 cm
Courtesy of the artist,
Hengesbach Gallery

dash, 2018
Acrylic on canvas,
250 × 200 cm
Courtesy of the artist,
Hengesbach Gallery

blur, 2018
Acrylic on canvas,
250 × 200 cm
Courtesy of the artist,
Hengesbach Gallery

Vera Palme

Bonn

The Owner, 2018
Oil on linen,
140 × 100 cm
Courtesy of the artist

The Owner, 2018
Oil on burlap,
55 × 100 cm
Courtesy of the artist

The Owner, 2018
Oil on linen,
45 × 55 cm
Courtesy of the artist

The Owner, 2018
Oil on linen,
45 × 55 cm
Courtesy of the artist

Chemnitz

Sven Väth, 2017
Oil and liquin on linen,
55 × 220 cm
Courtesy of the artist

politics, 2017
Oil on linen,
55 × 45 cm
Courtesy of the artist

politics, 2017
Oil on linen,
55 × 45 cm
Courtesy of the artist

politics, 2017
Oil and liquin on cotton,
55 × 45 cm
Courtesy of the artist

Wiesbaden

Still Life (III), 2019
Oil on linen,
100 × 140 cm
Courtesy of the artist

Still Life (II), 2019
Oil on burlap,
95 × 55 cm
Courtesy of the artist

Still Life (IV), 2019
Oil, stain on cotton,
50 × 40 cm
Courtesy of the artist

Still Life (VI), 2019
Oil on linen,
40 × 30 cm
Courtesy of the artist

Alexander Pröpster

Bonn

Summe meiner Teile (Nr. 504), 2016
Oil on paper,
450 × 210 cm
Courtesy of the artist

Holzwegbeschreibung (Nr. 515), 2019
Oil on paper,
150 × 210 cm
Courtesy of the artist

üt oder jüt (Nr. 451), 2016
Oil on paper,
100 × 70 cm
Courtesy of the artist

Dokumentation von Tieren, 2018/19,
Infrared camera shots,
15 × 20 cm, each
Courtesy of the artist

Chemnitz

Holzwegbeschreibung (Nr. 511), 2019
Oil on paper,
210 × 300 cm
Courtesy of the artist

Holzwegbeschreibung (Nr. 512), 2019
Oil on paper,
210 × 150 cm
Courtesy of the artist

In Frau Reethmayer's Garten (Nr. 509), 2016
Oil on paper,
150 × 210 cm
Courtesy of the artist

Holzwegbeschreibung (Nr. 514), 2019
Oil on paper,
210 × 150 cm
Courtesy of the artist

Dokumentation von Tieren, 2018/19,
Infrared camera shots,
15 × 20 cm, each
Courtesy of the artist

Wiesbaden

Holzwegbeschreibung (Nr. 510), 2018
Oil on paper,
210 × 300 cm
Private collection

Dokumentation von Tieren, 2016,
Thermal images,
4 × 5 cm, each
Courtesy of the artist

About Cycles (Nr. 508), 2016
Oil on paper,
210 × 300 cm
Courtesy of the artist

Franziska Reinbothe

Bonn

alle Augen auf, 2015
Acrylic on canvas, yarn,
150 × 130 cm
Courtesy of the artist,
Galerie Kim Behm, Mannheim

Untitled, 2016
Acrylic on canvas, yarn,
80 × 60 cm
Courtesy of the artist,
Galerie Kim Behm, Mannheim

sie bevorzugt wenig Kleidung, 2015
Diptych, acrylic on canvas,
ca. 130 × 100 cm
Courtesy of the artist,
Galerie Kim Behm, Mannheim

Chemnitz

melting, 2018
Acrylic on canvas,
ca. 140 × 80 cm
Courtesy of the artist,
Galerie Kim Behm, Mannheim

Untitled, 2019
Acrylic on canvas,
ca. 100 × 37 × 9.5 cm
Courtesy of the artist,
Galerie Kim Behm, Mannheim

Schwarz, in legerer Haltung, 2014
Acrylic on canvas, yarn,
ca. 180 × 180 × 20 cm
Courtesy of the artist,
Galerie Kim Behm, Mannheim

Zacken, 2018
Arylic on canvas,
ca. 84 × 73 × 12 cm
Courtesy of the artist,
Galerie Kim Behm, Mannheim

Wiesbaden

gesicherter Lawinenabgang, 2015
Oil and white paint on canvas,
ca. 110 × 86 × 12 cm
Courtesy of the artist,
Galerie Kim Behm, Mannheim

Untitled, 2016/18
Acrylic and forestry marker on canvas,
ca. 58 × 44 × 18 cm
Courtesy of the artist,
Galerie Kim Behm, Mannheim

Untitled, 2017
Chiffon, 120 × 100 × 4 cm
Courtesy of the artist,
Galerie Kim Behm, Mannheim

Who loves the Sun, 2018
Polyester, canvas, 90 × 70 × 4 cm
Courtesy of the artist,
Galerie Kim Behm, Mannheim

Daniel Rossi

Bonn

Untitled (Division), 2016
Acrylic, oil, latex and lacquer on polyester,
140 × 120 cm
Courtesy Galerie für Gegenwartskunst Bremen

Untitled (Caritas), 2017
Acrylic, oil, latex and lacquer on polyester,
111 × 111 cm
Courtesy Galerie für Gegenwartskunst Bremen

Untitled (Nike), 2019
Acrylic and oil on polyester,
170 × 150 cm
Courtesy Galerie für Gegenwartskunst Bremen

Chemnitz

Untitled (Destruction, Creation), 2017/18
Acrylic, oil and lacquer on wool,
205 × 160 cm and 210 × 147 cm
Courtesy Galerie für Gegenwartskunst Bremen

Untitled (Dress for Friese), 2018
Acrylic, oil and bitumen on polyamide,
56 × 43 cm
Courtesy Galerie für Gegenwartskunst Bremen

Wiesbaden

Untitled (Construction), 2017
Acrylic, oil and lacquer on wool,
215 × 135 cm
Courtesy Galerie für Gegenwartskunst Bremen

Untitled (Reversed), 2018
Acrylic and oil on polyester,
140 × 120 cm
Courtesy Galerie für Gegenwartskunst Bremen

Untitled (Rosa Decidua), 2019
Acrylic and oil on canvas,
170 × 155 cm
Courtesy Galerie für Gegenwartskunst Bremen

Markus Saile

Bonn

Untitled, 2018
Oil on wood,
31.5 × 26 cm
Courtesy of the artist

Untitled, 2019
Oil on wood,
81 × 76 cm
Courtesy of the artist

Untitled, 2019
Oil on wood,
33.7 × 28 cm
Courtesy of the artist

Untitled, 2016
Oil on wood,
93 × 124 cm
Courtesy of the artist

Chemnitz

Untitled, 2018
Oil on wood,
33 × 39 cm
Courtesy of the artist

Untitled, 2019
Oil on wood,
129 × 97 cm
Courtesy of the artist

Untitled, 2018
Oil on wood,
20 × 25 cm
Courtesy of the artist

Untitled, 2019
Oil on wood,
97 × 184 cm
Courtesy of the artist

Wiesbaden

Untitled, 2019
Oil on wood,
17 × 23 cm
Collection Gaby and Wilhelm Schürmann, Herzogenrath

Untitled, 2019
Oil on wood,
42 × 33.5 cm
Courtesy of the artist

Untitled, 2019
Oil on wood,
37 × 29 cm
Collection Gaby and Wilhelm Schürmann, Herzogenrath

Untitled, 2019
Oil on wood,
25 × 24 cm
Courtesy of the artist

Untitled, 2016
Oil on wood,
32 × 25 cm
Collection Kaufmann, Berlin

Moritz Schleime

Bonn

La Vieux Carre (Dösen), 2018
Oil on canvas,
60 × 50 cm
Courtesy Laden für Nichts

Painters Corner XI, 2019
Oil on canvas,
50 × 40 cm
Courtesy Laden für Nichts

The Dicks, 2016
Oil on canvas,
250 × 170 cm
Courtesy Laden für Nichts

Chemnitz

Lazyland (den Arsch voll Angst), 2018
Oil on canvas,
180 × 125 cm
Courtesy Laden für Nichts

West Ryder Lunatic Pauper Asylum, 2013
Oil on canvas, diptych
260 × 350 cm, total
Collection Hildebrand, Leipzig

Wiesbaden

Olympia, 2015
Oil on canvas,
180 × 260 cm
Collection Wolf, Chemnitz

Mezcal Sunrise, 2018
Oil on canvas,
60 × 50 cm
Courtesy Laden für Nichts

Painters Corner IX, 2019
Oil on canvas,
50 × 40 cm
Courtesy Laden für Nichts

Keine Pizza auf Ibiza (The Diary), 2018
Oil on canvas,
250 × 190 cm
Collection Schott, Leipzig

Jana Schröder

Bonn

Kadlites L25, 2019
Acrylic and graphite on canvas,
240 × 200 cm
Courtesy of the artist, Natalia Hug Gallery

Kadlites L26, 2019
Acrylic and graphite on canvas,
240 × 200 cm
Courtesy of the artist, Natalia Hug Gallery

Kinkrustation PB10, 2017
Papier-mâché, acrylic and oil on canvas,
240 × 200 cm
Courtesy of the artist, T293 Gallery

Kinkrustation PB11, 2017
Papier-mâché, acrylic and oil on canvas,
240 × 200 cm
Courtesy of the artist, Nino Mier Gallery

Chemnitz

Kadlites M5, 2017
Acrylic, graphite and lead pencil and oil on canvas,
200 × 155 cm
Courtesy of the artist

Kadlites M15, 2018
Acrylic and graphite on canvas,
200 × 160 cm
Courtesy of the artist, Natalia Hug Gallery

Wiesbaden

Kadlites M11, 2018
Acrylic and graphite on canvas,
200 × 160 cm
Courtesy of the artist, Natalia Hug Gallery

Kadlites M12, 2018
Acrylic and graphite on canvas,
200 × 160 cm
Courtesy of the artist

Kadlites M13, 2018
Acrylic and graphite on canvas,
200 × 160 cm
Courtesy of the artist, Natalia Hug Gallery

Daniel Schubert

Bonn

Untitled 20 – aus der Nivea-Serie, 2019
Acrylic on blue fabric,
220 × 147.5 cm
Courtesy of the artist, Galerie Gebr. Lehmann, Dresden, and Gerhard Hofland, Amsterdam

Untitled, 2016
Acrylic on canvas,
185 × 125 cm
Courtesy of the artist, Galerie Gebr. Lehmann, Dresden, and Gerhard Hofland, Amsterdam

Untitled, 2017
Egg tempera, crayon on canvas,
170 × 115 cm
Courtesy of the artist, Galerie Gebr. Lehmann, Dresden, and Gerhard Hofland, Amsterdam

Chemnitz

Untitled 25 – aus der Shimmer-Serie, 2018
Acrylic on canvas,
170 × 115 cm
Courtesy of the artist, Galerie Gebr. Lehmann, Dresden, and Gerhard Hofland, Amsterdam

Untitled – aus der Serie Lay in a Shimmer, 2019
Egg tempera on canvas,
210 × 150 cm
Courtesy of the artist, Galerie Gebr. Lehmann, Dresden, and Gerhard Hofland, Amsterdam

Untitled, 2016
Acrylic, tempera on fabric,
185 × 145 cm
Courtesy of the artist, Galerie Gebr. Lehmann, Dresden, and Gerhard Hofland, Amsterdam

Wiesbaden

Untitled 26 – aus der Shimmer-Serie, 2018
Acrylic on canvas,
170 × 115 cm
Courtesy of the artist, Galerie Gebr. Lehmann, Dresden, and Gerhard Hofland, Amsterdam

Untitled, 2017
Stretcher, canvas, acrylic, distemper, dimensions variable, ca. 115 × 170 cm
Courtesy of the artist, Galerie Gebr. Lehmann, Dresden, and Gerhard Hofland, Amsterdam

Kristina Schuldt

Bonn

Master, 2015
Oil and egg tempera on canvas,
50.5 × 40 cm
Private collection

reverse, 2016
Oil and egg tempera on canvas,
170 × 210 cm
Courtesy Galerie EIGEN + ART Leipzig/Berlin

Schlacht, 2019
Oil and egg tempera on canvas,
220 × 180 cm
Courtesy Galerie EIGEN + ART Leipzig/Berlin

Heim, 2019
Oil and egg tempera on canvas,
180 × 220 cm
Courtesy Galerie EIGEN + ART Leipzig/Berlin

Chemnitz

Einkaufswagen eine Treppe herabsteigend, 2017
Oil and egg tempera on canvas,
210 × 170 cm
Private collection, Zürich

Verwünschung, 2017
Oil and egg tempera on canvas,
210 × 170 cm
Private collection

Galerist, 2019
Oil and egg tempera on canvas,
100 × 90 cm
Courtesy Galerie EIGEN + ART Leipzig/Berlin

Wiesbaden

crossing, 2017
Oil and egg tempera on canvas,
210 × 170 cm
Private collection, New York

Nebelwand, 2018
Oil and egg tempera on canvas,
220 × 180 cm
Courtesy Galerie EIGEN + ART Leipzig/Berlin

RUN, 2018
Oil and egg tempera on canvas,
220 × 180 cm
Courtesy Galerie EIGEN + ART Leipzig/Berlin

Alicia Viebrock

Bonn

Untitled, 2019
Ink, acrylic and medium on canvas,
210 × 160 cm
Private collection, Munich

Untitled, 2019
Ink, acrylic and medium on canvas,
210 × 160 cm
Private collection, Frankfurt a.M.

Untitled, 2019
Ink, acrylic and medium on canvas,
240 × 190 cm
Private collection, Frankfurt a.M.

Chemnitz

Untitled, 2019
Ink, acrylic, oil and medium on canvas,
190 × 150 cm
Mondstudio Collection

Untitled, 2019
Ink, acrylic, oil and medium on canvas,
190 × 150 cm
Galerie FILIALE, Frankfurt a.M.

Mirto, 2018
Ink, acrylic and medium on canvas,
200 × 150 cm
Collection H. Brandl

Wiesbaden

Portal, 2018
Ink, acrylic and spray paint, medium on canvas,
190 × 150 cm
Private collection, Frankfurt a.M.

Untitled, 2019
Ink, acrylic and medium on canvas,
240 × 190 cm
Galerie FILIALE, Frankfurt a.M.

Untitled, 2019
Ink, acrylic and medium on canvas,
240 × 190 cm
Kienbaum Collection, Cologne

Stefan Vogel

Bonn

Ach- sowieso-- genau---, 2015
Ink, copies, fabric, glue, yarn, hot glue, linseed oil and oil on cotton fabric,
230 × 200 cm
Courtesy of the artist, Hildebrand Collection, Leipzig, Galerie Jahn und Jahn, Munich

Oh weh, 2017
Ink, paper, threads, typewriter, glue on cotton fabric,
200 × 230 cm
Courtesy of the artist, Hildebrand Collection, Leipzig, Galerie Jahn und Jahn, Munich

Salbe, 2018
Quadripartite, paraffin, paper, copies, concrete, Polaroids, wire, hair, threads, typewriter, staple gun, plaster, blistering ointment, dirt on glass,
200 × 240 cm
Courtesy of the artist, Matthias Jahn und Felicitas Kirgis Collection, Galerie Jahn und Jahn, Munich

Chemnitz

Und sie schälen traurig Pellkartoffeln, 2016
Paper, stain, yarn, copies, nicotine, staples, typewriter, red wine, dirt, tea on canvas,
200 × 230 cm
Courtesy of the artist, private collection, Galerie Jahn und Jahn, Munich

Gebrache, 2017
Paraffin, paper, threads, plastic, dirt, dust, metal, acrylic, lacquer, silicone, staples and typewriter on glass,
320 × 560 cm
Courtesy of the artist, Galerie Jahn und Jahn, Munich

es wird nicht besser, 2019
Photocopy, paper, glue, acrylic, tape, wall paint, oil paint, dirt, hair, typewriter, string, threads, synthetic material on polyester,
230 × 200 cm
Courtesy of the artist, Hildebrand Collection, Leipzig, Galerie Jahn und Jahn, Munich

Wiesbaden

Der rechte Winkel, der gekrümmte Zeigefinger und die ewige Baustelle, 2017
Paraffin, threads, stain, copies, dirt on glass,
140 × 170 cm
Courtesy of the artist, private collection, Galerie Jahn und Jahn, Munich

Sag's nochmal, 2018
Paraffin, yarn, staples, dirt, drippings, paper and hair on glass,
160 × 140 cm
Courtesy of the artist, private collection, Galerie Jahn und Jahn, Munich

Sag's nochmal, 2018
Ink, Polaroids, glue, mop, dirt, staple gun, synthetic enamel on cotton fabric,
230 × 200 cm
Courtesy of the artist, private collection, Galerie Jahn und Jahn, Munich

Jonas Weichsel

Bonn

Good Day today (David Lynch), 2019
Acrylic on rounded aluminium sheet,
54 × 37 × 3 cm
Courtesy of the artist, Galerie Thomas Schulte, Berlin

SC 60 (Goldgrün), 2019
Acrylic on aluminium, 60 × 42 × 1.3 cm
Courtesy of the artist, Galerie Thomas Schulte, Berlin

Terenz, 2013
Oil on canvas,
200 × 180 × 2.7 cm
Courtesy of the artist, private collection, Frankfurt a. M.

K. Michael Bergfeld, 2019
Oil on copper,
84 × 20.5 × 0.9 cm
Courtesy of the artist, Galerie Thomas Schulte, Berlin

United Europe Flag (A), 2019
Acrylic screen print on canvas,
72 × 104 × 1.3 cm
Courtesy of the artist, Galerie Thomas Schulte, Berlin

Chemnitz

Wandarbeit 5, 2019
Acrylic on wall,
220 × 80 cm
Courtesy of the artist, Galerie Thomas Schulte

TC Dia (W) Hansagelb/Heliogrün, 2019
Oil and acrylic on canvas,
76 × 47.5 × 1.5 cm
Private collection, Belgium

Collection II (Tilted), 2019
Acrylic on canvas,
200 × 216 × 2.7 cm
Courtesy of the artist, Galerie Thomas Schulte, Berlin

Wiesbaden

Große Flagge II, 2018
Acrylic on canvas,
240 × 170 × 2.7 cm
Courtesy of the artist, Galerie Thomas Schulte, Berlin

TC Dia (W) Coelinblau, 2019
Oil and acrylic on canvas,
76 × 47.5 × 1.5 cm
Courtesy of the artist, private collection, Milan

Finne, 2019
Acrylic (interference colour) on canvas,
210 × 15 × 1.3 cm
Courtesy of the artist, Galerie Thomas Schulte, Berlin

Glass Penny, 2019
Oil and UV printing on glass,
49 × 34 × 0.8 cm
Courtesy of the artist, Galerie Thomas Schulte, Berlin

Untitled III (Post Albers), 2019
Oil and acrylic on Alu-Dibond sheet,
50 × 40 × 1.3 cm
Courtesy of the artist, Galerie Thomas Schulte, Berlin

FC 68 Krapp (Peter F. Version), 2019
Acrylic on aluminium,
68 × 45 × 0.8 cm
Courtesy of the artist, Galerie Thomas Schulte, Berlin

Tristan Wilczek

Bonn

Untitled (Schema der Farbe Cynopreim), 2016
Acrylic, graphite and colour pencil on canvas,
200 × 150 cm
Gramse/Salz Collection, Cologne

Untitled (Ort, Raum, Gegend), 2018
Acrylic, graphite and colour pencil on canvas,
170 × 240 cm
Private collection Tobias Flessenkemper, Galerie Markus Lüttgen, Düsseldorf

Untitled (Blaupunkt), 2019
Acrylic, oil and graphite on canvas,
180 × 240 cm
Neumann Family Collection, New York

Chemnitz

Untitled (Instabile Landschaft), 2017
Oil and acrylic on canvas,
140 × 110 cm
Private collection, Cologne

Untitled (Aktiv, inaktiv), 2017
Acrylic, oil and graphite on canvas,
240 × 180 cm
Courtesy Galerie Markus Lüttgen, Düsseldorf

Untitled (Sequenz), 2019
Acrylic, oil and graphite on canvas,
140 × 110 cm
Courtesy Galerie Markus Lüttgen, Düsseldorf

Wiesbaden

Untitled (die leeren Zeichen 2), 2019
Acrylic, oil and graphite on canvas,
140 × 110 cm
Haas / Schaller Collection, Wiesbaden

Untitled (die leeren Zeichen 0), 2018
Acrylic and graphite on canvas,
140 × 110 cm
Courtesy Galerie Markus Lüttgen, Düsseldorf

Untitled (die leeren Zeichen 3), 2019
Acrylic and graphite on canvas,
140 × 105 cm
Courtesy Galerie Markus Lüttgen, Düsseldorf

Image Credits

Photo Credits

Mona Ardeleanu, Photo: Mona Ardeleanu, pp. 23–25

Israel Aten, Photo: Johannes Bendzulla, pp. 27–29

Paula Baader, Photo: Sören Beineke, pp. 30–33

Lydia Balke, Photo: Lydia Balke, pp. 34–37

Cornelia Baltes, Photo: Joe Clark, pp. 39–41

Jagoda Bednarsky, Photo: Hans-Georg Gaul, pp. 43–45

Viola Bittl, Photo: Wolfgang Günzel, pp. 47–49

Peppi Bottrop, Photo: Mareike Tocha, pp. 51–53

Andreas Breunig, Photo: Johannes Bendzulla, pp. 55–57

Paul Czerlitzki, Photo: Yann Bohac, p. 59 / Roman März, p. 60 / Marco Blessano, p. 61

Benjamin Dittrich, Photo: Björn Siebert, pp. 63–65

Jens Einhorn, Photo: Joachim Schulz, pp. 67–69

Jenny Forster, Photo: Thomas Lomberg, pp. 71–73

Pius Fox, Photo: Pius Fox, pp. 75–77

Max Frintrop, Photo: Ben Hermanni, pp. 79–81

Sabrina Fritsch, Photo: Achim Kukulies, Düsseldorf, pp. 83–85

Ina Gerken, Photo: A. R., pp. 87–89

Fabian Ginsberg, Photo: Michael Franz, pp. 91, 92 / Achim Kukulies, p. 93

Gregor Gleiwitz, Photo: Ivo Faber © VG Bild-Kunst Bonn, pp. 95–97

Lukas Glinkowski, Photo: Lukas Glinkowski, pp. 98–101

Sebastian Gögel, Photo: Andreas Wünschirs, pp. 103–105

Henriette Grahnert, Photo: Uwe Walter, Berlin, pp. 107–109

Dana Greiner, Photo: Dana Greiner, pp. 111–113

Vivian Greven, Photo: Vivian Greven, pp. 115–117

Toulu Hassani, Photo: Volker Crone, pp. 119–121

Sabrina Haunsperg, Photo: Ben Hermanni, pp. 122–125

Franziska Holstein, Photo: Björn Siebert, pp. 126–129

Aneta Kajzer, Photo: Aneta Kajzer, pp. 131–133

Sumi Kim, Photo: Sumi Kim, pp. 135–137

Maximilian Kirmse, Photo: Falk Messerschmidt, pp. 139, 141 / Thomas Krüger, p. 140

Li-Wen Kuo, Photo: Anders Sune Berg, pp. 143–145

David Lehmann, Photo: Clemens Schiesko, pp. 147–149

Benedikt Leonhardt, Photo: Carsten Humme, pp. 151–153

Florian Meisenberg, Photo: Florian Meisenberg, p. 155 / Dario Lasagni, New York City, pp. 156, 157

Monika Michalko, Photo: Jan Michalko, pp. 159–161

Hannes Michanek, Photo: Wolfgang Günzel, pp. 163–165

Simon Modersohn, Photo: Andreas Wemheuer, pp. 167–169

Bastian Muhr, Photo: Björn Siebert, pp. 171–173

Anna Nero, Photo: Anna Nero, pp. 175–177

Moritz Neuhoff, Photo: Tony Haupt, pp. 178–181

Vera Palme, Photo: Diana Pfammatter, pp. 183–185

Alexander Pröpster, Photo: Alexander Pröpster, pp. 186–189

Franziska Reinbothe, Photo: Falk Messerschmidt, pp. 191–193

Daniel Rossi, Photo: Christina Stohn, pp. 195, 196 / Franziska von Driesch, p. 197

Markus Saile, Photo: Markus Saile, pp. 199–201

Moritz Schleime, Photo: Stefan Fischer, pp. 203–205

Jana Schröder, Photo: Ben Hermanni, p. 207 / Johannes Bendzulla, pp. 208, 209

Daniel Schubert, Photo: Daniel Schubert, pp. 211–213

Kristina Schuldt, Photo: Uwe Walter, Berlin, pp. 215–217

Alicia Viebrock, Photo: Wolfgang Günzel, pp. 219–221

Stefan Vogel, Photo: Stefan Fischer, pp. 222–225

Jonas Weichsel, Photo: Jonas Weichsel, pp. 227–229

Tristan Wilczek, Photo: Ivo Faber © VG Bild-Kunst Bonn, pp. 230–231, 233 / Mareike Tocha, p. 232

Imprint

This catalogue is published on the occasion of the exhibition
Now! Painting in Germany Today

In co-operation with

Kunstmuseum Bonn
19/9/2019–19/1/2020

Museum Wiesbaden
20/9/2019–19/1/2020

Kunstsammlungen Chemnitz – Museum Gunzenhauser
21/9/2019–19/1/2020

Deichtorhallen Hamburg
7/2/–24/5/2020

Exhibition

Kunstmuseum Bonn
Stephan Berg, Director and Curator
Christoph Schreier, Deputy Director and Curator

Kunstsammlungen Chemnitz – Museum Gunzenhauser
Frédéric Bußmann, General Director and Curator
Anja Richter, Curator

Museum Wiesbaden
Alexander Klar, Director and Curator
Jörg Daur, Deputy Director and Curator
Lea Schäfer, Curator

Deichtorhallen Hamburg
Dirk Luckow, General Director and Curator
Bert Antonius Kaufmann, Chief Financial Officer
Annette Sievert, Exhibition management

Catalogue

Editor: Stephan Berg, Frédéric Bußmann,
Alexander Klar, Dirk Luckow
Editorial team: Lea Schäfer, Alexander Klar
Picture editor and Illustration sources: Lea Schäfer

Hirmer Verlag

Publishing project management: Kerstin Ludolph
Translations: Jane Michael, Renata Stein
Copy-editing: Chris Murray
Design and layout: Q, Wiesbaden
Production: Katja Durchholz
Lithography: Repromayer Medienproduktion, Reutlingen
Printing and binding: Printer Trento SRL
Paper: 150 g LuxoArt samt
Fonts: Beatrice, Blacker Text

Printed in Italy

Bibliographic information published by the Deutsche Nationalbibliothek: The Deutsche Nationalbibliothek lists this publication in the Deutsche Nationalbibliografie; detailed bibliographic data are available in the Internet at http://dnb.d-nb.de.

ISBN 978-3-89258-128-4 (German museum edition)
ISBN 978-3-89258-129-1 (English museum edition)
ISBN 978-3-7774-3419-3 (German bookstore edition)
ISBN 978-3-7774-3447-6 (Englishbookstore edition)

www.hirmerverlag.de

We would like to thank our sponsors and promoters

ART MENTOR FOUNDATION LUCERNE
Stiftung der Sparda-Bank West #15 JAHRE ENGAGIERT
HABBEL, POHLIG & PARTNER VERMÖGENSVERWALTUNG
Ministerium für Kultur und Wissenschaft des Landes Nordrhein-Westfalen
FREUDE. JOY. JOIE. BONN.
CHEMNITZ STADT DER MODERNE
CHEMNITZ KULTURHAUPTSTADT EUROPAS KANDIDAT 2025
FÖRDERKREIS DEICHTORHALLEN HAMBURG
Freunde des Museums Wiesbaden
KUNSTFREUNDE MUSEUM BONN
UBS
OLYMPUS
EY
cewe